EXILES

EXILES

LIVING MISSIONALLY in a POST-CHRISTIAN CULTURE

MICHAEL FROST

STRAND

Exiles: Living Missionally in a Post-Christian Culture
© 2006 by Hendrickson Publishers, Inc.
P. O. Box 3473
Peabody, Massachusetts 01961-3473

Published jointly, 2006, in the United States by Hendrickson Publishers, Inc., P.O. Box 3473, Peabody, Massachusetts 01961-3473, and in Australia by Strand Publishing, Suites 12–13, Fountain Plaza Business Centre, 148 The Entrance Road, Erina NSW 2250.

Printed in the United States of America

Fourth Printing — December 2007

Cover Photo Credit: Photodisc Photography/Getty Images. Used with permission.

Library of Congress Cataloging-in-Publication Data

Frost, Michael, 1961–
     Exiles : living missionally in a post-Christian culture / Michael Frost.
       p. cm.
     Includes bibliographical references.
     ISBN-13: 978-1-56563-670-5 (alk. paper)
     ISBN-10: 1-56563-670-8 (alk. paper)
     1. Postmodernism—Religious aspects—Christianity. 2. Non-institutional churches. 3. Christianity—21st century. 4. Christianity and culture. I. Title.
     BR115.P74F76 2006
     261—dc22
                              2006010724

Scripture taken from the HOLY BIBLE, NEW INTERNATIONAL VERSION. Copyright (c) 1973, 1978, 1984 by International Bible Society. Used by permission of Zondervan Bible Publishers. All rights reserved.

United States ISBN 978-1-56563-670-5
Australian ISBN 978-1-121202-84-1

To Carolyn Frost
in acknowledgement of her compassion for the urban poor,
her deep respect for the marginalized,
and her partnership with the forgotten.

CONTENTS

Part IV: Dangerous Songs

Note to the Reader

As will quickly become obvious, this book contains a good deal of pointed critique. Much of it I have shared in lectures and presentations around the US, Canada, Australia, New Zealand, and the UK. Some of my listeners have reviled it as "church bashing," while others celebrate it as prophetic. I have never claimed to be doing either. I have no stomach for unsophisticated church bashing. Announcing that the church is like an emperor with no clothes is easy enough. Any fool can do it. And besides, the church seems altogether unchanged by such announcements. As Neil Gaiman says, "It has always been the prerogative of children and half-wits to point out that the emperor has no clothes. But the half-wit remains a half-wit, and the emperor remains an emperor."

Neither have I ever made claim to being a prophet. A hundred years ago, Mark Twain debunked the over-valued place of the modern-day prophet with this scathing assessment: "I have done some indiscreet things in my day, but this thing of playing myself for a prophet was the worst." Believe me, I don't wish to be as equally indiscreet in this matter. I claim no greater insight or higher knowledge. Rather, my goal is to make a thoughtful evaluation of many facets of contemporary church and culture, and to offer helpful suggestions for Christians who wish to improve both of them in ways that are biblically sound and pleasing to God. Clearly, I am in sympathy with the multitudes of people who feel exiled outside of or, worse perhaps, within the traditional church, many whose company I have greatly enjoyed on my travels. Nevertheless, it is neither helpful nor truthful for one part of the body of Christ to dismiss the other parts as utterly defective and withdraw into a fortress constructed of self-righteousness. Thus, as a member and lover of the body of Christ, it is my hope that in this book I will engage and edify the entire church and "speak the truth in love" (Eph 4:15). Wherever I fulfill that marvelous directive from Ephesians, I give thanks, and wherever I fail it, I ask forgiveness.

Finally, I wish to thank those who have helped in the development of this book. Morling College generously granted me leave from classroom teaching to complete its writing. The Forge Missions Training Network has been a fertile and supportive community, and in particular its director, Alan Hirsch, my fellow conspirator and dear friend, gave invaluable feedback. I am indebted to Bob Maccini for his editorial comments. He has saved me much embarrassment. And I am especially grateful to Shirley Decker-Lucke from Hendrickson Publishers, who has supported my writing for some years now and who continues to encourage me to put it all down on paper.

PART I

DANGEROUS MEMORIES

1

Self-Imposed Exiles

The Memory: God Will Rescue the Exiled People

I know that men in exile feed on hopes.
—Attributed to Aeschylus (525–456 B.C.E.)

This book is written for those Christians who find themselves falling into the cracks between contemporary secular Western culture and a quaint, old-fashioned church culture of respectability and conservatism. This book is for the many people who wish to be faithful followers of the radical Jesus but no longer find themselves able to fit into the bland, limp, unsavory straitjacket of a church that seems to be yearning to return to the days when "everyone" used to attend church and "Christian family values" reigned. This book is for those who can't remain in the safe modes of church and who wish to live expansive, confident Christian lives in this world without having to abandon themselves to the values of contemporary society. This book is for those Christians who feel themselves ready (or yearning) to jump ship but don't want to be left adrift in a world where greed, consumerism, laziness, and materialism toss them about endlessly and pointlessly. Such Christians live with the nagging tension of being at home neither in the world nor in the church as they've known it. Is there some way of embracing a Christ-centered faith and lifestyle that are lived tenaciously and confidently right out in the open where such a faith is not normally valued? I think so, but it will require a dangerous departure from standard church practice. It seems that the church is still hoping and praying that the ground will shift back and our society will embrace once again the values that it once shared with the Christian community. But for many of us, and for those to whom this book is written, this hoping and praying is a lost cause. We acknowledge that the epoch of history that shaped the contemporary church has crashed like a wave on a shore and left the church high and dry. That epoch is known as the era of <u>Christendom.</u> Christendom has molded

- Not a golden age
- Past imagined to be better than it was.

our churches into their current form and abandoned them to a world that is completely over it all. I'm not the only voice, and certainly not even the most original voice, declaring that Christendom is over and that we too need to get over *it*.

"Christendom" is the name given to the religious culture that has dominated Western society since the fourth century. Awakened by the Roman emperor Constantine, it was the cultural phenomenon that resulted when Christianity was established as the official imperial religion, moving it from being a marginalized, subversive, and persecuted movement to being the only official religion in the empire. Whereas followers of Jesus at one time had met secretly in homes and underground in catacombs, now they were given some of the greatest temples and meeting spaces in the empire. They were, in a quite literal sense, handed the keys of the Roman kingdom. As G. K. Chesterton is noted to have said, "The coziness between church and state is good for the state and bad for the church."

By the Middle Ages, church and state had become the pillars of the sacral culture, each supporting the other. Even where there existed conflicts between church and state, it was always a conflict *within* the overarching con-

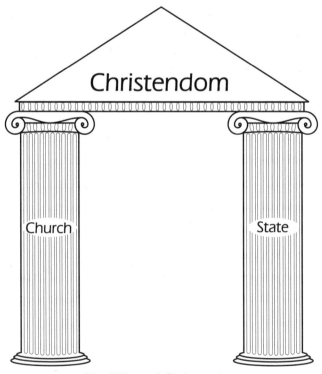

The Pillars of Christendom

figuration of Christendom itself. Christendom had by this stage developed its own distinct identity, one that provided the matrix for the understanding of both church and state. It had effectively become *the* metanarrative for an entire epoch. A metanarrative is an overarching story that claims to contain truth applicable to all people at all times in all cultures. And although the Christendom story no longer defines Western culture in general, it remains the primary definer of the church's self-understanding in almost every Western nation, including, and perhaps especially, the United States.

This metanarrative defined not only church and state, but also all the individuals and social structures in its orbit of influence. Members of this society were assumed to be Christian by birth rather than by choice. Christianity became an official part of the established culture of the empire. In some countries, the king or queen became the head of the church. In Germany, the church actually became a function of the state. The net effect over the entire Christendom epoch was that Christianity moved from being a dynamic, revolutionary, social, and spiritual movement to being a static religious institution with its attendant structures, priesthood, and sacraments.

Taken as a sociopolitical reality, Christendom has been in decline for the last 250 years—so much so that contemporary Western culture has been called by many historians (secular and Christian) the "post-Christendom" culture. Society, at least in its overtly non-Christian manifestation, is "over" Christendom. This is seen in isolated debates and struggles such as the place of prayer in schools and the "politically correct" innovation of renaming Christmas as a solstice gift-giving festival. It can also be seen in the removal of nativity scenes from shopping centers and the revocation of the normal rights and access to cultural events afforded to church leaders. When Roy Moore, chief justice of the Alabama Supreme Court, placed a 2.6–ton granite monument to the Ten Commandments in the rotunda of the Montgomery state judicial building, he had no idea how dead Christendom was, even in the South. Sure enough, two years later U.S. district court judge Myron Thompson ruled that the monument violated the U.S. Constitution's principle of separation of religion and government. Church attendance continues to decline across the West, nowhere more obviously than in Europe and Great Britain. At best, individual Christian congregations are respected and encouraged to continue their practice of corporate worship, but taken as a whole, the church is experiencing a sharp and dramatic deterioration in its influence and impact on Western society.

In the United States, mainline Protestants have never been a majority, but now they number some twenty-two million out of a population of 295 million. Even more troubling than the size of the church today are the results of George Barna's American church surveys. Following the attacks on the cities of Washington and New York on September 11, 2001, Barna asked a nationwide cross-section of Americans what they believed about issues associated with morality. While a majority denounced the terrorist attacks as evil, only a tiny minority (15 percent of adults and 4 percent of teenagers) actually believed in something called "absolute moral truth." Even among those who claimed to be "born-again Christians," less than one-third of adults and less than one-tenth of teenagers believed in such a thing.[1] The survey also found that for most Americans, religious faith is no longer a primary moral and ethical guide. When those surveyed were asked on what basis they make moral and ethical decisions, by far the most common response was "whatever feels right or comfortable in a situation" (38 percent of teens, 31 percent of adults). By contrast, only 13 percent of adults and 7 percent of teens said that they make decisions on the basis of principles taught in the Bible. In my own country, Australia, the impact of the church on mainstream culture is even more diminished, with the combined numbers of evangelicals, Pentecostals, and charismatics (those Christians who are generally most active in sharing their faith) making up just over 2 percent of the population.

Stuart Murray notes that the church in the United Kingdom is in even worse shape. According to Murray, if the current rate of decline in church numbers in the United Kingdom continues, "the Methodist Church will have zero membership by 2037 . . . the Church of Scotland will close its last congregation in 2033 . . . the Church in Wales will be unsustainable by 2020."[2] He also reports on the sad fortunes of the Salvation Army in the United Kingdom as well as an accelerating decline in the Church of England, leading him to announce that the United Kingdom is certainly well and truly in the grip of post-Christendom, which he defines thus:

> Post-Christendom is the culture that emerges as the Christian faith loses coherence within a society that has been definitively shaped by the Christian story and as the institutions that have been developed to express Christian convictions decline in influence.[3]

For many Christians, all this has been a matter of deep grief. There is barely a congregation or a Christian organization that has not publicly bemoaned the waning impact of the Christian story upon American or Western society. And although many Christian voices are calling us back to the days

---

[1]"Americans Are Most Likely to Base Truth on Feelings," The Barna Update n.p. [cited 21 February 2006]. Online: http://www.barna.org/FlexPage.aspx?Page=BarnaUpdate&BarnaUpdateID=106.

[2]Stuart Murray, *Post-Christendom: Church and Mission in a Strange New World* (Carlisle: Paternoster, 2004), 6.

[3]Ibid., 19.

were we ever supposed to?

when the church occupied a position of power and influence over Western society, nobody with any real sense of history believes that we can save Christendom. It has slid slowly into the sea, and with it all our hopes of ruling the West.

Suppose that when the fall of Rome happened, around 410 C.E., there was a small band of specialist Roman road builders supervising the construction of a Roman highway through what we now call Wales. In fact, imagine that you're one of these Roman road builders committed to creating one of Rome's greatest weapons in the conquering of the ancient world. Without roads, Rome's massive armies cannot be mobilized throughout unfamiliar and otherwise impassable routes. Rome succeeded to expand due in large measure to its master road builders. Now you find yourself far from home in a hostile and barbaric land. The road that you have been constructing runs south to north across the Welsh peninsula. It was destined to carry Roman soldiers to barracks across Wales to continue to subdue local communities. Now you find that there's no such thing as a Roman empire at all anymore. The Vandals and the Visigoths have sacked Rome itself. You and your team of construction workers are cut off from home, having created a now obsolete Roman highway. What do you do?

Surely this is the charge facing the church in the post-Christendom West. We have been building churches for an era that has slipped out from under us. The Christendom era, like Rome, has fallen. Now church leaders find themselves cut off and alone in an increasingly foreign culture that is antagonistic to them. The church no longer occupies the high ground. Christianity is believed by many to have been tried and failed. Says Mike Riddell,

> The Christian church is dying in the West. This painful fact is the cause of a great deal of avoidance by the Christian community. . . . Surely God will not let his church come to death? And yet the history of the church in North Africa teaches us that we cannot assume divine intervention to maintain the status of the ecclesiastical institution. It is not only possible for Christianity in the West to falter, it is apparent that the sickness is well advanced.[4]

However, there are other voices that express real hope—not in the reconstitution of Christendom, but in the idea that the end of this epoch actually spells the beginning of a new flowering of Christianity. The death of Christendom removes the final props that have supported the culturally respectable, mainstream, suburban version of Christianity. This is a Christianity

---

[4]Cathy Kirkpatrick, Mark Pierson, and Mike Riddell, *The Prodigal Project: Journey into the Emerging Church* (London: SPCK, 2000), 3.

expressed by the "Sunday Christian" phenomenon wherein church attendance has very little effect on the lifestyles or values or priorities expressed from Monday to Saturday. This version of Christianity is a façade, a method for practitioners to appear like fine, upstanding citizens without allowing the claims and teaching of Jesus to bite very hard in everyday life. With the death of Christendom the game is up. There's less and less reason for such upstanding citizens to join with the Christian community for the sake of respectability or acceptance. The church in fewer and fewer situations represents the best vehicle for public service or citizenship, leaving only the faithful behind to rediscover the Christian experience as it was intended: a radical, subversive, compassionate community of followers of Jesus.

[margin note: Jesus' teaching bites?]

Rediscovering Ourselves as Exiles

One such voice is Old Testament scholar Walter Brueggemann, who finds many parallels between the contemporary Christian experience of dislocation, uncertainty, and irrelevance and the experience of the Old Testament Jewish exiles in Babylon.[5] The Babylonian exile was an event that cast a long and dark shadow right across the history of Israel, affecting its theology, culture, and religious life. At the time, Israel had split into northern and southern nations, and both had been at the mercy of the marauding Assyrian and Egyptian Empires. The Assyrians had seen their empire begin to unravel, and the less powerful Egyptians were ready to pounce on the spoils. In the middle were the powerless nations of Israel and Judah. However, like a storm in the east, the Babylonian Empire was rousing and would eventually become so powerful as to sweep aside both the Assyrians and the Egyptians, capturing the Jewish nations in the process.

The death of Judah's King Josiah in 609 B.C.E. occurred as the Assyrian Empire was breathing its last before the advancing might of Babylon. The Egyptian forces decided to assist the Assyrians against their greater threat, the Babylonians, and on their way east they took control of Judah for four short years, between 609 and 605. The Babylonians, however, were expanding too rapidly for Egypt to contain, and during the reign of Jehoiakim the tiny nation of Judah would totally lose its independence to Babylon and finally disappear into the Babylonian Empire.

After an agonizing siege in which it was the only city in Judah to resist the Babylonian might, Jerusalem finally was razed in the summer of 587 B.C.E.

---

[5]Walter Brueggemann, *Cadences of Home: Preaching among Exiles* (Louisville: Westminster John Knox, 1997).

by Nebuchadnezzar's superior forces. And then began the citizenry's humiliation of living as exiles on the foreign soil of their conquerors. Carted east in a
massive repatriation program, the Jews were allowed to live in their own settlements in the capital and other Babylonian cities. They were free to build
houses, earn a living, and observe their own customs and religion, but they
could not return home to their desolated capital. Jehoiakim and his family
were "guests" in Nebuchadnezzar's household, and some Jews rose to high
positions in public service. Many became so accustomed to life in Babylon that
they refused to return to Jerusalem even when much later there was an opportunity to do so. They had sunk roots in the foreign soil, and Jerusalem held no
allure for them.

The experience that faced the Jewish exiles mirrors the church's experience today. In fact, the biblical metaphor that best suits our current times
and faith situation is that of *exile*. Just like the Jewish exiles, the church today
is grieving its loss and is struggling with humiliation. The ground has slipped
out from under the church. It has lost its footing and needs, as Brueggemann
puts it, to express a resentful sadness about what was, and now is not, and
never will be again. The passing of Christendom might be compared to the
fall of Jerusalem, and there is no going back. Exiles feel like a "motherless
child"—abandoned, rootless, vulnerable, orphaned. Brueggemann cites biblical material such as Lamentations as expressing the honest sadness of an
exilic people. But most pertinently he warns that the danger in exile is to become so preoccupied with self that one cannot step outside oneself to re-
think, reimagine, and redescribe larger reality. Such self-preoccupation very
rarely produces energy, courage, or freedom. What exiles yearn for is an invitation to live "freely, dangerous and tenaciously in a world where faith does
not have its own way."[6] And here lies the root of the problem of the church
today. Victimized by nostalgia and buffeted by fear, the church is focused too
much on merely holding the small plot of ground that it currently occupies
to confidently reimagine a robust future. The result is a retreat into some
fundamentalist us-versus-them model rather than "an endlessly cunning,
risky process of negotiation."[7]

I, for one, am happy to see the end of Christendom. I'm glad that we can
no longer rely on temporal, cultural supports to reinforce our message or the
validity of our presence. I suspect that the increasing marginalization of the
Christian movement in the West is the very thing that will wake us up to
the marvelously exciting, dangerous, and confronting message of Jesus. If we
are exiles on foreign soil—post-Christendom, postmodern, postliterate, and

---

[6]Ibid., 10.
[7]Ibid., 11.

so on—then maybe at last it's time to start living like exiles, as a pesky, fringe-dwelling alternative to the dominant forces of our times. As the saying goes, "Way out people know the way out."[8]

But if we can no longer rely on the buttresses built by Christendom, what kinds of things will provide us a framework for reimagining or rethinking the future of the Christian movement? Again, Walter Brueggemann says that such exilic rediscovering will require the use of intentional disciplines that in every case are marked by danger. Exiles are driven back to their most *dangerous memories,* their recollections of the promises made by Jesus and his daring agenda for human society. Exiles are prepared to practice a set of *dangerous promises,* promises that point to the kingdom and are caught up with the prevailing values of the empire. Exiles will mock the folly of that empire by offering a *dangerous critique* of a society wracked by greed, lust, selfishness, and inequality. And finally, exiles will sing a repertoire of *dangerous songs* that speak of an unexpected newness of life.[9] What makes these things dangerous is that they are practiced under the noses of those who don't care to hear them. When no one in the empire wants to be cast back to the radical story of Jesus or to see the biblical promises being enacted, the reaction can be brutal at worst, disdainful at best. How much more dangerous, then, it is to criticize the empire when everyone seems so satisfied with it as is. Exiles, like the prophets of old, are the troublers of the souls of those who serve this post-Christendom empire. And there is no more dangerous place than under the ire of a seemingly all-powerful empire. *Elijah (troubler of Israel)*

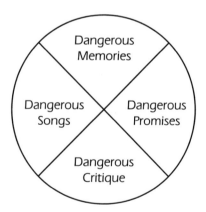

The Driving Forces for the Exile

---

[8]Bob Kaufman, "$$Abomus Craxiom$$," in *Solitudes Crowded with Loneliness* (New York: New Directions, 1965), 80.

[9]See Brueggemann, *Cadences of Home,* 134.

It is my intention to use this framework as the outline for my examination of living as exiles in a post-Christendom world today. We will look at the dangerous memories that will sustain exiles in the twenty-first century, and then we will explore the dangerous promises and dangerous critiques required by them. Finally, we will attempt to learn some dangerous revolutionary songs for exiles.

DANGEROUS MEMORIES

Exiles are driven back to their most dangerous memories. The inoffensive, insipid stories that we tell ourselves will fade away in the face of so stark an experience as exile. When the stakes are high, as they are for captives on foreign soil, exiles will fall back on their most potent memories. These are the elemental stories that galvanize a people to action, that fill them with courage and provide them a framework for dealing with the issues of captivity. Stories of the "good old days" when everyone attended Sunday school, or when traveling evangelists commanded audiences of thousands, will not do the trick. If our most dangerous memories revolve around a time when American Christians didn't drink or smoke or attend the cinema, then we will only ever be moved to nostalgia, not to action. Israel's dangerous memories included the stories of radical departures embraced by Abraham and Sarah and by Moses and Joseph and Jacob. By following the impulses of God's will in their lives, these great heroes spoke into the exiles' experience by demonstrating that God was present and powerful and active across geographic and cultural borders. They refuse to comfort those who would rather remain at ease in a foreign land. They unsettle the comfortable and rouse those yearning for a better day, a new day when God's name is vindicated and God's people blessed. Exiles must resist the temptation to forget completely but also must refashion more realistic and respectable memories. But the Christian's dangerous memories are those of a man who lived in nearly every way differently from the way we are told to live today. The stories of Jesus are an affront to the empire because they call us to abandon consumerism, greed, self-centeredness, and violence. And no empire based on these things wants to be reminded of them. Our dangerous memories are a threat to all who profit from the status quo.

Which are the Christian community's most dangerous memories? Surely they are the stories of the Incarnate One. The stories in the Gospels, far from being soothing bedtime stories for baptized children, are the most dangerous element of the Christian experience. They are radical, daring, unsettling, disturbing, even frightening. Our memories of God's human manifestation will continue to perturb us, inviting us to an alternative set of values that transcends our normal allegiance to our post-Christendom society. The Gospels are replete with stories that shake us out of our preference for the levelheaded, reasonable memories that the church often presents to us. Jesus is not levelheaded, nor is he reasonable. Just when we imagine we have him figured out and boxed in, he wriggles free, confounding our formulas and simplistic explanations. Let's face it: the Gospels aren't bedtime stories at all. Far from sending us drifting off to a carefree sleep, they trouble us, forcing us to reassess the deals we have done with the spirit of this age.

An illustration of the power of such dangerous memory can be found in Stanley Hauerwas's book *A Community of Character.* In that volume he exegetes Richard Adams's charming tale about traveling rabbits, *Watership Down.*[10] Adams's much loved book concerns Fiver, a small, nervous rabbit who develops a messianic hunch that something terrible is going to happen to his Sandleford warren. Fiver tells his brother Hazel, and they try to warn their aging Chief Rabbit, the Threarah, without success. Hazel and Fiver, marginalized as doomsayers, decide that they must leave, and they are joined by other strangely named rabbits: Bigwig, Dandelion, Pipkin, Hawkbit, Blackberry, Buckthorn, Speedwell, Acorn, and Silver. As they make their timely escape, their warren is destroyed by a housing developer's bulldozers. There is now no turning back.

So, the little band takes off across the countryside in search of a new home, Watership Down. As they make their escape, they must court many great dangers, the likes of which rabbits never encounter. They must cross a stream, traverse a bean field, and negotiate an open road. These are obstacles that rabbits normally must never approach. Everything within the DNA of a rabbit tells it to stop running, to dig deep into the cool, cool earth. Every rabbit's instinct is to hide underground. For Fiver and Hazel and their band to continue across the fox-infested open fields, they must countermand their every natural impulse. How are they to do it? The answer lies in a surprising quarter. The one thing that unites the band and fills them with courage are the stories they retell themselves, stories they heard as babies at their parents' knees. These stories all concern the clever rabbit folk hero El-ahrairah. The first such story told in *Watership Down* is the story of the "Blessing of El-ahrairah"

This story is the account of Frith, the god of the rabbits, allocating gifts to each of the species. In the story, each of the animals receives the characteristics for which we know them—the fox receives cunning, the cat eyes that can see in the dark, and so on. El-ahrairah is too busy dancing, eating, and

---

[10]Stanley Hauerwas, *A Community of Character: Toward a Constructive Christian Social Ethic* (Notre Dame, Ind.: University of Notre Dame Press, 1981).

mating and misses out on the best gifts. Realizing that rabbits will now be at the mercy of all the other gifted creatures, Frith grants him strong hind legs for escaping and declares that all the world will be the enemy of rabbits. He declares El-ahrairah to be the prince with a thousand enemies and pronounces, "But first they must catch you, digger, listener, runner, prince with the swift warning. Be cunning and full of tricks and your people will never be destroyed."[11] Such a story explains to Fiver and Hazel and the others the reason for their very being. It is their creation story, and El-ahrairah is their hero. This story is more than a simple explanation for why rabbits have strong hind legs; it describes the rabbits' task in life. It is not to try to make the world safe, but rather to learn to live in a dangerous world by trusting in stories, speed, wit, and each other. Says Hauerwas,

> I suspect it is not accidental that this is the first story told by the rabbits that left Sandleford, as all new communities must remind themselves of their origin. A people are formed by a story which places their history in the texture of the world. Such stories make the world our home by providing us with the skills to negotiate the dangers in our environment in a manner appropriate to our nature.[12]

What keeps the rabbits running, searching for their new home? It is the stories of El-ahrairah, their dangerous memories. These stories fill them with courage and provide them with answers for the dilemmas posed by life on the road. Whenever the rabbits are confronted by a challenge, they stop and rehearse the stories of their folk hero, the prince with a thousand enemies. They are, as Hauerwas refers to them, a story-formed community, and it is the stories that spur them on, driving them forward to the safety of Watership Down.

So too with the Jewish exiles in Babylon and the Christian movement today: we are a story-formed community. The Christian experience is not primarily formed by our liturgy, doctrine, or ecclesiology, as important as those might be. We are formed by the dangerous stories of our great hero. Just as the rabbits' instinct is to stop and dig, so too our very human instinct is to embrace safety, warmth, and security. Our all-too-human impulses push us toward being untroubled. We build houses, embrace respectability, and try not to stand out. We want to escape into the cool, cool earth rather than to cut out across the open fields, courting danger, negotiating challenges. So what will get us up and out of our safe warrens? What will continue to foster unease about being exiled in a post-Christendom world? Surely it will be the radical stories of Jesus, the prince with a thousand enemies.

---

[11]Richard Adams, *Watership Down* (New York: Avon Books, 1972), 37.
[12]Hauerwas, *Community of Character*, 15.

Jesus, fully human and fully divine

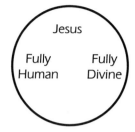

Some people separate the human and the divine

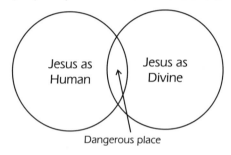

Dangerous place

The Danger of the Incarnation

Probably the most dangerous aspect of the Christ story is the very nature of the incarnation itself. Jesus models that it is possible to be both God and human at the same time. This is for us, certainly, the most terrifying thought. Throughout history the church has retreated into deifying Jesus so thoroughly that the human Christ can't be seen. If indeed Jesus is too human (or barely human at all), he calls from me a worrying response. He challenges my humanness and demands more from me than I can imagine offering. An overly deified Christ reduces my perceived response. To this otherworldly, superspiritual Jesus I simply have to offer my devotion, my worship, my adoration. By the grubby, human, peasant Christ I am challenged that maybe it is possible to be human and Godlike after all. Nowhere in Scripture is this more disturbingly presented than in Jesus' return to his hometown after the beginning of his messianic ministry. There, Jesus began teaching in the synagogue, and received what to me has always seemed a deeply shocking response. The locals, his old boyhood friends and neighbors, are offended and say,

> Where did this man get this wisdom and these miraculous powers? Isn't this the carpenter's son? Isn't his mother's name Mary, and aren't his brothers James, Joseph, Simon and Judas? Aren't all his sisters with us? Where then did this man get all these things? (Matt 13:54b–56)

How distressing to us that Jesus could be the Messiah, the human incarnation of God, second person of the Trinity for thirty years and *no one at home noticed!* No one in Nazareth smiles knowingly and says, "I always suspected there was something strange about that kid." Instead they wonder where he got all this messianic stuff. Somehow Jesus could be fully God and blend into Galilean society—hardly the most pious or sophisticated culture—without creating a ripple. This perspective on the incarnation bothers us because it dangerously invites us to follow Christ in all his ordinariness as well as all his righteousness. The incarnation demands that we neither retreat into a holier-than-thou Christian ghetto nor give ourselves over to the values of secular culture. And let's be honest: that is the most dangerous place of all. It is easier to imagine and embrace a closeted fundamentalism that retreats into a Christ-against-culture mindset. We can picture Jesus there, all holy and pure, unsullied by the world around him. We can also understand the capitulation to our host culture that some Christians make. It would be easy to join those Christians who abandon themselves to materialism, greed, and selfishness.

When responding as exiles in a post-Christendom world, we are used to seeing some respond with despair and grief (the fundamentalists) and others with assimilation to the dominant values. What is much more disturbing to us is the example of a God who does neither, but instead answers with a fresh, imaginative theological response. Jesus neither slides into compromise and sinfulness, nor fulfills our expectations of the holier-than-thou guru. The fact that both Matthew and Mark include this episode in their biographies of Jesus is remarkable. The story almost completely undermines claims about the divinity of Jesus. It is included because it is a dangerous memory for followers of Christ. We are called, like Christ, to be godly, but we are expected to live it out fully in the midst of others. There is no more dangerous path than the one trodden by Jesus.

DANGEROUS PROMISES

Recalling the stories of Jesus is one affront to the empire, but a second cause of annoyance to that empire is the resolute commitment by a few stouthearted souls to imagine a shift of power in the world, a shift from greed and self-righteousness to love and justice. The Christian movement must be the living, breathing promise to society that it is possible to live out the values of Christ—that is, to be a radical, troubling alternative to the power imbalances in the empire. In a world of greed and consumerism, the church ought to be a community of generosity and selflessness. In a host empire that is

living in a nostalgic past perhaps

committed to marginalizing the poor, <u>resisting the place of</u> women, causing suffering to the disenfranchised, the Christian community must be generous to a fault, pursuant of justice, flushed with mercy.

We are called by God to be God's and each other's companions. The term "companion" is rich in meaning, coming from the Latin *com panis* ("with bread"). We are called to deliver on the promise that we will share bread with others, that we will be *one* with each other. There are many names for this sharing: utopia, community, the kingdom of God. It is this sharing that Jesus calls us to. He does so in the sacramental feast known as the Lord's Supper. He breaks bread and shares it with us. Indeed he *is* the bread, the nourishment that binds us together in our mutual need of him. The Christian movement ought to offer the promise to others that we are the epitome of companionship. We, the church, are God's experimental garden in this world. A story from the country of my birth will express this. When the east coast of the island later to be called Australia was first settled by Europeans in 1788, it was discovered that the harbor at Sydney, <u>despite its beauty</u>, was no place for food production. Sydney is in fact built on a seam of sandstone, a clay shelf, that has been great for building a modern city but terrible for farming. So members of the new British colony nearly starved to death, stuck on the other side of the planet from their home. To stay alive they were entirely reliant on a steady stream of supply ships running back and forth from England to Sydney.   *metaphor*

Then in 1791 a <u>freed convict</u> named James Ruse petitioned the governor for a grant of land <u>northwest of the westernmost part</u> of the colony. He was to attempt to hack out of the virgin scrubland and soil the first viable crop-producing farm. His grand experiment was seen as an indicator of whether the new penal colony could survive without supplies from England. In fact, Ruse called his property <u>Experiment Farm</u>. In a sense, the whole colony held its collective breath and awaited the outcome. After a couple of encouraging seasons, Ruse eventually produced a bumper harvest. Experiment Farm was renamed Model Farm, for that's what it had become—a model for others to follow. Even today Ruse's original cottage at <u>Model Farm</u> is a national monument, symbolizing the hopes of the fledgling nation.

This, then, surely is the mandate of the contemporary church: to be a model farm, an example to others of the hope of the power of the gospel. We are to promise our host empire that the keys to the life abundant rest with us. Christ has delivered them to us. He has fashioned us into a people who belong to God ("Once you were not a people, but now you are the people of God" [1 Pet 2:10]). I've heard it said that the best way to critique the old is to fashion the new. What is needed is a community of believers who will fashion a new way of expressing their Christlikeness, a way of grace, mercy, forgiveness, and service. Said Lesslie Newbigin, "The only hermeneutic of the gospel is a congregation of men and women who believe it and live by it." This is our most dangerous promise, that the power of the Holy Spirit in our midst changes us, shapes us, remakes us as a collective of companions who share the bread of Christ among ourselves and beyond ourselves with others. It would seem that the poor reputation currently held by members of the Religious Right is due in part to the fact that they are eager to criticize public policy, but are unable to demonstrate the godly society that they demand of others. Rocked by financial and sexual scandals, the fundamentalist faction is ignored by many in contemporary society precisely because it cannot follow up its critique with the fulfillment of its dangerous promises.

In the book of Daniel, the fifth chapter is a critique of Babylon, while the sixth chapter is the promise of the exile who refuses to succumb to the rulers of the age. Daniel is cast into the lions' den because he refuses to bow the knee to a king who claims to be all-powerful and worthy of his worship. Daniel won't yield to the lordship of the Babylonian king, and he seems destined to pay the ultimate price. His miraculous rescue fills Christians the world over with the promise that God will vindicate those who remain loyal to him. Of course, many persecuted Christians around the planet have been as faithful as Daniel, and God has not shut the lions' mouths. Daniel 6 is not a promise that we will all triumph over our oppressors; rather, it is a theologically creative affirmation that the promises we make by remaining faithful to God's plan for us will bear fruit. The hope is that such faithfulness eventually will break the heart of the battle-weary King Darius, and that he too will burst forth with praise. This is a lesson more obviously learned by the Christians who remained true under Soviet oppression, or who do so today under the Chinese communist regime. Not all are rescued from the lions, but somehow, under God's great grace, their faithfulness eventually will elicit praises from the mouths of their oppressors.

Here in the post-Christendom West there is much talk about justice and peace, but the dangerous examples of Daniel and Jesus and our Chinese brothers and sisters reinforce that such criticism of our host empire must involve our actions and our lifestyles, not just our words. Vaclav Havel, the Czech poet, dissident, and prime minister, knew more about this than I when he said,

> There is such an enormous gap between our words and deeds! Everyone talks about freedom, democracy, justice, human rights, and peace; but at the same time, everyone, more or less, consciously or unconsciously, serves those values and ideals only to the extent necessary to defend and serve his own interests, and those of his group and state. Who should break this vicious circle? Responsibility cannot be preached: it can only be borne, and the only possible place to begin is with oneself.

Indeed, such promises must be enacted, not just proclaimed, even if it means that we might be headed for the lions' den.

Dangerous Criticism

The living out of these promises will mean that exiles must practice critical distance from their context. They must resist assimilation and refuse despair. Even though some Jewish exiles became very accustomed to the culture of their conquerors, settling into the cool, cool earth of Babylon, the faithful ones continued to practice a dangerous form of criticism. Of course, nowhere is this more powerfully seen in the Babylonian exile than in the example of Daniel. In fact, Daniel does the very dangerous thing that we see later in Jesus. He remains resolutely faithful to Yahweh and the Jewish law and yet he thrives in a foreign, ungodly society. While he prospers in Babylon, he doesn't grow too cozy with his host empire, asserting that its values are incongruous with God's governance. Other equally dangerous biblical examples include Joseph's role in Egypt and Esther's reign as the wife of a Persian king. All three characters flourish in pagan lands, and all three are used by God to bring glory to God's name. Of course, it should be noted that the book of Daniel, from which we derive nearly all our information about him, wasn't written during the Babylonian captivity, nor was it read by the Babylonian exiles. It was compiled much later and probably written to Jews dealing with similar issues of confinement by an oppressive regime. Nonetheless, the example of Daniel is designed to show how faithful followers of Yahweh respond in a pagan host empire.

In Daniel's case, we know little of his early career other than that he was an Israelite of royal or noble birth, and that he was carried into captivity by Nebuchadnezzar's army. Once in exile, he trained for the king's service and, following a custom of the time, was given the Babylonian name "Belteshazzar." We know him for his sagacity and his great skill as an interpreter of dreams, which eventually led to him occupying several leading governmental posts under the kings Nebuchadnezzar, Belshazzar, and Darius.

But one of the episodes for which Daniel is known by virtually every Sunday school scholar in history centers around his role as a critic of Belshazzar's court. In the fifth chapter of the book that bears his name, Daniel is ushered into the king's presence to interpret the bizarre vision of a disembodied hand that writes an unintelligible message on a wall. The language has stumped all of the king's seers and diviners, so Daniel is offered inducements to solve the riddle. Showing great pluck, Daniel doesn't resist translating God's rebuke of Belshazzar for his sacrilege and lasciviousness before declaring the supernatural message to be Yahweh's judgment on his reign. That very night Belshazzar is assassinated. The episode demonstrates that even though exiles may thrive in a pagan court, they are to never capitulate to the values of that court. Ironically, the king rewards Daniel for interpreting the very vision that spells the end of his life. The idea of being rewarded for critiquing a host empire seems remarkable, even unbelievable, but it fosters a hope that the godly will be blessed for taking the risk of speaking up for God's values in the face of great opposition.

That opposition is realized in Daniel 6, where Belshazzar's successor, Darius, is duped by jealous forces within the government to execute Daniel for his refusal to cease praying to Yahweh. It too is a well-known story and likewise demonstrates the power in the exile who refuses to bow to the prevailing culture. Daniel is kept safe in the lions' den, and then the Babylonian king, who was loath to throw him in there in the first place, says, "I issue a decree that in every part of my kingdom people must fear and reverence the God of Daniel," and erupts spontaneously in a hymn of praise:

> For he is the living God
>> and he endures forever;
> his kingdom will not be destroyed,
>> his dominion will never end.
> He rescues and he saves;
>> he performs signs and wonders
>> in the heavens and on the earth.
> He has rescued Daniel
>> from the power of the lions. (Dan 6:26b–27)

What are we to make of this? A pagan king is giving praise to the God of Israel! Like the rabbit stories of El-ahrairah, they are daydreams of the vindication of the powerless. Exiles, like the rabbits of *Watership Down,* have a thousand enemies in the highest places. In Daniel 6 we see a day when the exiles will speak critically into the center of ungodly power and triumph despite their enemies' foxlike cunning. Walter Brueggemann sees this dangerous criticism of power taking two broad forms. First, exiles must offer a *religious* critique of the empire:

> Every concentration of power needs its gods to bless it, to give credibility and legitimacy, to evoke loyalty and confidence. Every empire has such legitimating gods, however hidden they may be. But [says the exile] these gods are in fact a joke, because they have no power and they cannot save.[13]

---

[13]Brueggemann, *Cadences of Home,* 121.

In a post-Christendom world those gods take various forms. Perhaps there is no more powerful "religion" today than materialism. Like a pagan Babylonian religion, it demands all our attention, insisting on everything we have to offer, until in the end all our efforts are bent into its service. As a result, the empire thrives on inequality, injustice, oppression, and deceit. The greed inspired by such a world leads to environmental destruction, religious persecution, and apathy toward suffering. Today, we need tenacious followers of Jesus who are prepared to make fun of the powerlessness of these gods and their inability to save or to heal. This will take not only our words, but also our actions, our radical lifestyles.

And second, says Brueggemann, we must be prepared to voice a *political* critique against entrenched power. Once again, Daniel is a good example. He often announces the impending collapse of the empire, anticipating its shame and humiliation. His risky message to Belshazzar is that his empire had received all its greatness from Yahweh but had violated Yahweh's mandate by showing no mercy and no honor. By imagining itself to be autonomous, Babylon ensures its own destruction.

Something similar occurs in John's Gospel when Pontius Pilate, looking for a face-saving way to release his prisoner Jesus, offers him, beaten and humiliated, to the crowd. Their hunger to see Jesus crucified shocks even Pilate. Later, when he addresses his prisoner in private, Jesus refuses to answer him. Frustrated by his lack of cooperation or his refusal to beg for mercy, the governor boasts, "Don't you realize I have power either to free you or to crucify you?" Unperturbed, Jesus replies, through split lips and broken teeth, with a dangerous criticism: "You would have no power over me if it were not given to you from above" (John 19:10–11). By imagining himself to be autonomous, Pilate demonstrates his own folly, and Jesus calls him on it. Like Jesus, exiles must avoid such phony and seductive autonomy. All human life is at the mercy of God and is expected to yield to God's sovereignty and carry out the divine purposes of justice, mercy, and love. The host empire, including ours today, cannot keep its puny promises of life, and we, the people of God, must be prepared to say so. In a powerfully worded poem, Danish pastor Kaj Munk puts it this way:

> What is, therefore, the task of the preacher (or the church) today?
> Shall I answer: "Faith, hope and love"?
> That sounds beautiful.
> But I would say—Courage.
> No, even that is not challenging enough to be the whole truth.
> Our task today is recklessness.
> For what we Christians lack is not psychology or literature,
> we lack a holy rage.

The recklessness that comes from the knowledge of God and humanity.
The ability to rage when justice lies prostrate on the streets . . .
    and when the lie rages across the face of the earth—
        a holy anger about things that are wrong in the world.
To rage against the ravaging of God's earth,
    and the destruction of God's world.
To rage when little children must die of hunger,
    when the tables of the rich are sagging with food.
To rage at the senseless killing of so many,
    and against the madness of militaries.
To rage at the lie that calls the threat of death and the strategy of
destruction—Peace.
To rage against complacency.
To restlessly seek that recklessness that will challenge and seek to change
    human history until it conforms with the norms of the Kingdom of
    God.
And remember the signs of the Christian Church have always been—
    the Lion, the Lamb, the Dove, and the Fish . . .
        but never the chameleon.[14]

This is not a call to join a monastery or to escape to a kibbutz. We have to work and shop and live in the empire. Instead, it addresses our imagination, shaping and summoning us to another way, the way of Jesus, lived sincerely out in the open in the everyday. But surely today, of all times, someone must be prepared to cut through the imperial ideology and expose the true character of the empire. In a world where eleven million children die every year of preventable diseases, where thirty-five thousand people die each day of starvation,[15] where Christians from many nations are denied basic human rights, where the U.S. government holds international prisoners without charge or trial, where the AIDS epidemic continues across Africa unchecked, where possibly HIV-infected children are not tested for fear of increasing the damning statistics, who else would speak up but those who serve Christ? "To restlessly seek recklessness" is some vocation.

Dangerous Songs

Our current church culture, so wedded to Christendom thinking and now so out of touch with its host empires, avoids danger and stumps for gentleness, sentimentality, respectability. Nowhere is this more obvious than in

---

[14]Kaj Munk, http://kevinburt.typepad.com/the_nomadic_neophyte/religion/, cited April 4, 2006.

[15]http://www.starvation.net, cited March 31, 2006.

the songs we sing and the preaching we hear each Sunday. Our music is often insipid, cloying, and romantic. We sing pop-style love songs to Jesus, confessing our undying love for him in the same way that pop idols sing to a boyfriend or girlfriend. Where is the danger? Where is the responsibility? So many great revolutions have been birthed through the songs that their revolutionaries sang. The French revolutionaries sang in 1789 outside the Bastille. The Bolsheviks sang their radical songs in St. Petersburg. The American civil rights movement sang of liberty and righteousness in Alabama. The anti-Marcos revolutionaries sang through the streets of Manila. In South Africa, under apartheid, Christmas carols were banned because they evoked a revolutionary yearning for freedom and peace. That's how powerful the music of revolution can be.

Even more recently, we have seen the use of singing to rouse a new generation of Chinese into action. As China undergoes enormous economic and social change, it may surprise some people to learn that revolutionary songs still ring out over the capital, Beijing. Every morning for the past five years, in an ancient park called the Temple of Heaven, south of the Forbidden City, hundreds of people gather to sing. Armed with nothing more dangerous than a songbook, they sing revolutionary songs, some from before China's liberation, some from the time of the anti-Japanese war, and others written just after the communists came to power. These are the songs of the radical revolutionary past, before the Gang of Four and the Cultural Revolution, before the suffering and the corruption of modern China. These were the songs that imagined a radical, daring, magnificent future of equality and justice for all, and that, when sung today, hold the Chinese regime accountable, indicting them for their failure to deliver.

In his memoir of his time running a free medical clinic in one of India's largest slums, Gregory Roberts recalls the time he first heard the Blind Singers of Nagpur. Stumbling upon a late-closing nightspot on the outskirts of Bombay, he heard a choir of angelic voices singing in Urdu. He describes it this way:

> A gradual silence settled in the room, and then all of a sudden three men began to sing in powerful, thrilling voices. It was a luscious sound—a layered gorgeous music of passionate intensity. The men weren't just singing, they were crying and wailing in song. Real tears ran from their closed eyes and dripped onto their chests. I was elated, listening to it; and yet, somehow I felt ashamed. It was as if the singers had taken me into their deepest and most intimate love and sorrow.[16]

---

[16]Gregory David Roberts, *Shantaram* (Melbourne: Scribe Publications, 2003), 193.

Roberts then retells their sad story. While performing in a remote village, the traveling singers were caught up in a tribal battle and captured by marauding bandits. Along with twenty members of the village, they were captured, tortured, and had their eyes put out with bamboo rods. Now they travel around India, singing Urdu worship songs in nightclubs and cafés. Their effect is mesmerizing. While listening to their breathtaking performance, Roberts remembers a local philosopher leaning over and whispering in his ear, "The truth is found more often in music than it is in books of philosophy."

Compare these wild, rebellious songs to the lyrics of contemporary Christian worship songs. So many worshippers today sing, doe-eyed and sentimental, about their special love for Jesus (and his for them). Yet, in the past our brothers and sisters sang into reality a marvelous new world, a dangerous set of promises. Another exile, a revolutionary named Isaiah, writing in exilic times composed these words on behalf of God:

> For a long time I have kept silent,
> I have been quiet and held myself back.
> But now, like a woman in childbirth,
> I cry out, I gasp and pant. (Isa 42:14)

So, when the fierce Yahweh sings, he does so like a mother in labor. Now, that's my kind of singing! God's songs give birth to a new world, a new way of being his followers. And when we join in on the chorus of these rough, revolutionary songs, we share in the promise-making of God. We too declare our commitment to a new way, a way of justice, peace, mercy, and generosity. Why can't our corporate singing summon up a world where the poor are fed and the marginalized are welcomed at the table of the Lord? Why can't we sing about the world that Jesus dreamed up on the side of that mountain? Why does our singing so often seem so trivial? If you've ever seen the powerful and violent New Zealand film *Once Were Warriors,* you will have seen two very different types of singing.

Set in Auckland, the film deals with the Heke family, Maoris torn apart by violence, alcohol, and social dislocation. Beth Heke is a feisty, beautiful mother of five, married for eighteen years to her volatile husband, Jake, a muscular, explosive man. Jake spends most of his time at the local pub, getting drunk and proving his masculinity with his fists. Beth too experiences his wrath, and in one early and nearly unwatchable scene, Jake beats her senseless. But Beth is profoundly conscious of her warrior heritage. As a child, she was the chosen princess of her tribe, but she abandoned her destiny as a tribal leader by running off to marry Jake, whose family is descended from slaves. By rejecting her regal heritage she finds herself living a pointless suburban existence with Jake and her children, cut off from her tribal community. Jake leads her into a life of heavy drinking and loud parties. When drunk, Jake and his friends sing meaningless pop songs like the New Zealand novelty hit, "What's the Time, Mister Wolf?"

At the end of the film, after their daughter Grace's tragic death, Beth returns to the Maori longhouse (or *marai*) of her ancestors to bury her child. By returning her daughter to the spiritual home of her own childhood, Beth is seeking to reconnect to the history and community of her culture. Jake, instead, remains behind, drinking heavily in the pub with his friends, the jukebox blaring pointless pop songs. At the funeral Beth explains her heritage to her dead daughter and begs her forgiveness for taking her from the safety of the marai. Then the community erupts in traditional singing. These ancient songs offer the grieving family strength and communal power. Their singing is a protest against the violence, alcoholism, and futility of their urban existence. They sing up a new world, drawing on the anchors of the past. Meanwhile, Jake accepts free beer from his mates to drown his sorrow until the jukebox clicks over to another familiar song. "What's the Time, Mister Wolf?" begins to play. Grief-and guilt-stricken, Jake picks up a chair and smashes the jukebox. The silly novelty song offers no solace, no strength, no anchor in times of turmoil. His songs count for nothing. They mean nothing. They summon no change. They challenge no action. They are diversions from reality, not responses to that reality.

Like God singing in travail in chapter 42 of Isaiah, the Maori songs are pregnant with meaning and resounding with hope for Beth and her children. Surely Christian worship ought to do the same. I'm not necessarily advocating that we return to the rousing old hymns of Isaac Watts or Charles Wesley. Rather, I want to hear a new song, a revolutionary Christsong that summons from me greater faith in the new world that God is forming within us. Likewise, I want to hear a spoken word in the assembly that expresses danger, energy, possibility, an opening for newness. So much of our preaching is so overly concerned with the technical questions of getting the truth *right* that preachers have squeezed all the life out of the gospel. We have thought of the gospel as a fragile and precious object and have held it too tightly, rendering it shapeless and uninteresting. Much of what passes for gospel speech these days is not dramatic or artistic. It is bound by the reason of technique and overly concerned with concreteness. It seems stilted and mechanical. We believers hear it presented to us week in and week out, and by virtue of the very fact that we *are* believers, we put up with it. It is a truth greatly reduced, and it calls forth from us a faith greatly reduced also. Our struggle in the twenty-first century will be the struggle to maintain our commitment to the teachings of Jesus and the revelation of the gospel in the New Testament while endeavoring to rediscover a robust, poetic faith that abandons certitude and inanity.

Generously Angry

In England in 1922, young Eric Blair, with no idea what else to do with his life, followed in his father's footsteps and joined the Indian Imperial Police, serving as a subdivisional officer in Burma. By all accounts, he hated every minute of it, and finally he resigned and returned to England five years later at the age of twenty-four. Listless, unambitious, disheveled, and possibly depressed, he returned to a bedroom in his family's home. He lived there in obscurity for a year before he emerged in 1928, declared that he intended to become a writer, and headed off to Paris. Today we know him as George Orwell. His emergence in 1928 was as dramatic as the transformation of a caterpillar into a butterfly. The maudlin young Eric Blair disappeared into his bedroom one day, only to materialize a year later as the tenacious, prophetic writer Orwell. This is the same Orwell who wrote of the injustices of street life in Paris and London, who fought in the Spanish Civil War, and who poked fun at the horrors of Stalinism. We might well ask what happened in that bedroom that year in 1927. By Orwell's own account, he simply took to his bed with as many books by Charles Dickens as he could find. He was transformed by reading Dickens! *The Pickwick Papers, David Copperfield, Bleak House, A Tale of Two Cities, Great Expectations.* Immersed in these stories, Orwell developed the passionate zeal of a crusader for the poor and disenfranchised. These stories changed him and changed the course of his life. Writing much later, he said,

> Reading Dickens I see the face of a man who is always fighting against something, but who fights in the open and is not frightened, the face of a man who is generously angry.[17]

Dickens's stories became Orwell's dangerous memories. They brought him out in the open, campaigning for a greater cause. Orwell's own books, *Down and Out in Paris and London, Animal Farm, Nineteen Eighty-Four,* were uncompromisingly dangerous critiques of the world around him, but contained within their pages were the marvelous promises of a better world. If reading Dickens can do that for a person, what can reading Jesus do? I love Orwell's description of Dickens as one who is angry and fighting against this world, but who does so generously, out in the open, not lurking in the

---

[17]D. J. Taylor, *Orwell: The Life* (New York: Henry Holt, 2003), 57.

shadows. This is the honorable fight of the exile, to be generously, expansively, tenaciously angry.

Exiles are inspired by visions, ideas, and inspirations that spring pristine from the primary spring of truth and life: Christ himself. They have a word to say, not stained by this present, disintegrating society, but coming from the unquenched source of hope through which society might be reborn. Joseph Campbell spoke of people like this—he called them "heroes"—when he wrote,

> The hero has died as a modern man; but as eternal man—perfected, unspecific, universal man—he has been reborn. His second solemn task and deed therefore . . . is to return then to us, transfigured, and teach the lessons he has learned of life renewed.[18]

Campbell was not speaking in Christian terms, but he was on to something when he dared to hope for people who could taste of life as it was meant to be and speak into this fractured world about how to find it. For Christians, those lessons are found on the lips of Jesus, our dangerous memory. Furthermore, Campbell says,

> We have not even to risk the adventure alone; for the heroes of all time have gone before us; the labyrinth is thoroughly known; we have only to follow the thread of the hero-path.[19]

For followers of Jesus, it is he who has gone before us. He has trod the true hero-path. Campbell continues:

> The passage of the . . . hero . . . is inward—into depths where obscure resistances are overcome, and long lost, forgotten powers are revivified, to be made available for the transfiguration of the world. . . . [Now] it appears that the perilous journey was a labor not of attainment but of reattainment, not discovery but rediscovery.[20]

This is the work of the exile—not the discovery of a new gospel, or a new Christ, or a new Bible, as some more liberal thinkers have suggested, but the rediscovery of the original genius of the teaching of Jesus and the missional practice of the earliest Christians, all lived out boldly on the soil of a post-Christian empire. As that hoary old mystic William Blake once wrote,

> I will not cease from mental flight,
> Nor shall my sword sleep in my hand,

---

[18]Joseph Campbell, *The Hero with a Thousand Faces* (Commemorative ed.; Bollingen Series 17; Princeton, N.J.: Princeton University Press, 2004), 24.
[19]Ibid.
[20]Ibid.

Till we have built Jerusalem
In England's green and pleasant land.[21]

So this book is written to those who feel like exiles in a post-Christendom era. If you're like me, you have no stomach for calling the church back to the old ways that were developed during Christendom. We're out of our Sandleford burrow and heading across uncharted territory. How will we practice our critical distance from our context? How will we express our radical promises to this world? As mentioned earlier, we must begin by casting ourselves back to our most wonderful, but dangerous, memories. We must begin with the example of Jesus himself. Before we begin strategizing or scheming, we twenty-first-century Christians must reposition ourselves chiefly, first and foremost, as people of the way of Christ. And it's to his example that we now turn.

---

[21]Quoted in Malcolm Muggeridge, *A Third Testament* (London: Collins, 1978), 86.

Jesus the Exile

The Memory: Jesus Was a Radical and a Subversive

Jesus passed among the people
in a chef's hat
and they kissed His spoons and forks
and ate well from invisible dishes.

—Anne Sexton

The great Spanish painter Bartolomé Esteban Murillo was the youngest of fourteen children of a Sevillian barber, Gaspar Esteban, and his wife, Maria Peres. In 1627, his father died, and a year later came the death of his mother. Because his elder sisters and brothers had already grown up and left home, the ten-year-old Bartolomé was adopted into the family of his aunt, who was married to a wealthy Sevillian doctor. There he encountered a strict religious household and was often in conflict with his pious Catholic adoptive father. In pride of place in the sitting room of the doctor's house hung a large picture entitled *Jesus the Shepherd Boy.* Murillo said that the picture dominated the family, and its depiction of the young boy Jesus was in keeping with the devout tenor of the household. Murillo, himself later known for his religious paintings that emphasized the peaceful, joyous aspects of spiritual life, claimed that the picture haunted him for most of his years with the doctor's family.

The shepherd boy in the gilt frame stood bolt upright, straight and tall, his shepherd's crook like a sentinel's bayonet. Around his head beamed an obligatory halo. His eyes were lifeless, averted. His cheeks were rosy, and his complexion was unsullied. To the young Bartolomé, nothing could be further from his vision of a young Judean shepherd boy. One day when his adoptive family was out of the house, he removed the picture from the wall and began to work on it with his paint set. The stern, unflinching face was given a lively grin. The eyes were enlivened with mischief. The halo was transformed into a battered straw hat, and the plastered-down hair was now tousled and unruly. Jesus' crook was turned into a gnarled walking stick, and the somewhat limp lamb at his feet was altered into a troublesome dog. Though this painting is now lost forever, his efforts apparently were remarkable. His precocious talent and character were emerging even in childhood.

When the barber and his wife returned home, they were so disturbed by the sacrilege committed by their young charge that they forced him to carry the offensive work through the streets of Seville to shame him for his blasphemy. But far from humiliating him, the experience provided him his escape from their guardianship. A local religious icon painter, Juan del Castillo, was so impressed by the playful impression of Jesus that he took the boy into his home and apprenticed him, preparing him for his vocation as one of Spain's greatest religious artists.

I find myself regularly returning to this story as an emblem of my own life and ministry. I suspect that it has been my life's work to paint over the unreal, highly symbolic images of Jesus that many people carry and to seek to render something richer, more real, more inspiring than the porcelain icons that occupy the imaginations of many people today. I like to imagine myself as the mischievous and precocious young Bartolomé Esteban Murillo with my paint set on the living room floor, listening for the sounds of steps on the front path, hurrying in my work before I'm caught by the powers that be. But it's more than playfulness for me. It's my vocation of sorts, for I fear that our highly sanitized, domesticated images of Jesus derive not from the New Testament, but from two millennia of romantic Christian art and culture. And I'd go further and suggest that the degree to which we adopt a tame and insipid picture of Jesus is the degree to which we avoid the mission to which he has called us.

All Christian missional activity—our dangerous criticism, our dangerous promises—must emerge from our relationship to Jesus. He was the ultimate exile. Thinking equality with God a thing not to be grasped after, he humbled himself and allowed himself to be "exiled" on the earth. And like all good and faithful exiles, he enters fully into life in this host empire without giving himself over to it completely. It is the Spirit of Christ within each of us that gives rise to a missional lifestyle. And it is Jesus' actions and teaching that form our primary model for mission. Therefore, without question, the Gospels must be taken seriously as prescriptive texts for life, mission, and discipleship. Unfortunately, Jesus generally has been understood through dogmatic ontological frames (as in the creeds) or through the theological reflections of Paul (as in the Reformation). We need to recover the wonder of reading Jesus through the eyes of his earliest witnesses, the Gospel writers. There we find the nature of Jesus not so much reflected on or theologized about, but simply presented in all its strange glory. Jesus isn't romanticized in the earliest creeds. He is presented in flesh and blood, very real and very dangerous.

Sadly, the early church was quick to move beyond the very earthy, actional description of Jesus in the Gospels to a much more ontological one in the creeds. The ancient creeds developed in this period provide a small example of this evolution. The Old Roman Creed, composed in the mid-second century and from which we get the slightly more expanded Apostles Creed, reads like the summary of a story. It speaks of Jesus Christ,

> . . . who was born of the Holy Spirit and the Virgin Mary; crucified under Pontius Pilate and buried; the third day he rose from the dead; he ascended into heaven, and sits at the right hand of the Father. . . .

The later Nicene Creed, composed in the early fourth century, while containing many of the same elements found in the Old Roman Creed, reads more like a philosophical formula than a summary of a story. Jesus Christ is

> . . . light from light, true God from true God, begotten not made, of one being with the Father. . . .

The later Athanasian Creed is an even more striking example of the move toward doctrinally oriented conceptions of the faith. When the earliest witnesses to the Christ event sought to describe what they saw, they rarely took such a philosophical stance. They speak in very practical, plain language about what Jesus did and said. And this affects the way they saw mission. If the gospel is about a real man, eating, drinking, teaching, crucified, buried, resurrected, it locates the message in action. When we see Jesus as light from light, true God from true God, it dramatically changes our spirituality. Jesus becomes one to be worshipped, examined, reflected upon. The earlier creeds, however, present a lifestyle to be followed.

Even Paul, often co-opted by some in the church as an example of the more doctrinal approach, resolutely sees the gospel as consisting of the story of Jesus. This is Paul's Jesus—his messianic credentials, his physical descent from King David, his vindication/validation by the Spirit of God, and his resurrection from the dead. This looks very much like the gospel given to us in Matthew's Gospel, with its focus on the kingly rule of Jesus as displayed in his birth, life, death, and resurrection. The main emphasis is on historic events rather than on systematic theological ideas.

In Romans, Paul offers a brief summary of the missionary message. Romans 10:8–9 reads:

> But what does it say? "The word is near you; it is in your mouth and in your heart," that is, the message concerning faith that we proclaim: If you de-

clare with your mouth, "Jesus is Lord," and believe in your heart that God raised him from the dead, you will be saved.

Notice how the "message" of the church is completely located in the events of Jesus' life rather than in a philosophical statement about Christ's nature. Then, in 2 Tim 2:8, when Paul sees the end in sight and is handing over his mantle to the younger Timothy, he summarizes the essential issues: "Remember Jesus Christ, raised from the dead, descended from David. This is my gospel." The essence of the gospel, then, is in the very real and observable details of Jesus' life—his birth, his death, and resurrection. There is no deep reflection on the nature of creation, the fall of humankind in Adam and Eve's disobedience, or the system of sacrifices and atonement that had dogged Israel. The stuff of Christian mission finds its locus in the details of Jesus himself.

Yet another creedal summary is found in 1 Cor 15:1–5, where Paul reminds the church of the message that he first preached to them and by which they were converted:

Now, brothers and sisters, I want to remind you of the gospel I preached to you. . . . For what I received I passed on to you as of first importance that Christ died for our sins according to the Scriptures, and that he was buried, and that he was raised on the third day according to the Scriptures, and that he appeared to Cephas, then to the Twelve. . . .

Perhaps I am belaboring the point, but note the emphasis on events in this creed: Jesus' death, resurrection, and appearances. These events form the core of what Paul called the "gospel I preached to you." The importance of the aforementioned creedal statements should not be underestimated, for they are rare glimpses into the missionary proclamation of the first Christians, and of the Pauline missionaries in particular. In his letters, Paul (and the other apostles) had no reason to repeat the missionary preaching at great length. The gospel tends to be a shared assumption throughout the epistles, always in the background but rarely brought to the fore. Thus, the few hints that we have about what was "first delivered" are of paramount importance to anyone interested in a missional lifestyle. Martin Hengel, commenting on the missional preaching in the Acts of the Apostles, said this:

died in July

It is not a matter of chance that in his letters Paul sometimes refers by way of allusion to the narration of stories about Jesus. These allusions presuppose that the readers know more (1 Cor 11:23ff.; 15:3ff.; Rom 1:3; 15:8; Phil 2.; Gal 4:4 etc.). We must assume that in his mission preaching— which fades right into the background in his letters—Paul also of course told stories about Jesus, and primarily the passion story, the account of the crucifixion of Jesus. . . . These isolated references are therefore all the more important. In the ancient world it was impossible to proclaim as Son of God and redeemer of the world a man who had died on the cross . . . without giving a clear account of his activity, his suffering and his death.[1]

So Jesus defines the first missionaries totally. His lifestyle, his passion, his teaching became the template for the actions of the first Christians. In the same way today he should totally define those exiles seeking to follow him in a post-Christendom world. Our primary relationship with God is through the mediation of Jesus the Messiah, so his actions are central in Christian consciousness. Of course, this has a myriad of implications, but for one thing, it means that we can never get beyond the fact that we are disciples and therefore are directly connected to the messianic purposes in this world. We can never remove the historical Jesus from the foremost place in our thinking and actions.

I can't help but wonder which came first: the impulse to sanitize and tame Jesus by encasing him in abstract theology, thereby removing our motivation for discipleship, or our natural repulsion toward discipleship that forced us to domesticate Jesus to let us off the hook. Either way, when Jesus is just true light from true light, ethereal and otherworldly, we are only ever called to adore him. But when he is true human, one who loved and healed, who served and taught, who suffered and died and rose again, he becomes one we can follow.

The Bellini Syndrome

The little church of San Zaccaria in Venice houses one of great Renaissance masterpieces of religious art, Giovanni Bellini's *Madonna with Child and Saints*. It is about as good an example of the way the European church viewed the Virgin Mary and her child as any. In fact, it epitomizes Christendom's veneration of the baby Jesus. And yet, as wonderful a piece of work as it is, Bellini's picture couldn't be further from the real world of Jesus' ragged birth in provincial Bethlehem.

A Venetian himself, Bellini was in old age when he painted the picture over the altar there in 1505. As with Caravaggio's work, the first thing that strikes the observer about the painting, even before focusing on the details of the picture, is Bellini's breathtaking use of color. His canvas is infused with a rich, mellow glow that conveys a marvelous sense of warmth. It fills the niche in which the Virgin sits enthroned with a gilded atmosphere, typical of the best Renaissance work.

---

[1]Martin Hengel, *Acts and the History of Earliest Christianity* (trans. J. Bowden; London: SCM, 1979), 43–47.

Madonna Enthroned with the Child and Saints.
Giovanni Bellini (1430–1516), S. Zaccaria, Venice, Italy.
Photo credit: Scala/Art Resource, N.Y. Used with permission.

But as one draws closer, the strange details of the work become apparent. The Madonna sits on an ornate throne atop a pedestal, with the infant Jesus standing on her knee. She is presented as a typical sixteenth-century young Italian woman, her face serene and attractive. She wears a red dress and a modest white veil draped over her head. On her lap is arranged a dramatic sheet of blue taffeta, lending a regal air to her otherwise modest appearance. Mary seems aloof, distant, uninvolved in the pageantry around her.

At her feet an angel limply plays the violin, while before her four great saints of the church are assembled on either side of her throne. St. Peter, bald and white-bearded, swathed in a brown toga, holds a key, symbolizing his role as the doorkeeper to the kingdom of God. St. Catherine looks dreamily to the floor, holding a palm of martyrdom, and she stands opposite an equally languorous St. Lucia. Finally, St. Jerome, the scholar who translated the Bible into Latin, stands opposite Peter, engrossed in reading a large book. With his heavy white beard and striking red suit and hood, he resembles a modern-day Santa Claus.

It's understood that Bellini painted somewhere between fifty and seventy pictures of the Madonna and Child, and that he rarely painted them alone. He was never interested in producing intimate portraits of Mary and her child. For Bellini, every depiction of the Holy Family was to be accompanied by the splendor of the church's great saints, portrayed with dignity and repose. In nearly every case, the saints around her are painted in such a way as to form a triangle with Mary and her child at the apex. In another carefully arranged detail, Bellini never painted an odd number of saints. There are always two or four.

However, it's Bellini's depiction of the child Jesus that is strangely disturbing. Whereas Raphael or Botticelli was inclined to portray what seems to be a loving, warm relationship between mother and child, Bellini portrayed one that seems reverent, even distant. Mary's right hand hovers over the child's stomach, appearing to not even touch him, but merely to be ready should he topple. Her left hand likewise hovers beneath one his uplifted left foot, ready if needed. Her face looks away from the child, gazing placidly into space, serene, unimpressed. Bellini's portrayal of Jesus himself is a deathly one, his skin white-grey, like that of a corpse. In *Madonna with Saints,* Jesus stands almost like a tiny porcelain adult rather than a flesh-and-blood child. His blond hair crowns a face with downcast, heavy-lidded eyes. His right hand is raised, with his first two fingers and thumb positioned in the classic priestly blessing pose. Such an arrangement was by no means unique to Bellini. Thousands of images of the infant Christ display him with an adult face and his fingers raised to bless his onlookers.

Of course, Giovanni Bellini, like the many painters of religious art and icons of his time, wasn't pretending to paint an actual depiction of the birth of Christ in Bethlehem—obviously, the inclusion of the various saints confirms this. Rather, it is a symbolic representation of the *importance* of Christ's birth, confirmed by Peter, who symbolized the Roman Catholic Church, and Jerome, who symbolized the Vulgate, the Latin Bible. The church, the Bible, the Holy Mother, and, of course, the infant Jesus—these were the pillars of Christendom in 1505, and Bellini knew them well, placing them carefully in formation above the altar in the little church of San Zaccaria.

And yet, Christians today who look at this painting recognize that it is a far, far cry from the reality of the historical baby Jesus. Or do we? Every Christmas, both Catholics and Protestants send and receive Christmas cards depicting the baby Jesus lying serenely in a perfectly carved manger ("no crying he makes"), surrounded by majestically bedecked wise men, crowded under the Byzantine gables of a snow-covered stable. Our plastic nativity scenes reveal an equally unreal vision of the Bethlehem event, as we position our shepherds, wise men, cows, and sheep in a triangular shape similar to Bellini's arrangement of his saints. How far have we come since 1505? How much clearer is our vision of the Christ today than it was during the Middle Ages or the Renaissance? Surely the Jesus presented by Bellini and others of his time is adorable, but not real, not historical. In these depictions, Jesus doesn't ask for my discipleship, he simply asks for my worship.

And yet, as unpalatable as it might seem to many, in all likelihood Jesus wasn't born in a perfectly symmetrical A-frame stable. He probably wasn't born in a stable behind an inn at all. Those images have more to do with the English and Continental Christmas carols of the eighteenth and nineteenth centuries, whose writers imagined an inn in Palestine to look just like one in a quaint, snow-covered German village. When Joseph arrived in Bethlehem with Mary, as recorded in Luke 2:3–4, it's much more likely that he was taken in by members of his extended family. In fact, it would have been unthinkable in the Middle East, where hospitality had been elevated to a fine art, to imagine Joseph abandoned in the city of his forebears. More likely, he would have gone straight to relatives who would have fussed about his pregnant wife and provided a homecoming feast to this relative whom probably they had never met. Imagine a poor home in the Middle East filled with laughter, reminiscing, and storytelling, all happening around a low table loaded with simple fare.

A peasant home in those days would have had a guest room, and then one main room, which was both the sleeping space in the evening and the lounge area during the day. At night the animals would have been brought into this room in a lowered area at one end to keep them safe from the elements and possibly from poachers. When Joseph arrived, the city is indeed crowded with people registering for Augustus's census. The reference in

Luke 2:7 to the "inn" being full could also possibly be translated "guest room." In a city noted for its welcoming generosity, the chances are that Joseph's extended family had already offered its guest space to other visiting relatives, leaving him and Mary to bunk in the main room among the animals. Maybe there was a milking cow there and a donkey used as a beast of burden. Later in the evening, when Mary went into labor, the women of the home would have quickly shooed Joseph and the other men out to retire to a neighbor's home. Then these experienced midwives, some who themselves had traveled far to be there, assisted Mary as she gave birth to her son. Far from the sanitized pictures of Christmas cards or the lonely, filthy cave of revisionist historians, Mary's child would have been born surrounded by loving women, themselves all grandmothers, aunts, and mothers. Joseph and the other men would have been ushered back at the appropriate hour to ogle at the newly wrapped infant sleeping in the indoor animals' feeding trough (very ingenious of those resourceful women). Here, in a small house in a small village in Judea, the Savior is born, surrounded not by regally adorned saints, but by family and friends, now long since unremembered by history.

Furthermore, the first people to visit this new family were shepherds—the most unlikely candidates (Luke 2:8–20). In first-century Judea, shepherding was a somewhat disreputable profession. For a start, it didn't pay well and was a seven-day-a-week job. As itinerants, shepherds were rarely part of mainstream society, sleeping outdoors on the hills surrounding villages. In the eyes of religious authorities they were "sinners," because they were unable to keep the Sabbath. The term "sinner" was employed by these religious authorities to describe several types of people who were precluded from maintaining conventional, acceptable lifestyles: tax collectors, prostitutes, lepers, Gentiles, and, of course, shepherds. It becomes obvious in any study of Jesus' life and teaching that he had a strong preference for being with such people. It was rumored that Mary Magdalene was a prostitute. Certainly the disciple Matthew was a tax collector. Jesus touched and healed lepers and even valued the faith of a Gentile Roman centurion above anyone else's in Israel. How fitting, then, that at his birth he should be attended by such "sinners." Even the magi—now often called the "three wise men" (even though there's no indication that they were three)—must have been Gentiles, guided by God to adore his son, Jesus. Although, because of Herod's mandate to execute every Bethlehem boy under the age of two, it's likely that the magi didn't turn up until after Jesus had been weaned from Mary's breast.

No matter how much we might not like to acknowledge it, the incarnation of God in human form occurred in exceedingly ordinary circumstances. Jesus was born just another poor, rural child caught up in the global politics of Caesar Augustus and his very Roman wish to number all the subjects in his empire. To those others present at the moment of Jesus' birth, the entire event probably was most unremarkable. Of course, Mary and Joseph were aware of the astounding significance of the occurrence. They especially understood the shepherds' stories of angelic choirs, and we know that Mary "treasured up all these things and pondered them in her heart" (Luke 2:19). Barely a child herself, Mary remains mute in the face of these unfolding events, wide-eyed, overwhelmed, confused, keeping the whole story very much to herself. Hardly the serene, unruffled woman of religious art, she, and Joseph as well, must have marveled that lying amidst the ordinariness of cooing relatives and sleeping animals was, unbelievably, the Savior of the world.

It can't help but occur to even the most casual observer that the church even today still suffers from the "Bellini Syndrome." We still want to assist Jesus by making him grander, more "saviorlike," than he really appeared, and in doing so we domesticate him. Inadvertently, this was what the later creed writers were doing: seeking to make Jesus seem more marvelous that the bare facts of his life make him appear. Even today we want to wrench him from the pages of the New Testament, where he is presented as a real man who suffered and died and rose again. And yet, the incarnation remains an offense of monumental proportions. Theologically, the idea of God presented in human flesh is absurd enough (1 Cor 1:18–21), but as if to emphasize that the incarnation calls for action, not just reflection, God's human manifestation occurs in an exceedingly ordinary way. From our perspective, we assume that God's arrival on the earth ought to be accompanied by the kind of strange goings-on that we depict in nativity plays: cows that never poop, a baby that never cries, wise men's camels parked in the stable. Like Bellini, we want to add saints and symbols, positioned in a symmetrical, ordered fashion, each supposedly ordinary element really pointing to a greater, more spiritual meaning. The one thing that we can't bear for Jesus to be is *ordinary,* for his ordinariness invites us to follow him by providing us with a template of how to be Godlike even as an ordinary human being.

If the gospel refers to the events of Jesus' life that show him to be God's saving Messiah, then the appropriate response is *personal allegiance* to this Messiah, not merely a reliance on the benefits of his work. This is particularly clear in Paul's summary, in Rom 10:8–9, of the missionary preaching and the response that it demands. When someone learns of the resurrection/ exaltation of God's Christ, that person is to make a pledge of personal loyalty to him in the words "Jesus is Lord."

Eating and Drinking Yourself to Death

Any basic study of the Gospels shows how the lordship of Christ is revealed or couched in everyday and ordinary places. Like Esther or Daniel or Joseph, Jesus thrives in his host empire while always maintaining an appropriately godly distance from it. Nowhere is this more obvious than in how he ate and drank, and with whom he did so. In fact, it's hard to read the Gospel accounts and not be aware of the centrality of food and drink in Jesus' life. Any understanding of Jesus requires that we look at his unique table manners.

Today, in just about every culture, as in Jesus' time, the table is a focus of community life. At the table, when food is shared and eaten, we find a community's (or a family's) nature concentrated into its essence. As guests in a family's home, when we eat at their table, we see things about their family life that it might take weeks of involvement to discover otherwise. Somehow, the sharing of a meal highlights things about each other not revealed in other activity. Food and drink are the lubricant of genuine community and, strangely, the revealer of its nature. Have you ever attended a church service and seen everyone on their best behavior, with certain people taking certain functions whether they be upfront or behind the scenes? You think you know something about these people when you see them at worship. You might believe them to be a male-dominated community, under the authority of properly accredited men. You might believe them to be ordered, tranquil, and composed. You might conclude that their children are polite and unobtrusive. But if you're invited to join them for a fellowship meal in the hall, you might encounter the emergence of another community altogether. Here, you might discover that this community is really very matriarchal, and that their children are boisterous and playful. You might discover that those men who dominate the proceedings in the church service are passive and irrelevant over the meal table. Eating together seems to distill an extract of the nature of those who share the meal.

The table is remarkably central to all the important events in our lives. We create all sorts of tables too—tables in the kitchen, formal tables, tables by the river or under the stars. The communal table transcends people's personal differences and encourages social skills and conviviality. There's nothing quite like it. It is the same the world over, especially in the Middle East, where business is conducted over a meal, where contracts are signed and commercial agreements are sealed based on conduct at the table. In fact, at the table there is a series of unwritten and often unspoken expectations and courtesies that set the reputable and the disreputable apart. The nineteenth-century traveler H. B. Tristram described a Middle Eastern banquet this way:

Entertainment is a public affair. The gateway to the court, and the door . . . stand open. . . . A long, low table, or more often merely the great wooden dishes, are placed along the centre of the room, and low couches on either side, on which the guests, placed in order of their rank, recline, leaning on their left elbow, with their feet turned away from the table. Everyone on coming in takes off his sandals or slippers and leaves them at the door, socks or stockings being unknown. Servants stand behind the couches, and placing a wide, shallow basin on the ground, pour water over it on the feet of the guests. To omit this courtesy would be to imply that the visitor was one of very inferior rank. . . . Behind the servants the loungers of the village crowd in, nor are they thought obtrusive in doing so.[2]

SIMON'S DINNER TABLE

Tristram's description conjures images of Jesus eating in the home of Simon the Pharisee (Luke 7:36–50), a prime example of the kind of trouble Jesus got into over meal tables. At this feast, Jesus was reclining as Tristram describes when a woman known to all as a "sinner" began to wash his feet, not in water but in expensive perfume. She does so partly because Simon has refused to offer this courtesy to Jesus on his arrival. She is also obviously motivated by deep gratitude for the grace that Jesus had shown her some time prior to this event. When Jesus, now a noted rabbi, refuses to reject this "sinful" woman's display at the table of a religious leader such as Simon, he himself is immediately branded as disreputable. But rather than being shamed by convention, Jesus rebukes Simon for judging him, for refusing to offer him the basic courtesies associated with a dinner party, and for condemning the repentant woman. But Jesus goes even further: he favorably compares the woman with the Pharisee, concluding that she has acted honorably and Simon has not. The strong implication is that Simon is ungrateful for the grace shown to him.

It's hard for us to imagine how badly Jesus is behaving. Today, if a host treated us as badly, we would have little problem walking out or expressing our dissatisfaction. But in Jesus' time the guest at any table is expected to show appreciation for the hospitality, no matter how meager it might be. These expectations are codified in an unwritten law. The host is expected to disparage the quality of what is being offered as inadequate for the rank and importance of the guest. And regardless of what the host is serving, the guest

---

[2]H. B. Tristram, *Eastern Customs in Bible Lands* (London: Hodder & Stoughton, 1894), 36–38, cited in Kenneth Bailey, *Through Peasant Eyes* (Grand Rapids: Eerdmans, 1983), 4.

is expected to repeatedly claim to be unworthy of the host's hospitality. For Jesus to dare to complain about the indecorum of his host's actions is simply unbelievable! Archaeologist Nelson Glueck relates an experience of being entertained by an Arab family in the ancient ruins of Pella on the bank of the Jordan:

> We were met and entertained at lunch by Dhiab Suleiman, the [headman] of the village. It mattered not that he was poorly clothed, his house small, his people poverty-stricken. . . . We were exchanging polite conversational amenities with a prince of Pella. We drank his coffee. . . . We dipped pieces of his fragrant, freshly baked bread into a dish of sour milk, and ate the eggs which he boiled and peeled for us. We exclaimed honestly over the goodness of it all. . . . We under no circumstances could have refused his hospitality or stoned him with disdain or pity for his slender provender. I have forgotten many splendid feasts, but I shall never forget the bread we broke with him.[3]

If the rules of hospitality and acceptance are so great and overpowering, what does Simon's table reveal about Jesus? Why does he so overtly break the ancient custom of the guest and revile his host? Obviously, the answer doesn't simply lie in the fact that Simon has been an inadequate host. In fact, it resides in the very character of Jesus himself, and this meal, the sharing and receiving of common food and drink, distills it marvelously. In any confrontation with Jesus, the only options are faith or offense. Jesus clearly knows himself to be God's unique agent who mediates forgiveness, and therefore he expects humble and, indeed, costly devotion. At Simon's table he is revealed to be this agent. He pronounces forgiveness over the penitent woman and demands similar fidelity from Simon, revealing that the Pharisee loves him little because he has little sense of his need to be forgiven. Simon's table also reveals Jesus' freely offered gift of salvation, which must be received by faith. The table also reminds us of Jesus' valuing of the inherent worth of women. Even at a banquet of men he acknowledges this "sinful" woman as a champion of faith, repentance, and devotion.

In as ordinary and everyday an event as a meal, the true nature of Jesus as the Messiah is revealed in all its unlikely guises. Fawned over by a woman of ill repute, her tears staining his feet, her long, thick, black hair mopping up oil and tears and dust, Jesus emerges clearly as the Messiah. Over a table of bread and sauces, maybe lamb and spices, he demands the costly allegiance of all present. In the ancient world, when kings and emperors demanded similar allegiance, normally it was done on the battlefield, an army ready to enforce

---

[3]Nelson Glueck, *The River Jordan* (Philadelphia: Westminster, 1946), 175–76, cited in Bailey, *Through Peasant Eyes*, 15.

their ruler's decree. From the lips of the Christ comes such a command, not trumpeted on the battlefield, but at, of all places, an ordinary dinner table.

The Disciples' Takeout Snack

In Luke 6, Jesus again attracts criticism over his eating habits, or in this case, his disciples' eating habits. Walking through the ripening fields of barley one Sabbath, just as harvest time was to begin, Jesus and his friends are hungry, perhaps even starving. They were a poor, itinerant community, traveling in the hottest part of the year. In Palestine's warm Jordan Valley barley ripens during April, whereas in Transjordan and the region east of the Sea of Galilee wheat is harvested in August. So we don't know exactly where or when this band of pilgrims arrives by the field ready to be harvested, but we do know that they were hungry enough to pick the heads of the grain, rub them between their hands to remove the chaff, and eat. Of course, Jewish law had made provision for people in such a condition. It was strictly forbidden to harvest and steal another person's crop, but quite acceptable for starving travelers to take a few handfuls of grain.

> If you enter your neighbor's grainfield, you may pick kernels with your hands, but you must not put a sickle to the standing grain. (Deut 23:25)

Imagine the hot summer sun beating down on these famished travelers as they munch the dry grain, thankful for the generosity of the farmer. And yet even this simple roadside meal is the object of concern for religious leaders. The Pharisees find yet another reason to condemn Jesus, and again it revolves around eating. By means of their hairsplitting legalism, these men were constantly burying God's law under the heavy load of their traditions. They confront Jesus, blaming him for allowing his disciples to profane the Sabbath by "working" on it. They knew full well that the rabbis had drawn up a catalogue of thirty-nine principal works, subdivided into many categories, so that, for example, plucking the heads of grain was considered reaping, while rubbing out the grain was considered threshing. They had Jesus on a technicality, and they were quick to pounce.

Jesus' response is breathtaking in its audacity. He reaches back into Jewish history and quotes an episode when King David and his starving soldiers arrive at Nob and ask the priest to provide them with bread (1 Sam 21). The priest Ahimelech confesses that he has no bread to share, only the twelve consecrated loaves arranged on the altar to symbolize the tribes of Israel. Though such bread should never be eaten, David, God's anointed future leader of Israel, receives it because of the extreme circumstances that had led to the starvation of his retinue. According to Jesus' logic, if an exception can be made to the law (not to eat consecrated bread) when God's anointed leader needs it, then now is indeed such a time as that. In other words, he is equating himself with David, Israel's greatest king and his own forebear. But, as usual, he goes even further. Lest the comparison be lost on the Pharisees, he makes it explicit: "The Son of Man is Lord of the Sabbath" (Luke 6:5). If Jesus acts short-tempered, he does so in the face of the religious exclusionism practiced by the Pharisees at the expense of "sinners" and outcasts.

If the meal at Simon's home reveals Jesus' rightful ability to forgive sins, then this roadside snack reveals his rightful lordship even over the law of Moses. Both claims, of course, are shockingly blasphemous to the Pharisees. Eating these two meals alone would have been enough for Jesus to get himself killed.

Zacchaeus's Table of Repentance

Later, when Jesus arrives in Jericho, he simply reinforces the generally held suspicions that he isn't holy enough to be a proper rabbi. Jericho was a wealthy and fashionable city, home to many affluent traders and businessmen. Herod the Great had built a grand winter palace with ornamental gardens near the city's famous palm and balsam groves that yielded lucrative revenues. One resident of Jericho was Zacchaeus, a tax collector, who had grown powerful and wealthy through his association with the Roman authorities. We know little about him really (see Luke 19:1–9), but we can reasonably assume that he lived a decadent lifestyle, living high on the hog from his ill-gotten gains at the expense of others. What we do know for sure is that as soon as Jesus lays eyes on him, he invites himself to dinner.

Naturally, this was a shock to all who heard of it. Jesus arrives in one of the region's wealthiest cities and invites himself to stay with one of its most well-to-do citizens. At one stage of his journey Jesus and his hungry friends are rubbing grain in their hands; at another stage he's living in luxury in the home of Zacchaeus the tax collector. Like the shepherds at Jesus' birth, like the weeping woman at Simon's home, like the "Sabbath-breaking" disciples, Zacchaeus is openly regarded as a "sinner" by those around him. He is a collaborator with the invading Roman Empire. He profits from the suffering of his people. And it is to him that Jesus turns.

The meal at Zacchaeus's home reveals something further about the character of Jesus. It dramatically illustrates that when someone has a faith encounter with Jesus, he transforms that person's will and priorities. Overwhelmed by the grace of Jesus, that he would be willing to share the table of a social outcast like himself, Zacchaeus bursts forth with a pledge to deliver half of his wealth to the poor and to repay those whom he has swindled four times the amount that he owes them.

Jesus forgives. Jesus fulfills or completes the law of Moses. Jesus empowers us to repentance and new life. How are these doctrinal statements revealed in the instances that we have examined? Through the sharing of a meal. In this way, the Gospel writers not only teach us theological truths about the Christ, but also they show us how these truths are to be conveyed. After reading about the incident at Simon's table, I should desire the forgiveness that Jesus offers, and also I should see something of how to "be Christ" to the sanctimonious and to the penitent. When reading the short account in which Zacchaeus appears, I should feel led to repent of my own greed, and also I should learn something of the grace-filled power of accepting another's hospitality, no matter how unseemly the host might be. In this way, I am learning *about* the gospel, and I am learning *to do* the gospel.

The Wedding Table at Cana

Of all Jesus' meals, with the possible exception of his final one, the wedding at Cana is the most surprising. That is probably because it is such an unlikely setting for the first recorded miracle of the Messiah. Being in Galilee in the north, Cana would have been a typically small, unsophisticated northern village. Many years before, owing to pressure by the non-Jewish nations further to the north, Galilee found itself somewhat cut off from the rest of Jewish Palestine, surrounded by the Samaritans, the Phoenicians, and the Syrians—all Gentile nations. As a result, when the process of Hellenization was at its peak, Galilee became an easy target, so to speak, almost completely losing its Hebrew flavor and ethos, though remaining nominally Jewish. During the revolts of the Maccabeans (from 167 to 143 B.C.E.), faithful Jews in Galilee were actually withdrawn south to avoid "contamination" from the irreligious culture of the northerners. When the Maccabeans finally won independence, Galilee had to be repopulated with righteous Jews. This, together with the cultural diversity of its population, contributed to the contempt felt by southern Jews toward Galileans.

All this accounts for the somewhat humorous conversation between Philip and Nathanael in John 1:43–51. Having recently encountered Jesus, Philip excitedly invites Nathanael to meet the rabbi for himself, saying, "We have found the one Moses wrote about in the Law, and about whom the prophets also wrote—Jesus of Nazareth, the son of Joseph." Nathanael exclaims, "Nazareth! Can anything good come from there?"

Later, when Nicodemus is defending Jesus before the Pharisees, suggesting that they at least look further into Jesus' claims, they dismiss the idea out of hand, mocking Nicodemus: "Are you from Galilee too? Look into it, and you will find that a prophet does not come out of Galilee" (John 7:50–52).

And as we've already seen, even the Nazarenes themselves were skeptical, wondering where Jesus got all these ideas. "Isn't this the carpenter? Isn't this Mary's son and the brother of James, Joseph, Judas and Simon? Aren't his sisters here with us?" (Mark 6:3). They knew full well that none of their neighbors or friends grew to be great rabbis and religious leaders, let alone claim to be the Messiah.

From all this we can reasonably assume that a Galilean wedding was a rough-and-ready affair. Like many Middle Eastern weddings, it could go on for up to eight days, and it included an orgy of eating and drinking and wild celebration. In that culture, a father prepared for his daughter's wedding on the day she was born. Each year, when he was fermenting his family's barrels of table wine, he would draw out an extra barrel for his young daughter's wedding day and keep it aside. Since girls often were married as young as fifteen or sixteen, most diligent fathers would have cellared around fifteen or sixteen barrels of wine, some now superbly aged. At a daughter's wedding banquet it was customary to bring out the wine in order of maturity so that the best wine was served first. The new wine was brought out much later, by which time everyone probably was too inebriated to notice the difference.

In John 2, we have the account of a Galilean wedding in which the wine ran out. Maybe that was because the guests had consumed all sixteen barrels of wine, making it quite a sodden affair indeed. Or maybe it was because the father of the bride was irresponsible and had not prepared adequately for his daughter's feast. Or maybe it was because this was a poor family without the necessary means to provide for their guests. In any case, as we've already noted, the inability to provide food or wine for guests is one of the greatest social embarrassments that any host could bear. The daughter would also have to bear the shame of the community, bring remembered for her inferior banquet. It's hard for us today to feel the magnitude of the dilemma, but suffice it to say that Jesus' mother is profoundly conscious of the humiliation that her friends will experience. In this well-known story, Mary calls the problem to the attention of Jesus, who at first cryptically (or comically) resists her unexpressed request for help before miraculously producing over one hundred-twenty gallons of beautifully aged wine from water used by pious Jews for ceremonial washing. In other words, he uses the very symbols of the religious separation between the holy and the profane to further lubricate a drunken Galilean shindig. In doing so, he establishes a theme that, in the hands of his enemies, will dog him for the rest of his public ministry:

> The Son of Man came eating and drinking, and you say, "Here is a glutton and a drunkard, a friend of tax collectors and 'sinners.'" (Luke 7:34)

The table at Cana is an affront to us at many levels. Simply the presence of alcohol disturbs many Christians, but at another level the miracle is a disconcerting one. We later see Jesus heal incurable diseases, cast out legions of demons, and alter natural elements—feeding thousands from a few small portions, calming a raging storm at sea—with authority and power. His decision to dramatically and conspicuously raise Lazarus from the dead right under the noses of his detractors was the final straw for those who saw him as a religious and political threat to Israel. These miracles all seem necessary and important. But to inaugurate his public ministry with a party trick in Galilee does seem frivolous, even indulgent. But that's only to us Westerners, who have never been embedded in Jesus' culture. The table at Cana reminds us that Jesus is as much interested in our social embarrassment as our infected bodies or our empty stomachs. The miracle is a perfect one to begin with, really. It shatters the age-old partition between the sacred and the profane. It sacralizes the everyday wonder of being part of a community that celebrates and eats and drinks together. It includes hardworking, nonreligious "sinners" in the circle of God's care and protection. Is it any wonder that the one accused of being a glutton and a drunkard should give his followers something remarkable to do to celebrate his ongoing presence with them even after his death and resurrection? He tells them to eat and drink in remembrance. Now that's cheeky.

The Christian communion table, then, is not a holy, untouchable artifice, but rather a feasting place, a place to enjoy the presence of the one who eats and drinks with us. Today, however, we have turned it into something like the stone water jars used for ceremonial purification rites that Jesus found in Cana. The communion table now represents the separation between the holy and the unholy rather than a place where everyone can share in the bounty offered by the falsely accused drunkard and glutton. Just as Jesus filled those jars with rich, full-blooded red wine, likewise he dares to fill the communion table with a satisfying, nourishing, luscious feast of love and hospitality.

Sharing Our Tables

Born Michelangelo Merisi in 1571, he eventually became known by the name of the township of his birth, Caravaggio. After a lackluster apprenticeship, he ventured to Rome, and by the age of twenty he was causing scandal, not only because of his volatile character and temper, but also because of his controversial painting methods. It was his express aim to make paintings that depicted what he called the "truth," and he was critically condemned for making his pictures of religious subjects look natural and everyday. In spite of these adverse reactions, Caravaggio was commissioned to produce a number of large-scale paintings. And even though many of his works were rejected by patrons on the grounds of indecorum or theological incorrectness, some people were beginning to see his style as a welcome antidote to Mannerism, the limp style of creating dreamy-eyed, highly stylized, religious images. Caravaggio's biblical characters looked like ordinary people, their faces animated by fear or anger or compassion. He brought the otherworldly realm of the Bible right into the streets and the meal tables of seventeenth-century Rome.

Nowhere is that more powerfully seen than in his two paintings, both titled *Supper at Emmaus* (1601 and 1606). Based on the episode recorded in Luke 24, both are examples of Caravaggio's virtuoso talent. They depict the meeting of two disciples with the resurrected Christ. After traveling with him for some time, the two come to recognize him only during a meal in the way he blesses and breaks the bread. The interesting thing about these two paintings is that they are composed in almost exactly the same way, with Jesus seated at the center, blessing the food, flanked by the surprised disciples. It's the slight differences that are most interesting.

Caravaggio (1573–1610), **Supper at Emmaus (1601).**
National Gallery, London, Great Britain. Photo credit:
Nimatallah/Art Resource, N.Y. Used with permission.

In the first picture, the disciples look like ordinary laborers, one about to spring vigorously from his chair, the other waving his arms wildly, both of them amazed at the realization that they are sharing a meal with the resurrected Christ. Over Jesus' right shoulder, the innkeeper watches passively, observing the dramatic moment of recognition. On the table is an impeccably rendered still life of bread, poultry, fruit and wine. The picture is lent great emotion with chiaroscuro and powerful foreshortening. The light that falls sharply from the top illuminates the scene with all the suddenness of the moment of recognition. It captures the climax of the story, the moment at which seeing becomes recognizing. So, typical of Caravaggio, the lighting in the painting is not merely illumination, but also an allegory. It models the objects, makes them visible to the eye, and is at the same time a spiritual portrayal of the revelation, the vision, which will be gone in an instant.

Caravaggio (1573–1610), **Supper at Emmaus (1606).**
Pinacoteca di Breva, Milan, Italy. Photo credit:
Scala/Art Resource, N.Y. Used with permission.

Five years later, during a particularly turbulent time of his life and after his rejection by many church patrons, Caravaggio returned to the same subject and virtually repainted it, this time creating an entirely different impression. A different theology is at work behind it. This painting is more restrained in color and action. The disciples, though still appearing to be surprised, are more reserved and natural in their reactions. The overall impression of the picture is more reverential, less symbolic and melodramatic than the first version. Instead of a sumptuous still life, the table is set only with bread, a bowl, a tin plate, and a jug. The innkeeper, though repositioned over Jesus' left shoulder, looks very similar to the earlier painting.

Perhaps the major difference in the second picture is that includes a new, fifth character. Behind the disciples and the innkeeper, positioned in the shadows, is an elderly maid, her face heavily lined and downcast. She holds an empty bowl and seems too preoccupied with her own thoughts to be paying the dinner party any mind at all. Her inclusion is strange. She doesn't appear in the first version, and her presence in the upper right corner seems to unbalance the composition. The 1601 version is perfectly composed, balancing one of the disciple's waving arms with the innkeeper's passive stance. The 1606 version seems awkwardly composed. The maid's upper torso floats at the edge of the action. She could be removed with no effect on the overall composition. Who is she, and why did Caravaggio include her in this second version? She has been the source of much speculation by art historians throughout the years, so allow me to add to the conjecture. Perhaps she is the prostitute from Simon's table, or the tax collector Zacchaeus, or the shepherds from Bethlehem. Maybe she represents the unremembered, everyday people who seemed to find their way to Jesus' table. Look carefully at the elderly maid. She seems burdened with a lifetime of woes. In Jesus' time, it was definitely a man's world, and she is a poor, elderly woman, a maid, perhaps with no family to care for at home.

The inclusion of the maid would have offended some of the church leaders for whom Caravaggio worked. Whereas Giovanni Bellini had surrounded the infant Christ with saints and scholars, Caravaggio surrounds the resurrected Christ with the poor, the uneducated, the forgotten. Some scholars have suggested that perhaps the maid represents Caravaggio himself. Just as she is an outcast—a poor woman in a rich man's world—so too was Caravaggio feeling increasingly alienated from the church in 1606. A radical in a time of conformity, passionate and innovative, Caravaggio represented everything that the church stood against. As a bisexual of questionable morals, with a violent temper and a predilection for fighting duels, whose work was continually questioned, he knew what it was like to be held with suspicion by the church. The realism with which Caravaggio treated even religious subjects disturbed his patrons greatly, and here in *Supper at Emmaus* (1606) the outsider is included at the table of the resurrected one, as with a tranquil gesture he blesses the bread.

I find myself returning again and again to this work, my eyes drawn to the worried waitress. She represents the field of mission to which all of us are called. If Jesus is the locus of Christian mission, the maid represents its subject. In this savage, corporatized, militarized world she represents the people in occupied Iraq, Palestine, Kashmir, Tibet, and Chechnya. She might be the aboriginal people of Australia, or the Ogoni of Nigeria, or the Kurds in Turkey, or the Dalits and Adivasis of India. The worried maid represents the millions who are being uprooted from their lands by dams and development projects, or the poor who are being actively robbed of their resources and for whom everyday life is a grim battle for water, shelter, survival, and, above all, some semblance of dignity. She represents your neighbor and mine. She focuses my attention on the ostracized gay community, the homeless, the addicted, and all those who clamber at the margins of society and yearn for a place at Jesus' table, though they might not yet recognize their desire to share Christ's food.

Exiled for Us All

Jesus "exiled" himself into the world surrounded by ordinary people, many of them outcasts—exiles themselves, if you will. As he grew to adulthood, his wonderful messianic character was revealed by the tables at which he ate. He sups with elderly maids, with bisexual painters, with longhaired prostitutes, with hungry fisherman, and with filthy-rich charlatans. The gospel is revealed on his lips and through his actions, nowhere more powerfully than in his agonizing death and marvelous resurrection. On the cross, Jesus in effect becomes the ultimate exile, separated from his Father in heaven: he cries out, *Eloi, Eloi, lama sabachthani*—"My God, my God, why have you forsaken me?" His exile is complete. Like Jews carted off to Babylon, Jesus is ejected from his Father's presence by his choice to bear the burden of our sin and die a humiliating death on a Roman cross. At that moment he can no longer see or sense his Father's attendance, and the affliction of this exile is almost too great to bear. By dying for us, he purchases our redemption, ensuring that though we might feel exiled from the world around us, we will never be cut off from God and his remarkable, undying love. Jesus suffers a self-imposed exile on our behalf. Our faith in him ensures that there will always be a home for each of us in the presence of God and his only Son, Jesus. Having found such a home, we also find that the sting of exile in this post-Christendom world is numbed for us. We then are freer to follow Jesus' example as he models for us the profound power of sharing a table with the marginalized and the despised. This surely is the locus of missional activity—grace, love, hospitality, generosity. With Jesus at the center of our imaginations, such elements are not optional for modern-day exiles, but unavoidable.

Following Jesus into Exile

The Memory: Jesus Is Our Standard and Example

The friends of God should love him to the point of merging their love with his with regard to all things here below.

—Simone Weil

Recently in Texas I met a young Christian who mistakenly thought that I was interested in cool new ways of doing church services. It's an occupational hazard, I'm afraid. When I mention that I write and speak about innovative, missional modes of church, people seem to hear "funky, hip, new, ultra-relevant worship styles." Nothing could be further from my thinking, but the young Texan, excited by my use of the term "innovative," told me about his minister, who does interesting things to enhance the impact of his sermons. It turned out that one of his minister's most "innovative" techniques was to drive a tank on to the platform of the church sanctuary.

"A tank?" I gasped, incredulously.

"Yeah," he replied, "a member of our church works with the military and managed to arrange a tank to be driven right up to the pulpit. Our minister emerged and climbed down onto the platform and began preaching."

I was stunned. First, I was trying to imagine a church building big enough to allow a tank to be driven from backstage onto the platform. But second, I was amazed that such a display was considered acceptable, let alone innovative. I asked the young man, "Do you think Jesus would do such a thing?"

The question surprised him initially, particularly because he thought that I would be impressed by the story. But after some thought, he reluctantly admitted that maybe Jesus wouldn't use a symbol of military might and temporal power to enhance the authority of his teaching. In fact, the more you think about it, the more you realize that everything about Jesus is contrary to the symbolism employed by the minister that Sunday. Jesus humbles himself and embraces the frailty of humanity. What's more, he embraces the abject defenselessness of the life of a poor Galilean carpenter. His public ministry, though clearly demonstrating the supernatural might of the kingdom of God, eschews any recourse to earthly symbols of power. The more you know about the exile Jesus, the more you cannot possibly picture him driving an armored personnel carrier. The kind of power demonstrated by Jesus is the more radical force of humility, peace, love, and mercy. Military forces are needed today only because humankind will not live as God intended in the first place.

Driving a tank into the pulpit might be cool (well, it would certainly grab everyone's attention, I suppose), but is it a reflection of the Christ? A tank is a symbol of destruction. Jesus was a man of peace, a man who brought healing, restoration, and reconciliation to those whom he served. What has happened that a Christian minister, presumably a keen student of the Gospels, could think that driving a tank was an appropriate illustration of the ministry of Jesus? How vigilant we must be to ensure that we don't allow our impression of Jesus to be held captive by the prevailing mores of our secular culture! Rather, it is essential that we continue to return to the Gospels to ensure that the reverse occurs: to allow Jesus to hold our hearts and imaginations captive in response to the dominant thinking of our time. For exiles trying to live faithfully within the host empire of post-Christendom, the Gospel stories are our most dangerous memories. They continue to fire our imaginations and remind us that it's possible to thrive on foreign soil while serving Yahweh, but it's the kind of thriving that often rejects popular wisdom. These stories are the standard by which we judge all other stories, all other descriptors of life today. If, after reading these dangerous biblical stories, you can't imagine Jesus the Messiah as a televangelist, strutting around on stage in a flashy suit, playing it up for the cameras, then you are forced to reject this image and seek another mode of being Christ today. If you can't picture Jesus driving a tank or pouring millions of dollars into new church-building projects, then you are forced to allow the dangerous ancient stories to judge the insipid contemporary ones.

Hypnotizing Chickens

How did the contemporary church get to be like this? How did we end up with armies of church leaders who resemble corporate executives and act as if church is a global business? How is it that the subversive, radical nature of the life of Jesus has been so domesticated that we find ourselves in our current position, with Christians living in ghettos and losing touch with our most dangerous memories? The Bellini Syndrome is alive and well, even today. We have preferred the adorable alabaster Jesus to the flesh-and-blood radical Messiah. We have imprisoned him in a stained-glass cell and want only to worship him, never to follow him. Well over one hundred years ago, Henry Drummond could say,

> In many lands the churches have literally stolen Christ from the people; they have made the Son of Man the priest of an order; they have taken Christianity from the city and imprisoned it behind altar rails.[1]

If we are to be faithful exiles, like the Hebrew exiles in Babylon, we must be thrown back to our most challenging and inspiring memories. For the Hebrews, that canon of memory included the radical stories of their pilgrim ancestors, but especially it included the remarkable exodus narrative, which filled them with hope that just as God had rescued them from Egypt, so also God would one day rescue them from Babylon. We must not be mesmerized by life here in Babylon. Nor must we become content with the values of Babylon or the symbols of temporal earthly might. We must hold resolutely to our dangerous memories of the Messiah, who dwelt on foreign soil and demonstrated supremely what the exile's life must be like.

In his wonderfully creative book *Orbiting the Giant Hairball,* Gordon Mackenzie discusses the way organizations mesmerize their workers into becoming like zombies, slaves to the corporate ethic, but devoid of their individual, one-of-a-kind energy, the very energy that the corporation needs to reinvent itself. He illustrates this with a delightful story of his father's country vacation on his aunt and uncle's farm in 1904. The aunt and uncle had a son the same age as Mackenzie's father, and when together, the two of them became real troublemakers. One Sunday morning as the family was preparing to drive their horse-drawn carriage to church, the boys feigned stomach cramps and were told to stay home and rest. As soon as the carriage rounded a bend and disappeared from sight, the ten-year-old boys were out of bed, looking for trouble. Mackenzie takes up the story:

> Wanting to impress my father, a city boy, the cousin asked, "Do you know how to mesmerize a chicken?"
>
> "Mesmerize? Uh-uh. What's that?"
>
> "Follow me."

---

[1] Cited in John Ridgeway, "The Vision for Missional Communities," unpublished policy paper, Navigators USA, 2005.

The cousin led the way to a ramshackle chicken coop out behind the farmhouse. There he selected a fine white hen. He carried her under his arm to the front of the house, produced a piece of chalk and drew a short line on the porch. He stood the creature over the chalk line and held her beak to it. After a moment or so, the boy slowly removed his hands. The chicken stood motionless, beak to the chalk line, hypnotised. My father hooted with glee.

"Let's do another one! Let's do another one!" he pleaded.

The two boys ran back to the hen house for another chicken. And another. And another. Before long the hen house was empty, and the front porch was filled with 70 or so dead-silent, stark-still chickens straddling chalk lines, beaks seemingly glued to the porch.[2]

It's a charming story of tomfoolery that gets even funnier when the aunt and uncle return home with the Scottish Presbyterian minister, who thought that the boys had missed church because they were ill. Embarrassed by his son's deception, the father bounded onto the porch and place-kicked chicken after chicken back into consciousness, feathers, clucking, and cursing filling the air. But it's a subversive story because it challenges us to consider the degree to which we too have been mesmerized by the prevailing culture. Mackenzie makes the point:

The same thing that happened to those chickens can happen to you. When you join an organisation, you are, without fail, taken by the back of the neck and pushed down and down until your beak is on a line—not a chalk line, but a company line. And the company line says things like, "This is our history. This is our philosophy. These are our procedures. These are our politics. This is simply the way we are."[3]

How easy is it for the church to be pushed down by our host culture—pushed down to the chalk line and made to embrace the philosophies, procedures, and politics of that empire. To continue with Mackenzie's imagery, the wonderful thing that the dangerous stories of Jesus does is to place-kick us off the porch, to snap us back to consciousness and remind us of reality. Anyone who thinks that driving an armored personnel carrier into church is a Christlike thing to do is a person whose beak has been jammed onto the chalk line for far too long.

---

[2]Gordon Mackenzie, *Orbiting the Giant Hairball: A Corporate Fool's Guide to Surviving with Grace* (New York: Viking Penguin, 1998), 51–52.
[3]Ibid., 52.

In Imitation of Christ

In the previous chapter we looked at the offense of the incarnation of Christ. That one doctrine alone seems to bother us more than any other. It reminds us of the radical capacity of Jesus the man to seamlessly embrace humanity and divinity equally and successfully. His example, though impossible to duplicate, is nonetheless a rallying point for us to seek to emulate his lifestyle. In the incarnation, God enters fully into close relational and physical proximity to humanity in the pursuit of reconciliation. Likewise, if exiles today are to model their lives and ministries on that of the exile Jesus, they must take a stance that promotes proximity between themselves and those among whom they live.

I have been taken to task by some Christians who insist that the incarnation of Christ is such a unique and unrepeatable event that it is biblically unorthodox to refer to *incarnational* living today. Christ is the only incarnation, they argue, and we cannot reincarnate him today. While I agree that *the* incarnation is unique, I see nothing unorthodox about inviting believers to model their lives after that of Christ. In fact, I think that this is just an exercise in semantics. Even if you don't like the term "incarnational," there can be no doubt that the Scriptures call us to emulate the lifestyle of Jesus, which includes both his capacity to enjoy life and his willingness to suffer. Speaking of his impending death, Jesus says, "Whoever serves me must follow me; and where I am, my servant also will be" (John 12:26). Christians must be prepared to go where Christ would go: to the poor, to the marginalized, to the places of suffering. They must be prepared to die to self in order to follow Jesus' radical lifestyle of self-giving and sacrifice. Further, both Peter and Paul insist on making Jesus the template for Christian living:

> To this you were called, because Christ suffered for you, leaving you an example, that you should follow in his steps. (1 Pet 2:21)

> Follow my example, as I follow the example of Christ. (1 Cor 11:1)

Paul makes this point even more strongly in Philippians, in which he tells us that our "attitude should be the same as that of Christ Jesus" (Phil 2:5). We often assume that this passage then commends to us Jesus' humility, which is clearly present in the text. But Jesus' humility is commended to us insofar as it is expressed in his commitments to *identification* and *relinquishment.* First, to follow Jesus' example means that we should share his profoundly humble identification with sinful humankind (Phil 2:7b–8a). Second, those of us who wish to emulate Jesus should be aware of his equally humble willingness to empty himself and make himself nothing for the sake of God's redemptive purposes (Phil 2:6–7a). The greatest example of both is his humiliating death on the cross (Phil 2:8b). To embrace an incarnational ministry, then, involves a willingness to relinquish our own desires and interests in the service of others. Of course, our suffering doesn't atone for the sins of others, as Christ's did, but our self-emptying or sacrificial love will direct people to the higher and more efficacious sacrifice of Christ. The exile will be called to also suffer, relinquishing wealth, worldly power, and position. Pity, condescension, or paternalism misses the mark; only a compassion *that acts* is acceptable in incarnational ministry. Thus, following Jesus' example, incarnational Christian witness will include the following four aspects:

1. An active sharing of life, participating in the fears, frustrations, and afflictions of the host community. The prayer of the exile should be, "Lord, let your mind be in me," for no witness is capable of incarnationality without the mind of Jesus.

2. An employment of the language and thought forms of those with whom we seek to share Jesus. After all, he used common speech and stories: salt, light, fruit, birds, and the like. He seldom used theological or religious jargon or technical terms.

3. A preparedness to go to the people, not expecting them to come to us. As Jesus came from the heavens to humanity, we enter into the "tribal" realities of human society.

4. A confidence that the gospel can be communicated by ordinary means, through acts of servanthood, loving relationships, good deeds; in this way the exile becomes an extension of the incarnation in our time. Deeds thus create words.

So, if we take the incarnation seriously, we must take seriously the call to live incarnationally—right up close, near to those whom God desires to redeem. We cannot demonstrate Christlikeness at a distance from those whom we feel called to serve. We need to get close enough to people that our lives rub up against their lives, and that they see the incarnated Christ in our values, beliefs, and practices as expressed in cultural forms that make sense and convey impact.

When one theologian e-mailed me about what he believed to be my inappropriate use of the term "incarnational," I replied by asking him what term he would use to describe the biblical, Christian impulse to draw near to those who don't know Christ, and for him to give me examples of how he did this in his own life and ministry. He didn't reply. I've come to discover that there is a whole world of professional Christians who live primarily in the church or the Christian academy, and who determine what is the so-called true and proper terminology or the correct biblical procedure for mission, but who never seem to embody the ideas that they describe. On the other hand, there are theologically untrained people who are reading the Bible and intuiting new ways to create proximity with not-yet-Christians. These exiles often don't feel appreciated or understood by the conventional church. They have been marginalized by their other Christian friends who thought their ideas and lifestyle too radical or too unsafe to accommodate. But they are on to something, and in their unorthodox practice reside the seeds of the survival of the Christian movement.

Third Places

Many of these amateur missionaries are discovering that the best place for building proximity with members of a host culture is in a *third place*. The term "third place" was coined by sociologist Ray Oldenburg and appeared in his 1990 book *The Great Good Place,*[4] a celebration of the places where people can regularly go to take it easy and commune with friends, neighbors, and whoever just shows up. The subtitle of his book says it all*: Cafés, Coffee Shops, Community Centers, Beauty Parlors, General Stores, Bars, Hangouts and How They Get You Through the Day.* According to Oldenburg, third places are those environments in which people meet to develop friendships, discuss issues, and interact with others. Sometimes referred to by other sociologists as "social condensers," these places have always been an important way in which a community develops and retains cohesion and a sense of identity. Oldenburg says that these third places are crucial to a community for a number of reasons:

- They are distinctive informal gathering places.

- They make the citizen feel at home.

- They nourish relationships and a diversity of human contact.

- They help create a sense of place and community.

- They invoke a sense of civic pride.

- They promote companionship.

- They allow people to relax and unwind after a long day at work.

- They are socially binding.

---

[4]Ray Oldenburg, *The Great Good Place: Cafés, Coffee Shops, Community Centers, Beauty Parlors, General Stores, Bars, Hangouts and How They Get You Through the Day* (New York: Paragon House, 1989).

- They encourage sociability instead of isolation.

- They make life more colorful.

- They enrich public life and democracy.[5]

In Oldenburg's thinking, our first place is the home and the people with whom we live. Our second place is the workplace, the place where we spend most of our waking life. But the third places in our society are the bedrock of community life and all the benefits that come from such interaction. It might be a restaurant or a bar. It might be a social group such as a Rotary or Elks club or a quilting circle or a water-skiing community. It might be a physical location such as a coffee shop or a beach or a mall. Your third place is the *Israel's* place where you just like to relax and be you. All societies have informal *Gate* meeting places, such as the Forum in ancient Rome or the contemporary *of the* British pub. In other societies it might be the gathering of elders at the city *city.* gate or the casual lounging of warriors around the campfire. Oldenburg concludes that for the healthy functioning of a community, we all need such third places, places of easygoing conviviality and safety.

Oldenburg sees several essential ingredients for well-functioning third places:

Third Places

- They must be free or quite inexpensive.

- Food and drink, though not absolutely essential, are important factors.

---

[5]This list doesn't appear in Oldenburg's book, but is a summary of his argument.

- They must be highly accessible to neighborhoods so that people find it easy to make the place a regular part of their routine.

- A lot of people should be able to comfortably walk to the place from their home.

- They should be places where a number of people regularly go on a daily basis.

- They should be places where a person feels welcome and comfortable, and where it is easy to enter into conversation.

- A person should expect to find both old and new friends on each trip to the place.[6]

You can understand why businesses such as Starbucks have latched on to this concept. They have invested greatly in seeking to be a third place for American culture, knowing that it can be very lucrative for a business to be seen this way. By providing free wireless Internet access, comfy lounges, cool music (in some stores even downloadable music), they are attempting to be the place that America likes to be when not at home or work.

Third places are the most significant places for Christian mission to occur because in a third place people are more relaxed, less guarded, more open to meaningful conversation and interaction. Contrast that with the situation in many homes today. People enter their houses by driving discreetly into the garage, the automatic door closing quietly behind them. Their kids play in yards enclosed by tall wooden fences. The quest for privacy is taken to an even higher level by people who choose to live in gated communities. We have people over to our homes only if we already know and like them. We tend to have perfunctory conversations with neighbors. Many people don't even know their neighbors' names, and a great many of them are perfectly happy this way. The home—the first place—is becoming less and less a place for proximity and intimacy. Likewise the second place. The workplace is more often than not a place where conversations and personal interactions are purely functional. We speak about what needs to be discussed in order to get the job done. Over lunch, work colleagues might ask each other how their weekend was or comment on an important news item. But often colleagues are guarded at work, and the conversations are kept casual.

It's in the third place that we let those guards down. It's here that we allow people to know us more fully. It's here that people are more willing to discuss the core issues of life, death, faith, meaning, and purpose. For example, have you worked with a colleague whom you considered to be fairly

---

[6]Again, this list is a summary and doesn't appear as such in Oldenburg's book.

buttoned-down and straight-laced, until the annual Christmas party, when after a few drinks this person is dancing on the tables and telling uproarious (often dirty) jokes? Or what about the office clown who's always making light of every issue at work, until at a bar after 5:00 p.m. one Friday this comedian tearfully opens up to you about a personal tragedy? Why? Because there seem to be different rules about the appropriateness of intimate conversation at work than there are in a social context.

Any cursory reading of the Gospels will reveal Jesus' interest in being in third places. In the previous chapter we explored his enjoyment at sharing food with so-called sinners. In a society where every third-place experience revolves around food (the Middle East), Jesus finds himself at the center of a place where people feel free to, well, just be! I would argue that in today's society, any attempt to model your life on the life of Christ must include a genuine attempt to hang out regularly in third places. Genuine incarnational living demands it. Missional proximity can best be developed in bars, pubs, gyms, grocery stores, beauty parlors, community groups, and coffee shops.

I've seen such missional proximity built in some of the most surprising places. Nowhere was this more charmingly exhibited than my visit one weekend to Pittsburgh's Hot Dogma, a New York–style hot dog restaurant in downtown Oliver Street. The brains behind Hot Dogma is frankfurter aficionado Tim Tobitsch. Originally from New Jersey, Tim went to college in Pennsylvania and was distressed to find that the only hot dogs served in the student cafeteria were slimy chicken by-product franks on limp buns. Yearning for a proper New York–style hot dog, Tim began cooking the genuine (garlicky) article on a George Foreman grill in his dorm room. Soon students were flocking for real New York dogs with all the trimmings. One such student was Megan Lindsay, who upon graduation moved to Pittsburgh, where she became involved with a house-church movement called Three Nails. There she became inspired to create a third place where she could meet locals and share something of the love of Jesus with others. Together with another Three Nails member, Craig Niblack, recently graduated from Pittsburgh's Carnegie Mellon University with an MBA, she put in a call to her old college friend, Tim the frankmeister. Would he move to Pittsburgh and help start a missional business? And more importantly, would he bring his New York-style hot dogs with him? Tim was inspired by Megan's vision for a missional proximity space in Pittsburgh (he was also motivated by having been unemployed since graduation). Tim's hot dogs, Megan's high energy, and Craig's business savvy added up to a powerful combination.

As a non-American, whose appreciation of the hot dog is pretty low, I was inspired by Tim's love of the frank. He can tell you why his spicy, all-beef, natural-casing dogs are the best. He can tell you the best way to eat them—with mustard, sauerkraut, and New York–style red-onion sauce (they list ketchup on the menu, but in very small print). I was equally inspired by Megan's heart to serve God through her business. Even though the restaurant's atmosphere is downright playful, with tabletops adorned by artwork reproducing the Mona Lisa, the American Gothic couple, and other classic images—all with frankfurters slipped into the picture—the team has tried to build an ambience in which people feel welcome to hang out. There's a comfy couch, books and games, and free wireless Internet access. Every other Tuesday live music invigorates the lunch hour.

After my visit to Hot Dogma, Tim and Megan took me back to one of the house-church meetings connected to Three Nails. In a small house in Pittsburgh's culturally diverse South Side, a group of ten or so twenty-somethings gathered around plates of biscuits and chicken while encouraging one another's faith and studying the Bible. There are nearly a dozen such groups connected to Three Nails. Twice monthly the groups combine for a jointly conducted worship service, usually held in traditional, grand old Episcopalian churches and featuring a powerful ancient-future vibe. The link between Hot Dogma and Three Nails is a reciprocal one. Hot Dogma has pledged 15 percent of its profits to support Three Nails financially, while members of the church regularly work in the restaurant or bring their friends there.

Listening to Megan describe her excitement at serving food, showing love, and expressing faith through Hot Dogma, I could imagine Jesus there at one of the brightly painted tables, telling stories, inspiring the downcast, healing the brokenhearted. I could picture him serving up Hot Dogma franks such as the Texan (with chili, cheddar, and jalapeños), the Mexican (in a tortilla with black-bean salsa and guacamole), or the El Greco (with feta cheese and artichoke hearts). I could picture him showing hospitality and generosity in the darkened streets of downtown Pittsburgh in the arrowhead formed by the merging of the Allegheny, Monongahela, and Ohio Rivers.

Other Christians have developed similar spaces for proximity. In the heart of Tacoma, Washington, a church called Zoe has redeveloped the disused Longshoremen's Club into a music venue and drive-thru restaurant. As the decaying downtown area comes back to life, thanks mainly to the restorative work of the University of Washington, Zoe has created a brilliant third place for the many artists, musicians, and bohemians moving down river to escape skyrocketing prices in nearby Seattle.

In Athens, Ohio, Christians seeking to develop a meaningful third place for building relationships with not-yet-Christians have established Donkey Coffee, an uptown café specializing in free-trade coffee and featuring a very cool ambient space for artists and students from the nearby University of

Ohio. The café itself is divided into four main areas. The porch is a smoking area. The front area facing a window is usually filled with people chattering or reading books. The middle section has big, comfortable couches and provides space for customers to play board games, drink coffee, and hang out. Finally, there's a windowless dungeonlike area that feels like your parents' basement. Called Donkey Backstage, this area features live music or poetry every Friday and Saturday. The live music creates a very relaxing chill-out vibe.

The guys at Donkey also offer Athens residents and Ohio University students a social conscience, not only through their commitment to free-trade produce, but also through things such as its regular "justice table," where customers can read about community events and issues of global justice. And as anyone from Ohio will tell you, Donkey is one of the coolest cafés in the state.

In Sydney's western suburbs you can find something similar at Mars Hill Café ("Where thinkers drink"). Kevin Crouse and the rest of the team at Mars Hill are committed Christians who see the coffee shop as the best forum for building missional relationships with the neighborhood. As in many cafés, when you order your coffee or meal at the counter, you get a little sign on a stand that you place on your table so your server can find you to bring your order. At Mars Hill, instead of the signs being the usual numbers, they are quotations from well-known philosophers such as Socrates, Wittgenstein, Sartre, Hume, and Hobbes. The staff will then casually ask you whether you agree with the quotation and engage the table in friendly conversation about meaningful topics. Any casual visit to the coffee shop will reveal that the owners are interested in the large philosophical issues of life (different coffee combinations are named after great thinkers). But to discover that they are Christians would take some time. Like Donkey Coffee in Athens, Mars Hill is not an overtly Christian coffee shop. It's a very cool venue that features art, poetry, live music, and robust discussion that just happens to be run by Christians.

Back in Pittsburgh, Jesse and Sherry Holeczy and Josh and Danna Cascone own In the Blood Tattoo and Piercing, a tattoo parlor on the city's South Side. Deeply committed to Christ, they obviously exude his love and grace because their parlor has become a hangout for a whole community of recovering alcoholics, working people from the neighborhood, college students, single moms, a punk-rock band, and a pierced and spiky-haired collection of iconoclasts. Who would have imagined that a tattoo parlor could be a missional third place? But that's what it's become. It has become a haven for people of all kinds of backgrounds. By emulating Christ's mercy and kindness, they have fashioned a supportive and safe space for dozens of leather-clad, pierced and tattooed people who normally wouldn't be churchgoers.

The Holeczys and the Cascones decided to begin a Monday night Bible study for anyone who might be interested. Today, around forty people study the Bible with them every week, right there in the tattoo parlor, and a bunch of them have connected to a nearby church called Hot Metal Bridge. Josh Cascone's upper left arm is emblazoned with a large cross and the word "Forgiven." When I met him, I commented on how simple and beautiful his tattoo was and what a talking point it must be. He smiled—and offered to tattoo me any time I wanted.

Too Busy to Be in Third Places

Whenever I speak about the need to focus our energies in third places, many well-meaning Christians can't help but agree. It makes perfect sense that if we want to influence people in the way Jesus did, we should create proximity in the places where people relax and find meaning. But for many Christians this poses a great dilemma. Whether it's as simple as joining the local jogging club or as complex as owning a third-place business, most Christians can't do it because they simply don't have the time. The reason for this is that for most Christians their church has become their third place. Their churches soak up every bit of their spare time. All their social networks revolve around church. They belong to the church-based women's or men's group. Their kids play for the church softball team and attend the Friday night youth group. In fact, the most committed Christians end up on various committees and panels and usually find themselves out several nights a week and on weekends involved in church activities. How could they ever find the time to hang out in third places?

Some hardy souls, convinced that it's where they would find Jesus, venture out and join a secular club or regularly stop by the same coffee shop each week. But because most of their spare time is committed to church, they can manage to be in these secular third places only occasionally. The key to building missional proximity is frequency and spontaneity. By seeing people several times a week, casually and unrushed, you usually find that after a period of time you're invited to a party here or a barbecue there. The most important events often are the spontaneous ones that you get caught up in because you're *there*. And you need to be there frequently to get caught up in such a way. One evening I was enjoying a drink at the bar of an Italian restaurant with my friend and coauthor Alan Hirsch in Ann Arbor, Michigan. He and I were speaking at a conference in town. Without warning, we were approached by another patron, who invited us to join his party for a drink. "It's very sad," he said, "Laverne is moving to San Diego, and we're seeing her off." Turning to Laverne (whom I had never met before), I asked her why she was heading for San Diego. "Love," was her one-word reply. She was grinning from ear to ear. "That's a good reason," I said. We were swept up in this farewell party simply because we were there. We struck it lucky. If we were locals, we might have had to be at that bar regularly for a long time before making such a connection.

However, if I'm busy several nights a week and all weekend with my church activities, how can I possibly develop a commitment to such frequent proximity? Our churches, under the guise of doing the work of Christ, are inadvertently sucking us away from the very people that Jesus would want us to hang out with. It's as if we've had our beaks held down on the chalk line until we acquiesced and agreed that God wants us to be so busy with church work. Read the dangerous stories in the Gospels, and then tell me that Jesus wants you to be so busy with church activities. Read those radical stories of the one who was accused by religious people of being a drunkard and a glutton. I'm convinced that those stories, if taken seriously, will propel you out of organized Christianity and into the third places in your neighborhood.

A Baptist minister once told me about how he was so chronically busy that he didn't even have time to cut his lawn. Months had gone by, during which he was so busy with church meetings and activities that he literally didn't have a moment to get the lawnmower out. Then one Friday night he remembered that they were having a backyard barbecue the next day. Small children couldn't possibly get around in his overgrown lawn. He finally had no choice. He got his lawnmower out of the shed, and using a flashlight held over his head to shine on the grass, he began cutting the lawn in the middle of the night. Halfway around his front lawn, he looked across the street to see his neighbors peering through the curtains at the comical image of the minister cutting the lawn at night by flashlight. He realized there and then that the credibility of his faith to his neighbors was shattered. Who would want to participate in a religion that kept you so busy?

Exiles have figured out that churches don't value people who won't turn up for every meeting, attend every event, and locate all their significant friendships within the congregation. They have decided to slip away from the ever-spiraling vortex of so-called Christian fellowship. It sucks you in, demanding everything of you, leaving you completely socially disconnected from your neighbors, your community. And it won't be appeased by a half-hearted allegiance. It demands your all, always. Note how many ministers refer to serving as a church usher, attending Sunday school, or joining a church committee as "the Lord's work." Exiles, having read the dangerous stories of Jesus, have decided that the best way to do the Lord's work is to follow him out into the third places in their community.

Practicing the Presence of Christ

Finding proximity with not-yet-Christians is one thing, but while doing so, exiles have realized that they are to practice the presence of Christ right there under people's noses, where the wonderful aroma of Jesus can be sensed. An old saying has it that for many people, the only Bible they will ever read is the lives of their Christian friends. And it's true. When we allow our lives to be "read" by people with whom we have proximity, they need to be able to see the story of Jesus unfolding in our pages. This doesn't mean that we need to wear cheesy Christian T-shirts or start preaching the gospel at every opportunity. It means that, like the guys at Mars Hill Café, our allegiance to Christ unfurls slowly, over multiple interactions, by which time the reader is so far into the book of our life that they can't put it down. Practicing the presence of Christ means being a living example of the life of Jesus. This raises the stakes enormously. It means that our lives need to become increasingly aligned with the example of Jesus. It doesn't require sinless obedience—as if that's possible anyway. It means, though, increasingly becoming people of justice, kindness, mercy, strength, hope, grace, generosity, and hospitality.

For exiles, practicing the presence of Christ will mean more than was intended by the phrase coined by Brother Lawrence in his much-loved book of a similar name, *The Practice of the Presence of God.* In that book, Brother Lawrence was referring to the cultivating of a rich, daily, inner experience of the love of God in our lives. Practicing the presence of God is "to take delight in and become accustomed to his divine company, speaking humbly and conversing lovingly with him all the time, at every moment, without rule or measure."[7] His method of doing so is one of the classic examples of Christian spirituality, and it will be worth summarizing here because these skills of personal spirituality are important for exiles. But bear in mind, the missional practice of the presence of Christ will include outer actions and behaviors as well as the inner beliefs and practices prescribed by Lawrence.

Brother Lawrence of the Resurrection was born Nicolas Herman in France in 1611. When he was a young man, he was seriously wounded during military service, and during his period of convalescence, after begging God for his life, he pledged himself to religious service. God obviously made good on the deal, and Herman recovered and went on to fulfill his side of the bargain, initially trying to live the life of a religious hermit, and then in 1640,

---

[7]Brother Lawrence, *The Practice of the Presence of God: With Spiritual Maxims* (Grand Rapids: Revell, 1999), 36.

at the age of twenty-six, entering the Order of Discalced Carmelites ("discalced" means "barefoot") in Paris as a lay brother. For his religious name he took "Lawrence." For fifteen years he worked as a cook in the monastery kitchen, at times preparing meals for over one hundred friars. In later life, due to severe sciatic gout, he was unable to stand for the many hours required to cook. He spent the remainder of his years as a sandal maker for the barefoot Carmelites (go figure!) until his death at the age of seventy-seven.

In spite of his cloistered life, the disciplines of the monastic life did not appeal to him for two broad reasons. First, he found himself unable to connect with God through the disciplines of meditation, contemplation, silence, and written prayer. He found them overly complicated and requiring too great a level of theological sophistication. Second, he believed that connectedness to God ought to be accessible to even the most ordinary person. If this connection was possible only for monks of uncommon devotion, then he didn't see it as a very useful religious system at all. As a result, he set about developing a series of exercises, easily learned by anyone and practicable in any circumstances. In effect, he was creating an egalitarian system for the devotional life, freeing religious service from the monastery and inviting anyone, of any background, to experience the presence of God in daily living. He wrote,

> I gave up all devotions and prayers that were not required and I devote myself exclusively to remaining always in his holy presence. I keep myself in his presence by simple attentiveness and a general loving awareness of God that I call "actual presence of God" or better, a quiet and secret conversation of the soul with God that is lasting.[8]

In all things, Brother Lawrence sought to maintain a constant awareness of God's gracious presence in his life. He called this "the practice of the presence of God" and describes it this way:

> The holiest, most ordinary, and most necessary practice of the spiritual life is that of the presence of God. It is to take delight in and become accustomed to his divine company, speaking humbly and conversing lovingly with him all the time, at every moment, without rule or measure, especially in times of temptation, suffering, aridity, weariness, even infidelity and sin.[9]

Lawrence's practice of the presence of God involved five simple skills (simple to explain, though not necessarily that easy to master). Let's look at them one by one.

---

[8]Ibid., 53.
[9]Ibid., 36.

Seek God's Presence: Guard Your Heart with Extreme Care to Retain Purity

Lawrence understood that it is impossible to seek God's presence while also seeking after sinful human desires. He had a very robust, refreshing understanding of human sin. He knew that it's impossible for us not to sin, that sin will always be a reality in the human experience, but that in order to experience the presence of God, we must regularly confess our sin and recognize that God's presence is achievable in spite of it. The quest for sinless perfection (so much a part of the monastic movement of that time) was folly to Lawrence. Listen to his marvelous testimony of God's grace:

> I consider myself as the most miserable of all human beings, covered with sores, foul, and guilty of all sorts of crimes committed against my King; moved by sincere remorse I confess all my sins to him. I ask him pardon and abandon myself into his hands so he can do with me as he pleases. Far from chastening me, this King, full of goodness and mercy, lovingly embraces me, seats me at his table, waits on me himself, gives me the keys to his treasures, and treats me in all things as his favourite; he converses with me and takes delight in me in countless ways, without ever speaking of forgiveness or taking away my previous faults. Although I beg him to fashion me according to his heart, I see myself still weaker and miserable, yet ever more caressed by God. This is what I see from time to time while in his holy presence.[10]

Here we find a perfect balance between a heightened awareness of his human inadequacy and an equally sharp awareness of God's tender and unearned grace. In order to practice the presence of God, exiles need to be ruthlessly honest about their sinfulness, keep short lists of unconfessed sin, develop accountability relationships with more godly and experienced mentors, and seek to abide in God's unfathomable grace.

See God's Presence: Keep the Soul's Gaze Fixed on God by Faith

Brother Lawrence developed the phrase "keep the soul's gaze fixed on God" to describe the practice of seeing God in every aspect of life. By this he meant that we are to cultivate a capacity to see God's presence shining through even the most mundane or profane activity, whether it be making sandals or cooking (Lawrence's two main activities) or any other ordinary task. This sacralizing of the everyday allows the exile to see that God doesn't live in church buildings or cathedrals, but that God's presence can be seen in

---

[10]Ibid., 54.

art, beauty, work, food, grief, pain, and joy. By fixing the soul's gaze on God by faith, we are freed to see God in distinctly nonreligious categories and to help not-yet-Christians to connect to a God who can be encountered even if they've never been to church.

Live God's Presence: Do All for the Love of God

Doing *all* for the love of God includes all things, both the so-called sacred and the secular. Nothing is to be excluded. According to Brother Lawrence, the practice of Christian spirituality does not demand isolation or retreat. He believed that all of our everyday activities hold the potential to become what he called "little acts of communion with God." It is an all-encompassing, expansive vision of the world. Lawrence saw every single activity as a chance to glorify God. In fact, in his understanding, God's presence charges all our activities with glory—so much so that our sanctification isn't based on the actual activities that we perform, but rather on our preparedness to do them for God rather than for ourselves.

Whereas the monastic community of which he was part saw the Eucharist as the ultimate expression of God's sacramental activity on the earth, and therefore as the ultimate human activity, Brother Lawrence enjoyed a much more holistic spirituality. For him, performing the ordinary tasks of cooking was as wondrous and beautiful an opportunity to experience God as was the Eucharist. In fact, after participating in the Eucharist one day, Lawrence wrote,

> Possessed thus entirely with the greatness and the majesty of this infinite Being, I went straightway to the place that duty had marked out for me— the kitchen. . . . I flip my little omelet in the frying pan for the love of God, and when it's done, if I have nothing to do, I prostrate myself on the floor and adore my God who gave me the grace to do it, after which I get up happier than a king. When I can do nothing else, it is enough for me to pick up a straw from the ground for the love of God.[11]

and,

> The times of activity are not at all different from the hours of prayer . . . for I possess God as peacefully in the commotion of my kitchen, where often enough several people are asking me for different things at the same time, as I do when kneeling before the Blessed Sacrament.[12]

and,

---

[11]Ibid., 116.
[12]Ibid., 115.

> We must never tire of doing little things for the love of God, who considers not the magnitude of the work, but the love.[13]

This kind of spirituality sets the religious life free from the monastery and invites the ordinary cobbler, cook, and gardener into the life of Christian service. Exiles know that their daily lives, whether as lawyers, builders, or stay-at-home parents, are opportunities to serve God. Their spirituality is based not on distinctly religious activities in especially recognized religious zones, but rather on the ability to recognize God's grace in every sphere of human existence—eating, drinking, working, bathing, sleeping, all with God, and thus to God's glory. To the untrained eye, the difference is unobservable; a casual observer could hardly tell the difference between a Christian and non-Christian doing the same things. But internally, the difference is significant.

Speak in the Presence of God: Offer Short Prayers to God

Lawrence's genius was his ability to set religious practices free from the realm of the "professional Christian." One didn't need to be a monk or a hermit to commune with God. Nor did one need to memorize lengthy prayers and petitions. Lawrence insisted that any believer can practice the presence of God by offering regular short prayers of the simplest nature. He offered the following short phrases as examples:

> To those who set out upon this practice let me suggest a few words, such as "My God, I am wholly Yours," "O God of love, I love You with all my heart," "Lord, make my heart even as Your own," or other such words as love prompts at the moment. . . . Before beginning any task I would say to God, with childlike trust: "My God, since you are with me, and since I must apply myself to these duties by your order, I beg you to give me the grace to remain with you and keep you company. Even better, my Lord, work with me, accept my efforts and take possession of all my affections. . . ." Moreover, as I worked, I would continue to hold familiar conversation, offering to Him my little acts of service, and entreating the unfailing assistance of His grace.[14]

After completing his tasks, Lawrence gave thanks for all the good that was accomplished. He also asked pardon for all his shortcomings. Like Tevye in *Fiddler on the Roof,* Lawrence might have appeared to be talking to himself, but actually he was talking to God. The focus of his conversation included his aches and pains, his joys and trials, as well as the most mundane

---

[13]Ibid., 98.
[14]Ibid., 12.

aspects of everyday life. Tevye could even joke with God. Likewise for Lawrence, anything could be a topic of conversation with God.

Treasure God's Presence: Value the Presence of God More Than Anything

Jesus says, "For where your treasure is, there your heart will be also" (Matt 6:21). When we value the presence of God more than anything, we will set our minds and our hearts on pursuing this one thing above all else. But, Lawrence is quick to explain, we should not do this for our own pleasure or benefit alone. His primary motivation for pursuing God is that this is what God wants more than anything else:

> There is no way of life in the world more agreeable or delightful than continual conversation with God; only those who practice and experience it can understand this. I do not suggest, however, that you do it for this reason. We must not seek consolations from this exercise, but must do it from a motive of love, and because God wants it.[15]

Which of us could live as devotedly as Brother Lawrence? So convinced was he that God derives such pleasure from our attention and our interest. It is God who seeks us out for relationship. It is God who yearns for intimacy with sinful humankind, even in the most regular, everyday activities of our lives. These five practices will ensure that exiles live God-connected lives even if they're not attending regular or mainstream church services every Sunday. But these are practices that, as we noted earlier, can be invisible to the casual observer because they are inner disciplines, exercised by our imaginations and our hearts. I want to add some other, outwardly expressed disciplines to ensure that we practice the presence of Christ in plain sight of not-yet-Christians. These practices will be explored in greater detail throughout the rest of this book, but suffice it at this point to say that demonstrating the presence of Christ will involve the following:

- **The practice of hospitality**: sharing our homes and our tables with others

- **The practice of generosity**: giving our resources to those in need, especially the poor and marginalized

- **The practice of justice**: offering our energies in the creation of equitable political environments

---

[15]Ibid., 57.

- **The practice of environmental stewardship**: being committed to caring for the fragile ecosystem in which we live

- **The practice of mission**: being prepared to be sent into all the world so that people might know that Christ is Lord of all

Perhaps you've seen the episode of the irreverent animated series *The Simpsons* in which young Bart Simpson is discussing his family's faith with his father, Homer:

BART: What religion are we?

HOMER: You know, the religion with all the well-meaning rules that don't really work in real life.

Ouch! But the "religion" of Jesus (not that it's a religion at all, but the term is current coinage) is anything but a series of rules that don't work in real life. The lifestyle that he calls forth from us is one energized by love, sacrifice, kindness, and grace. It is the most "useful" lifestyle of all because it sets us back on the road that we were intended to travel in the first place. It is no easy matter, of course, but whether we practice this life in a tattoo parlor, a hot dog restaurant, a coffee shop, a scrapbook club, or a parents' group, its inherent quality will direct people to the one who made us the people we are today—to the indwelling power of the Spirit of Jesus.

Naked and Empty-Handed

And yet, as strong as we might be, thanks to that indwelling spiritual power, if we take the incarnation seriously, we are led into a mission that renounces any reliance on temporal or earthly power. This is my big problem with the tank-driving minister. For over two thousand years the church too often has abused its earthly power and position. It has established a power base that at its worst has given us the Crusades and the Inquisition, and at its most benign leaves us with multimillion dollar church facilities that reek of wealth and privilege. Regardless of how much many affluent pastors might love their state-of-the-art air-conditioned church sanctuaries with their coffee bars, bookshops, and valet parking lots, we cannot forget that Jesus died on the cross naked and empty-handed.

On my first trip to Rome, I scheduled time to visit Vatican City to see St. Peter's Basilica, the Sistine Chapel, and the Vatican Museum. I remember imagining them to be faith-inspiring buildings. I quite often feel very close to God in art galleries, so I figured that the church's most famous art collections would be especially spiritually uplifting. I couldn't have been more wrong.

For me, the Vatican smacks of wealth, power, and unbridled human grandeur. Massive monument after massive monument overwhelms the visitor, all paid for by previous popes, all established as memorials to their greatness. I couldn't sense any personal connection to God. In fact, I almost wept to imagine the poor, scorned Galilean carpenter wandering unnoticed through the marble halls of St. Peter's. Jesus called us to take up our cross and follow him. And it is important to note that for all the discreet medieval art of the Vatican Museum, Jesus died stark naked, covered by nothing but his own dried blood. His hands held no miter, no staff, no symbol of power. They were empty but for the nails, as big as our thumbs, that anchored him to that cross.

This reflection on the Vatican is offered with no particular malice toward Catholicism. I have felt the same way in Anglican Cathedrals (and Crystal Cathedrals, for that matter) and Baptist megachurches. Many people outside the church, whether Christian or not, feel the same way. They cannot equate the radical young Middle Eastern rabbi with the religion of wealth and power that claims him as their leader.

Consider the extraordinary success of Dan Brown's book *The Da Vinci Code.* It plays heavily on a general assumption among readers that the church's wealth and power have blinded it from understanding the humble reality of its founder. A publishing phenomenon, this "airport thriller" has broken all records for book sales in recent years. It begins with the death of Jacques Sauniére, renowned curator of the world famous Louvre Museum in Paris. Unknown to most of the world, Sauniére was a prominent member of the Priory of Sion. This priory is a secretive esoteric religious group that has existed for centuries. Many of the priory's leaders have been among the most prominent, powerful, and influential persons in history. The priory has been the guardian of a secret so important that some of its members, like Sauniére, will chose death rather than reveal it.

You don't even need to have read the book to know that the secret has to do with the assertion that Christ was not divine, that he married Mary Magdalene and had a child by her. The book asserts that Jesus' offspring landed in France and have been protected ever since by the priory, headed at one stage by Leonardo da Vinci, who hid various clues to this dreadful truth in his paintings, particularly his *Last Supper.*

Sauniére is murdered by an agent of the Christian church because it has the most to lose if the priory's secret is revealed. His unwitting niece and a Harvard professor become caught up in the intrigue. They inadvertently uncover the church-shattering secret and thereafter are hunted by both the police and the aforementioned assassin sent out by the church to keep the truth from coming to light. And here's the most sinister aspect of the book. At one level Brown's book might simply be a riveting page-turner of a thriller (it's certainly that), but at another level it plays into our worst fears that the church is built on a fissure of lies and half-truths, and that it will stop at nothing to keep the deception a secret. Millions of readers of *The Da Vinci Code* might be of two minds about the divinity of Christ, but I guarantee that they're certain that the Christian church would stop at nothing to maintain its position of power and wealth in society today. Even if it required the use of hired killers, the church—not unlike the CIA, MI5, and FSB secret intelligence agencies—would do anything to protect its ever more fragile interests.

This plays into the classic postmodern belief that the truth can never be found at the center of society. It's assumed these days that powerful hegemonies such as the legal system, the political system, big business, and the church can never be trusted because they have too much to lose if the truth were told. In other words, whatever such powers say to us is designed to maintain the status quo, with them retaining their power. It's assumed by many young people in particular that church leaders know that the Bible and canon law are full of lies and manipulations of the truth. These leaders can't tell the truth, because if they did, they'd be out of a job. They have too much to lose to be considered trustworthy. I have read many books about ancient mysteries, contemporary scholars, rare documents, greedy collectors, and the obligatory quasi-academic protagonist, but *The Da Vinci Code* has cornered the market by tapping into our general distrust of religious and civic institutions. The plain truth is there, it says, but we can't expect those who profit from the lies to tell it to us.

Conversely, many others believe that the truth can come only from the margins, from those who have nothing to lose by telling it the way it really is. Only the most marginalized people—the gay and lesbian community, artists, filmmakers, the poor, the young—can show us the way forward. This can be a terribly naïve view, of course, but it's worth taking into account. Many surveys across the West indicate that although the church scores very poorly on the trustworthiness index, Jesus is still regarded very highly. No doubt, one of the reasons for this has to do with his impeccable revolutionary "street cred." Jesus is the archetypal poor, marginalized radical. He didn't profit in any way from what he taught. In fact, he suffered unspeakably for it. Despite the strange current interest in Che Guevara, who was more profiteering mercenary than pure-minded revolutionary, other heroes such as Mohandas Gandhi, Martin Luther King, Andrei Sakharov, Nelson Mandela, Aung San Suu Kyi, and Arundhati Roy have not benefited personally for their beliefs. They are universally respected for their strength, courage, and integrity. A new Christian movement is required, one that recovers the essential powerlessness of the revolutionary. It was Martin Luther King who was noted as having said, "The real revolutionary is the one who has nothing to lose."

[handwritten marginalia: What will happen when their respect makes them mainstream endless cycle of the fringe]

Note the underground churches of China, or the persecuted church of Burma, or the cell churches of Latin America. Note the simple little projects like Hot Dogma or Donkey Coffee. They are small, fragile experiments. They are collectives of brave souls, trusting God and stopping at nothing to embody (incarnate) the gospel of Jesus. Part of their very great impact is that they have no temporal wealth or power. They are forced to rely on God. As John Eldredge says,

> God is calling together little communities of the heart, to fight for one another and for the hearts of those who have not yet been set free. The camaraderie, that intimacy, that incredible impact by a few stouthearted souls—that *is* available. It is the Christian life as Jesus gave it to us. It is completely normal.[16]

After hearing me speak this way, a gentleman gave me a small book titled *When the Church Was Very Young,* by Ernest Loosley.[17] He said he thought I'd like it. I opened it and scanned the contents page. Each chapter began with the phrase "When the Church Was Very Young, It Had . . ." and concluded with things such as "No Buildings," "No Denominations," "No Fixed Organisation," "No New Testament," "No Dogmatic System." I thanked the gentleman, saying that the book looked right up my alley. He smiled and told me to look at the year of its publication. To my amazement, its release date was 1935. We have always known that the Christian church should be an underground movement. Old Ernest Loosley knew it as long ago as 1935. We also know that where the church is growing most dynamically around the world today, it is doing so in places where it has no buildings, no seminaries, no clergy, no money. It is the church's very marginalization that commends its message to the world.

Naming the Name of Jesus

If we take seriously the call to follow Jesus into exile, we will find ourselves developing closer proximity with our neighborhood. It's simply unavoidable. It will involve divesting ourselves of much of the baggage that traditional churches have loaded on us. It will mean wriggling free of the demands that churches have insisted we fulfill. It will mean practicing the presence of Jesus in our inner life as well as through our outward actions. By

---

[16]John Eldredge, *Waking the Dead: The Glory of a Heart Fully Alive* (Nashville: Thomas Nelson, 2003), 11.

[17]Ernest Loosley, *When the Church Was Very Young* (London: Allen & Unwin, 1935; repr., Auburn, Maine: Christian Books Publishing House, 1988).

living expansive lives of justice, kindness, hospitality, and generosity, we model the life of Jesus to those who would never attend a church service or read the New Testament. And, of course, we would do this without recourse to large buildings, well-funded programs, and other expressions of institutionalism. We will, like Jesus, go naked and empty-handed to others, with no motive other than to show grace and practice mercy. Well, whether we like it or not, sooner or later someone is going to ask us why we live the way we do. And at that point, exiles must be prepared to name the name of Jesus in contexts where his name might never be heard. In other words, even though many exiles balk at the thought of evangelistic activity, having been so thoroughly turned off by the abusive behavior of evangelists whom they have observed in the past, they need to acknowledge that the proclamation of Jesus will naturally flow from the living of an incarnational lifestyle.

Let me give an example. One of Australia's finest modern novelists is Tim Winton. He is a big, barrel-chested man who lives on the wild, isolated northwestern coast of Australia. Western Australians have the reputation of being "hard"—heavy drinkers, quiet-spoken, not given to displays of sensitivity. Although Winton's characters sometimes embody this taciturn, emotional remoteness, he himself is both emotionally sensitive and deeply spiritual, a committed Christian in a part of the world where religion often is seen as weakness. Asked once by a television interviewer about his faith, he didn't defend it with theological erudition or philosophical argument. Instead, he told the story about his father, a tough frontier policeman who was hit by a drunk driver in the 1960s, when Tim was just five years old. His father spent weeks in a coma before recovering enough to return home, a mere shadow of his former self. As a boy, Winton remembered the experience vividly:

> I remember the day that they brought him home, and he was sort of like an earlier version of my father, a sort of augmented version of my father. He was sort of recognizable, but not really my dad, you know? Everything was busted up and they put him in the chair, and, you know, "Here's your dad." And I was sort of horrified.[18]

Another image that stayed with the young Tim Winton was that of a local Western Australian man, Len Thomas, who came to the house every day to carry the disabled policeman from his bed to the bathroom. There he would strip him down, place him in the bath, and wash his wasted body. Still a very large man, Winton's father was too heavy for his wife to get him to the

---

[18]"Tim Winton," Enough Rope with Andrew Denton n.p. [cited 17 January 2006]. Online: http://www.abc.net.au/tv/enoughrope/transcripts/s1227915.htm.

bathroom. Len Thomas, a member of the local church, had turned up un-expectedly, offering to help. As Winton remembers it, it was a very unusual thing for a macho Australian to do in the 1960s—to gently carry another man and place him in the bath and tenderly clean his naked body. It had a powerful effect on the young boy:

> And this weird, kind of strangely sacrificial act, where he'd come and wash another grown man and carry him to bed and look after him in a way that Mum just physically couldn't do. Something, you know, it really touched me, in that regardless of theology or anything else, watching a grown man bother, for nothing, to show up and wash a sick man . . . you know, it really affected me.[19]

For Winton, the sacrifice made by Len Thomas was explanation enough of his Christian faith. Len had embodied (incarnated) the gospel for young Tim Winton, and it spoke louder than a thousand sermons from a thousand pulpits. As deeply unsettling as this image of Jesus might be to us, it is no less provocative than Jesus' own decision to bathe his disciples' feet in John 13. Peter's reaction to Jesus—"No, you shall never wash my feet"—clearly indicates how shocking it was. In the Middle East the feet are considered to be a very private part of the human anatomy, and great discretion is attached to them. For Peter, to have a man of honor wash his feet is akin, I suppose, to having a burly, Western Australian man bathe your broken body.

Winton doesn't say whether Len Thomas ever explicitly told him about Jesus, but it was obvious to him that this neighbor was motivated by his Christian faith. His presence, his proximity, his powerlessness all spoke volumes. This mirrors the Franciscan mantra "Preach the gospel always, and if necessary, use words." It also reflects Peter's words in 1 Pet 2:12: "Live such good lives among the pagans that, though they accuse you of doing wrong, they may see your good deeds and glorify God on the day he visits us." In fact, later in this letter, Peter dares to suggest that wives can win their un-believing husbands over to faith without words at all, but merely by their ex-amples of purity and reverence (1 Pet 3:1–2).

This seems extraordinary, and it appears to contradict Paul's declaration in Rom 10:17: "faith comes from hearing the message, and the message is heard through the word about Christ." I see no contradiction at all, but simply two sides of the same coin. For too long the church has been preach-ing to a world that will no longer listen. As a result, many exiles are nervous about "preaching Christ." As I mentioned, I acknowledge that they have been turned off by exploitative and manipulative evangelistic methods and

---

[19]Ibid.

repelled by an oversimplification of the gospel to a few short points in a brief tract. They would rather perform acts of service than "share the gospel" with someone, for fear that they might become the very thing they wish to avoid: a narrow-minded, bigoted fundamentalist. This is an overreaction, though I understand where it comes from. But exiles need to be careful not to throw the baby out with the bathwater. As we go about our lives, like Len Thomas, practicing proximity, presence, and powerlessness, there will undoubtedly come a time for proclamation. It probably won't take the form of an uninterrupted monologue. In all likelihood, it will occur over multiple conversations, over a period of time, with those whom we live among. But it will be the kind of private discourse that is intimate, personal, and life-changing, precisely because it has emerged out of a loving, long-term, trusting relationship between equals.

Sharing the Message

"Evangelistic"	"Incarnational"
monologue	dialogue
presentation with doctrinal points	exchange of ideas
formulaic	communicated through various conversations & experiences

Many Christians have been trained in how to "give a gospel presentation" during which they are expected to work through six or seven doctrinal points toward the conclusion that their listener pray a "prayer of salvation" to accept Jesus as their Lord and Savior. It sounds good, which no doubt is why so many have undertaken such training. But friendships and conversations rarely go this way, opening up to an opportunity for someone to burst into an extended monologue about their beliefs. Ideas often are transferred from person to person through the engagement of life with life, through a variety of experiences and circumstances, and through myriad conversations. This isn't to say that exiles shouldn't be ready to speak about Jesus. Quite the contrary, exiles need to be more than prepared to talk about him, but to recognize that such a discourse should be respectful, kind, and conducted with humility. As Paul says, "Let your conversation be always full of grace, seasoned with salt, so that you may know how to answer everyone" (Col 4:6). But such a conversation, when sweetened by an incarnational lifestyle, will be given added potency when it appears on the lips of men and women whose lives represent such a demonstrable goodness akin to that of their Lord, Jesus.

Living such a delicious lifestyle will require us to make and keep a number of promises to our host empire. When we find ourselves on foreign soil, in exile in a post-Christendom empire, we should make such dangerous promises as the pledge to be authentic, true, generous, inclusive, welcoming, and kind, to stand with Jesus in a radical new lifestyle of grace and love. Making these promises is dangerous only when people watch us to see whether we keep them or not. And watch us they will. I think that many people are sick of the Christian movement but nevertheless remain fascinated by Jesus. Subconsciously, some people watch Christians in the hope that some of them will actually prove that such promises can indeed be kept.

When Prince Charles married Lady Diana Spencer in July 1981, they emerged from St. Paul's Cathedral and made their very public trip to Buckingham Palace in an open car, waving and smiling to the crowds that thronged the route to greet the newly married royal couple. The next day, the Fleet Street press reported every word that Charles and Diana had said to each other, both in the car and on the balcony of the palace, even the most furtively whispered conversations. How did they know what Diana shyly said to her new husband in their wedding car? It was later revealed that every newspaper had expert lip readers positioned at various places along the route reading every word that passed between the two newlyweds. Such was the price she paid for her relationship to the future king of the United Kingdom, a price later shown to be far greater than anyone should bear.

So it is likewise for exiles "wedded" to Jesus, the king of heaven. People watch us. Many of them genuinely want to see whether the teaching of Jesus is, as Homer told Bart, a bunch of well-meaning rules that don't really work in real life. Or is it possible that Jesus' followers can make *and keep* the daring promises to which he has called them? It is to those dangerous promises that we now turn.

PART II

DANGEROUS PROMISES

4

Exiled from a Hyper-Real World

The Promise: We Will Be Authentic

> I would rather be with someone who is real than
> someone who is good.
> —Attributed to Philip Yancey

W hat kinds of promises emerge from the exile's decision to follow Christ in the midst of the host empire? In this section we will observe five important promises. All of them are related to the kind of community that we are seeking to fashion in the soil of post-Christendom. Exiles are called to action based on the following promises:

- **We will be authentic.** In a world of hyper-reality, themed environments, false celebrity, and fake experience, exiles will live out the promise of being honest, genuine, and real.

- **We will serve a cause greater than ourselves.** Exiles will not throw themselves headlong into the standard operating policy of the empire by being primarily concerned about their own needs. They will band together to fashion communities of love and service.

- **We will create missional community.** Exiles will hold out the promise that it's possible for humans to unite with others, offering their individual gifts and learning from each other, while committing to a common task.

- **We will be generous and practice hospitality.** Beyond conventional hospitality, exiles will put themselves at the service of the hungry and the needy.

- **We will work righteously.** Exiles promise to do everything, including the most secular work, as an expression of their being sent by God into the nooks and crannies of the host empire.

In our world today—post-Christendom and postmodern—we find ourselves a far cry from the simpler times during which Jesus lived. As exiles, trying to negotiate our way through the twenty-first century, with Jesus as our guide and our dangerous example, we find ourselves up against challenges that we can't imagine Jesus having to deal with. We stare vacantly at our WWJD ("What would Jesus do?") wristbands, wondering just what Jesus would do when confronted with the befuddling complexities of contemporary culture. No wonder so many Christians opt to withdraw, to burrow deeper down inside their warrens in the hope that they can avoid contamination from the onslaught of the post-Christendom West. Likewise, the temptation to give in and be swept along by the prevailing mores is perfectly understandable. Swimming always against the constantly shifting flow of culture is exhausting, and it's not incomprehensible when Christians throw their hands up and just stop swimming.

And yet, abandoning ourselves to the current is hardly what Jesus did. Exiles, following his example, are forever seeking to forge another way forward. Neither hiding from nor embracing the values of contemporary society, they seek to thrive within their host culture without becoming slaves to it. No easy feat, as we've already noted. Like Joseph in Egypt, Esther in Persia, or Daniel in Babylon, we are called to the ongoing and risky negotiation of engagement and resistance. And yet our decision to follow Christ implies that we will make a series of promises to our host empire. These promises include our declared intent to be people of love, justice, generosity, and hospitality. These are dangerous promises because making them is easy, but keeping them is risky and daring. It is to the first of these promises that we now turn: *we will be authentic.*

In an empire of fakery and phoniness, the followers of Christ will dangerously promise to be a community of authenticity and honesty. One of the greatest obstacles to faithful Christian living today is the thorough pervasiveness of our Western obsession with hyper-reality. This is the current obsession with mass-produced and packaged products that, though artificial, purport to be even better than the real thing. For example, "freshly squeezed" orange juice packed with sugar and extra vitamins and minerals. Or talk-show hosts who speak to us as though we were close personal friends. Or tanning studios. Or bacon-and-cheese flavored snacks. As we are seeking to live an exilic, missional lifestyle, we are surrounded with news reports about celebrities' plastic surgery disasters. Or commercials for miracle weight-loss programs. Or new mass-produced products promising to have been made by poor villagers in South America. One critic has referred to this as the "cool-whip culture"—a culture in which banana-flavored desserts haven't had anything resembling a banana anywhere near them. The banana flavoring tastes more like a banana than a, well, banana. Everything is more "real" than real. We find ourselves talking about the love lives of movie stars as if we know them personally. Hearing suburban housewives explain, "Gwyneth is struggling with depression after the birth of her daughter," you'd think we were discussing someone we actually knew and cared about. We routinely discuss the intimate details of the personal lives of Brad and Angelina, or Jessica and Nick, but we don't even know the most casual details about our neighbors' lives. We use artificial sweeteners, artificial creamers, artificial butter, artificial soft drinks (what on earth is actually in Coke and Dr. Pepper anyway?).

We thrill to the opportunity to eat a seafood meal at the local Joe's Crab Shack. You'd think that it's a ramshackle dive that might fall down any minute, if you hadn't seen it being built just eight months ago by a speedy professional crew that travels around the country building Joe's Crab Shacks. Or maybe you're not in the mood for shellfish, especially 1,200 miles from the nearest ocean. Just down the road is the Cracker Barrel Old Country Store, a homey, weathered place where a welcoming fire emanates from gas nozzles. On the walls at Cracker Barrel hang nearly a thousand pieces of suitably worn Americana, lovingly collected and restored. Each one has a bar code. We're used to franchised Italian, Mexican, and Thai restaurants that have a faux authentic vibe to them, and we give up on ever having a genuine eating experience again. As an Australian, my "favorite" fake eating experience is the oh-so down-under Outback Steakhouse.

Trying to be authentic in a world of fakery is, for many, harder than avoiding pornography, drugs, or abortions. Why is the church so obsessed with these issues and yet so wholly uninterested in critiquing its own capitulation to hyper-reality—Teflon facades, Max Headroom–like televangelists, million-dollar smiles. The pastor's family is often even happier than the Brady Bunch. From pulpits around the country we hear too-good-to-be-true anecdotes dished up as expressions of everyday Christianity. The heroes of these stories are more morally upright than George Washington and are always amply rewarded for their integrity. Every prayer gets answered. Every cent poured into the church coffers is returned a hundred-fold to the giver. We think we know that all of it is untrue, but in this day of hyper-reality, we're as inclined to suspend disbelief as long as we do for an infomercial for a new fat-draining grill. We're used to being told that everything tastes better, feels better, looks better, thanks to this new product—even if that new product happens to be Jesus. We're used to taking the pretense at face value.

Signs of the Real

The French postmodern philosopher Jean Baudrillard once presciently said,

> By crossing into a space whose curvature is no longer that of the real, nor that of the truth, the era of simulation is inaugurated by a liquidation of all referentials. . . . It is no longer a question of imitation, nor duplication, nor even parody. It is a question of substituting the signs of the real for the real.[1]

"It is a question of substituting the *signs of the real* for the real." Surely this sums up our current dilemma. So much of our world is designed to look and feel real without ever being so. Watching the recent and compelling "reality TV" atrocity *I'm a Celebrity—Get Me Out of Here!* you could be forgiven for buying wholeheartedly into this bleak perspective. Baudrillard was commenting on our own construction and consumption of a hypermodern nonreal. So-called reality TV, a perfect example of such, in general is an entertainment that grabs more headlines than "real" news. And yet the sole component of *I'm a Celebrity* is the entirely contrived setup of a bunch of rather dim famous people whose task is simply to be, to exist in front of the cameras in a bizarre parody of "normal" reality. What is more disturbing is Baudrillard's point about the realm of pure simulacra being beyond parody, in that reality TV is considered as newsworthy and therefore as real as an earthquake or a military coup.

The reality-TV tsunami has washed over us, and we are drowning in the swirling waters of counterfeit "reality." Ever since television executives realized that Western audiences can't get enough spurious, fraudulent nonsense on television, they have produced virtually every imaginable rendering of the reality genre, developing some of the most crass and simplistic nonsense ever to air on television. And international audiences have gobbled it up.

When former British paratrooper Mark Burnett bought a British idea for a show in which contestants were stranded on an island and forced to vote each other off in order to survive, he opened the floodgates on reality TV. Burnett's program *Survivor* was a ratings smash, which in turn spawned *Temptation Island.* In this version of the show, happy couples are separated and placed on different islands with beautiful members of the opposite sex who try to lure them to break up with their partners. Now, television wasn't just fooling with contestants' minds, it was interfering with their relation-

---

[1]Jean Baudrillard, *Simulacra and Simulation* (trans. Sheila Faria Glaser; The Body, In Theory: Histories of Cultural Materialism; Ann Arbor: University of Michigan Press, 1995), 22.

ships. It couldn't be more crass, but it was Fox's highest-rated series in 2001 and now has over eleven foreign editions.

The link between reality TV and soft-porn titillation was confirmed with the success of *The Bachelor,* in which twenty-five beautiful women get to date one man, and at the end of the series he chooses the winner and marries her. While totally demeaning the concept of marriage, it too was a hit. Nothing is sacred. But even this idea could be devolved further, and we soon had the phenomenally successful *Joe Millionaire,* in which a handsome, $19,000–a-year construction worker pretends to be a millionaire. The girls who competed for his vote would not be aware of the scam until the final episode. The show rated its socks off. Reality TV was reaching new heights (or depths, depending on your view). Since then, the reality genre has merged with the quiz show/competition concept and given us *The Weakest Link, Who Wants to Be a Millionaire? American Idol,* and *The Amazing Race.* These "reality" programs have since been followed by shows with titles such as *101 Things Pulled from the Human Body* (for example, a piece of two-by-four removed from a woman's ear canal, and a swordfish sword removed from a man's eye), *Last Comic Standing* (a comedy talent quest), *World's Nastiest Neighbors* (as it sounds), *Plastic Surgery Nightmares* (also as it sounds, and a big ratings win), and the atrocious *The Simple Life,* in which pampered New York socialite teens are forced to live on a farm for the length of the series.[2]

In the meantime, FM-radio jocks have been pushing the hyper-reality envelope even further, with multiple dating competitions leading to on-the-air weddings. In fact, on-the-air wedding ceremonies are now so common as to be completely meaningless. Nighttime radio announcers have been lambasted for their despicable antics, including broadcasting their listeners having orgasms or tricking loved ones with heartless pranks. In a recent innovation, radio announcers have been putting listeners through lie-detector tests and asking them deeply personal questions in an attempt to embarrass them before their partners. It's the ultimate in hyper-reality: breaking up with your wife because you discovered she'd been unfaithful via a radio program lie-detector test. Imagine explaining that to the kids.

It all sounds dreadful, doesn't it? So why do audiences enjoy it so much? I don't think it's too simplistic to conclude that reality TV works because it offers a fragmented and disconnected Western audience the opportunity to vicariously enter into a pseudo-community via the television set or the radio. As I noted before, in many suburban communities we don't even know our

---

[2]For a very useful article on this subject see Mark Seal, "Reality Kings," *Vanity Fair* (July 2003): 121–25 and 151–55. For lists of the mainstream reality TV shows see the website www.realitytvworld.com.

neighbors' names, let alone how they live or what they do with their spare time. Mundane reality TV such as *Big Brother* cashes in on our sense of isolation. Week in and week out, we are subjected to watching ordinary people lie around a house, crammed with cameras, talking about their sex lives, their political views, their relationship hang-ups. We watch people cook, eat, empty the garbage, and fall in love (or lust, as the case may be). *Big Brother* is about as uninteresting as reality TV gets, and yet, particularly in the United Kingdom, Europe, and Australia, it has rated consistently well, especially among younger audiences.

One reason for this is that the hyper-reality of the program is only increased when the audience is invited to meddle in the show. *Big Brother, American Idol,* and *Last Comic Standing* allow viewers to vote people out of the show. Viewers can actually impact the lives of the contestants. There is a sense of involvement in the lives of the viewers' favorite characters. Much of this current situation is forecast in Peter Weir's clever (and ahead-of-its-time) film *The Truman Show* (1998). Popular culture is interesting in its ability to be strikingly self-conscious. It can be extraordinarily self-reverential and cuttingly self-critical. *The Truman Show* does both, though more of the latter. Truman Burbank (played by Jim Carrey) has unknowingly grown up in a hermetically sealed film studio, his whole life being the subject of the longest-running reality-TV show in history. When he finally discovers the true nature of his world, he bravely ventures forth out into the real world, disregarding the protests of the show's creator. Though thoroughly engrossed in his journey of discovery, viewers switch off once Truman has left the set. The final line, from a member of the audience is, "Oh well, what else is on?" We think we have a level of intimacy with reality-TV stars, but a few days after a show ends we have forgotten them and moved on.

Also, reality TV makes the world a very simple place. Even a cursory viewing of *Survivor,* for example, reveals that the complexities and messiness of life (even life on a deserted island) are papered over by clever editing and high production values. We cannot bear complexity and intricacy, even though they are a normal feature of real life. In the editing room, relationships on *Survivor* or *Temptation Island* are reduced to simple stereotypes. There are good guys and bad guys. Jealousy, affection, anger, and humor are reduced to typical responses, sound bytes, and emblematic images, never fully conveying the multifaceted nature of contestants or the complexity of the situations in which they find themselves. The reason: the messiness of life wouldn't make good television.

What can we conclude from all this? People want it real, but not too real! We have become masters of consuming fake realism. We want a sanitized, processed, and highly polished representation of something that *approximates* reality. But in fact, reality is a frightening prospect for us, and we don't really expect that what will be presented to us on the small screen will be real. In his highly influential book *Amusing Ourselves to Death*,[3] Neil Postman concludes that the medium of television is by its very nature unable to convey complexity and seriousness. The ephemeral nature of television, because of its incredible volume and prevalence in society, is the basic tenet of Postman's argument here. By its very nature, Postman says, television is incapable of presenting true public discourse, which relies on arguments that don't necessarily have the entertainment quotient necessary for the medium. Even current affairs and news programs (and channels) limit their exploration of stories to sound bites and thirty-second to six-minute reports. Postman's controversial conclusions included the view that evangelists had no business on television because the medium itself undermines the confidence that the audience has in its content. We don't believe the claims made in infomercials, news broadcasts, or reality-TV programs, but we passively agree to consume them *as if they were real.*

It reminds me of the protagonist's wife in *Fahrenheit 451*, who, when asked about the company she had entertained that evening replies, "Oh, you know—the gang," with an airy wave at the wall-encompassing television screen. As I write this, millions of teenagers are completely consumed with *American Idol.* They behave as if they actually know the contestants personally, using their first names only (in the same way they are introduced on the program). They speak of them in the kind of intimate language that we reserve for speaking about acquaintances and colleagues. I know for a fact that a month or two (if that long) after the series ends, they will have virtually forgotten all about the contestants. What happens to a culture that can so quickly relate to television characters and then so quickly dispense with them? And does this affect the quality of viewers' personal relationships with "real" people? The cultural repercussions of the reality-TV craze are yet to be realized. It will be interesting to watch them as they unfold.

Of course, blogs are another form of hyper-reality. Shorthand for "web logs," blogs are online diaries written by all kinds of people who want to share their inmost thoughts and beliefs and everyday lives with the rest of the world. They come in a variety of types. There is the very personal "this is my life" kind of blog—a diary of what I did today. Then there's the propaganda style of blog, written by politicians, writers, academics, and religious leaders, designed to promulgate the author's ideas on particular issues. There are blogs about sports, sex, relationships, faith, church, terrorism—in fact, you name

---

[3]Neil Postman, *Amusing Ourselves to Death: Public Discourse in the Age of Show Business* (New York: Viking Penguin, 1986).

it. There are photoblogs with little text but the host's happy snaps on display for the world to see (supermodels seem to favor this kind of blog). There are even moblogs—photoblogs featuring shots taken by mobile phones.

What all blogs have in common is the host's/author's basic belief that his or her life or thoughts about life are worth sharing with anyone who will log on. It's either the most astonishing universal display of narcissism or the most liberating opportunity for the ordinary and the everyday to be celebrated. On one level it looks like the liberation of the ordinary, but at another level it's an expression of hyper-reality: it looks like we're meeting people via the Web, but really we're meeting only the acceptable persona that they want displayed to the world. Some observers estimate that there are about fifty thousand blogs in cyberspace. Celebrities, techno-geeks, students, journalists, house-wives, and priests all blog. I was briefly the subject of an international blogging debate after a speaking tour of the United Kingdom. Several people who attended a lecture that I gave in London were not happy with what I presented, and they said so on their blogs. Of course, they are quite within their rights to do so. Any public lecture is open to criticism and reaction. It was what happened next that astonished me. A minor debate stretched across the planet, with scores of people logging onto these blogs to discuss me and my ideas. Some of these people knew me personally or had read my books, but most of those who made entries had never met me, heard me speak, or read anything that I've written. This didn't stop them from morphing into fiery, opinionated, outspoken critics. It was like a global game of Telephone, in which with each entry my persona and my ideas were shifting and chang-ing shape. What really happened in that lecture in London was now irrele-vant. Through the anonymity and freedom of the Internet, strangers were now discussing someone they don't know with people they've never met as though it was an intimate, private conversation.

Some blog sites are like individualized reality-TV shows. They garner their own audience of regular visitors and create pseudo-cybercommunities of strangers across the planet. At its best, a blog is a medium for self-expres-sion, a way to publish your ideas aside from the slow and cumbersome nature of traditional publishing. At its worst, a blog can be self-entertainment, irre-sponsible and unaccountable. Self-tailored entertainment is the new craze among postmodern people who are anxious to make their mark on the media. Media-hungry, narcissistic people are starring via reality TV and the Web, reflecting back images of themselves. One interesting and disturbing trend on the Internet is the explosion of amateur pornography. It is estimated that close to one-fourth of all pornographic material available on the Web is posted by ordinary people filming and photographing themselves or others for a worldwide audience.

The Emergence of the New Realism

Baudrillard's ominous warning seems ever more concerning. Our substitution of the real with *signs* of the real occurs not only on television every night. It finds its way into the food we eat ("I Can't Believe It's Not Butter!") and the furniture we buy (a Pottery Barn "authentic" Mayan chest, apparently carved by the humble villagers of Cusco, for example). We regularly encounter commercials for luxury cruises to remote, untouched Caribbean island communities, or "accurate" reconstructions of Elizabethan villages, and we wonder about the degree to which we ever really encounter the authentic.

But it seems that at last there is a backlash against all this faux reality. Just before we all completely drown in a sea of postmodern hyper-real angst, it seems we are seeing the reemergence of the real. Sociologists, ecologists, and even advertising companies are heralding a new movement of realism. In a world of hyper-reality, there is an emerging search for authenticity, the championing of real food, culture, politics (rather than *Realpolitik*), and entertainment by a demographic that author David Boyle refers to as "New Realism." In his book *Authenticity: Brands, Fakes, Spin and the Lust for Real Life,* Boyle says this group of new realists is easily recognizable: they want to know where their food comes from and what's in it; they want politicians to come clean about the lies that they've told and musicians to play rather than mime at their concerts; they want to speak to a person rather than a machine when they call a helpline; they seek out local produce and frequent farmers' markets as a means of revitalizing community agriculture and bypassing supermarket monopolies.

According to Boyle, new realists are serious about the environment. They place a heavy emphasis on relationships and they value women's points of view, as well as having a commitment to spirituality and psychological development. They are disaffected with the large institutions of modern life, including both left and right in politics, and they reject materialism and overt displays of status. They're very grounded and practical people. In their book *The Cultural Creatives,*[4] Paul Ray and Sherry Ruth Anderson present their studies on this demographic. Even though Ray and Anderson refer to this emerging group as "cultural creatives," I'll stick with Boyle's "new realists" because it's a more helpful descriptor. These new realists span quite a range of ages, eighteen through seventy, so this is not a generational movement. There are fewer liberals than conservatives, and fewer people who don't see

---

[4]Paul H. Ray and Sherry Ruth Anderson, *The Cultural Creatives: How 50 Million People Are Changing the World* (New York: Harmony Books, 2000).

themselves as either left or right. This is about a new kind of politics. They come from all across the United States, according to Ray and Anderson, and are represented by all ethnic groupings and all income levels, from working class to highly affluent. They are seeing the world differently from the mainstream and are demanding the following:

- Ecologically sustainable products and services, and concern for the whole planet

- An insistence on authenticity, personally, at work, in business and politics

- Bringing women's issues into public life

- Reporting the news differently, to see the big picture, and first-person stories, and good news too

- Bringing spirituality into American life

Ray and Anderson claim that these so-called new realists make up as much as 26 percent of the U.S. population. They also claim that in the early 1960s, people who shared the same values as today's new realists numbered less than 5 percent of the population. If they're right, that is shockingly quick social change. Not only is the speed of this emergence stunning, but also its breadth is catching even the most alert observers by surprise. Officials of the European Union, hearing of the numbers of new realists in the United States, launched a related survey in each of their fifteen countries in 1997. To their amazement, the evidence suggested that there are at least as many new realists across Europe as Ray and Anderson report in the United States. And yet, what unites them primarily as a single "movement" is their shared assumption that there is something wrong with this world, and that one of the chief ways to fix it is to strive for greater *authenticity.* Boyle describes them this way:

> The New Realists increasingly want "real" food—maybe organic—that tastes of something, doesn't involve the genes of fish for temperature control, and comes from a real place somewhere on the map. They don't want the kind of consumables leached of flavor and interest in the form of pills or tubes that the experts used to tell us represented the future of food because the Apollo and Gemini astronauts used them.

> They want the real sound of people working, not the fake, recorded mutter that the BBC shelled out £2,300 for in 2000 when they worried that their accounts department was too quiet.

Or the fake smells that London Underground tried in their tunnels the same year.

Or the fake places that all look the same, with the same global storefronts in every town and city around the world, in the cheapest international style of glass and concrete.

Or fake politicians whose slightest utterance is tested before focus groups and scripted, and who—like George W. Bush—even have the word "Wow!" on the teleprompter.

Or the fake relationships people create online, never having to meet, using fake names—sometimes even breaking up real flesh-and-blood relationships in the process.

Or fake community activity, like the Holiday Bowling Lanes in New London, Connecticut, which social theorist Robert Putnam describes in his book **Bowling Alone,** with giant TV screens above each lane, where the players never talk to each other between turns, but just stare sadly upwards.

Or the kind of world where, except for the very rich, most of us will have to rely on virtual bankers, virtual doctors, virtual pharmacists, virtual carers and virtual teachers.[5]

However, the new realists also want to use the Internet and credit cards; many have a soft spot for electronically generated dance music; most would like to hang on to their cars; and many find that monopolized supermarket produce is tasty and convenient after a hard day's work. The emphasis is on searching for and maintaining authenticity—the real, the local, the genuine, the handmade. But is this actually a *movement,* or simply boring middle-class lifestyle hypocrisy?

Some say the answer is neither. The word "movement" suggests a group of people with definite aims and an agenda for change. The amorphous New Realism is more fittingly described as a general tendency in thought, action, and consumption. Large numbers of Westerners are tiring of the hyper-real. They are collectively yearning for something richer and more authentic. And though it's easy to label the new realists as hypocrites (as many commentators have), the paradoxes in the New Realism outlook are more kindly understood as a result of consumer confusion rather than a blatant attempt to have their cake and eat it too. Anyone who has tried to employ the notion of "ethical living" (whatever that means) while also trying to maintain even what

---

[5]David Boyle, *Authenticity: Brands, Fakes, Spin and the Lust for Real Life* (London: Flamingo, 2004), 10.

would be considered an average lifestyle recognizes the dilemmas and confusions that such lifestyle choices bring. We would all like to encourage local farming and agriculture as much as possible, but when the supermarket is open "24/7" and accepts credit cards, the weekly farmers' market can pale by comparison. However, there is a danger that the search for authenticity can itself become a form of elitism: when wealthier people eat "handcrafted rustic" wholegrain bread rather than its mass-produced white-flour counterpart, it becomes clear that much so-called authenticity can only be bought at a price. Similarly, seeing a country in a truly authentic way means avoiding the discount package deals and family-friendly tour companies that make it possible for many people to get away in the first place. Such harsh realities are not lost on the new realists, who, though striving for a form of altruism, prefer to have a choice than no options at all.

Boyle would claim that new realists recognize these paradoxes. As he puts it,

> It's a new kind of humanism that defends human choice against the giant corporations and the technocrats who would find it cheaper just to use machines or computers to interact with us. . . . It's an attitude that doesn't condemn extra thick-skinned tomatoes, extra-ripe bananas, decaffeinated coffee beans—but does condemn the economic processes which mean they drive out the real stuff.[6]

So the protest is not against people's own choices, but rather against the lack of choice that we face when deciding how to live, the lack of choice that makes it much more difficult to find a genuinely ethical investment fund or an independent bookshop than it is to buy into the mass-produced alternative. The new realists despise the lack of choice generated by the economic monopolization of the world by multinational interests.

However, even the notion of authenticity is being picked up, rebranded, and sold back to us by those very forces that the new realists seek to avoid. Wander into any big-name supermarket and you are sure to find a plethora of authentic local produce—"local" meaning specific to its place of origin. So there is Italian balsamic vinegar, Wensleydale cheese, Chilean wine, and authentic Thai cuisine. And this is where the nonreal real comes in. All of these products are real and to a certain extent authentic, but their mode of sale—designed to within an inch of its life—negates whatever authenticity the original product would have had to begin with. There is something decidedly unreal about the mass presentation of such "authentic" foods. At a time when Christian Dior makes woolly hats and when a vacuous celebrity's plastic

---

[6]Ibid., 295.

breasts are headline news, the hunt for authenticity can seem a bit like a fool's crusade. And if the definition of authentic living is restricted entirely to what we buy, then it is indeed a fool's crusade to attempt to purchase our way out of a lack of lifestyle choices. New Realism could develop into a systematic and active critique of the way the world is run and the way humans regard themselves and each other.

The Exile's Quest for the Authentic

As exiles, we should welcome the emergence of New Realism with open arms. In fact, exiles ought to be at its forefront, valuing and promoting that which is truly authentic. As much as the complexities of hyper-reality might seem foreign to the world of Jesus, the response of exiles can nonetheless be modeled on his example of integrity, truth-telling, and authenticity. And yet the recent history of the church is strewn with examples of inauthenticity. Take, for example, the recent craze for praying the obscure prayer of Jabez in 1 Chron 4:10. Taken completely out of context, exegeted to within an inch of its life, and promoted as a "key" to unlocking God's blessing in one's life, the prayer of Jabez became the latest artificial mechanism for short-circuiting the genuine ongoing work of communion with God ("I Can't Believe It's Not Prayer!"). Though we have Jesus' own template for prayer, which includes doing God's will and seeing the kingdom come, we seem to prefer the shorter, more-to-the-point request for blessings or "enlarged borders" (nudge nudge, wink wink). For some reason, we think that God can't see our greedy hearts or our lazy attitudes, but is marshaled into action by a magic prayer.

Part of the pervading phoniness about many Christians' lives is that there seems to be an assumed difference between our public worship experience and our private lifestyle and practices. And by this, I'm not simply referring to standard, garden-variety hypocrisy. The claims of the Christian life are so great that none of us can live up to them—the very reason for Christ's redemptive death. Of course, there'll be a gap between what we believe we should be doing and the degree to which we can do it. However, I'm referring more to the wholesale disconnect between our public and private faiths.

The monumental damage done to children by inauthentic Christian parents is obvious and lamentable. Why can't Christian communities be places of truthfulness and vulnerability? Why must they so often be places of unreality? Not that long ago, a friend of mine informed me in hushed yet outraged tones that her rector had used the term "crap" in one of his sermons. He was a new rector, and his "disgusting" language raised all kinds of nostalgic feelings in my friend for the previous rector (about whom my friend had often complained in the past!). It got me thinking. What else can't you do in church that you can do in other everyday activities in life? I have another friend who brings her Scottie dog to our church every Sunday. He sits quietly at her feet and sighs deeply through his nose every so often. When I told one of my students about our church's regular attendee, the Scottie dog, he told me that his church had recently debated long and hard about whether a blind member of their church could bring his seeing-eye dog to the church services. No dogs, no crap. What next?

Why, when we know that God sees everything and knows all, do we fool ourselves into thinking that we should behave differently in church from the way we live any other time of the week? We don't, as many preachers mistakenly imply, come to church to *meet with* God. God lives not in churches, but in our hearts and imaginations. This idea that God is more attentive to our language inside the walls of a church than outside is a silly one. Even in the Old Testament, when there was an assumption that God dwelled in temples and holy places, there is a disarming openness and honesty before God in public proclamation and prayer. The prophets spoke to God frankly, sometimes disturbingly so, demanding that God know exactly how they felt. Sometimes they're self-centered, vindictive, and outright childish. Sometimes, though they might not say the word "crap," they do express the most shocking rage toward God. Jeremiah and Job make astonishing accusations against God. Jeremiah accuses God of having let him down "like a deceitful brook" and charges God with enticing him unwillingly, overpowering him, and humiliating him. Job famously fires off a volley of complaints to God. Says Old Testament scholar Vic Eldridge,

> Job [claims] God has shot his arrows at him (6:4), made him suffer months of emptiness and nights of misery (7:3), scared him with dreams and terrified him with visions (7:14). He calls out in protest, "Will you not look away from me for a while, let me alone until I swallow my spittle? (7:19). God, he claims, has worn him out, shrivelled him up, torn him in his wrath, given him up to the ungodly, seized him by the neck and dashed him to pieces, set him up for target practice and slashed open his kidney. And that's only in chapter 16![7]

This may not be appropriate language for church services today, but it is a brutally frank and open exchange between God and his followers. Commenting on Ps 137, where the psalmist concludes the passage with the hateful "Happy shall they be who take your little ones and dash them against the rock," C. S. Lewis said that at least the psalmist meant what he said! And there's the point. God seems quite able to accept honesty in place of propriety.

[7]From an unpublished sermon by Vic Eldridge, former principal of Morling Theological College, Sydney.

Nehemiah naïvely prays for personal glory: "Remember me with favor, my God, for all I have done for these people" (Neh 5:19). And listen to how he prays for his enemies: "Remember Tobiah and Sanballat, my God, because of what they have done; remember also the prophet Noadiah and how she and the rest of the prophets have been trying to intimidate me" (Neh 6:14).

Or how's this for a politically and theologically incorrect prayer: "Hear us, our God, for we are despised. Turn their insults back on their own heads. Give them over as plunder in a land of captivity. Do not cover up their guilt or blot out their sins from your sight, for they have thrown insults in the face of the builders" (Neh 4:4–5). And just in case you thought no one could curse their enemies quite like Nehemiah does, wait until you get a load of Jeremiah raging against those who've opposed him:

> Should good be repaid with evil? Yet they have dug a pit for me. Remember that I stood before you and spoke in their behalf to turn your wrath away from them. So give their children over to famine; hand them over to the power of the sword. Let their wives be made childless and widows; let their men be put to death, their young men slain by the sword in battle. Let a cry be heard from their houses when you suddenly bring invaders against them, for they have dug a pit to capture me and have hidden snares for my feet. But you, LORD, know all their plots to kill me. Do not forgive their crimes or blot out their sins from your sight. (Jer 18:20b–23a)

Wow! That's hardly an appropriate prayer for this Sunday's worship service, is it? And yet God chooses to have published in his Word these deeply flawed expressions of anger or sadness by his followers. Of course, Jeremiah's prayer begging God not to forgive sinners stands in stark contrast with Jesus magnificent prayer on the cross, "Father, forgive them, for they know not what they do." Commenting on Jeremiah's prayer, theologian John Bright makes the following point:

> That is not at all Christlike, but all too like you and me. Yet for all his outbursts of very human passion, and for all his bitter complaint against God and destiny, here was one who suffered brutal suffering for the sake of the Kingdom of God; who made himself obedient unto death; who, when his spirit flinched and he fain would have turned tail and fled, nevertheless found it within himself to say, "Not my will, but thine, be done" and so take up his cross.[8]

Jeremiah, Nehemiah, and Job were counted as great men of God. God did not count their frankness against them, but rather understood their

---

[8]John Bright, *The Kingdom of God: The Biblical Concept and Its Meaning for the Church* (Nashville: Abingdon, 1957), 120.

frustration and loved them in spite of their anger. I think that God prefers honesty to respectability any old day.

Shiny Happy People

Most new realists have what Hemingway once indelicately called a "built-in, shockproof crap detector." They can see the reality behind the saccharine smiles of fake, patronizing Christians. Exiles share this view, embarrassed themselves about so much of the fraudulent nature of contemporary church life. Walter Brueggemann, from whom I've borrowed the exile metaphor, spoke of this phoniness in his Lyman Beecher Lectures at Yale University.[9] He said that from his experience, the two primary reactions many Christians have to church services generally and preaching specifically is an overriding sense of alienation and rage. When the language used by clergy and worship leaders is always loaded with hyper-real images and unlikely expectations, audiences slowly develop, first, a feeling of alienation. Public Christian discourse seems to regularly concern itself with happy Christian families, answered prayers, and parables with an obvious moral inserted in the punch line. For example, the vast majority of Protestant clergy are married, and their sermon illustrations about love usually reflect their own relationship to their spouse or their children, depicting their family in the sweet, sentimental glow of a Norman Rockwell painting. It's not hard to see how alienating it would be for a single person to never hear faith expressed in terms that made sense of his or her experience, let alone for those of us struggling to stay married or to deal with rebellious teenagers, blended families, divorce, or extended-family disputes.

And at a more general level, public Christian discourse often expresses the Christian experience in equally alienating ways. We become used to hearing our leaders speak of how "God turned up" in a certain situation, and although we're never entirely sure what that means, we play along, happy to know that God turns up dramatically in other people's lives but acutely aware that it rarely happens in ours. We hear our leaders say, "Then God said to me . . . ," and we listen, amazed that certain people have direct access to the very voice of God but aware that we ourselves haven't heard God's stentorian tones. Of course, in most cases the leaders that use such phrases hear God speak in the very everyday ways that we do—through the Bible, through the coalition of circumstance, through the advice of godly friends. But from the pulpit this isn't made explicit. It's often what's *not* said that conveys so much in the public realm of Christian speech.

---

[9]Published as *Finally Comes the Poet: Daring Speech for Proclamation* (Minneapolis: Fortress, 1989).

Some years ago the rock band R.E.M. had a hit with the cheesy song "Shiny Happy People" ("People, people, throw your love around / Love me, love me, take it into town"). With distinctive backing vocals from Kate Pierson of the B52s giving it a real novelty feel, the song is a parody of the superficial brightness of the self-satisfaction and success of American life. It's only really the "winners" in life who pretend to be shiny and happy. Perhaps there are many shiny happy people in church, but those of us who aren't shiny and don't feel perpetually happy eventually develop a strong sense of alienation. We're not able to play the game with any sense of integrity. As Brueggemann suggests, we are left with a sensation of numbness and ache, yearning for something richer, more textured, more real. This takes me back to the elderly maid in Caravaggio's painting of the supper at Emmaus. She looks neither shiny nor happy; in fact, she looks miserable, worn down, ignored, burdened. Although a subversive painter such as Caravaggio can place her at Jesus' table, welcomed into the presence of the Christ, I find it very difficult to imagine her among the smiling, nattily attired male leadership of the contemporary church. She might be the recipient of some church-based service—a soup kitchen or a shelter for the homeless—but as a partner in equal standing, valued, acknowledged, listened to? I doubt it.

Ultimately, says Brueggemann, all this alienation and numbness leads to a sense of rage—unspoken, silent rage. We become angry with a God who "turns up" regularly to others but never to us. We think it unfair that some families apparently are richly blessed by God, but ours is monumentally ordinary, even though we've said our prayers and raised our kids in the church. There doesn't seem to be genuine access and equity within the Christian community. We suspect that our work—as a teacher or nurse or lawyer or parent—is every bit as godly and kingdom-expanding as that of the clergy, but it's never acknowledged. We suspect that we are not much more or less righteous than our leaders, but that is never expressed. We suspect that God is interested in more than our weekly attendance and our regular offerings, but no one ever explicitly says so. And soon we begin to doubt ourselves and wonder if our very ordinary and everyday existence is really important—to God, to our church leaders. The unexpressed rage sits heavily in our chests. Some leave church for good, but many just keep attending, either for the sake of the kids or because leaving would draw more attention than they want. So, at the local level of the suburban church, all this alienation and rage lead to the classic disconnect between my faith and my life. More than a generation ago, Keith Miller wrote in *The Taste of New Wine,*

> Our modern church is filled with many people who look pure, sound pure, and are inwardly sick of themselves, their weaknesses, their frustration and the lack of reality around them in the church. Our non-Christian friends feel

*either "that bunch of nice untroubled people would never understand my
problems"; or the more perceptive pagans who know us socially or profes-
sionally feel that we Christians are either grossly protected and ignorant about
the human situation or are out-and-out hypocrites who will not confess the
sins and weaknesses (they know intuitively) to be universal.[10]*

In the meantime, at the macro level of national Christian leadership,
whether denominational or political, we are observing another level of disconnect. The link between Christian triumphalism and the politics of oppression
becomes even stronger and more concerning. Many American Christian political leaders, claiming to speak for Christ, are opposed to gun control and
support the death penalty. And we can't picture Jesus endorsing such a stand.
Some purportedly Christian social policies often value the rich at the expense
of the poor and favor corporations at the expense of individuals. They tend to
eliminate virtually all regulations that protect the environment, worker safety,
and public health. And in an effort to fulfill the dominionist belief in the
manifest destiny of "Christian" nations (read "pro-U.S." nations), they value
an aggressive foreign policy. When the Religious Right in the United States is
possessed of absolute moral righteousness, it tolerates no dissent. Exiles
struggle to see Jesus seated at the table of such muscular American Christian
politics. The alienation and rage just sets in further.

If I see one more televangelist sitting at a fake kitchen table in a fake
kitchen, having a fake conversation about the Bible with his wife, I think I'll
scream. The sheer artificiality of it all—the lace curtains and faux colonial
table for two—isn't fooling anyone outside the church. So, how did we get
here, with our obsession with shiny happy Christianity? Any cursory reading
of the Bible will reveal that it is peopled with characters that are anything
but. From Abraham to Jacob to Moses, God's special people have been of
questionable credentials, people whose behavior has at times been more than
suspect. Even the prophets, so often quoted by shiny happy preachers today,
were hardly as two-dimensional as they're made out to be. Hosea married a
prostitute and was abandoned by her, Ezekiel was bizarre in his eccentricity,
Jeremiah was a melancholy. Even the apostle Paul, often epitomized as a
shiny happy Christian hero, was a religious vagabond, rejected by his community (and probably his family), destitute, itinerant, mocked. Arguing
against the attacks of Corinth's "superapostles" (themselves pretty shiny and
happy from all accounts), Paul takes up the story himself:

*I have worked much harder, been in prison more frequently, been flogged
more severely, and been exposed to death again and again. Five times I re-*

---

[10]Keith Miller, *The Taste of New Wine* (new rev. ed.; Orleans, Mass.: Paraclete,
1992), 19.

ceived from the Jews the forty lashes minus one. Three times I was beaten with rods, once I was stoned, three times I was shipwrecked, I spent a night and a day in the open sea, I have been constantly on the move. I have been in danger from rivers, in danger from bandits, in danger from my own countrymen, in danger from Gentiles; in danger in the city, in danger in the country, in danger at sea; and in danger from false believers. (2 Cor 11:23b–26)

The last point is particularly cutting. Falsity within the Christian community is as great a danger to Paul as shipwrecks and bandits, which themselves were a very real and ever-present menace to the itinerant. Paul, whose personal presence appeared to disappoint the Corinthians, would rather boast "of the things that show my weakness" (2 Cor 11:30).

Earning the Right to Be Reheard

Exiles will not sit in churches passively and put up with the phoniness, but neither will they simplistically take their bat and ball and go home. Too many people, alienated and angered by the contemporary church, have just left, contributing to the decline of the Western church. Exiles might well leave (or be thrust out), but if they do so, it will be to forge a new way, to fashion communities of honesty, openness, hospitality, and genuine love. Within this landscape, exiles now realize that they must earn a right to be heard in this postmodern world. Political or economic clout won't be enough. In fact, it might even work against their cause. Like the escaping rabbits of Sandleford, indeed like Jesus himself, exiles recognize that being powerless in a temporal or political sense is not such a bad thing. It forces us back to our core beliefs, our dangerous stories. When we have no impressive buildings and no swollen budgets to sustain our work, often only then do we realize that the best we have to offer this post-Christendom world is the quality of our relationships, the power of our trustworthiness, and the wonder of our generosity. Unfortunately, in post-Christendom the new realists are over the church's claims, presuming the church to simply be a powerful institution desperate to ensure its own survival. We need to earn the right to be reheard. Is it too simplistic to say that we earn that right through our authentic lifestyles? In a culture yearning for authenticity—the real—the pressure is on us in the Christian community now more than ever to put our time and our money where our mouth is and live what we preach. As power and plausibility structures crumble, as the myth of the external "expert" erodes, access and permissions are guarded. The new realists are inherently suspicious and cynical. The search is on for authenticity, and this is a search we should welcome. Exiles will pour their time and energy into developing communities of authenticity. They will embrace the scrutiny of this world and live up to our culture's expectations, if not to be perfect, then to be genuine.

Those Christians for whom their outer and inner worlds are not in sync are a roadblock to the cynical or inquisitive new realists. Furthermore, this lack of genuine authenticity is toxic to the Christian life. Do we truly live out that which we claim to believe? If we talk about humility, are we humble? If we talk about forgiveness, do we forgive? If we talk about love, do we really love? If we value justice, equity, peace, and generosity do we practice them? If David Boyle's assessment of the new realists is correct, they are not expecting perfection, any more than they can be perfect, but they do anticipate (and rightly so) that people with high ideals will be actively working to live them out in some way.

They are also opposed to the lack of choice we are offered by multi-national interests. When major corporations confront us with a lack of choice, it makes it much more difficult to live genuinely ethical lives by buying ethical products and services. It's their economic monopoly that creates the stranglehold that the multinationals have on goods and services that limits us living a more authentic lifestyle. As Christians, we need to be prepared to acknowledge and share this perspective. We at least need to be trying to make economically, politically, and socially responsible choices in what we eat, wear, and drive and where we live. Of course, such choices should always have been important to us, but today such choices are not just ethical, they are *missional*. Exiles from the phoniness of church must take the lead and operate at the forefront of the New Realism agenda, promoting authenticity, honesty, and genuineness.

Birds of a Feather?

The challenge to missional exiles in the current cultural landscape is to form such communities, whether they do so in small groups in private homes or in more public contexts. Where they meet, when, and how often is not my primary concern. My chief interest is that we see a flourishing of myriad new Christian faith communities that embrace the following six values:

1. To seek an approach to spiritual growth that values inward transformation over external appearances

2. To value a spirituality that seeks not to limit our God-given humanity, creativity, or individuality; to value diversity and difference over conformity and uniformity

3. To enjoy from-the-heart, honest dialogues and avoid relationships marked by superficiality and hidden agendas

4. To strive to be completely honest with God and appropriately transparent with others about our inmost thoughts, hopes, dreams, emotions, shortcomings, failings, transgressions, struggles

5. To seek to welcome back mystery and paradox over easy explanations; to live with questions that have no easy answers

6. To work to honestly recalibrate our lifestyles, diets, spending patterns, and commitments to reflect our hope for a more just, equitable, and merciful society

One step in this direction has been the recent development within the church of Life Transformation Groups. Small groups of three meet weekly to read the Bible, pray together, and ask each other a series of "character conversation questions," basically an accountability contract that invites all three members to be frank and open about their failings and receive the encouragement to continue to shape their lives to the will of God. Some might find the specific questions somewhat conservative in their tone (why, for example, nothing about global justice or compassionate living?). Admittedly, they're not my cup of tea (but maybe that's because I find it hard to "pass" many of them), but their popularity is indicative of the desperate yearning within the Christian community for accountability, discipleship, and nurture.[11]

---

[11]Life Transformation Groups were developed by Neil Cole, the executive director of Church Multiplication Associates (CMA). CMA Resources provides cards that list the "Character Conversation Questions" for small-group interaction. See "Resources Available through CMA," CMA Resources.Org, under "Life Transformation Group Cards" [cited 17 January 2006]. Online: http://www.cmaresources .org/resources/allproducts.asp. The questions are also listed in Cole's book *Cultivating a Life for God* (Carol Stream, Ill.: ChurchSmart Resources, 1999). They are as follows:

- Have you been a testimony this week to the greatness of Jesus Christ with both your words and actions?
- Have you been exposed to sexually alluring material or allowed your mind to entertain inappropriate sexual thoughts about another this week?
- Have you lacked integrity in your financial dealings or coveted something that does not belong to you?
- Have you been honoring, understanding, and generous in your important relationships this week?
- Have you damaged another person by your words, either behind their back or face to face?
- Have you given in to an addictive behavior this week? Explain.
- Have you continued to remain angry toward another?

I heard of a church that has divided its building into zones for its worship services. There are lines marked on the floor by masking tape to indicate whether you're sitting in a "hot" zone or a "cool" zone. Sound bizarre? The hottest zone is the one nearest the platform at the front. You're expected to sit there if you're really ready to get into worship. There's lots of hand-raising, dancing, and gutsy singing happening up front. The second zone from the platform is for those who are feeling okay about their relationship with God and are pretty open to what might happen during the service. The third zone—a cool zone—is at the back of the hall. It's for those who are happy to be in church but unable or unprepared to give themselves fully to the worship experience. Parents with young kids who need attention often sit back there. So do people who've brought friends who are feeling wary. Or others who just don't feel very close to God at the moment sit back there. Then, at the very rear of the building, there's the coolest zone. It has a few room dividers separating it from the rest of the hall. There are a bunch of lounges, magazines, and a coffee machine there. This zone is for those who are not at all ready to worship, but just want to be with the Christian community. They chill out, maybe enjoy the music or catch some of the teaching, but overall they just hang with other believers (many unbelievers sit back there too).

How often have you felt uncomfortable in church because everyone is getting into the singing or the teaching, but you're not engaged? Have you felt inferior? Churches have a way of making us feel that if we're not part of the crowd, there's something spiritually defective about us. Sometimes I don't feel close to God and don't want to sing my lungs out. Sometimes I don't care what the preacher has to say. I'm not like that all the time, but there are stages and seasons when I'm feeling flat or sad or distant from God. It would be nice to feel like I had the freedom to be true to myself and to God and not fake it for the sake of corporate solidarity.

In a magnificent book on the church, Jürgen Moltmann identifies the principle that undergirds much of how we do church today as "birds of a feather flocking together." In explaining, Moltmann says,

> "Birds of a feather flock together." But why? People who are like us, who think the same thoughts, who have the same things, and who want the same things confirm us. However, people who are different from us, that

---

- Have you secretly wished for another's misfortune so that you might excel?
- (Create a personalized accountability question.)
- Did you finish the reading and hear from God? What are you going to do about it?
- Have you been completely honest with me?

You've got to hate that final question!

is, people whose thoughts, feelings and desires are different from ours, make us feel insecure.[12]

Next time some plucky worship leader berates you for not singing loud enough or joyously enough, think of birds of a feather. We've all got to be equally happy? Equally devoted? Equally studious? Anyone who isn't feeling upbeat about God makes the rest of us feel insecure. Note the way we often treat people in deep grief or depression, or people who are openly rebelling against God. Our distance from them emerges from our own insecurity.

This has serious implications for the church. If the church is simply a community of like-minded people inviting other like-minded people to join them, then it will always be severely impeded in its attempt to impact our world. The church, then, according to Moltmann, has no ego-strength, no self-confidence. It's a form of self-justification. Moltmann proposes that the biblical mode is very different. Instead of being birds of a feather, the church should embrace Paul's injunction for the church: "Accept one another, then, as Christ has accepted you, to the glory of God" (Rom 15:7). Accepting others isn't just some wise and useful injunction for the good of the church. The acceptance of others emerges directly out of our having been accepted by Christ. When we know that Christ has accepted us, we are freed from the need for self-justification. This liberates us to accept others. Says Moltmann,

> Accept one another "as Christ has accepted you." Only this attitude can give us a new orientation and break through our limitations so that we can spring over our narrow shadows. It opens us up for others as they really are so that we gain a longing for and an interest in them. As a result of this we become able actually to forget ourselves and to focus on the way Christ has accepted us.[13]

I don't think that we should stay sad or despondent, wallowing in our distance from God. Good Christian faith communities will be concerned about the spiritual growth of its members. We want to grow to be more like Jesus. But along the way we have our ups and downs. Whether you think "zoning" church services is a good idea or not, we have to think about ways to show that we accept one another. The medium is the message. The church that I was just referring to is sending an important symbolic message to their members: you are accepted no matter where you are along the journey! Many of us have decided to leave institutional Christianity to be part of fashioning such communities. We exiles have found that the constraints of the structures of

---

[12]Jürgen Moltmann, *The Open Church: Invitation to a Messianic Lifestyle* (trans. M. Douglas Meeks; London: SCM, 1978), 30.

[13]Ibid., 30–31.

mainstream churches have precluded us from finding (or building) this kind of acceptance and nurture. The missiologist David Bosch described such an authentic Christian community in the following way:

> The new fellowship transcends every limit imposed by family, class or culture. We are not winning people like ourselves to ourselves but sharing the good news that in Christ God has shattered the barriers that divide the human race and has created a new community. The new people of God has no analogy; it is a "sociological impossibility" that has nevertheless become possible.[14]

This makes the exile's heart skip a beat. We "prove" the gospel by being a people who believe it and live by it. In this way we will say more to this host empire than a thousand televangelists or a million direct-mail campaigns. Surely, then, these exilic communities must work on having the following seven characteristics:

1. It will be a community of heartfelt praise, not the fake mouthing of sentimental worship songs.

2. It will be a community of authenticity and truth, not public pretense.

3. It will be a community that does not live for itself, but genuinely serves others.

4. It will be a community of missional engagement with its host empire, not retreat into a religious ghetto.

5. It will be a community of mutual responsibility, not privatized religion.

6. It will be a community of hope, not intimidation and alienation.

7. It will be a community of justice, not lip service and phony left-leaning pronouncements.

We do well to conclude with Brian McLaren's warning: "I tend to notice that when people use the words 'authenticity' and 'community' a lot, both tend to leave the premises. It's easy to use authenticity and community as new marketing tools to win customers to our product; as soon as that happens, we violate authenticity and community. I think we get closer to both by pursuing love—by practicing the virtues found in I Corinthians 13."[15]

[14]David Bosch, "The Structure of Mission: An Exposition of Matthew 28:16–20," in *Exploring Church Growth* (ed. Wilbert Shenk; Grand Rapids: Eerdmans, 1983), 239.

[15]Brian McLaren, "What About Authenticity?" A New Kind of Christian n.p. [cited 21 February 2006]. Online: http://www.anewkindofchristian.com/archives/000150.html.

5

The Exile's Esprit de Corps

The Promise: We Will Serve a Cause Greater Than Ourselves

Americans are right that the bonds of our communities have withered, and we are right to fear that this transformation has very real costs.

—Robert Putnam

A second promise held out by exiles is that we will serve a cause greater than ourselves. In an empire of self-centeredness and greed someone must model an alternative: the creation of communities of service, love, and justice. In the 1970s and 1980s the term "community" was in vogue with theologians, church leaders, psychologists, sociologists, and self-help authors right across the Western world. We were told how much we need to be in community. It was mentioned that the human being is a herd animal, and we cannot live for any length of time in isolation. Life is not meant to be done alone. We need fellow travelers, supporters for the journey of life. Nearly every church was using the term "community" in its advertising and promotional material. Some even used it in the name of the church itself.

I have to admit that I went in for this stuff in a big way. In the 1980s I read Scott Peck's *The Different Drum* and was deeply moved by his definition of "true" community. He wrote about an experience of human togetherness the likes of which I'd never known, but for which I yearned deeply. Up to that point, my experience of church community had been that of a generally warm, outwardly friendly society with pretty rigid rules about who was "in" and who was "out." After reading Peck's take on the subject, I realized how deeply I hungered for the kind of human connection that he wrote about. According to Peck, the characteristics of true community are these:

- Inclusivity, commitment, and consensus

- A sense of realism

- The ability to be contemplative and self-aware

- A feeling of safety in all members

- The ability for members to experiment with new types of behaviors

- The ability to fight gracefully

- A place where all members are leaders

- A spirit of peace[1]

This didn't sound like any church that I'd ever been part of. I became strongly committed to trying to build a community like this, centered on Jesus, but inclusive and welcoming. A small band of Christians joined me in that experiment. We regularly referred to our community as being hard at the center and soft at the edges. In other words, our commitment to Christ and his teaching was hard and nonnegotiable, but at the edges of our community we provided multiple portals or entry points. We sought to be nonjudgmental, open, vulnerable, and consensual. We threw ourselves enthusiastically into the work of building community. We read the work of theologians Robert Banks (*Paul's Idea of Community*), Henri Nouwen (*Reaching Out*), and Jean Vanier (*Community and Growth*). We studied the Acts of the Apostles, particularly the first chapters concerning the community of grace that emerged in Jerusalem in the early months of the Christian movement. We followed Scott Peck's mandates:

> Community is and must be inclusive. The great enemy of community is exclusivity. Groups that exclude others because they are poor or doubters or divorced or sinners . . . are not communities; they are cliques—actually defensive bastions against community.[2]

> The members of a group in some way must commit themselves to one another if they are to become or stay a community. Exclusivity, the great enemy to community, appears in two forms; excluding the other and excluding yourself. A friend correctly defined community as "group that has learned to transcend its individual differences." But this learning takes time, the time that can be bought only through commitment.[3]

---

[1]M. Scott Peck, *The Different Drum: Community Making and Peace* (New York: Simon & Schuster, 1987).

[2]Ibid., 61.

[3]Ibid., 62.

We found ourselves cycling through the very same movements that Peck said we would as we moved from noncommunity to true community. He wrote that for any group to achieve community in the truest sense, it must undertake a journey that involves four stages: *pseudo-community,* where a false niceness reigns and all members are on their best behavior trying to fake community as best they can by not raising important issues or expressing their true frustrations with each other; *chaos,* when the skeletons finally come out of the closet, and the masks of pretense are stripped away; *emptiness,* a time of quiet and transition; and finally, *true community,* marked by both deep honesty and deep caring. Says Peck,

> Community is a spirit—but not in the way that the familiar phrase "community spirit" is usually understood. . . . The members of a group who have achieved genuine community do take pleasure—even delight—in themselves as a collective.[4]

It was pretty heady stuff, and we saw some real movement toward our goal. We developed community-building skills that have served us even until this day. We picked up people who'd been judged and found wanting by their former churches. We congratulated ourselves for our capacity to accept all comers and to fashion lost and lonely people into important members of our community.

But along the way I was regularly disquieted by visitations from slightly older people who came to our community to take quick look at how we were doing and if it was working. I discovered that most of these older people were survivors of similar community-building experiments from the 1970s. They had become jaded and cynical by their own experiences of the so-called radical discipleship movement of that era. They told me that they too had worked on fashioning inclusive community, and that they too had experienced periods of success such as my community was currently experiencing. But they eyed me with suspicion and told me that it wouldn't last. Their marvelous experiments had come undone, leaving many idealistic young people wounded or exhausted.

So I went back to study the Acts of the Apostles, and I realized that the blissful early days of the Jerusalem church were also short-lived. In fact, I realized that the inclusivity of sharing possessions, eating together, and gathering under the apostles' teaching, as delicious as it seemed, was actually a contravention of Jesus' command for them to take the gospel to the very ends of the earth. As I read on, I realized that the early Jerusalem church was in fact a community in transition. Once a traveling missionary community of

[4]Ibid., 73.

disciples, centered on Jesus, it had become a static group, camped in Jerusalem. But this was not its intended future. After the persecution that resulted from Stephen's bold and offensive ministry (Acts 6–7), the church was scattered, and through that dispersion it rediscovered its original mandate: to be a missionary people, a community on the move. I began to fear that we had lost something important in all our work in building community. I began to wonder whether Christians don't do well to build community as an end in itself. We build community incidentally, when our imaginations and energies are captured by a higher, even nobler cause. Though it took me a while, I came to realize that Christian community results from the greater cause of Christian mission. My ongoing reading led me to the discovery that what I was originally yearning for was not the therapeutic community that Scott Peck spoke about, but rather the missionary community that the apostle Paul writes about.

This isn't to suggest that some of Peck's characteristics listed above aren't worthwhile descriptors of true community. I still desire to be part of a community like that. But I have come to realize that aiming for community is a bit like aiming for happiness. It's not a goal in itself. We find happiness as an incidental by-product of pursuing love, justice, hospitality, and generosity. When you aim for happiness, you are bound to miss it. Likewise with community. It's not our goal. It emerges as a by-product of pursuing something else. Those who love community destroy it, but those who love people build community. Then my dear friend and fellow conspirator Alan Hirsch, with whom I wrote *The Shaping of Things to Come*,[5] introduced me to the much more radical concept of *communitas*. His reading in anthropology led him to this idea, which offered me a much more useful way of seeing the relation between mission and community.

Not Community, Communitas

Alan Hirsch's research led him into the idea of communitas through the work of British-American symbolic anthropologist Victor Turner, who first used the term in his 1969 book *The Ritual Process*.[6] Born in Glasgow, Turner and his wife, Edith, moved in 1950 to Africa to live among and study the Ndembu, a tribe in Zambia. There they analyzed rituals and the symbolic meanings that are derived from them. Though he was to move to

---

[5]Michael Frost and Alan Hirsch, *The Shaping of Things to Come: Innovation and Mission for the 21st-Century Church* (Peabody, Mass.: Hendrickson, 2003).

[6]Victor Turner, *The Ritual Process: Structure and Anti-structure* (Chicago: Aldine, 1969).

the United States in 1961, teaching at Stanford, Cornell, and the University
of Chicago, during which time he returned to Africa to study the Gisu of
Uganda, Turner's work with the Ndembu was central to his later thinking
and writing.

Of particular interest to us in trying to understand his use of the term
"communitas" are his studies on the initiation rites used by the Ndembu, and
later, the Gisu. What mattered to Turner was not so much the symbols or
rites themselves, but rather the roles of the symbols in specific social situations. He concluded that initiation ceremonies were not simply religious or
cultural sidelines to the structure of tribal society; they were central to maintaining social stability. For example, in one of his famous studies he found
that the Ndembu used several kinds of trees for young women's rituals. One
of the tree species that were used produced a milky white sap, while another
seeped a dark red liquid. The Ndembu took the different saps as symbolic of
breast milk and menstrual blood, and by so doing they attributed various
symbolic meanings to these trees, meanings that reinforced the roles of
women within society and sustained cultural solidity.

Turner also explored the nature of male initiation rites among the
Ndembu. Before him, pioneer anthropologist Arnold van Gennep had identified three universal stages to such rites: separation, liminality, and reintegra-
tion. The Ndembu were no different. Young men of a certain age were
removed from mainstream society while they undertook the ordeal of induc-
tion into adult life. This period of separation, during which the initiates were
considered no longer children but not yet adults, was called liminality by van
Gennep. A liminal stage is a stage of transition, a period that is neither one
thing nor the other. Turner focused a good deal of his later thinking on this,
the second stage of rites of passage. Liminality, he said, was a stage in which
the initiates lived for an extended period in a spatial, social, and spiritual
threshold. Cast out of the village and made to live in the jungle, fending for
themselves and being visited regularly by the community's holy men to be
taught the lore and learning of adulthood, the initiates found themselves on
this threshold.

After a period on this threshold, the young men were then reintegrated
into mainstream or normal society with a new status. They were men in full
standing, no longer boys living in the world of women. But Turner's chief interest was with the middle stage. He believed that young tribesmen, while
in this liminal, or "limbo" stage, discovered a depth of community so great
that it transcended what we normally mean by that term. He observed
that the initiates developed a potent and distinctive form of social community that led to a spontaneous experience of intense intimacy and equality. It
was an undifferentiated, egalitarian, nonrational community. In the period

of liminality, the initiates progressively achieved a release from conformity to general norms and experienced a profound and collective sentiment for each other. This sense of "supercommunity" also included or was stimulated by the quest for and presence of a sacred space, god, or spirit. Initiates refer to a transforming experience of connection with oneself, with others, and with the universe. Thought by Turner to most approximate a religious experience, he called this wonderful experience of interconnectedness between initiates "communitas."

In short, Turner's concept of communitas denotes an intense feeling of social togetherness and belonging, often in connection with religious rituals, in which people stand together "outside" society, and society is strengthened by this. Communitas is the opposite, in many ways, of normal society, but with each one feeding and enriching the other. Societies need the liminal experience of communitas because it pushes society forward, nurturing it with the freshness and vitality that come from the deeper communion that is experienced there. But societies obviously need the stability of normal life. In anthropological terms, normal life can be characterized as *structure*, while communitas is a form of *anti-structure*. Turner explains,

> I have used the term "anti-structure" . . . to describe both liminality and what I have called "communitas." I meant by it not a structural reversal . . . but the liberation of human capacities of cognition, affect, volition, creativity, etc., from the normative constraints incumbent upon occupying a sequence of social statuses.[7]

It is the liberation experienced in communitas that sows the seeds of cultural regeneration back in normal society. Turner then went so far as to detach the phenomena of liminality and communitas from rites of passage and dared to suggest that it is possible for societies to regularly experience them, not just at early adulthood. The social modes of normal society (structure) and communitas (anti-structure) can and do exist simultaneously in a society, and no society can function adequately without this dialectic.[8] In fact, Turner dared to suggest that in the dialectic between communitas and normal society resides the hope for the future of that society.

> People or societies in a liminal phase are a kind of institutional capsule or pocket which contains the germ of future social developments, of societal change.[9]

---

[7]Victor Turner, *From Ritual to Theater: The Human Seriousness of Play* (New York: PAJ Publications, 1982), 44.

[8]See Turner, *Ritual Process,* 129.

[9]Turner, *From Ritual to Theater,* 45.

Community vs. Communitas

Community	Communitas
inward focus	social togetherness outside society
focus on encouraging each other	focus on the task at hand
safe place	pushes society forward
something to be built	experienced through liminality

This is so different from what we have usually identified as "community," particularly the way the church has used this term. So-called Christian community often is portrayed as an inwardly focused gathering of people committed to one another, to encouraging one another and building one another up. It is often referred to as a "safe place," a place where members can be open and vulnerable together and receive support, understanding, and mutual care. I have no objection to these things at all. In fact, I hunger for them. But I think that the church has made them an end in themselves. We are regularly told to "build" community, to meet new people, to welcome visitors, as if this is our purpose as a church. And as Brian McLaren suspects, the churches that talk so much about it often aren't doing it. This is because community is not an end in itself; rather, it is a means to an end. Initiates, experiencing communitas, might find all the elements of mutual support and care mentioned above, but they find them as part of a group of people undergoing a shared ordeal. In other words, you can't have the marvelous experience of communitas without being in a liminal state. Many churches want the exquisite experience of rich, deep relationships, but they aren't prepared to embrace the challenge of coming out of mainstream society. When in a liminal stage, coping with the difficulties and ordeal of being outside the structure of normal society, people find themselves thrown together in a richer, deeper, more powerful sense of togetherness. Not community, communitas!

The Communitas of Christ

Although this symbolic anthropology may seem somewhat obscure, the concept of communitas isn't as unusual as it first appears. We all know that when people are thrown into a challenge—an ordeal, to use Turner's expression for it—they develop a much deeper sense of communion. Surely we can recall periods of our lives when this was true. Think of any group of people in a liminal state, and in all likelihood they will have experienced a deeper sense of community than those in mainstream society. Have you ever been on a short-term mission trip overseas and felt such a special, intimate, profound sense of connection with your fellow travelers? When building houses in Mexico or working in orphanages in Haiti, we connect with other Christians at a level entirely different from the one experienced each week in our local church. This isn't just because of the exotic location or the spicy food. It's because we are in a liminal state. We are not living at home, nor are we really living in Mexico. We are in transition, a resident in neither place, really. This sense of liminality, fueled by the challenge of completing certain set tasks, fosters communitas. Even if we find ourselves on a team with people we don't particularly like or whose company we don't much enjoy, the experience of liminality eventually sweeps away our petty differences, bonding us strongly, because we are forced to rely on each other simply for survival.

Christians who have just returned from such trips regularly bemoan the fact that the intensity of communion that they felt with others overseas is completely absent in their churches. This is exactly what Victor Turner called the dialectic between structure and anti-structure, between normal society and communitas. Those who have emerged from a liminal state are able to bring a challenge to normal society about the meandering ordinariness of life. In African tribal societies, when the newly initiated young men return from their ordeal in the wild, they are flushed with the vitality and excitement that come from surviving the rite. Their returning energy and their critique of normal tribal life is an annual shot in the arm to the tribe, reminding them of their core values and pushing them forward as a society. Ideally, this should be the experience of our churches. As people undergo liminality and communitas in whatever forms, they should be able to return to normal, structured church society and engage in this important dialectic. As noted earlier, Turner said that those who've tasted communitas are like a capsule that contains the germ of future development and change. It's disturbing to hear young people, recently returned from an experience of liminality and communitas, complain that their church doesn't understand their experience and provides no forums for them to talk about it.

Exiles are in a liminal state. In fact, liminality defines totally the experience of exile. Those of us who have come out of the mainstream church find ourselves, like the escaping rabbits from *Watership Down*. We have been thrown together with other fellow travelers, and we're on the road, not knowing entirely what will happen. My concern is that too many exiles are taking this journey alone. When taken in company with others, this journey holds the promise of a deeper communion, a more committed society of friends who encourage each other and build each other up. This communion between fellow travelers will allow for a sense of security, but it will be the kind of safety that travelers find together on the road. The dangers are still there, but we are safer and stronger together than traveling alone. And our experience together will contain that germ for widespread change in the mainstream church.

This is obviously the sense of companionship that Jesus' first disciples felt. With Jesus at the center, they experienced a liminality and communitas so exquisite that it eventually spoke so profoundly into normal, mainstream society that it altered the history of the world forever. Although we sometimes mistakenly imagine the company of Jesus to be a happy band of vagabonds traveling carefree around Palestine, we need to remember that the twelve apostles, in particular, had left everything to follow Jesus. They were like the African initiates. They had separated themselves from mainstream society at great personal cost. They are a perfect example of a liminal society.

In John 6, after Jesus has miraculously fed the five thousand and then walked on water, he believes that it's time to deliver some of his most uncompromising teaching to his followers. Since they had experienced such amazing displays of his power, it seems reasonable to expect that they would be very receptive to his message, but instead John tells us that "many of his disciples said, 'This is a hard teaching. Who can accept it?'" (John 6:60), and that "from this time many of his disciples turned back and no longer followed him" (John 6:66). Jesus' "hard teaching" has the effect of separating out the true disciples from those who were interested in his miracles but not ready to cross onto the threshold of liminality. Turning to the Twelve, Jesus asks, "You do not want to leave too, do you?" Peter's answer is that of a true exile: "Lord, to whom shall we go? You have the words of eternal life" (John 6:67–68). For Peter, there was now no turning back. He had thrown his lot in with Jesus and this motley band of fellow disciples.

In Matt 19, Jesus has his well-known encounter with a rich young man, during which he provocatively suggests that in order to receive eternal life, the man should sell all his possessions and give the money to the poor. When the wealthy man declines to do so, Jesus reflects on how difficult it is for a rich person to enter the kingdom of God. The disciples are astonished, and they question him on this, with Peter blurting out, "We have left everything to follow you! What then will there be for us?" (Matt 19:27). Jesus, of course, goes on to promise a great heavenly reward to the disciples, but the point here is that Peter was profoundly aware of his own exiled—liminal—status. He had left everything: his job, his community, his family.

Only in this liminal state could these disciples experience the awesome power of communitas. Men who otherwise would have nothing to do with each other are thrown together by their shared devotion to Jesus, and as they journey together, they develop a depth of relationship that literally turned the world upside down. Take, for example, the companionship between just two of the disciples, Simon and Matthew. We know that Matthew was a tax collector also called Levi, and that Simon was known as a Zealot. As a tax collector and a Zealot, they couldn't have been further apart on the spectrum of Jewish society. As already noted, tax collectors were collaborators with the occupying Roman forces. Charged with collecting the excessive Roman tax from their compatriots, men like Matthew also extracted a healthy commission from their Jewish clients. With the might of Rome behind them, some tax collectors were able to extort great sums of money from the Jews. Earlier, we looked at the example of Zacchaeus, who was keenly aware of the degree to which he had fleeced his fellow citizens.

Zealots like Simon, on the other hand, were archpatriots. Opposed to Roman rule, they were like urban guerrillas, performing acts of terrorism against both the Romans and their Jewish agents. The Zealots were known for their use of what we today call a stiletto blade. They would conceal the long, thin blade in the folds of their robes while they looked for opportunities to get close to a Roman soldier or a tax collector. If they could stand next to a soldier in a crowded street, they would quietly slip their blade up under his ribs and be gone before he hit the ground. It was not uncommon that after a street crowd had gathered and then dispersed, a Roman corpse was left in its wake. (I've always wondered if there was more to it than his stature that got Zacchaeus up that sycamore tree.)

It's amazing, then, to consider that Jesus invites both a tax collector and a Zealot into his company. Under any other circumstance it was a recipe for disaster, but the presence of Jesus, his teaching on love and forgiveness, and the exciting communitas fostered by their shared life on the road transform these two men into brothers-in-arms. By the time they gather together after Jesus' ascension, the band of disciples had grown to about 120 people and shattered social conventions by including women (Mary Magdalene, Mary the mother of James, Salome, Joanna), Pharisees (Joseph of Arimathea, Nicodemus), and other previously unnamed men (Matthias, Joseph called Barsabbas). It also included a reinstated Peter and a once-doubting Thomas. Their sense of companionship is not diminished after the physical departure of Jesus; rather, through the book of Acts we see it grow to include people from all across the world.

Nowhere is this phenomenon more keenly displayed than in Luke's descriptions of the missional communities of Paul. In referring to Paul's missional communities, I mean his band of fellow missionaries, but also the local missional communities that he plants and nurtures around the Mediterranean. The intense feeling of togetherness and belonging that he shares with them is evident in the tone of personal greetings to them in his epistles. Reading Acts 20–21, about Paul's farewell journey from Philippi back to certain arrest in Jerusalem, one can't help but be struck by the quality of his relationships with the Christians in Philippi, Troas, Tyre, and especially Ephesus. Knowing that arrest in Jerusalem would in all likelihood mean his eventual execution, Paul's friends in these towns do all they can to dissuade him from his task. They do so out of deep love for him. The image of Paul and the Ephesian elders who have traveled to meet him in Miletus en route to Jerusalem is particularly poignant. After Paul's farewell speech, they all kneel together to pray. Then they embrace him and kiss him and weep openly, knowing that they will never see him again. The depth of their love for each other was forged in the fires of their liminal experience as followers of Jesus in a pagan city such as Ephesus. It was communitas.

Paul also develops this same sense of communitas with his co-workers Barnabas, Timothy, Silas, Aristarchus, and John Mark, among others. His references to them in his letters are touching. Together they experience and survive beatings, shipwrecks, imprisonment, and long, hazardous journeys through bandit-infested territory. There is nothing sweeter or more satisfying than the love that fellow exiles share with each other. Paul clearly put a high premium on it. When John Mark deserts Paul's band in Pamphylia to return home to Jerusalem (Acts 13:13), he breaks the code of a liminal community. To take Victor Turner's example again, it would be like a young Ndembu boy abandoning his cohort of fellow initiates to return home to his mother. He would be shamed by the tribe for the rest of his life. Likewise, John Mark's desertion is unforgettable to Paul. In communitas the stakes are higher. There is a challenge to be undertaken, and everyone must play his or her role. Later, when Barnabas proposes that they bring John Mark on their next journey, Paul will not relent (Acts 15:36–41). The deserter doesn't get a second chance. It's easy to simply think of Paul as a hard-hearted autocrat who can't forgive the failings of his brother, but I think that there's more going on. In communitas the desertion of a partner is devastating. It's like a member of a football team just giving up halfway through the final game. Communitas isn't a warm, relaxing space where you can come and go as you please. Communitas requires commitment, integrity, hard work, and courage. In short, communitas is about love. I find Paul's attitude toward John Mark harsh, yes, but understandable. You have to have experienced communitas to share my view.

Natural Expressions of Communitas

Many people undergo something of a communitas experience in their daily lives. Sporting teams, theater companies, orchestras, bands, dance troupes—these kinds of societies all know something, perhaps just a whiff, of the concept of communitas. When a group of musicians or dancers are performing, every member must play his or her part well, not just individually, but in concert with the others. This sense of interdependence can be very exciting. Jazz musicians speak of the almost spiritual nirvana they sense when all members of the band are playing in perfect harmony. Any member of a sports team can recall something of the profound sense of intimacy felt with teammates when individual contributions to the game create a force greater than the sum of their parts. When an amateur theater group begins rehearsals, it can be just a rag-tag assembly of would-be thespians. But on the stage, galvanized by the urgency of the impending opening night, they are transformed into something else. With the script as their guide, they are forced together by the "ordeal" of knowing that soon they will be giving public performances. One young amateur actor once told me that he felt a greater sense of belonging and acceptance in his theater company than in his church. I suppose he thought that it had to do with the quality of the people in the theater as compared with those in the church. But the fact remains that churches are full of marvelous, kind, caring people, every bit as accepting as theater people. The fundamental difference is that churches are working on community, while an amateur theater group is a kind of communitas.

Turner himself was onto this phenomenon. Later in his career he began to apply his theories to American subcultures, such as artists. In his essay "Liminality and Communitas" he notes,

> Prophets and artists tend to be liminal and marginal people, "edgemen," who strive with a passionate sincerity to rid themselves of the clichés associated with status incumbency and role-playing and to enter into vital relations with other men in fact or imagination.[10]

He believed that artists, including actors, musicians, dancers, painters, and so on, were the very people most capable of propelling society forward, because they had stepped into a liminal state and had experienced a communitas unlike anything possible in normal society. If you've spent any time with artists of any kind, you know what he means. When artists meet for the first time, they share the knowing smile of someone who has stepped out of the respectability of mainstream suburban life. Their shared liminality opens them up immediately to each other. Although until recently strangers, now they are family.

---

[10]Victor Turner, "Liminality and Communitas," *Creative Resistance* n.p. [cited 17 January 2006]. Online: http://www.creativeresistance.ca/communitas-toc/communitas-toc.htm.

Something similar can happen with journalists. In 2003 seven journalists from the *New York Times* broke the story of Jayson Blair, a *New York Times* reporter who in six months on the paper managed to produce thirty-six articles containing fabricated information or plagiarism. It is one of the most shocking cases of journalistic malfeasance in American history. There aren't any comparable cases of such widespread, almost sociopathic, fraud as the Blair case. When the seven *New York Times* investigators began their inquiries, it gradually emerged that both the executive editor and the managing editor of the paper were complicit in a culture that allowed a fraud such as Blair to thrive. It became obvious to the journalists that they might actually lose their jobs by writing the exposé. Instead, after several weeks of nerve-wracking and exhausting work, their final article led to the resignations of Blair and the two top editors. After their ordeal, one of those journalists, David Barstow, said,

> One of the great things about journalism is that when you're thrown into really difficult stories under tight deadlines you forge these amazing friendships. This experience will bond me to these guys forever. We were in a foxhole, and we'll always remember that.[11]

This is no different from men and women who have served together in the armed forces, particularly those who saw combat together. On Veterans Day we see them gathering for their street marches, nodding with an unspoken respect to each other. They have known a liminality unlike anything the rest of us can imagine. They were separated from mainstream society, sent to a foreign land to undergo a life-and-death ordeal, and then returned to us as different people. Those of us who have known nothing but civilian life can never fully appreciate their experience. It is to each other, to the communitas, that they must turn for real understanding.

As long ago as 1465, this kind of battlefield camaraderie was described by the French knight Jean de Brueil:

> Battle is a joyous thing. We love each other so much in battle. If we see that our cause is just and our kinsmen fight boldly, tears come to our eyes. A sweet joy rises in our hearts, in the feeling of our honest loyalty to each other; and seeing our friend so bravely exposing his body to danger in order to fulfill the commandment of our Creator, we resolve to go forward and die or live with him on account of love. This brings such delight that anyone who has not felt it cannot say how wonderful it is. Do you think someone who feels this is afraid of death? Not in the least! He is so

---

[11]Seth Mnookin, "Scandal of Record," *Vanity Fair* (December 2004): 167.

*strengthened, so delighted, that he does not know where he is. Truly, he
fears nothing in the world.*[12]

Some might be squeamish about what seems like the glorification of war,
but I don't mean in any way to be lionizing the horrors of mortal combat. I
am willing, though, to be reminded of the powerful connection that people
develop when faced with awesome odds. It's the same connection that ex-
plorers such as Shackleton or Peary or Lewis and Clark felt with their men.
The sense of communitas that Shackleton developed with his crew was legendary. He pledged them his life that he would not let one of them die, and
when his *Endurance* expedition got into deep trouble, he and a few others
traveled thousands of kilometers in an open boat and then traversed a moun-
tainous island to get help for them, as they waited out a dreadful winter in an
overturned row boat. In return, his crew loved him beyond words. It's the
same connection that the suffragette Emmeline Pankhurst and her fiery
daughters, Christabel and Sylvia, developed with their "troops" who fought
against a British society that wouldn't grant women the vote. When one of
their number, Emily Wilding Davison, threw herself in front of the king's
horse, Anmer, as it rounded Tattenham Corner in the 1913 English Derby,
male society was shocked by the lengths to which these women would go
(Davison in fact died four days later from injuries sustained in the collision).
For the suffragettes, though, the movement was a war, and the communitas
that developed was every bit as great as that between male combatants during
military campaigns.

It is the same depth of connection that occurs with women's movements
across the world today. Often it is women, and more specifically mothers,
who are at the forefront of the fight for peace or social justice. Whether it be
in Chile or Rwanda or Darfur, mothers often are the ones thrown into a
liminal state where they discover communitas and the power to fight for
change. Nowhere has this been more celebrated that in the Four Mothers
Movement in Israel. Between 1985 and 1997, the conflict between Israel and
its northern neighbor, Lebanon, had become a silent war. Each year, some
twenty-five to thirty young Israeli soldiers were killed along the border. At
the same time, hundreds of thousands of Lebanese were displaced or killed. It
was rarely or never reported—a war that nobody seemed to care about. All
that changed in 1997 when two Israeli army helicopters collided on their way
to Lebanon, killing the seventy-three Israeli soldiers on board.

The passivity that had existed since 1985 evaporated. It was four
women—four mothers of Israeli soldiers—who lived, as they still do, in the

---

[12]Quoted in Robert Bly, *Iron John* (Dorset: Element Books, 1991), 155.

north of the country who decided that they had had enough. Their simple demonstration was to stand in the middle of a major intersection and demand that their government explain why, after seventeen years, they were still sending soldiers to die in Lebanon. The effect was staggering. In a nation whose parents had always passively accepted the fact that the military was central to the establishment and continuation of the state, suddenly four women were standing against the status quo. The Four Mothers immediately received tremendous public attention. It touched a vital nerve inside Israel, and their numbers grew tremendously and very quickly. Though initially a women's group, today, about 40 to 50 percent of the Four Mothers are men. Their success has spawned nine more women's peace groups in Israel. The Four Mothers movement has refused to join forces with conventional political parties. Its members remain liminal, and their liminality has swept many up in the marvelous communitas of protest.

Similar groups have developed in Northern Ireland, where both Catholic and Protestant mothers have been at the forefront of peace and reconciliation movements. In the 1970s, Betty Williams and Mairead Corrigan were united by a terrible accident that propelled them both into the public eye as peace activists. Corrigan's sister and three children were run down by an out-of-control car, its driver an IRA gunman shot dead while outrunning British soldiers. The three children were killed and Corrigan's sister, dreadfully injured and unable to cope with her grief, took her own life some time later. Williams, one of the first bystanders to arrive at the scene of the accident, joined Corrigan in forming the Community of Peace People. Initially a women's movement, it said "Enough!" to the never-ending cycle of violence and vengeance that gripped Northern Ireland. Ignored by the male-dominated political parties, the Peace People captured the imaginations of thousands of ordinary Irish parents. When Williams and Corrigan were awarded the Nobel Peace Prize for their peace-building work in 1976, Irish politicians were forced to take them seriously. In Cambodia, it is women who lead many of the effective trade unions, fighting for better working conditions for their colleagues. It is women's groups that fight and lobby the government against the epidemic of domestic violence. A women's media center has been established to raise awareness of the unacceptable levels of rape that beset Cambodian families. During the recent national election, thousands of women were marshaled as independent observers at polling stations and to scrutinize the vote-counting process. In Argentina in the 1970s, a group of white-scarved mothers assembled every week in Buenos Aires's main square, under the glare of soldiers of the monstrous military dictatorship of General Videla, to display pictures of their missing children. Their children were numbered among the thirty thousand *desaparecidos*—literally, the disappeared—under that regime. Called the Madres de la Plaza de Mayo, these mothers banded together to remain the only people in the world to hold Videla's henchmen accountable.

Thrown together by their liminal state, forced to work against cultural forces massed against them, women's groups around the world know the same kind of communitas that the thirteenth-century French knight Jean de Brueil spoke of earlier. Communitas is not an exclusively male experience by any means. It is an intimacy, a connection, that is more than the warm, inner glow experienced by many groups within our society today. It is hardened by battle, softened by true and genuine partnership, and forged by a shared vision for a better world.

This kind of intimacy was captured charmingly but powerfully in the third installment of Peter Jackson's epic *Lord of the Rings* film trilogy. In *The Return of the King,* after Frodo and Sam have finally destroyed the ring and Mordor has been defeated, the four hobbits return to normal life in sleepy Hobbiton. There, they find themselves at a large wooden table at a noisy, bustling inn. The other drinkers are laughing and carousing, going on with life as they had always known it. But Frodo and his friends have experienced an adventure like no other. They have looked death in the face many times, and by rallying together, they have not only survived, but also triumphed over evil. What of this experience could their friends and neighbors possibly understand? As they raise their tankards of ale to their lips, they look at each other—a long, knowing look. As their eyes meet, something unspoken is powerfully communicated. They *know* each other. No words can express what they're thinking, but they know each other's thoughts. This is the society found only in communitas.

The Lord of the Rings films are by no means the only ones that celebrate communitas. In fact, I perceive that an astonishing number of movies have a communitas at their core. So many, in fact, that I suggest that their popularity tells us something about the deep yearning for communitas that we all share. We love watching films in which a band of friends find deeper connection through the challenges thrown at them by an external threat, precisely because we desire that same connection with our own friends. War movies such as *Band of Brothers, Saving Private Ryan,* and *Blackhawk Down* work because not only do they attempt to depict war accurately, but also they focus primarily on the intensity of the relationships among the soldiers. It is an intensity forged by their shared experience of combat. In *Saving Private Ryan,* the band of soldiers are stunned to learn that their captain (played by Tom Hanks) is in fact a schoolteacher in civilian life. In the liminal experience of war he has been changed, enlarged, by the ordeal of combat leadership.

In buddy movies such *Boys on the Side, Thelma and Louise,* and *Ocean's 11* (and *Ocean's 12*), the characters undertake a challenge and develop ever-deeper intimacy as the story unfolds. The same can be said for *The Matrix* trilogy and *O Brother, Where Art Thou?*

Even more powerful, and common, are those films where characters who are opposites are thrown together. In *Rain Man,* a selfish, immature young man named Charlie Babbitt (played by Tom Cruise) is forced to drive his autistic older brother, Ray (played by Dustin Hoffman), across America to retrieve his inheritance. By the end of the journey, Charlie has been transformed by the relationship that he has developed with his brother. In the cult classic *The Princess Bride,* an unlikely band of adventurers (a pirate, a vengeful Spaniard, a giant, and a princess-to-be) are bound together in their attempt to overthrow an evil prince. A similarly unlikely bunch comes together to build a baseball diamond in a cornfield in *Field of Dreams.* And, of course, just about every *Mighty Ducks*–style sports film capitalizes on our desire to see a rag-tag bunch of also-runs transformed into a force greater than the sum of the individual parts. The granddaddy of them all, though, is *The Wizard of Oz,* in which each character literally contributes a different part to the body as a whole: the Scarecrow's brain, the Tin Man's heart, the Lion's courage, and Dorothy's sense of destiny.

These movies speak to us because they depict the very sense of intense intimacy and equality between the characters that we yearn for among our friends: a friendship that is spontaneous, immediate, egalitarian, and nonrational, forged by worthy challenges and trials. In short, human beings deeply desire communitas.

Liminality Is the Key

My quest in the 1980s and 1990s to build true community was only slightly misguided. The hunger for community is a legitimate one, but to pursue it for its own sake is the mistake. When we seek to build community without the experience of liminality, all we end up with is the kind of pseudo-community that pervades many churches. It's more like a support group than a communitas. In David Fincher's incendiary film *Fight Club,* the main character/narrator, played by Edward Norton, is lost in a quagmire of materialism and meaninglessness. He has an odious job as a recall coordinator for a major automobile company and tries to fill the void in his life by buying new furnishings and appliances for his Ikea-inspired home. The pain is too great, though, leading to a numbing cycle of sleepless nights and pointless days. When he tries to get some prescription drugs for his insomnia, his doctor refuses, unsympathetically comparing his psychological "pain" with the real physical pain experienced by victims of testicular cancer. In reaction, Norton's character then attends a support group for cancer sufferers and soon finds himself becoming addicted to a variety of support groups. For the first time in his life, he gets in touch with his emotions and cries freely. However, Marla Singer (played by Helena Bonham Carter), another tourist in the land of genuine suffering, spoils this therapeutic release for him by holding up a mirror to his dishonesty.

Norton's character wants the kind of community that he can find at a support group. And for a time it is helpful, but it has its limits. He can never fully realize the kind of community he desires, because he is not on the same threshold as the other members of the group. He and Marla don't actually have cancer or alcoholism. They can look like sufferers, faking it for a period, but ultimately the ordeal of cancer is not one that they can share. For communitas to develop, the members of a group must all be involved in the same challenge. In Terence Malick's war film *The Thin Red Line,* Captain Staros (played by Elias Koteas) refuses to order his men over a ridge, knowing that it is securely held by well-armed Japanese forces. Despite several orders from above, he steadfastly refuses to give the word to charge the hill. Later, when he is relieved of duty, he talks to his men, declaring that they are like his sons. They gather around to say farewell him, knowing that he has shared their ordeal and saved them from certain death. This scene can be juxtaposed with a later one, where, after the campaign has ended, the new captain, Captain Bosche (played by George Clooney), who has never seen action, gives the men a speech in which he says that they should look at him as if he were their father. Staros's speech is heartfelt and moving; Bosche's speech is shallow and ridiculous.

Building community for its own sake is like attending a cancer support group without having cancer. It's like asking solders you haven't fought with to imagine that you are their father. And it's like your church demanding your allegiance and your weekly attendance without giving you a cause to work toward. It's no different to the church holding endless Bible study groups or hearing countless sermons for the purpose of learning information that will rarely be utilized. Have you ever noticed how many men attend worship only occasionally and begrudgingly, but when there's a church cleanup day, they'll turn up joyfully and work hard all day? Such workdays create a mini-communitas. So do short-term mission trips and youth mission trips. So does church planting. But weekly church services do not. It's like sitting at the apostles' feet and drinking in their teaching in Jerusalem in the first century. It serves a useful purpose, but the ultimate purpose of the Jerusalem church was to go and make disciples of all nations. There's no question that the apostles' teaching was essential, but not as an end in itself. Their teaching was meant to mobilize ordinary believers to go into the world, baptizing new disciples and teaching them all that Christ commanded them. As we noted earlier, it wasn't until persecution drove the first Christians out of Jerusalem that they discovered their purpose and that purpose threw them together into a liminal state as a missionary movement.

Attending a respectable middle-class church in a respectable middle-class neighborhood isn't a liminal experience. Joining a peace movement in a nation obsessed with military might is. Traveling to Indonesia to help with the international relief effort after a tsunami is. Joining a church-planting team is. Standing with mothers in the middle of a busy intersection to protest the deaths of their sons is. Why do our churches often miss this experience of communitas? For no other reason than that they often avoid liminality, opting for safer, more secure environment.

I'm not for a minute suggesting that Christian communitas shouldn't address the need that all of us have for safety. Indeed it should. However, it should fashion safe spaces not as alternatives to missional engagement in our world, but as parallel experiences to that engagement. Whenever I have led or been part of a mission team, we have ensured that there are protocols for those who are tired, emotionally depleted, or spiritually dry to retreat and be replenished. But this hasn't stopped the mission from continuing. It happens in parallel with the ongoing purpose of the team.

A Christian Communitas

Alan Hirsch, who did much to introduce me to this idea, defines Christian communitas this way:

> Communitas in the way I want to define it is a community infused with a grand sense of purpose; a purpose that lies outside of its current internal reality and constitution. It's the kind of community that "happens" to people in actual pursuit of a common vision of what could be. It involves **movement** and it describes the experience of **togetherness** that only really happens among a group of people actually engaging in a mission outside itself.[13]

The "grand sense of purpose" is the key. As Hirsch says, communitas just "happens" when a society of believers commits itself to that grand purpose, to that external mission. Lesslie Newbigin was right twenty years ago when

---

[13]Alan Hirsch, *The Forgotten Ways: Reactivating the Missional Church* (Grand Rapids: Brazos, forthcoming).

he observed that the two moods of the church were timidity and anxiety. Timidity squashes our missional impulse. It causes us to withdraw from any grand purpose for fear of upsetting the delicate balance of conflicting egos currently residing in each church. Christians surround themselves with fellow churchgoers, so that their church's only goal is to maintain equilibrium. The church's anxiety fosters its awkward reputation in the wider community. Says Alison Morgan in *The Wild Gospel,*

> Anxiety . . . means that insofar as we do engage with the world out there, our contribution is mostly a worried attempt to restrain it; afraid for our children, we strive to uphold the moral standards of a sliding culture by campaigning against abortion or disapproving of stories about wizards. The result is that we keep our moral and spiritual integrity, but our witness is lost.[14]

Such timidity and anxiety leave the church as nothing more than a retreatist, frightened, ineffective organization. Morgan adds, "We have set up private clubs for those whose leisure interest is religion."[15] How, then, could a settled, safe church community really encounter anything like communitas unless it has taken the step into liminality? This is the very step that the great heroes of the faith have taken, heroes lionized by the church, but heroes whose example has been forsaken. They moved out of the safety of institutional Christianity and forged new Christian communitates (the plural of communitas).

It reminds me of one of Søren Kierkegaard's parables. Noticing that a flock of wild geese had settled on his property on their long flight south for the winter, Kierkegaard was intrigued when they didn't fly on as the weather turned colder. In fact, this flock sheltered in his yard and waited out a relatively mild winter on his pond. At first, the Danish philosopher was delighted to have his own resident family of geese. Then he was disturbed to notice how, with the onset of each subsequent winter, as other wild geese flew south, his geese would rankle and squawk and fuss among themselves. The honk of the wild geese flying overhead awakened within his geese some primal urge to fly, but they never did. Some flapped their big wings and took to the air briefly, but they returned and enjoyed the safety of Kirekegaard's farm. Then, he reports, came a winter when the honking wild geese overhead raised no reaction at all from the land-bound flock. They pecked at the earth, oblivious to the call of the wild overhead. For Kierkegaard, this described the

---

[14]Alison Morgan, *The Wild Gospel: Bringing Truth to Life* (Oxford: Monarch Books, 2004), 189.
[15]Ibid.

Danish church in the nineteenth century, and it might well describe the Western church today. Some churches will still hear the wild honking, and their feathers will bristle, their heart will skip a beat, their lungs will fill with air, ready for the long flight ahead of them. But their feet don't leave the ground. They love to read about the Christian heroes who have forged new movements, addressed grand plans, planted new churches, fed the hungry, fought for justice, but they prefer the security of the farm. Sadly, some other Christians can't even hear the call at all.

Mission—Our Raison d'Être

As I've said many times now, exiles have come out of the burrow. They have heard the call of the wild and realized that they cannot develop the magnificent sense of communitas that they need from within the existing mainstream church. This isn't to say that it's impossible to do. Many Christians will feel called to remain within institutional Christianity, trying to shoo the domesticated geese into the sky every winter. Exiles do not feel similarly called. They can't be placated by the promises of church leaders who think that by creating a committee for communitas within the church they'll keep the exiles happy. Creating communitas—something we all desire—is not necessarily about developing new programs. It's about a band of Christians discovering their grand sense of purpose and pursuing it. As Mennonite missiologist James R. Krabill says,

> Being more missional might actually mean doing fewer things. There is a Latin American proverb that says, "If you don't know where you're coming from, and if you don't know where you're going, then any bus will do." Some congregations are clearly riding too many buses! What they need is not more **flurry,** but more **focus.** Becoming disciplined about being a missional church can provide such a focus.[16]

For Christians, communitas emerges naturally when we commit ourselves to a mission beyond ourselves. It's as simple as that. This is why people often say that they prefer, say, their amateur theater group to their church. The theater group has a defined mission. So it is with your local branch of Greenpeace or Amnesty International. They have a much grander purpose than just meeting regularly. Like the Four Mothers movement or Shackleton's attempt to cross Antarctica, their raison d'être defines them totally and creates the social conditions for genuine community to grow. We have

---

[16]James R. Krabill, "Does Your Church 'Smell' Like Mission? Reflections on Becoming a Missional Church," *Mission Insight* 17 (2001): 14.

known all along that the raison d'être of the church is mission—sharing the good news of Christ, feeding the hungry, clothing the naked, visiting the imprisoned, working for justice. It is in the service of these goals that we will find communitas with our fellow workers.

Some people have challenged me in the past that the raison d'être of the church is not mission, but worship. We are called by God to worship him and enjoy him forever, they say. Yes, ultimately I agree that the highest post to which we've been called is that of true worship of the one and only living God. However, if we take Paul's definition of worship seriously, we might look at the concept quite differently. In chapter 12 of his letter to the Romans Paul says,

> Therefore, I urge you, brothers and sisters, in view of God's mercy, to offer your bodies as a living sacrifice, holy and pleasing to God—this is true worship. (Rom 12:1)

In the church we are so blinded by the contemporary use of the term "worship" that we take it to literally mean nothing more than the corporate singing of praise to God. When someone says that our reason for being is to worship, we can be fooled into thinking that our highest calling is corporate singing. I'm not against corporate singing, of course, but according to Paul, my spiritual act of worship involves sacrificing my body, my volition, my actions. He then goes on to counsel the Romans about what this would look like in practice. He lists the following acts of true Christian worship:

- To not conform to the norms of society (v. 2)

- To humbly express spiritual gifts in practical ways (vv. 3–8)

- To love others (vv. 9–10)

- To be spiritually zealous, hopeful, patient, and prayerful (vv. 11–12)

- To be hospitable and generous (v. 13)

- To live in harmony, with munificence and charity toward unbelievers (vv. 14–21)

So this is worship! We have to stop isolating mission from worship, and acknowledge that when I act charitably toward someone, I give glory to God. When I share with someone about my friendship with Jesus, I am worshipping God. Mission, then, is an expression of Christian worship. In fact, I'm prepared to say that it is *the* central and *most* powerful expression of worship. In Romans, Paul's argument about worship continues throughout chapters 13–15. He persists in emphasizing the rule of love as an expression of worship. We are to love those in authority by submitting to them lawfully (Rom 13:1–7). We are to be gracious to new believers (Rom 14:1–12) and work to maintain unity in the church (Rom 14:13–23). Why? Paul concludes,

> May the God who gives endurance and encouragement give you the same attitude of mind toward each other that Christ Jesus had, so that with one mind and one voice you may glorify the God and Father of our Lord Jesus Christ. Accept one another, then, just as Christ accepted you, in order to bring praise to God. (Rom 15:5–7)

What gives praise to God? It's our acceptance of others. Our works of generosity and hospitality are acts of worship. It is ironic, isn't it, that in many churches people who won't even speak to each other are joined together in hymn singing or contemporary worship, not knowing that their actions undermine the very words they are singing? Exiles, tired of meaningless corporate singing, long to be involved with fellow followers of Jesus in shared tasks of generosity or hospitality.

Acts of Worship

Nearly twenty years ago Johannes Verkuyl, Dutch missiologist and former missionary to the East Indies, wrote that he believed that Christian mission had four indispensable and interdependent dimensions: proclamation, service, community, and the struggle against injustice. In 1986 he wrote,

> If the creation of fellowship belongs to the heart of the Kingdom of God,
> then missions and evangelism do not occur if that aspect of community
> formation is disregarded or ignored.[17]

I copied this quotation in my Scott Peck days and had it pinned to a notice board. In those days, I took Verkuyl to mean that if we build community
first, mission will naturally follow. I now realize that that's not true. Too
many groups throughout history have done this and never made it to mission. Too many mainstream churches are trying to get their so-called internal
life right before reaching out to others. They'll find that they'll never get the
internal stuff right. If you focus on community formation solely, you almost
never get to any mission. Now I think that Verkuyl, a resilient old warrior-
missionary who endured incarceration by the Japanese in 1940s, had a more
nuanced perspective in mind, but back then I saw it as a simple cause-and-
effect movement from community to mission. Now I'm convinced that
when we get our thinking right about Jesus, he propels us into mission—that
is, into the service of others, a cause greater than ourselves. Knowing that
cause, that mission, and, together with others, embracing the challenges
involved naturally lead to communitas.

Verkuyl saw those four dimensions as essential and interconnected. You
can't prioritize one over the others. Proclamation, service, community, and
the fight for justice are equally important, but the organizing principle is the
grand purpose to which we feel called. Many exiles leave the mainstream
church and engage in the kinds of things we've looked at already: living an
authentic life, struggling for global justice, showing compassion, pursuing
vocation as a way of doing God's work. But often they do it alone, imagining
that it's either the conventional church or no church at all. My encouragement to them is to band together with others, maybe just a handful, and
serve a cause greater than themselves. Include some Christians and perhaps
some nonbelievers who share your values of faith, justice, and integrity. Then
commit yourselves to serve others. It doesn't have to be as dramatic as standing up to an Argentine dictatorship or destroying a ring in Mount Doom in
the heart of Mordor. It could be any small, brave experiment that Jesus
leads you to.

But more than this, our liminal, missional experiences contain the very
stuff required for the transformation of the mainstream church. Remember
that Turner believed that experiences of communitas by people who stand
together "outside" society strengthen that society. The church needs exiles to
have the liminal experience of communitas because it pushes the church for-

---

[17]Johannes Verkuyl, "My Pilgrimage in Missiology," *International Bulletin of
Missionary Research* 10, no. 4 (1986): 151.

ward, bothering it with the freshness and vitality that come from the deeper communion of mission. The liberty experienced in Christian communitas plants the germ of cultural regeneration back into the mainstream church. In fact, as we noted earlier, Turner dared to suggest that in the dialectic between communitas and normal society resides the hope for the future of that society. So it is in the Christian sector of society. If only the mainstream church leadership could grasp this idea.

6

Fashioning Collectives of Exiles

The Promise: We Will Create Missional Community

Christianity has not been tried and found
wanting; it has been found difficult and left
untried.

—G. K. Chesterton

If I've convinced you about the joys of communitas and the need for us to
embrace mission as a liminal experience, then let me push it one step further. Exiles have, more often than not, left the mainstream church or are
hanging in there out of habit or a long-standing sense of joyless duty. But
neither are they at home in the host empire of post-Christendom. Nevertheless, they have experienced communitas on short-term projects such as mission trips or community service. They know what it *should* be like to be in
league with fellow travelers, surfing the edges of liminality, tasting the freedom of noninstitutional religious service. But they rarely found it or find it
in their churches. It's my personal experience that a great many exiles have
found their way into parachurch and missionary organizations where they do
experience liminality and communitas by serving the poor, working with
young people, planting churches, evangelizing, regenerating urban neighborhoods. Quite unconsciously, they have followed the still, small voice into
missional activity where excitement, hard work, and the very real threat of
failure are their constant companions. But they have been fed the lie that
these liminal, missional experiences aren't really the *stuff* of church. They are
sidelines, outreach activities of the genuine article. Real church is about the
more stable, regular, weekly gathering of believers.

Whenever I have spoken to mainstream church leaders and clergy about
communitas, I have sensed a resistance, sometimes even an out-and-out rejection of what I'm saying. But when I address regular church attenders or especially parachurch or missionary workers, the reaction is overwhelmingly

positive. Parachurch youth workers, urban missioners, cross-cultural missionaries, church planters—these people have tasted of the joys of communitas and are spoiled from ever being happy simply to attend a religious meeting as the sum total of their Christian experience. We continue our look at the exile's dangerous promises. One of those promises, I strongly believe, is the decision to fashion alternatives to the empire's current churches. To do so will require that exiles create missional communities.

Church as a Liquid, Missional Experience

Exiles are not content to believe that the liminal experiences of Christian mission can be only an occasional feature of our lives as Christians. Why can't the liminal, missional work that we're engaged in with others be the field in which our experience of churching occurs? Exiles are brave enough to make this choice. They have stopped playing at church each Sunday and discovered that their missional experience with others *is* their church.

For example, I remember meeting Shaun Tunstall, from the city of Brisbane on the east coast of Australia, who, in his mid-twenties and living with dyslexia and ADD, finally decided he would stop attending church. He couldn't sit still during church services, and he wasn't wired to take in information from half-hour sermons. He wasn't getting anything out of the meetings, even though he had been attending church weekly since he was born. Now, flushed with frustration and early adult rebellious energy, he decided to stop going to church. Instead, Shaun decided that he would take his powerboat out on Brisbane's Pine River and go waterskiing on Sunday mornings. He gathered a group of friends, some Christian, some not, and headed off to the river for a relaxing day of waterskiing. But after reversing the trailer down the boat ramp and edging the craft into the water, he became wracked by guilt. It was a beautiful Sunday morning, and every week of his life he had been in church. Now here he was about to go waterskiing. He expected one of God's vengeful lightning bolts to burst from the clear, blue sky and sink his boat at any minute. So, in an attempt to salve his conscience, he grabbed a pocket Bible from his car and announced to his friends that he would like to mark the day by reading a short passage of Scripture. You can imagine his friends' surprise. After reading the shortest psalm he could find, he reflected briefly about the beauty of God's grace and then asked the guys if there was anything he'd like them to pray about. Stunned by these proceedings, his friends, especially the non-Christian ones, eventually offered up needs they had that Shaun could pray about. Then they went waterskiing all day.

Next week, twice as many people turned up. Shaun read a brief passage, shared a few thoughts about it, and asked for prayer points. He did this for weeks. The numbers kept increasing, and soon he had a community of over fifty people who would meet by the river, share a short devotion, pray together, and enjoy God's creation. Soon, people started becoming Christians. After a while, they started breaking for lunch at some picnic tables by the Pine River, where they would break bread and drink wine and remember Jesus' sacrificial love. They shared a meal together and took up a collection each week and gave the money to the poor. They took it upon themselves to become the "chaplains" to the general river community. Now they are known as the people who tow broken-down boats back to the boat ramp. They provide free parts and repairs for other boats that have given up the ghost. They eat together, they serve the poor, they share Jesus with others, they celebrate the Lord's Supper, they serve their general community. And all along, Shaun's parents and church friends are hoping that he'll come to his senses and start attending church again!

In Vancouver, Canada, Marion and Kellie work with teenage mothers. They care for pregnant teenagers, showing them unconditional love and support, offering them practical medical and prenatal information, as well as listening to their fears and hopes for the future. Often they are invited to be the teenagers' support person in the delivery room and can be called out at any time to drive one of their girls to the maternity ward of the local hospital. They have created a community of young women, some pregnant, some new mothers, who meet together for mutual support and lots of laughs. Many of these young mothers, if they aren't already Christians, become Christians through Marion and Kellie's example of love and grace. As they "graduate" out of the program when their babies reach a certain age, many of the young women then sign on as co-workers with Marion and Kellie. As much as they are encouraged to attend mainstream churches, the teenage mothers find a greater sense of acceptance in the community. The group also provides them a place to contribute to the lives of others, making a difference to other girls who've been in the same place they have. Marion once told me that she feels more "churched" by her community of young mothers than anywhere else. So, what stops us from simply acknowledging this band of companions as a church in their own right?

Jeff Dennis moved into West Fillmore in inner-city Chicago thirteen years ago to establish a traditional Navigators ministry among men there. It was his vision to fulfill the standard Navigators brief of sharing Christ, discipling new believers, and encouraging the churches, but he soon realized that the men of the Fillmore area were more concerned about finding a job than finding Christ. After trying (and failing) to establish a manufacturing company (plastics), Jeff turned to providing job training for the community. Primarily this meant teaching "employability skills" (interviewing skills, resolving conflicts on the job, etc.) and basic life skills, as well as math, reading, and writing.

I met Jeff at a conference in Ann Arbor, Michigan. His ministry had blossomed, and a number of other Navigators staff members had joined him in Chicago. Now, as well as teaching job skills, he is heading up a small employment agency that provides jobs for the community. To fund all his staff and programs, Jeff, along with another Navigator, Peter Payne, created Breaking Ground Inc., a construction program that employs local men to build homes for neighborhood families. Not only does Breaking Ground provide affordable homes for the community, but also it provides jobs and job training to local men, many of whom are ex-offenders without skills. Plus, guys like Jeff and Peter get to mentor the men in the frequent teachable moments of each workday.

Breaking Ground has boomed in recent years. In December 2004 the team completed their first ten homes in the rundown neighborhood of South Spalding. Because of the multiple subsidies that they arranged, families were able to buy these four-bedroom houses for less than $100,000. Their monthly payments are comparable to what they were paying in rent. Ten families' lives have been transformed, and the block where the houses were built—once a virtual slum—has been revitalized. Jeff and Peter believe that where multiple new houses are built on the same street or the same block, there is an instant upgrade in that community. Families who pay for their own home act differently than they did as tenants. They learn to fix things, mow the lawn, and pick up the trash. They call the police when drug deals and gang activity happen nearby. They take a greater pride in their street and their general neighborhood. In 2005 Breaking Ground is planning a new development of 130 homes.

But more than this, they started a weekly meeting called Valid Concerns. It's a mix of a twelve-step program, a community support group, and a Bible study. Many of those who attend are workers from Breaking Ground, many of whom are ex-offenders or substance abusers. The leader, an ex-offender himself, is a deeply committed Christian man whose life has been transformed by Jeff's ministry. Together, group members encourage one another's faith, study the Bible, hold each other accountable to a holy lifestyle, and "do life" together. As Jeff and I spoke about the group, I told him that it sounded like a really wonderful church-planting project. At first he balked, not really seeing it as a church, but just a support group. But the more we talked, the more he came to see that it was every bit a church. He said, "I have never wanted to start a church, but I see that I need to be free from the old, failing model. Valid Concerns is every bit a New Testament type of church."

In his book *Liquid Church,* Pete Ward argues that there needs to be a shift from solid church to liquid church. He defines solid church in formal, institutional parameters: a more-or-less coherent congregation with a distinct organizational structure meeting in a particular place at a particular time. In solid church, faithfulness tends to be equated with church attendance; success is measured in terms of numbers; worship and teaching are standardized, producing a bland and inoffensive diet of middle-of-the-road music and safe spirituality; and membership has become an exclusive and self-serving commitment, little different sociologically from membership in a golf or tennis club.

Solid Church vs. Liquid Church

Solid	Liquid
formal	informal
institutional	fluid
organized congregation	relationship with others through communion with Christ
structured time & place	flexible to needs of community
faithfulness = attendance, success = numbers	not about the building, but the spiritual activity
worship & teaching are standardized	church is a verb, not a noun
membership is exclusive & self-serving	fundamental motivation is mission

According to Ward, liquid church, by contrast, takes its identity from the informal and fluid notion of believers in communication with each other. This rather simple idea, if carried through in practice, has significant implications. First, liquid church is not an institution, but something that we "make with each other by communicating Christ."[1] It exists in networks of relationships. Second, the basis for church life is found not in organizational patterns or buildings, but in people's spiritual activity. Ward reemphasizes the suggestion that "church" should be understood as a verb rather than a noun ("I church, you church, we church"). It might not seem all that radical, but rarely is it seriously embraced by many Christians today. Third, liquid church does not have to take the form of a weekly congregational meeting:

---

[1]Pete Ward, *Liquid Church* (Peabody, Mass.: Hendrickson, 2002), 2.

"Worship and meeting will be decentered and reworked in ways that are designed to connect to the growing spiritual hunger in society."[2] This points to the fundamental motivation behind the idea of liquid church, which is mission.

The glue that unites Shaun and his band of river dwellers is their common sense of mission and the need to share resources with each other to achieve their missional objectives. Likewise with Kellie and Marion. Their group needs each other because they have taken on the missional task of loving unloved teenage mothers. A shared sense of mission often takes a group to a liminal space, and when there, they are compelled by circumstance and common goals to draw on and from each other. Ward's provocative suggestion is that we simply acknowledge these myriad groups for what they are: churches—liquid, missional churches.

The Way It Is around the World

In Kenya I once attended a prayer meeting of church leaders and pastors, all seated in a large circle around an austere theological college lecture room outside Nairobi. I noted that the man next to me was much taller, darker in skin tone, and more lithe than the Kenyans who had been hosting me during my visit. During the prayer time I opened my eyes and looked down to see that he had a dreadful scar on his left foot. His disfigurement was so noticeable that I, perhaps rather rudely, asked him about it when the formal time of prayer had ended. He smiled accommodatingly and told me that it was a bullet wound. He then turned his face to show me another terrible scar on his right cheek, a wound that later I heard was caused by a machete. In his soft, gentle way he then told me that he was not, in fact, Kenyan at all. He was a Sudanese soldier who had been injured in the bitter civil war in his country. He had escaped over the border into a teeming refugee camp in northern Kenya, where he heard about the grace of Jesus for the first time. He converted to Christianity and now spends his time evangelizing other refugees and planting churches in the massive camps.

Hearing of the conference that I was attending, he had walked and hitch-hiked to Nairobi. In that typically self-effacing African manner, he told me that he was very inadequate at church planting. "Why," he confessed, "I have only managed to plant five churches since I got started." When I asked him to explain his "inadequate" church-planting method to me, he said that basically he preached the gospel until he had a dozen or so new converts, then he

---

[2]Ibid., 2.

introduced them to each other, spent time teaching them basic doctrines, provided them with Sudanese-language Bibles, established some simple leadership structures, and then he left them to preach again until he had another dozen new Christians. Having heard me speak at the conference in Nairobi, he was convinced that I must have been a much more "successful" evangelist than he was.

When we hear stories like this, it's very easy to dismiss their veracity. We've heard about great so-called revivals in Africa with thousands upon thousands of people becoming Christians, and we wonder if there's anyone left to evangelize in southern and eastern Africa. We've heard the comment that the African church is a mile wide and an inch thick, meaning that millions there call themselves Christian, but their faith is shallow and easily mingled with African tribal beliefs and practices. Perhaps also, we rather prejudicially imagine that life is simpler for Sudanese refugees than it is for us, and that launching groups of a dozen or so new believers there isn't as difficult or as legitimate as planting "real" churches in the West. But it's important to remember that most of the churches being planted in Southeast Asia, South America, China, and Africa—that is, most of the churches being planted across the world—are planted this way. They have no buildings, no seminaries, no full-time paid clergy. These nondenominational, nonstructured, nontraditional churches now represent one of the fastest-growing sectors of the Christian movement. David Barrett, professor of missiometrics at Regent University, Virginia Beach, and publisher of the *World Christian Encyclopedia,* and Todd Johnson, former director of the World Evangelization Research Center in Richmond and now Research Fellow in Global Christianity and Director of the Center for the Study of Global Christianity at Gordon-Conwell Theological Seminary, published a report in 2001 that noted the emergence of these churches, a movement they call the "neo-apostolics." This movement is marked by four primary characteristics:

1. They reject denominationalism and restrictive, overbearing central authority.

2. They seek a life focused on Jesus.

3. They seek a more effective missionary lifestyle.

4. They are one of the fastest growing movements in the world.

Barrett and Johnson estimate that this neo-apostolic group now numbers over twenty thousand movements and networks with a total of 394 million Christians worldwide. Further, they are predicting that by 2025 there will be something like 581 million Christians associated with this move-ment—120 million more than all Protestant movements put together.[3]

And according to many sources, the vast majority of that growth is ap-pearing in non-Western countries. In his profoundly illuminating book *The Next Christendom,* Philip Jenkins, professor of history and religious studies at Penn State University, provides readers with an important secular study of the social impact of the growth and spread of Christianity. Jenkins says that currently we are living through one of the transforming moments in the his-tory of religion worldwide, wherein the Christian center of gravity has shifted from the West to Africa, Asia, and Latin America. In fact, Jenkins dispenses with the East-West dichotomy in preference for a North-South framework. Christianity, he says, has been a distinctly Northern religion, flowering in Europe, Scandinavia, Russia, the United States, and Canada. Now, in terms of numerical growth at least, the emerging Christian world will be anchored in the Southern continents. Says Jenkins, "By 2050, only about 1/5 of the world's 3 billion Christians will be non-Hispanic Whites. . . . The era of Western Christianity has passed within our lifetimes."[4]

Jenkins notes that Catholic growth has been particularly dramatic in Af-rica, usually in former French and Belgian territories. In 1995 there were six-teen million Catholics in all of Africa; today there are 120 million. In 1940 Latin America had barely one million Protestants; since 1960 they have grown at a rate of 6 percent annually, and today there are about fifty million Protes-tants. Pentecostals account for 80 to 90 percent of the growth since 1950. In Asia Protestantism continues to flourish. Today there are almost twice as many Presbyterians in South Korea as in the United States. Jenkins goes on to project that the largest Christian communities in 2025 will be the United States, Brazil, Mexico, Philippines, Nigeria, Zaire, Ethiopia, Russia, China, and Ger-many (using U.S. government statistics).[5] He illustrates the shift:

> By mid-century there are likely to be more Christians in Uganda than Ger-many or Britain, perhaps more than the largest 4 or 5 European nations combined. By 2050, the Philippines should be the 3rd or 4th largest num-ber of Christians on the planet. Today the Philippines has more Catholics than any individual European state and they are growing fast.[6]

In many cases, the Protestant growth, which in the South is markedly Pentecostal, is characterized by the kinds of church-planting strategies

[3]"State of Christianity 2001," under "World," [cited 17 January 2006]. Online: http://www.jesus.org.uk/dawn/2001/dawn07.html.
[4]Philip Jenkins, *The Next Christendom: The Coming of Global Christianity* (Oxford/New York: Oxford University Press, 2002), 3.
[5]Ibid., 90.
[6]Ibid., 91–92.

described by the Sudanese soldier-pastor I met in Nairobi. I have sat with church leaders in Tanzania, Zambia, Cambodia, Vietnam, and Brazil who have explained a similar method. When the evangelist has led a handful of people to put their trust in Christ, he or she (usually he in the South) gathers them, equips them, and then leaves them to their own devices, relying on the evangelist's occasional return visits. As fragile as it sounds, God is blessing this new movement in astonishing ways.

And yet, for all our concerns about the frailty of a dozen or more new believers churching together, we can't help but acknowledge that this is precisely the method that Paul used on his missionary journeys. It's true that in some settings Paul spent a considerable amount of time, but we can't find him staying any longer than eighteen months or two years with a new church. In many cases he stayed just long enough to establish a core group, train leaders, and establish some basic structural rules for living together. Beyond that, these new congregations relied on visiting apostles and occasional letters. It seems no more precarious a strategy than the approach taken today in Vietnam or Brazil. It's just that in the West we are so used to the infrastructure available to churches that we cannot imagine churching without them. But buildings, seminaries, paid clergy, conferences, books, and other resources are luxuries for the church of Jesus, not necessities. We can rightly be thankful to God for their prevalence in the West, but we had better realize that there are now more Christians around the world doing without them than with them.

At an international Christian conference in South East Asia recently, several members of the underground church in China appeared on the platform to report on the situation for the church in their country. They asked their audience to pray for them because the communist government has imposed restrictions on them that made being an effective church difficult. In particular they reported on three impositions that they wanted lifted: (1) no unauthorized assembly of more than fifteen people is allowed; (2) no unauthorized church buildings or sanctuaries can be erected; (3) no unauthorized formal training of leaders is permitted. As they spoke, it occurred to those gathered that these restrictions were the very things that forced the Chinese underground church to be the dynamic and powerful force that it has become. The first imposition forces churches to embrace a cellular-division model of church growth. As a congregation reaches twenty or so members, it must divide into two and launch a new congregation. The second imposition compels the church to meet in homes, restaurants, karaoke bars, and other private spaces. The third restriction drives congregations to equip their own indigenous leadership without the help of formal schools or seminaries. The bitter irony was not lost on many there that day: the communist government is actually forcing the Christian church to rediscover its original genius as a missional movement.

We Make It Too Hard

Why is it so much more difficult in the West? Why can't we imagine being a community of Christ's followers without a building or formally trained and accredited clergy? Whenever I raise this issue in seminars, people regularly remind me that house-based groups of fifteen or so without proper accreditation and training can lead to heresy and cultish practices. But the fact remains that nearly every major heresy that has beset the Christian church has come from recognized church bodies whose leaders were properly accredited by their sponsoring hierarchies. Conversely, virtually every new movement among people hungering for a deeper knowledge of God has been rejected, quashed, or destroyed by the "church" of its day, and its leaders have famously been excommunicated or martyred for following the missional impulse of God. Being part of a recognized denomination or organization by no means guarantees biblical purity. The fledgling churches living out their faith in those Sudanese refugee camps are every bit as legitimate as the congregation of Canterbury Cathedral. It's just our insecurity that causes us to think otherwise. As an Indian church planter was noted to have said, "You have a Bible? You can read? Then you can start a church."[7]

We have been told for so long that we can't possibly be all that God wants us to be without a properly ordained minister, or without a purpose-built facility, or without the support and assistance that a denominational leadership structure can offer us. Of course, it should be no surprise that we've been told that by seminary professors, ordained clergy, and denominational leaders. Many people have too much to lose if we rediscovered what the church around the Southern continents is discovering. Let me make myself clear on this matter. I am not suggesting that there is anything inherently wrong with seminaries, denominations, church buildings, and the rest of the massive infrastructure that the church in the West has at its disposal. What I'm saying is that our reliance on them is limiting our spiritual growth. We are not fully realizing our calling to be the church of Jesus Christ as long as we rely on money, buildings, and paid experts.

And we are exporting this unhelpful reliance on structures around the world. On a recent visit to Ho Chi Minh City in Vietnam, I encouraged a group of underground church leaders in a darkened booth in a nearly empty karaoke bar. When I told them that they didn't need the trappings and accoutrements of the church in the United States, they burst into disbelieving laughter. I reiterated, "You have all the resources you need right now from

---

[7]Quoted in Felicity Dale, *Getting Started: A Practical Guide to Planting Simple Churches* (Dallas: House2House Ministries, 2003), 165.

the Holy Spirit to be everything God wants the church of Vietnam to be." It took quite some convincing. They were certain that they should aim for the kind of "blessings" experienced by the American church to finally fulfill their calling to fully be the church of Vietnam.

To put it in terms of Pete Ward's thinking, the Vietnamese leaders were yearning to become solid church instead of liquid church. Only we in the West who have come to realize that solidity comes with too many unwanted strings attached can see the marvelous opportunities available to liquid-church movements. In solid-church thinking, a church must be planted in a certain time and place and remain there henceforth and forever. Why do Western Christians love having plaques and foundation stones attached to their very solid buildings? Because they speak of permanence, immovability, reliability. But who's to say that it's not perfectly legitimate for God's "church" to burst forth in this neighborhood for a season and subside before bursting forth somewhere else? Why can't we think liquidly, of Christian communities rising, receding, spilling into the cracks and taking myriad shapes in equally myriad people groups and places? With such a liberating ecclesiology, exiles are able to recognize the "church" in all sorts of weird and wonderful expressions. We need as equal a shift in our perspective as those leaders in Ho Chi Minh City. We need to rediscover that the six, eight, ten, or thirty of us who do life together as followers of Jesus have every spiritual resource we need to be his church at this time and in this place.

To Yearn for the Wide, Boundless Ocean

One of the most intriguing thinkers of the twentieth century was the dashing and adventurous French pilot and writer Antoine de Saint-Exupéry. His novel *The Little Prince* is apparently the third most widely read book in the world after the Bible and the Koran. In a posthumously published collection of his wise sayings and thoughts called *Citadelle*, he said,

> If you want to build a ship, don't summon people to buy wood, prepare tools, distribute jobs and organise the work; teach people the yearning for the wide, boundless ocean.[8]

In the West, the mainstream church is too focused on motivating its members to embrace the technicalities of shipbuilding without ever having first inspired them with a yearning to sail the high seas. Exiles, though, live for the sea. They have tasted the pleasure of noninstitutionalized friendships

[8]Antoine de Saint-Exupéry, *[Citadelle] The Wisdom of the Sands* (trans. Stuart Gilbert; Chicago: University of Chicago Press, 1984), 54.

and the freedom of conscience that they now enjoy. They trust God enough to believe that God will build the church and that the gates of hell will not prevail against it, and that the form that God's building takes might disturb or frighten many Christians. God is building the church in karaoke bars in Ho Chi Minh City, in refugee camps in northern Kenya, by the Pine River in Brisbane, and among teenage mothers in Vancouver. Exiles, who have that hunger, have a responsibility to pass it on to others, to teach them to yearn for the boundless ocean. How? The missionary outfit Third Place Communities, based in Hobart, Australia, has a set of commitments that help sustain their missional lifestyle. Let's take a brief look at them.[9]

Let Jesus Be Your Reference Point

Some years ago I heard Scott Peck say that he felt that the Gospels were the best-kept secret in Christianity, and I'm inclined to agree. As we saw in the first part of this book, the dangerous memories that we have of the life of Jesus become the reference point for exiles. Our identity is bound up in our understanding of who he is and what he does and says. When we become obsessed with the Jesus of the Gospels, we cannot but yearn for the high seas. He is free—marvelously, frighteningly free—from the strictures of institutional religion. What would Jesus do? If we're serious about answering that question, we could find ourselves in the most liminal, missional experiences of our lives. Exilic leaders will teach their friends to marinate their lives in the Gospels themselves.

Embrace a Radical Spirituality of Engagement

Following Jesus means engaging meaningfully with the lives of others. How could we possibly believe that we could model our lives on him and remain distanced from the poor, the confused, the struggling, and the lost? Following Christ means more than not drinking or not swearing in polite company. It means facilitating a program for teenage mothers. It means preaching the gospel in a refugee camp. Jesus' life is not primarily marked by retreat, reflection, and solitude. Although he did have such experiences, for him they were rarities, punctuation points in a life of engagement, action, connection. In Matt 9:35 we are told that "Jesus went through *all* the towns and villages, preaching in their synagogues, preaching the good news of the kingdom and healing *every* disease and sickness." This is an awesome itinerary, and it indicates a high spirituality of engagement. The exilic leader will

---

[9]I am indebted to Darryn Altclass of Third Place Communities for these suggestions. They are drawn from the unpublished notes from a seminar entitled "The Habits of a Missional Leader," one of the best presentations of missional church principles that I have ever heard.

take a stance that assumes that engagement is normal and retreat is an occasional but necessary feature of spirituality.

BE INSPIRED BY PREVENIENT GRACE

In two of my previous books, *The Shaping of Things to Come* (coauthored with Alan Hirsch) and *Seeing God in the Ordinary*,[10] I have explored the issue of prevenient grace at length. To believe in prevenient grace is to assume that God goes before us even into the most irreligious situations and creates fields or environments in which our Christlike example can be received. Think of the verb "prevene." It is related to the idea of "convene." When one convenes a meeting, he or she opens that meeting and conducts it. But someone had to prevene that meeting before it began. A hall had to be booked, an agenda had to be determined, seats had to be set out. To prevene is to go beforehand and prepare in advance. Says the writer of Ecclesiastes, "He has made everything beautiful in its time. He has also set eternity in the hearts of men; yet they cannot fathom what God has done from beginning to end" (Eccl 3:11). It's the eternity in our hearts that draws us into the search for God, the very same God who is searching after us always. Exiles acknowledge that. They go confidently into the world on the assumption that God goes beforehand. Our job, then, is not to make things happen, but to cooperate with God, who is already making them happen.

FOLLOW THE MISSIONARY GOD INTO STRANGE PLACES

If exiles are looking for where God is already working, they might be surprised by what they find. They might find God in the bar or the biker gang, in the strip club or the casino. Of course, they might find God evangelizing refugee camps, but also working in the Green movement or protesting against the WTO. No one in Jesus' time would have thought to find God eating with tax collectors or playing with children. God shattered the preconceptions of religious people then, and does so today. I have met bands of exiles heading up a biker gang in Melbourne, Australia; running a dance venue in Pomona, California; hanging out in an inner-city bar in Birmingham, England; heading up a public art co-op in San Francisco; managing a skateboard park in Gisborne, New Zealand; running a pub in Bradford, England; managing a mobile drop-in center in Toronto, Canada; and managing a floating café on a canal in Amsterdam, Holland. I know people who, following God's missional impulse, have developed Christian collectives in busi-

---

[10]Michael Frost, *Seeing God in the Ordinary: A Theology of the Everyday* (Peabody, Mass.: Hendrickson, 2000).

nesses such as a shoe store in San Francisco, a record store in Brisbane, a sporting goods store in Mission, Canada, a hot dog restaurant in Pittsburgh, and an Italian restaurant in Melbourne.

Inspire People around You to Do the Same

Here's the rub. Exiles are finding themselves falling into the cracks between a host empire that they cannot embrace and a church that they cannot relate to. Many leave the church and find themselves enjoying the freedom of being released from the many commitments that churches require of them, but they also find themselves adrift, alone on the high seas in a very small craft with very few, if any, sharing the journey with them. As we noted the preceding chapter, what we yearn for is a band or a collective of like-minded souls with whom we can embrace a challenge, an ordeal of sorts, that can ignite our passion for humankind and for our Lord and Savior, Jesus. Exiles want what they haven't found in their churches: a free, organic, egalitarian communitas bound together by a common cause, a cause greater than themselves, a cause for justice, grace, and peace. If this describes your yearning, I hate to break the news to you, but no one is going to create such a communitas for you. Exiles, sick of mainstream churches but tired of going it alone, have to embrace the challenge to fashion collectives of exiles and lead them into mission. You might establish a mission to teenage mothers or develop a small business that provides opportunities to help the environment or serve the poor or befriend the lonely. You might simply water ski every Sunday or start a discussion group in an independent bookstore. But whatever you do, be prepared to lead others into a deeper communion with each other and with God. Before you know it, you might have fifteen people, and not long after that you might end up with more than a bunch of people. You might have a collective of exiles bound together by a common cause. Dare I say it? You might even have incidentally planted a *church*.

When Is a Bunch Actually a Church?

This is the question I am asked more than any other. When is a group of exiles more than just a bunch of believers who happen to have bumped into each other at a conference or a social gathering? I mean, if occasionally I have a drink at the local pub with a few other Christians, are we the church? Are we churching? Are we an expression of the church universal? Are we a local church? Some exiles have tried to convince me that because Jesus promised that he will be with us whenever two or three meet together in his name, that any such gathering is church. I love the freedom offered by Jesus' statement in Matt 18:20, that his followers don't need a special building or an ancient liturgy or a large quorum to know that he is with us, present in our midst. But if the sum total of my communal experience of following Jesus is limited to occasional, irregular gatherings of people who have neither asked for a commitment from me nor offered any to me, surely something is missing. Taking Jesus' one statement and building a whole ecclesiology on it is naïve, even dangerous. In fact, I think that it can be cogently argued that the whole of the New Testament was written to communities of believers, not individuals, and that the epistles especially are written with the obvious assumption that followers of Jesus will be in committed collectives of fellow believers.

So, Christianity is a communal faith. There can be no question of that, really. But exiles have fled the "solid church," with its static structure of weekly standardized meetings, safe spirituality, inoffensive values, and exclusive and self-serving membership. They feel liberated from the sterility of institutional religion. How can exiles go back to safe, conventional churches? Well, maybe what's required is a rediscovery of what actually constitutes a biblical ecclesiology. When exiles have experienced a missional communitas, their appetites are whetted for an ongoing experience of communal, Jesus-centered faith, but they don't want the whole package of the traditional church. Often exiles will pose the question this way: "What's the bare minimum that a group of exiles must do or be in order to church effectively?" The question isn't put as a means of avoiding commitment or effort, but rather as an attempt to recover the simple, unadulterated freshness of the original Christian project.

Some years ago, New Zealand church leader Michael Riddell explored this very question in his groundbreaking book *Threshold of the Future*. Having detailed several missional or experimental church projects, Riddell distills a list of fifteen indicators or common features of these emerging models. They include an emphasis on relationship, honesty and reality, dynamic ecumenism, countercultural values, and laughter, with little emphasis on buildings, size, and structures.[11] Although I resonate with Riddell's list of

---

[11]Michael Riddell, *Threshold of the Future: Reforming the Church in the Post-Christian West* (London: SPCK, 1998), 168–71. Riddell's full list of fifteen indicators is summarized as follows:

1. High premium placed on relationships
2. Commitment to honesty and reality
3. Minimal organizational structure
4. Connection of the community's worship and faith life with the everyday cultural experience of the participants
5. Commitment to communal openness and inclusivity
6. Dynamic ecumenism
7. Commitment to mission
8. Ability of members to laugh and cry together

indicators, I see them more as descriptors of the communal life of certain missional churches than as the universal characteristics of the emerging models of missional church. I prefer to explore the issue with broader brush strokes, looking for general principles that can be applied to myriad churches regardless of, say, how much laughter and tears they experience or how minimal their structures are.

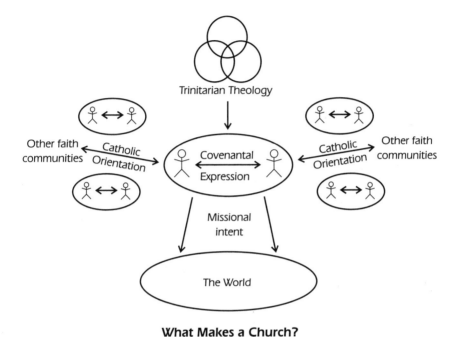

What Makes a Church?

So here's my attempt at posing the "bare minimum" requirements for a missional communitas or a group of believers to church together effectively.[12]

---

   9. Scripture respected and allowed to speak in an inductive and topical manner
   10. The surrounding culture taken seriously not only as a mission field, but also as a potential source of God's activity
   11. Little importance placed on buildings
   12. Intentional small size to allow greater intimacy and flexibility
   13. Appreciation of genuine spirituality
   14. Presence as gracious spaces of refuge
   15. Countercultural with respect of Western values such as materialism and individualism

[12]In *The Shaping of Things to Come*, 76–81, Alan Hirsch and I offer a simple, three-sided framework for churching: communion, community, commission. Although I think that this framework still holds, I'm aware that many parachurch agencies can embrace these three commitments without necessarily emulating the

I've managed to get it down to four criteria. Of course, other authors will suggest other criteria, but my four requirements for elevating a bunch of believers into the wonderful project of churching together are, put simply, these:

1. Trinitarian in theology

2. Covenantal in expression

3. Catholic in orientation

4. Missional in intent

Let's look at these more fully.

Trinitarian in Theology

At the core of Christian belief stands the Trinity, and its rediscovery and centrality in the life of a group of Christians provide both the framework for genuine community and the spiritual glue for it. God as Father invites us to be his apprentice-children (as we saw earlier); God as Son inspires us to participate in the extension of the kingdom around the world; God as Holy Spirit directs us to acknowledge Jesus as Lord and offers us every good gift in living it out.

In a time of religious pluralism, our belief in the Trinity is a resource that actually furnishes the grounds for what Kevin Vanhoozer calls a "harmonious reconciliation rather than a violent repression of the plurality that so marks our age."[13] In fact, Vanhoozer claims, quite rightly, that despite accusations of narrowness and intolerance, Christian faith can address the problem of pluralism via the doctrine of the Trinity far better than other religious claims. In his book *The Trinity in a Pluralistic Age,* a number of scholars argue that Trinitarian theology does this in several ways:

- Thinking of God as Trinity can help counteract the rampant individualism of our day. The self-giving love of the Trinity encourages us toward compassion and reconciliation (which are included in proclaiming the gospel).

- Compassion and relationship are intricately linked. Because God is one-in-three in eternal relationship, we can be certain of the basis of God's compassion toward us and others.

---

depth of communal, worshipful, missional life we see in Paul's churches. Nonetheless, I suggest that readers consider that section in *The Shaping of Things to Come* alongside the points I'm about to make in the rest of this chapter.

[13]Kevin J. Vanhoozer, ed., *The Trinity in a Pluralistic Age: Theological Essays on Culture and Religion* (Grand Rapids: Eerdmans, 1997), x.

- A Trinitarian-based theology respects and learns from otherness (pluralistic) while holding that one message is true for everyone (exclusivistic).

- Trinitarian theology restores a sense of mystery to our understanding of God and rejects the ill-fated attempts by the Enlightenment at absolute certainty/foundationalist thinking, which has also been so thoroughly rejected by postmoderns. When they think that they're discarding Christianity, they are really only rejecting the Platonic-Aristotelian philosophical framework of the Middle Ages. In this way, a recovery of Trinitarian thinking helps us rescue Christianity from the postmodern critique.

- Because the Trinity is a mystery revealed to us despite our idolatory and self-righteousness, our gratitude as recipients of divine grace motivates us to show respect towards those whose beliefs differ from our own.

- The life of the Trinity is an interpersonal fellowship in which we, by grace, participate (as insiders), and at the same time the life of the Trinity provides a model for human living (as we look from an outsider's perspective).

This last point is key.[14] We participate in the Trinity as God's children and Jesus' joint heirs, and we also stand back at a distance, observing the interaction between the three persons of the Trinity, learning from their community as a model for ours. Since God's nature is communal, exiles should not imagine that they can live this life of faith alone. A traditional hymn describes the mirror images of the interrelationships within the Trinity and within Christian communities:

Blest be the tie that binds
Our hearts in Christian love;
The fellowship of kindred minds
Is like to that above.

Covenantal in Expression

One of Christianity's most famous and effective exiles was a sixth-century Italian hermit named Benedict. He lived in a time when the European church was compromised by wealth and power and so grossly in league with the state as to make it virtually a secular department of the legal and political system. True followers of the exile Jesus were disgusted by the pallid state of the church and left in droves, most finding their way into monasteries

---

[14]See Richard Bauckham, "Jürgen Moltmann's *The Trinity and the Kingdom of God* and the Question of Pluralism," in Vanhoozer, *Trinity in a Pluralistic Age*, 155–64.

or, like Benedict, into solitude. As a monk, Benedict lived in a hermitage, ministering only to those who sought him out for wisdom or spiritual succor. However, his study of the Scriptures and his genuine attempt to live out the life of Christ in solitude left him with the conclusion that Jesus' teaching required him to be in contact with other people. He realized that one cannot do Christianity alone. He began organizing fellow exiles—hermits—into communities, channeling their passion for Jesus into a form of communitas.

Benedict's simple plan was to foster households of twelve people each,[15] bringing hermits, monks, and other exiles from the corrupt institutional church to live together in Christ, supporting each other to live out the teachings of Jesus. Benedict's households were communities of intimacy, openness, love, and gentleness. He established leaders in each house, godly people, able to encourage the household as described by Paul in 1 Thessalonians:

> Instead, we were like young children among you. Just as a nursing mother cares for her children, so we cared for you. Because we loved you so much, we were delighted to share with you not only the gospel of God but our lives as well. . . . You are witnesses, and so is God, of how holy, righteous and blameless we were among you who believed. For you know that we dealt with each of you as a father deals with his own children, encouraging, comforting and urging you to live lives worthy of God, who calls you into his kingdom and glory. (1 Thess 2:7–8, 10–12)

And then Benedict did a striking thing, much copied down through history. He developed an order for each house, a set of rules that would ensure a godly cohesion among all the members. Each member of the household was to make a pledge of loyalty to the others, and they to him. In making this pledge, each new member was promising to embrace the order that governed the community for the good of all. The Rule of St. Benedict is now famous, but try to imagine it as a religious and social experiment embraced by fellow exiles in the sixth century. Benedict began his list of rules with the following encouragement:

> We are, therefore, about to found a school of the Lord's service, in which we hope to introduce nothing harsh or burdensome. But even if, to correct vices or to preserve charity, sound reason dictates anything we do is too stringent, do not at once fly in dismay from the way of salvation, the beginning of which cannot but be narrow. But as we advance in the religious life and faith, we shall run the way of God's commandments with expanded hearts and unspeakable sweetness of love; so that never depart-

---

[15]Initially, Benedict's community houses were for men only, but today there are many more women than men in Benedictine houses across the world.

ing from His guidance and persevering in the monastery in His doctrine till death, we may by patience share in the sufferings of Christ, and be found worthy to be coheirs with Him of His kingdom.[16]

Then follow seventy-three rules covering everything from how much food the community was to eat, to how the community was to care for the very young or very old (with kindness), to how women were to be treated (with special attention), to how to deal with those who fail to keep the rule (with grace), to what work to undertake, to how to elect a leader. They might seem old-fashioned and overly restrictive today. The slavish allegiance to rules like these was partly the very thing that the Reformers railed against. But the idea of a collective of exiles, escaping a corrupt church and resisting the forces of secular culture, living in harmony to serve Christ is the very thing we need to recover today. In Rule 72 Benedict wrote,

Let our members put their zeal for Christ into action by being careful to prefer one another to themselves. Serve your brothers and sisters with pure and sincere love. Fear God and obey your leaders with sincere and humble affection. Never let anything be exalted above Christ. And may he bring us as a people together to eternal life.[17]

Who wouldn't desire such "expanded hearts and unspeakable sweetness of love"? Throughout the Christian movement there have been similar orders—the Franciscans, the Dominicans, and other Mendicant orders—all with their own particular rule. The Poor Clares, named for their founder, Clara Offreduccio, embrace the following rule: "Bless people. Eat with them. Heal the sick. Preach the gospel." Many of them were responsible for the regeneration of the church and the flowering of Western culture.

It's true, as Martin Luther and John Calvin and the other Reformers pointed out, that we are saved by faith, through God's grace revealed in Jesus Christ. Many exiles entered these orders in an attempt to earn their salvation by good works, self-discipline, and suffering. But in Christ we are free from such a dreadful, never-ending rowing toward God. God has drawn near, shown his love through Jesus, and redeemed us from sin and death. But that doesn't mean that exiles today won't see the need to band together with fellow travelers and fashion "households" of acceptance, love, nurture, shared goals, common projects, communal life. As Tom Sine says,

---

[16]"The Holy Rule of St. Benedict," St. Benedict's Abbey n.p. [cited 21 February 2006]. Online: http://www.kansasmonks.org/fr___abbey.html Our Way of Life/ Rule of St. Benedict. The quotation comes from the 1949 edition of The Holy Rule of St. Benedict, translated by Rev. Boniface Verheyen of St. Benedict's Abbey, Atchison, Kansas.

[17]Ibid.

We will need to aggressively work for the re-monking of the church to enable followers of Jesus Christ to intentionally set the focus and rhythm of their lives out of biblical calling instead of cultural coercion.[18]

And what is "re-monking"? Stuart Murray, in his very helpful book, *Post-Christendom*, takes up Sine's idea by suggesting that a post-Christendom church might reimagine itself as "a monastic missionary order, communities of encouragement, support and training from which we emerge to live as Christians in the workplace and to which we return for reflection and renewal."[19] I don't propose (and neither does Murray, from what I can work out) that we all need to live in the same house (though if you want to, go right ahead—I couldn't think of anything worse!). Rather, I think it means finding a group of comrades who will be bound to you by a "rule," a set of common values and commitments. And when you find it, you'll realize there is nothing sweeter.

In my own community, smallboatbigsea, a collective of exiles based on Sydney's north shore, we have developed a simple rule or order to our communal life. It is summarized by the acrostic BELLS.

- **Bless. We will bless at least one other member of our community every day.** This will take different forms. We might simply send an e-mail expressing our affirmation. We might write a letter, deliver a gift, say a word of encouragement. It might sound difficult, but you'd be surprised how easy it is once you've got into the hang of it. And it's marvelous to be in a community of such support and consideration.

- **Eat. We will eat with other members of our community at least three times each week.** In our community we all eat together every Sunday night, each of us bringing a plate of food to share with the others. Also, we are divided into groups of three that meet weekly for mutual accountability, discipleship, and nurture. Those smaller cells usually meet over a meal or coffee (my group meets for breakfast each week). So, two meals a week are already locked in. It's very simple to ensure that we share one more meal with someone else in our collective.

- **Listen. We will commit ourselves weekly to listening to the promptings of God in our lives.** Again, this will take different forms for different people. Some of us are very spiritually intuitive and hear from God in visions, pictures, and other ecstatic experiences. Others of us make our weekly commitment to search out God's voice in less spectacular ways. We will ensure

[18]Cited in Heather Wraight, ed., *They Call Themselves Christians: Papers on Nominality Given at the International Lausanne Consultation on Nominalism, December 1998* (London: Christian Research, 1998), 109.

[19]Murray, *Post-Christendom*, 280.

a weekly time of solitude to listen to God. We will take a prayer walk, find time alone in a special place, use prayer beads, and so on.

- **Learn. We will read from the Gospels each week and remain diligent in learning more about Jesus.** Of course, we encourage our members to read the whole Bible and to have a regular rhythm of biblical study. But in our attempts to be a Jesus-centered collective, we emphasize a weekly exploration of the Gospel stories about him.

- **Sent. We will see our daily life as an expression of our sent-ness by God into this world.** Earlier we looked at the dualism that has beset the mainstream church, a dualism that assumes that our life outside church is irrelevant to the extension of God's kingdom. We looked at being apprentice-children and doing the work of God through things such as truth-telling, building, healing, and naming. At smallboatbigsea we are committed to looking out for ways in which our daily lives can be expressions of our "sent-ness," our mission as agents of God's grace on this planet. This will include acts of hospitality and the just stewardship of our resources, as well as working for justice and striving for global peace. A great framework for thinking of our sent-ness can be found in the text that Jesus used to describe his own sense of being sent to the world. In Luke 4:18–19 Jesus outlines his ministry to include: sharing the gospel ("good news to the poor"), attacking the consequences of poverty ("release to the captives"), overcoming disability and illness ("recovery of sight to the blind"), defeating the causes of poverty ("liberation to those who are oppressed"), and celebration and reconciliation ("proclaiming the year of the Lord's favor").

As mentioned earlier, we all meet together each week to share a love feast. That weekly meal is conducted along the same BELLS rule, but at this time it is more like a liturgy. We gather and bless each other, speaking words of encouragement and affirmation over one another. For visitors, people whom we don't know very well, we have a list of generic blessings drawn from Scripture, such as the Aaronic blessing or Paul's blessing to the Ephesians, or from other sources, such as Celtic or traditional church blessings. Then we eat. Oh, how we eat! Magnificent food and cheap wines are placed on the shared table. During the meal, we break bread and dip it in wine to celebrate Jesus' presence with us and to remember his sacrificial death on the cross. Everyone brings something to share with others, and as we consume it, we naturally express our gratitude to God and each other, asking others for the recipe of the delicious creations that we are enjoying.

After the meal, we spend time listening to God and sharing with each other anything we've heard God say to us that week. Then we have a time of shared learning, conducted by various members of the tribe. Some deliver short monologues; others lead us in a more interactive learning time. Finally, we leave time for people to share how the shadow of God's work was revealed in their sent-ness that week. People talk about their work as healers or truth-tellers or builders and are affirmed for the efforts that they have undertaken. In this way, we try to break down the dualism that occurs in many churches, where our daily lives are completely irrelevant to our Sunday experience.

Experiments like this are taking place all over the world. In downtown Austin, in historic Old Enfield, about two miles from the University of Texas, you'll find Oak Grove Abbey. Housed in a beautiful six-bedroom mansion built in 1937, Oak Grove Abbey is a monastic community modeled on the traditional monasteries of old, but with a very contemporary vibe (the abbey even has a deck and a solarium!). Launched by Greg Willis as a missional project a few years ago, the abbey is designed to fashion a missional community that develops holistic ways of living and learning together, while encouraging its members to learn the "native language" of postmodern Austin as they work in and serve the local community. It does this by expecting the following practices from its members:

- Each participant is required to either have a flexible part-time job that is highly relational (coffee shop, bookstore, etc.) or time devoted to a particular craft that may become a small business (making clothes, etc.).

- Each participant is required to share common household duties, such as cleaning, cooking, and gardening, on a rotating basis.

- Each participant is required to maintain a series of communal learning assignments, which will include reading, regular seminars, group discussion, and writing as set by the leaders.

As in any monastic community, a structured daily rhythm is central to the Oak Grove Abbey way of life. Each day contains morning, midday, and evening prayer. There are also designated times for working, seminars, reading, and common meals. I haven't visited Oak Grove Abbey, but I did meet Greg in Dallas, and we have remained in contact. Here he describes the first Holy Week at the abbey:

Palm Sunday—Sean pieced together a wonderful liturgy, including responsive reading, singing, and casual reflection. We raised the palms of our hands in worship. Definitely launched the week with the right spirit of organic reverence.

Monday—Sean and Melissa included black mission figs with our evening meal, and we discussed the cursing of the fig tree over dinner. Our less Christianized friend Callaway informed us of a tongue-in-cheek website called godhatesfigs.com.

Tuesday—We walked in circles around the Abbey, imagining ourselves walking back and forth about Jerusalem and listening to Jesus' many teachings and encounters with the Jewish religious elite. We noted that Jesus' rhetoric no longer held any punches as He confronted hypocrisy with "reckless abandon." We could feel the tense inertia leading towards His arrest and death.

Wednesday—Melissa retold the story of Mary anointing Jesus' feet with expensive nard. She noted that the disciples misunderstood her and judged her critically, but Jesus was moved by her unique intuition and extravagant act of worship.

Thursday—Sean took his small group of high school boys to the upper room of the Abbey as they relived that beautiful evening together. I had an opportunity to tell the story with my coworkers and to make a small gesture (less vulnerable than feet washing) that communicated to them that I care about them deeply.

Friday—Jolie prepared a Seder meal and rehearsed the major details of Passover. Our understanding of the Lord's Supper was greatly enriched by realizing the obvious moments that Jesus would have used to offer His New Interpretation of the bread and the wine. No Jewish person would ever have forgotten the radical way in which He demonstrated His fulfillment of these time-honored rituals! After dinner, we observed the Stations of the Cross using contemporary icons.

Saturday—The day of waiting. Fittingly, we aerated our garden to prepare the soil for planting.

Easter—We went to the park where Melissa had invited some of the underprivileged children she teaches to come with their families. Although it was cold and windy, the few kids who came (including Connor) had a great time running around on the playground. Sean and Melissa gave the breakfast leftovers to homeless people. That afternoon, Jolie led Connor through the story that goes with the Resurrection eggs. We had a big celebration dinner, where each of us summarized what we had done throughout the week. This gave us a good context for truly tasting the Victory of the empty tomb! We were especially glad to have my friend Tim with us for the retelling. After dinner, we watched **Romero** on the big screen. Profound and unsettling—you should see it.[20]

---

[20]"First Holy Week at the Abbey," n.p. [cited 17 January 2006]. Online: http://oakgroveabbey.com/news/index.php?id=8. On similar monastic communities see Rob Moll, "The New Monasticism," *Christianity Today* 49, no. 9 (September 2005), 38–40.

Similar new monastic experiments are happening around the United States, including Simple Way in Philadelphia, Camden House in Camden, New Jersey, and Rutba House in Durham, North Carolina. I consider such communal life to be covenantal in nature. That is, the commitment to celebrate Christ's presence, to share life with each other, and to embrace mission together is more than a promise or a pledge. It is a covenant, like a marriage, a union of more than one party centered on shared values and commitments. There is more going on than the acts of worship or gathering or mission themselves; it is a symbol of what is taking place and has taken place invisibly in our spirits. We have been joined together in a spiritual communion. The community itself is a holy thing, much more than a gathering of like-minded people, but it requires the explicit commitment of the members to God and to each other and to the world they have been sent to serve.

Catholic in Orientation

To be catholic in the true sense of the word is to be conscious of your place in the universal church, across both time and space. Churching involves a gracious recognition of the small part that our community plays in the millennia-long project of Christian mission. Rejection of the wider body of Christ and withdrawal into some haughty rarefied atmosphere wherein we assume that we've "got it" and everyone else is wrong is neither helpful nor honest. When we church, we should have an eye to some level of connectivity with other brothers and sisters. You might be surprised to hear me say this, since the whole tone of this book so far may seem to imply that we need to give up the mainstream church as a lost cause. I have never once said that the church is a lost cause, nor have I ever encouraged anyone to leave the church for dead. However, I am keenly aware of the hundreds of thousands of exiles who have done so, as well as those who are attending traditional churches while in internal exile. I'm sympathetic to their frustrations and motivations, and I'm eager for them to hold on to their passion for Jesus and their love for humankind without losing heart while adrift in the sea of postmodern culture. When exiles band together to church with each other in the ways that I've described, I believe that they have something of an obligation to speak back into the regular church.

Remember Victor Turner's belief that liminal communities push the mainstream forward, bringing it vitality, innovation, and creativity? Every new exilic community does the same to the church. The Benedictines and the Franciscans did. So did the Reformers and the Anabaptists. So did the Enthusiasts such as Wesley, Whitefield, Harris, and the Methodists. And the Booths and their Salvation Army. And the Pentecostals. The liberty experienced in Christian communitas sows a seed of cultural regeneration back into the mainstream church. The church is growing across the world and has grown across time. Exilic communities are aware of their place in it. They are global in their perspective and will actively support overseas missions. They are local in their expression and will just as actively seek to serve the other traditional churches in their midst.

This isn't to say that the more traditional church will necessarily be receptive to you. Many people have trouble identifying a group of Christians as a church if they don't have a building, a certificate of denominational authenticity, or an ordained leader. We have had more than one person join our community and report that their Christian friends in the mainstream church have warned them away from us, suggesting that we might not even be Christians. But we mustn't allow ourselves to be marginalized into closed, secretive communities. I say live it out large, loud, and wonderfully free in Christ, doing our level best to bless other churches in any way we can.

Missional in Intent

This might go without saying, given the previous chapter, but we church best with those with whom we share a common goal or mission. I especially wanted to discuss communitas before looking at ecclesiology. In fact, I believe that our proper understanding of Christ (Christology) leads us into an appropriate commitment to mission (missiology), which forces us to develop the means of a common life together (ecclesiology). It must happen in that order. Too many churches begin by trying to artificially develop an ecclesiology, determining first where to meet, what songs to sing, what to preach, how to have small groups and leadership structures. Instead, as we noted Antoine de Saint-Exupéry saying, to build a ship, you must first create a hunger for the sea. That hunger comes from our familiarity with Jesus. His Spirit will force us out onto the rising tide, and it's then, and only then, that we will need to develop the most appropriate structures for worship, communal life, and leadership. Many of these structures are negotiable, and they differ around the world and from denomination to denomination. God is blessing churches whose worship style and leadership arrangements are as different as chalk and cheese. It's not that important. What's more important, in fact essential, is our familiarity with Jesus and the heartbeat of mission that it fosters.

You might disagree with my brief list and think that certain other elements should be included. In the Church of England report *Mission-Shaped Church,* the authors identify five essentials quite similar to mine. They say that emerging or missional expressions of church are (1) focused on God as Trinity, (2) incarnational, (3) transformational, (4) disciple-making, and

(5) relational. The authors have also identified several key indicators for each element.[21] I have no objection to this list, and I'm thrilled to see such an august body as the Church of England being prepared to endorse communities, Anglican or not, that have these five elements at their core.

A Day by the Sea

The community at smallboatbigsea isn't the epitome of everything that a group of exiles churching together should be. Often I'm loath to talk about them for fear that they'll feel like they're just a case study or an exhibit for others to examine. They're my dearest friends and my life companions. They share with me a Trinitarian theology, a sacramental rule for our common life, a connectivity to the wider church, and a commitment to both global and local mission. But we make mistakes. We fall short of our ideals. Sometimes we let each other down. Nevertheless, we press on, and oftentimes we get it just right.

A little while ago, we baptized my youngest daughter, Fielding. Our whole community met in a grassy park on the edge of Sydney Harbor. From the park, there is a steep sea cliff down to a very small, enclosed sandy beach, accessed by a narrow wooden staircase. As we approached the stairs, each of was given a handful of frangipani flowers to carry onto the beach. It was a gorgeous summer day, and the waters of Sydney Harbor shimmered in the bright sunlight. The few sunbathers on the sand below might have thought it strange to see scores of people of differing ages proceeding down the rickety stairs with flowers in their hands. Some bystanders showed quite a bit of interest in us. One woman asked me if we were an extended family disposing of the ashes of a deceased relative. "Close," I thought. After all, baptism is about dying to one's past and embracing new life in Christ. She hung around to watch the proceedings. My oldest daughter, Courtney, noticed some of her old school friends sitting on the beach, and they informally joined the crowd. There we were, a strange but beautiful collection of exiles, thrown together by a common cause, celebrating the flowering of a wonderful, passionate young woman's faith.

Jackie, a DJ and psychology student who has mentored Fielding, spoke about her faith and her beautiful character, recommending Fielding to us as a woman of joy and passion. Katrina, a young mother in our community

---

[21]Mission and Public Affairs Council of the Church of England, *Mission-Shaped Church: Church Planting and Fresh Expressions of Church in a Changing Context* (London: Church House, 2004).

whose children have brought much happiness to Fielding, read from the
Scriptures. Carolyn prayed for her daughter, and I explained the ancient rite
of baptism and why we were doing this, before we all moved to the water's
edge. Once there, everyone cast the frangipanis on the water, and Fielding
and I waded in, surrounded by floating stars of white and bright yellow.

After I had immersed her in the salty water, Fielding was swept up into
the fresh air, the rushing water scattering the frangipanis around us. I looked
out to the community gathered on the shore. Dave, the personal photogra-
pher for the mayor of Sydney, was snapping shots of everyone. Barbara, old
enough to be Fielding's grandmother, with whom she shares duties in the
children's program we run on Sundays, was beaming with pride. Greg, a so-
licitor, was explaining what was happening to his little daughter, Hannah.
Amy, a social worker, had brought a teenage relative along and was talking
with her about what Fielding had just done. Susan, a nurse, gave Fielding a
candle as a gift.

Later, we opened picnic baskets, spread out blankets, and did what we do
best: we ate and laughed and talked and played with the children. We blessed
each other. We heard from God in the beauty of fellowship, the lapping of the
water on the sand, and the toughness of a young woman's pledges of discipleship. We swam in the harbor, and threw balls on the beach. The portable
stereo played some cool beach music, and we hung out and celebrated with
Fielding and enjoyed companionship with one another. And all along I
thought, "I am so glad that I church with these people. It's way better than
just being a bunch."

7

Exiles at the Table

The Promise: We Will Be Generous and Practice Hospitality

> For it is only in company that eating is done
> justice; food must be divided and distributed if it
> is to be well received.
>
> —Walter Benjamin

There's a fabulously evocative scene in the marvelous French film *Amélie* in which two wine glasses levitate slightly above a restaurant table. They are being blown gently up above the table's surface by the billowing tablecloth, which has caught a slight breeze coming across the balcony. Of course, for such a quirky thing to happen, the wind would have to be perfectly pitched under the cloth. Too hard, and it would blow the fragile glasses over; too soft, and they would hold the cloth firmly in place. The film is full of such wonderfully unlikely images.

But what delighted my wife and I so much about that scene was the fact that we had eaten one of the best meals of our lives at that very table on that very balcony overlooking Paris. Patachou is a restaurant perched on the top of a steep embankment in Montmartre; its balcony, seeming to teeter on the precipice, looks out over the City of Light below. We ate the works that night—appetizers, duck, cheese, wine, crème caramel—and it was sensational. All the while, dark purple clouds bruised the horizon as a ferocious storm gathered from the west. Just as we drained our glasses of the dregs of our cheap(ish) red wine, the most astonishing thunderstorm swept in over the city and bucketed rain over Montmartre. Our waiter ushered us into the safety of the main restaurant, and we all laughed out loud at the ferociousness of the rain—each of the falling drops seemed as big as a child's fist. Later, as the storm eased, we made a dash through the drenched cobblestone streets, shimmering in the moonlight. From Montmartre we took the Metro to the Pont Alexandre across the Seine.

We'll never forget it. It was a feeling of exhilarating aliveness, even bliss. It was the sensation of blood surging through our veins, our bodies charged with the excitement of a terrific storm, a delicious meal, a romantic evening. I'm still conscious of the sense of gratitude that I feel toward God for so wonderful an experience. In fact, it seems like a sacred event, a moment when we touched God. Why can't a superb meal on a glistening, rain-soaked balcony be seen as a religious experience? It's really about having the eyes to see God's grace in the ordinary things of life. Instead of thinking of ordinary, everyday activities such as eating as mundane and unholy, let's consider how we might see them as opportunities to bring God and his grace into our everyday world.

The Deadly Sin of Gluttony

Of all the meals we've eaten in our lives—around two hundred thousand by the time we're forty years of age—how many of them felt sacred? How many of them felt like moments in which we connected with God, our world, and our tablemates? How many of them were charged by gratitude, love, astonishment, and joy? And conversely, how many of them stand out as experiences of sheer indulgence and surplus—meals at which we ate so much that we felt sick, guilty, and disgusted with ourselves? Many of the exiles whom I have met have become sick of the excess and the thoughtless, cavalier way of dealing with food as entertainment. Across the Western world there is an obesity epidemic. For example, some estimates have it that more than 60 percent of all Americans are overweight or obese, including 37 percent of children and adolescents. Obesity has been linked to hypertension, heart disease, adult onset diabetes, stroke, gall bladder disease, osteoarthritis, sleep apnea, respiratory problems, lower back pain, various forms of cancer, and much more. In fact, if left unabated, obesity will surpass smoking as the leading cause of preventable death in the United States.

And all the while, overweight people are lining up at fast-food outlets to "supersize" their meals to include a liter of soft drink and a bucketful of fries. Each and every day of the year, a quarter of all Americans will eat at a fast-food restaurant. In fact, McDonalds alone serves more than forty-six million people each day in 118 countries—more than the populations of Canada or Australia or Spain. And it's getting worse. In 1972 Americans spent $3 billion a year on fast food. Today it is more than $110 billion, with 40 percent of American meals being eaten outside the home (a man in California once told me that he hid his wife's birthday and Christmas presents in the oven because he knew she'd never look there!). In his shocking documentary about fast food, *Super Size Me,* filmmaker Morgan Spurlock showed first-grade children a series of pictures of famous people and asked them to identify as many as they could. Not one child could identify the picture of a bearded, long-haired Jesus figure. Every one of them not only recognized Ronald Mc-Donald and Wendy, but also became visibly excited by the image.

There is very little that is sacred about meals anymore. Our parents didn't slaughter the animal we are eating (incidentally, in the United States we consume more than one million animals an hour). We as a family didn't pray throughout the year that our crops wouldn't fail. We didn't pitch in at harvest time to bring the crop in for sale. Often, our parents didn't cook the meal from scratch, preferring packaged and precooked meals. Many families don't eat together around a table; some family members take their plates to their room, while others perch them on their laps in front of the television. The closest we might get to sacred eating is Christmas or Thanksgiving, but so many of our everyday eating habits treat food and cooking as annoyances or interruptions.

The biblical word for all this indulgence is, of course, gluttony. The medieval church considered it one of the seven deadly sins, and yet, while the Scriptures do contain warnings against immoderation in the consumption of food and drink, they are surprisingly few in number. In most cases, the Bible counsels against overindulgence because of the negative ramifications of overeating or overdrinking. Proverbs 23 contains several such warnings, but they are not of the "all gluttons go to hell" variety. In the most quoted verse on this topic, Prov 23:19–21 says,

Listen, my son, and be wise, and set your heart on the right path. Do not join those who drink too much wine or gorge themselves on meat, for drunkards and gluttons become poor, and drowsiness clothes them in rags.

Put simply, if you're regularly drunk or if your diet is poor, you will not be able to work efficiently and will end up broke. It's very practical advice against leaving your farm or your workbench to indulge in long, sodden lunches and not fulfilling your professional duties. By no means an injunction against eating well or enjoying wine, these verses offer the simple advice that we should work hard and avoid the injurious influences of drunkards and gluttons. In fact, chapter 23 of Proverbs has some charmingly useful advice about moderation. The writer compares eating at the tables of a king and of a stingy man and is critical of both for different reasons:

When you sit to dine with a ruler, note well what is before you, and put a knife to your throat if you are given to gluttony. Do not crave his delicacies, for that food is deceptive. (Prov 23:1–3)

Do not eat the food of a begrudging host, do not crave his delicacies;
for he is the kind of person who is always thinking about the cost. "Eat
and drink," he says to you, but his heart is not with you. You will vomit
up the little you have eaten and will have wasted your compliments.
(Prov 23:6–8)

On the one hand, don't be seduced by the gluttonous tidbits and luxuries served by kings, but on the other hand, don't waste your time on the par-
simonious offerings of the tight-fisted host. What marvelous balance! Back in
chapter 2 we observed the strict rules of hospitality employed in the Middle
East in Jesus' time and even today. Guests were expected to engage in loud
displays of appreciation regardless of how meager the meal might have been,
while all along the host downgrades the quality of his hospitality as being inadequate for the importance of the guest. Eating and drinking at the table of
a stingy person would be a waste of your compliments. You would feel sick,
almost to the point of vomiting, that you had to compromise yourself by
praising the miser's hospitality. The writer of the proverb is demanding that
we not linger at the table of indulgence and excess any longer than we do
at the table of miserliness. Eating at the table of a poor person, one who
couldn't afford much of a meal, is different. As custom has it, you must show
appreciation for all expressions of genuine hospitality, no matter how paltry.
What is not to be tolerated is a meal prepared by a person who could afford
much but who offers little.

At the Table of the Exile

As exiles, we can rightly look to the example of great biblical exiles such
as Joseph, Esther, Ruth, Daniel, Jesus, and Paul to see how we should eat. We
have already examined Jesus' approach to the table. His eating habits caused
no end of trouble during his lifetime, and they reveal to us the nature of genuinely exilic living. The other biblical exiles are good examples also. Let's
look at a few of them.

Joseph's Storehouses of Egypt

It's well known that Joseph was the eleventh and favorite son of Jacob,
sold into Egypt by his jealous brothers. Most people know about his rocky
rise to power as an exile in Egypt, punctuated by deception, imprisonment,
and remarkable good fortune. At age thirty, after his wise service in the court
of Pharaoh, he is elevated to rule over the nation. Genesis 41 describes

an exile with unbelievable power in a foreign land. He wears the Pharaoh's signet ring and appears in a wardrobe of fine linen and a gold necklace. When he went about the city in his imperial chariot, the crowds stood aside as his drivers shouted, "Make way!" He is given an Egyptian name, "Zaphenath-Paneah," and he marries Asenath, who is the daughter of an Egyptian priest, and fathers two sons. For a man of God, he is remarkably at home in his host empire.

Yet it's important to note that much of Joseph's success as an exile revolves around food. His very promotion to political power is predicated upon his God-given interpretation of Pharaoh's dream about the coming years of abundance and famine. Forewarned by Yahweh, Joseph knows that he must ensure restraint and discipline during the seven imminent years of plenty, so he effectively implements a strategy of food preservation and the necessary infrastructure for its storage. He is dizzyingly successful at this. Among a people that otherwise would have squandered their excess food, Joseph creates a new culture of moderation with the responsible regulation of national resources. He fashions a wealthy, developed nation with a capacity to preserve, not fritter away, its prosperity.

When the years of plenty gave way to seven years of prophesied famine, Egypt was well positioned to ride it out. But more than supplying the needs of Egyptians, Joseph's storehouses were full enough to alleviate the suffering of surrounding nations as well, including the prime minister's homeland of Canaan. The stories of how Joseph's brothers traveled from famine-ravaged Canaan to Egypt to purchase grain and how they were initially deceived and toyed with by their brother and later forgiven and blessed by him are well known. The exile, though initially ejected from his family and his nation, shows himself to be a man of generosity, hospitality, and good management of resources.

Surely today, in a world where thirty-five thousand people die of hunger each day, exiles will, like Joseph, be concerned with the equitable and responsible distribution of resources. Even if we live in a host nation that squanders its wealth and wastes its food, we can be galvanized into action by the ancient Egyptian prime minister Zaphenath-Paneah, who said to his brothers, "For two years now there has been a famine in the land, and for the next five years there will be no plowing and reaping. But God sent me ahead of you to preserve for you a remnant on earth and to save your lives by a great deliverance" (Gen 45:6–7).

Exiles do well to adopt a similar attitude, even if they don't have the political clout of a prime minister. If our host empire is not generous, it is our duty, like Joseph, to do our best to fashion a culture of generosity, temperance, moderation, and equitable aid toward foreign nations.

The Vegetarian Daniel

From the beginning of the book that bears his name, we learn that the exile Daniel was chosen to embark upon three years of language and cultural training at the Babylonian court of the King Nebuchadnezzar before entering royal service. Like all such acolytes, Daniel was given a Babylonian name ("Belteshazzar") and assigned a certain diet in keeping with the customs and habits of the Babylonian people. No doubt such an opportunity was a great honor, and the allocated food intake was generous. But Daniel resolves "not to defile himself with the royal food and wine" (Dan 1:8). The term "defile" is a loaded one, implying that there is something sacrilegious about Nebuchadnezzar's menu. But is that really the case? Ingratiating himself to one of the court officials, Daniel conspires with him to adjust his diet as a test to prove the good sense of Yahweh's dietary laws: "Please test your servants for ten days: Give us nothing but vegetables to eat and water to drink. Then compare our appearance with that of the young men who eat the royal food, and treat your servants in accordance with what you see" (Dan 1:12–13).

Naturally, after the allotted period of ten days Daniel and his vegetarian friends were healthier and better nourished than the other imperial students. This story opens the book of Daniel and establishes the relationship that the exile Daniel enjoys with the royal court of Babylon. Without capitulating to the mores of the court, he thrives physically and spiritually, and thereby he remains an affront to the values of that court. Just as centuries later Jesus would declare that his disciples were to be in the world but not of it, Daniel epitomizes the exile's dislocation and power. He doesn't belong in Nebuchadnezzar's court, and the imperial provisions don't belong in his belly. And yet Daniel's abstinence isn't a federal case. He quietly, subversively, designs his own menu and proves to the court that God's plan for healthy eating is the better.

Is vegetarianism, then, the divine plan for exiles? Not strictly. In all likelihood, Nebuchadnezzar's rich menu was full of carbohydrates and fat as well as containing certain foods not permitted by the law of Moses. Daniel's only recourse, short of instructing the royal kitchen how to prepare another menu altogether, was to eat simply prepared vegetables and to drink water. He doesn't feel the need to withdraw from the court. It's possible today, with the dietary laws of Israel now relaxed, for us to do likewise, to enter fully into a post-Christendom world without having to eat everything that's offered to us by advertisers, fast-food restaurants, and our friends. And we should be as equally vindicated as Daniel by appearing more healthy and better nourished than others. And yet how can we claim such a thing when churchgoing folk are just as obese as others?

Exiles will enjoy a good, healthy diet. They will eat in moderation, not stoically denying themselves all gastronomic pleasures, but enjoying delicious, fresh, tasty food just as God intended.

Paul and the Missional Table

Paul was an exile. He entered a self-imposed exile from the rigid and deeply disciplined Pharisaism of his adult life and embraced a newly found freedom in Christ without ever abandoning himself to the values of the Roman Empire. Like Jesus' eating habits, Paul's table manners are a window into his ministry. Rigorously trained to avoid contamination from unbelievers and pagans, Paul broke with all convention and regularly enjoyed the company and the hospitality of Gentiles. It's hard to fully comprehend how disturbingly radical it was for a Pharisee to share a table with a pagan, but Paul's eating habits have a distinctly missional motivation. He explains his new lifestyle this way:

> Though I am free and belong to no one, I have made myself a slave to everyone, to win as many as possible. To the Jews I became like a Jew, to win the Jews. To those under the law I became like one under the law (though I myself am not under the law), so as to win those under the law. To those not having the law I became like one not having the law (though I am not free from God's law but am under Christ's law), so as to win those not having the law. To the weak I became weak, to win the weak. I have become all things to all people so that by all possible means I might save some. I do all this for the sake of the gospel, that I may share in its blessings. (1 Cor 9:19–23)

His freedom in Christ allows him to enter fully into the worlds, customs, and practices of whomever he feels led to serve, whether Jew or Gentile. In fact, he goes further in 1 Cor 11:1 when he urges the Corinthians to actually follow his example of missional socializing with unbelievers. Now, this was a very tricky thing to suggest in Corinth at that time, as the city was awash with pagan religions of every variety, all of which were committed to their particular festivals, feasts, and sacrifices. It was virtually impossible at that time to purchase meat in the marketplace that hadn't previously been used in a ritual sacrifice to some exotic deity. Animals were presented at temples, prayed over, slaughtered, and then afterward sold to butchers who carved the meat and sold it in open, fly-infested street stalls. The Christians in Corinth were anxious that this meat, innocent though it appeared on the butcher's table, had been cursed by the prayers and rituals of the pagan religions. It was easy enough for them to avoid such meat, though. In a city as large as Corinth, with a sizable Jewish population, there would have been a number of kosher providers who offered meats uncontaminated by the idol worship of the city. The problem only arose when Corinthian Christians were invited to eat at the table of another member of society. There was no question that meat served by non-Christian friends or in public restaurants was highly likely to have been previously offered to idols. What to do?

Can Christians eat meat served by pagan associates? Will the meat be contaminated by demons or cursed by foreign deities? Will Christians lose their salvation if they ingest food sacrificed to idols? If they eat the nonkosher meat, are they implicitly participating in the unrighteous practice of idol worship? These are important questions, and they deal with a much broader issue than simply idol-sacrificed animals. The question is really about whether Christians will be "contaminated" by their association with unbelievers. Because if Paul agrees that they cannot eat such meat, it effectively means that the Christian community will become closed off from mainstream society, a Christian ghetto raising its own Christian meat and avoiding all contact with unbelievers.

Paul addresses the issue at length in chapters 8–10 of 1 Corinthians. In his response, he avoids actually instructing the Corinthians definitively whether they should or shouldn't share so-called tainted food with unbelievers. He argues for a freedom and a flexibility that allow the matter to be determined on a case-by-case basis, but by no means does he rule out the possibility that at times the most missionally appropriate response will be to share a table with Gentiles, eat their meat, and impart the love of Christ to them. This is the gist of 1 Cor 10:31–11:1. What we eat or drink is not the most important thing; rather, we should be about seeking the good of others. Says John Dickson,

> Paul insists that our social lives be governed not by "purity rules" but by three simple but profound goals. Firstly, we should live with a desire to bring glory to the one true Lord: "So whether you eat or drink or whatever you do, do it all for the glory of God" (1 Cor. 10:31). . . . If there is just one God to whom all people owe their allegiance, and if the worshippers of that God are to promote his glory throughout the world, then it makes sense that our social lives—our "eating and drinking"—should be aligned to this reality. If God is glorified by your going to such banquets, says Paul, then go; if God will be glorified by your avoiding such banquets, then avoid them. Live for God's honor.[1]

There is a refreshing, down-to-earth practicality about this approach. Paul knows that he is not spiritually contaminated by nonkosher meat. He has nothing to fear. But also he is conscious that eating such meat can sometimes

---

[1]John Dickson, *Promoting the Gospel* (Sydney: Blue Bottle, 2005), 57.

do great harm to the reputation of God. His flexibility is based on the freedom from condemnation that he has experienced in Christ. And his approach to eating with unbelievers is rooted in a desire for those who don't know Christ to encounter him. Dickson continues with Paul's three rules:

> The second and third goals unpack what it means to shape your social life around the glory of God. Paul states the second goal in the next verses 32–33: "Do not cause anyone to stumble, whether Jews, Greeks or the church of God—even as I try to please everybody in every way." . . . This verse, then, is not simply about upsetting people; it is about acting in a way that puts their salvation at risk. In the context of 1 Corinthians 8–10 Paul means that the Corinthians' dining habits must not threaten anyone's experience of salvation—whether Jews, Greeks, or the church of God. What Paul states negatively in verse 32 he states positively in verse 33. Here he offers a third goal of Christian living. Not only are we to avoid jeopardizing the salvation of others; we are to actively pursue that salvation: " . . . even as I try to please everybody in every way. For I am not seeking my own good but the good of many, so that they may be saved."[2]

This is how Paul eats. His table life is arranged primarily to give glory to God, and secondarily to actively promote faith in the lives of others. In this way, today exiles are encouraged to share their tables with those who don't know Jesus. Allow your generosity and hospitality to so captivate your guests that they want the same conviviality, joy, freedom, and faith that you have. Paul recognizes that Christianity in a ghetto is not Christianity at all. If we retreat into our own compounds and eat our own meat, sharing our tables only with other Christians, our faith becomes nonmissional—an enormous offense in Paul's eyes. We should eat out in the open, where others can see and join us, celebrating life and liberty in Christ. But we should also be conscious that our behavior might cause new Christians to falter in their faith, so we must remain altogether other-centered in our culinary practices.

A Convivial Table

The examples of the exiles Joseph, Daniel, and Paul teach us different things about eating in a foreign empire. Joseph teaches us to fashion an empire that is concerned with the fair and wise distribution of food; Daniel reminds us to eat in such a way as to be as healthy and vital as we possibly can so that our lifestyles will glorify God; Paul instructs us to be responsible in our freedom and to share food with those who don't know our Lord and Sav-

---

[2]Ibid., 59.

ior. In effect, what all three have in common is that they see food and eating as missional activities that enact some change on the host empire in which they find themselves. We have much to learn from them. In order to recover some of their wisdom, it will be important to consider the place of food and the meal table in our society today.

You might recall what we noted earlier about third places being great zones for building relationships with not-yet-Christians. Two of the core ingredients that make third places fertile for mission are food and alcohol. Although it makes many conservative Christians uncomfortable, it's a fact that many not-yet-Christians really open up about important issues over a meal and a few drinks. They are used to lowering their defenses at a dinner party. They see nothing unusual about deep and genuine conversation being lubricated by great food and wine. Just as Paul said to the Corinthians, be prepared to eat and drink whatever it takes "so that some might be saved." This is not a license for drunkenness or gluttony, but rather a call to recognize that over a meal or a few drinks after work some of our not-yet-Christian friends will be more prepared to discuss faith issues. In this context, Paul's advice about not causing people to "stumble" (1 Cor 10:32) isn't about us offending non-Christians with our eating habits; rather, it's about affecting the faith of weaker believers who can't appreciate the freedom that we have in Christ. I've never known non-Christians to be offended by my decision to drink or to abstain from alcohol.

The place of a meal in this context is essential. A shared table is a profoundly special place for people in the West today. Everyone is a food critic! We love cooking, whether it's in our kitchens, on television, or in a coffee-table cookbook. Nigella Lawson, Jamie Oliver, and Martha Stewart are culinary heroes for millions of Britons and Americans. Many people today like to talk about food (before and after), experiment with new kinds of food, cook food with friends, eat out a lot, do gourmet and ethnic cooking, and try natural foods and health foods. They cook to show love and to show off! At this time in our culture, the shared table is a perfect place for the kind of missionary eating that Paul speaks about in 1 Corinthians.

The problem with all this is the fact that many Christians don't actually go to third places. In fact, as I said earlier, for many Christians, the church is their third place. All their leisure time is spent at church meetings or gatherings, belonging to church-based committees and occasionally socializing with our church friends. While not-yet-Christians are connecting over take-out Thai or whipping up a Moroccan couscous dish or barbecuing Atlantic salmon steaks, Christians are out several nights a week at church services, small groups, and leadership committee meetings. They have no time to engage meaningfully in third places, so the kind of exciting missionary table fellowship that Paul practiced is lost to them. Even when we do invite non-Christians to our table, often it's on our terms. We invite them to *our* church breakfasts or *our* evangelistic dinners or *our* potluck suppers. When it's on our terms, the guest rarely fully relaxes.

Exiles have freed themselves from the busyness of church activity precisely so that they can share food with their friends, neighbors, and work colleagues in a more mutual fashion. A meal should be an equalizing experience. It should be a time when people *share* in the truest sense of the word. Only when a guest feels welcome, honored, and safe will he or she open up to the host. The exile will be as equally concerned about creating such safe, welcoming spaces as about entering into such spaces created by non-Christians. And that means freeing our social calendars and enjoying the company of people who don't share our faith. We should cook the freshest, healthiest fare, complementing it with great wine, supporting small businesses and family farms. Our menus should reflect our concern to avoid products made in countries that lack fair labor laws or produced or stored in ecologically unsafe ways. The exile's table should be a place of justice, generosity, laughter, safety, and conviviality. Serve up something delicious, and then just watch the conversation flow and trust God to stick his nose in somewhere.

Denial and Freedom

In each of the three exilic case studies that we examined, we can see an interplay between denial or abstinence and freedom in the case of food. All three individuals understood the value and power of abstinence. Denying oneself a pleasure need not necessarily mean that we are narrow-minded fundamentalists. In fact, only when pleasures such as eating are balanced in a rhythm of freedom and responsibility can we enjoy them all the more for what they're worth. When I give myself over to avarice and gluttony, eating everything I want whenever I want, the beauty of godly feasting is lost because each meal blurs into the previous one. Likewise, if I had sex with hundreds of partners in a wave of lust and avariciousness, it would be difficult to engage in the sacredness of sex with a partner whom I love deeply. The undisciplined and uncontrolled search for pleasure makes that which is potentially sacred ordinary and mundane. By denying ourselves, we heighten the importance and the wonder of the experience. For Paul, eating was more than refueling. It was a chance to glorify God, to share his faith with others or to encourage the faith of a fellow believer. He embraced freedom within the constraints of abstinence.

There's a scene in Bernard Malamud's novel *Dubin's Lives* in which the hero, a shy, withdrawn professor of literature who has rediscovered the power of lust while studying the life of D. H. Lawrence, seduces a young woman and convinces her to go to a hotel room with him. Flushed with the thought of a successful sexual conquest, the professor begins to undress before glancing out the window of his hotel room. Outside he sees a synagogue, and through its window he sees a group of old men at prayer. The image of these devout men takes the wind out of his sails. He cannot continue with the seduction. Sometimes we resent the power that religious faith has to rein us in when we're hell-bent on pursuing pleasure, but this is one of its greatest gifts to us. It heightens our enjoyment of life by placing healthy restrictions on pleasure—not dour, draconian, life-denying restrictions, but godly brakes on our potentially uncontrollable gluttony. Breaking away from the fear-based rules of the Pharisees is important, but denying ourselves certain pleasures can lift an ordinary meal into the realm of sacred ecstasy.

A marvelous expression of this idea is found in the film *Babette's Feast*. It's the story of a Parisian woman who, escaping political tyranny in France, finds herself in exile in a tiny, austere Lutheran village in Denmark. There, she merges unobtrusively into the puritanical community, with her only tie to France being a lottery ticket sent to her every year by an old friend. After fourteen years of austerity, she wins the prize money of ten thousand francs. Her subsequent decision to spend the entire sum on a magnificent French banquet seems astonishing, but not when seen in the light of her years of exile in the dour, austere stuffiness of her village. She has had enough soulless cooking and tasteless food.

Her banquet is a triumph of culinary art. Its preparation is almost a religious experience, but sadly, only one of her guests recognizes the meal as the masterpiece that it is. After Babette's fourteen years of self-denial in exile, her feast is a celebration of sacrifice, festivity, fine food, and hard work. It is a powerful reminder that the act of savoring must entail a degree of gratitude. Enduring her plain drudgery for so long only serves to heighten Babette's banquet to the realm of the sacred. Her costly feast is a holy event only because of her years of self-denial.

Many of our choices to resist flagrant pleasure seeking are like spiritual calisthenics, exercises that strengthen our capacity to control our basic instincts. The wonder of that night I shared with my wife, Carolyn, at Patachou, the Montmartre restaurant, was heightened precisely because we don't eat like that every day of the week. Exiles should eat a healthy diet, bearing in mind that there's nothing more attractive than a healthy food-lover. Like Daniel, exiles today can demonstrate the goodness of their religion by enjoying life, eating well, sharing their table with unbelievers, and working to create a just world where the poor are fed and the earth's resources are distributed fairly. Says John Piper,

> God is glorified in us when we aim our behavior at being most satisfied in him. We may do this by grateful eating or by grateful fasting. His gifts leave a hunger for him beyond themselves, and fasting from his gifts puts that hunger to the test.[3]

So, let's start by getting our own food intake right, not just for the sake of our bodies, but as an expression of our devotion to God. Here's some commonsense advice for good nutrition and culinary pleasure:

- **Drink more water.** We need about eight glasses a day to aid in digestion, improve our skin, give us more energy, and keep headaches at bay. A well-hydrated body is better able to draw all the vitamins and minerals from its food intake.

- **Eat slowly and take pleasure in your food.** If we quickly gobble our food, our brain doesn't catch on in time and can't tell us when we're full. That way, we eat too much, too quickly. Eat delicious meals slowly, taking pleasure in your food and thanking God for his generosity in providing it. Ease up on the salt and use herbs and spices to add flavor. Savor it. The world is full of starvation. We dishonor the hungry by not responsibly enjoying the bounty that is available to us in the West.

- **Eat "real" food rather than low-calorie food.** In an effort to sell you fat-free or low-fat products, manufacturers often have to remove the most flavorful aspects of the food—the fat! To reintroduce more flavor, they often use chemical additives. Because of this, "real" full-fat food is much better for you than these low-fat versions. To keep your heart healthy, enjoy small quantities of real chocolate or olive or vegetable oils rather than relying on the fake fat-reduced stuff.

- **Eat smaller meals more often.** Instead of skipping breakfast or lunch and gorging yourself on sweets or fast food, discipline yourself to eat three decent-sized, healthy meals every day.

- **Don't overdo the carbohydrates.** Carbohydrates such as pasta and potatoes activate your de-stressing hormones, so you often feel sleepy and sluggish after eating them. For this reason eat them at the end of the day, not for lunch.

- **Resist alcohol on an empty stomach.** If you take a drink on an empty stomach, your blood sugar will drop and your energy levels will crash.

---

[3]John Piper, *A Hunger for God: Desiring God through Fasting and Prayer* (Wheaton, Ill.: Crossway, 1997), 46.

The next thing you'll want to do is eat something, anything. Usually what you'll eat will be salty nuts, chips, or fast food. Use alcohol as an accompaniment to a great meal. And avoid drinking during daylight. And don't drink cheap wine or tasteless beer. If you do drink, make sure it's a hearty stout or lager, or a glass of rich, full-bodied South Australian cabernet or shiraz, or a Californian pinot noir, or a Chilean or South African chardonnay.

- **Lower the caffeine.** Caffeine, the Christian's drug of choice, produces adrenaline, which stresses you out even more, and it's highly addictive. Stick to one or two cups a day, and make sure that it's good quality, Fair Trade coffee. Or drink herbal tea or hot water with a slice of ginger or lemon, which should make you feel calmer and sleep better.

- **Eat more protein.** Fish and other seafood, eggs, lean meat, pulses, nuts, and grains give us energy and are great for controlling moods because they have amino acids that produce hormones that make us feel good. Protein picks you up.

- **Eat a lot of fruit and vegetables.** You've probably heard this many times before, but it's always a good reminder: we should eat five portions of fruits and vegetables every day to prevent heart disease and cancer. The bad news? Fries don't count as a vegetable.

The Ferocious Power of Hospitality

So, like the exile Paul, we should eat communally with both fellow believers and unbelieving friends as a missional practice to "prove" the power of the gospel. And like the exile Daniel, we should eat responsibly and healthily to demonstrate the inherent goodness of life in God. In addition, like the exile Joseph, we should work at ensuring that the poor, the marginalized, the dispossessed, and victims of an unjust global economy have enough to eat. Those facing loneliness, poverty, or alienation must not be strangers to us. The God of love and compassion is calling followers to break down the walls of isolation and alienation that entrap so many people. We've already looked at ways we can help create a more just world. But locally, remember that meal times provide excellent spaces for genuine friendship, solidarity, and mutual compassion. The Bible is full of examples of people who were prepared to risk a great deal to show hospitality and got more than they bargained for. At Mamre, Abraham welcomed three strangers to dinner, who turned out to be two angels and the Lord God, who announced that Sarah would miraculously become pregnant with a son (Gen 18:1–15). When a widow from Zarephath offered food and shelter to a stranger, that stranger turned out to be Elijah, a man of God, who then raised her son from the dead (1 Kings 17:9–24). When two disciples were traveling to Emmaus from Jerusalem, where their teacher, Jesus, had been executed, they invited a stranger to stay with them for the night. As the stranger broke bread at supper with them, their eyes were opened to him being their risen Lord (Luke 24:13–35). An oft-quoted text in this regard, though, comes from Jesus' parable of the sheep and the goats, found in chapter 25 of Matthew:

> Then the King will say to those on his right, "Come, you who are blessed by my Father; take your inheritance, the kingdom prepared for you since the creation of the world. For I was hungry and you gave me something to eat, I was thirsty and you gave me something to drink, I was a stranger and you invited me in, I needed clothes and you clothed me, I was sick and you looked after me, I was in prison and you came to visit me." (Matt 25:34–36)

In a world where so many are alone and isolated, words are not enough. One Christmas we took our children to an inner-city church that provides a free Christmas dinner for the homeless. We arrived in the early afternoon and spent the rest of the day carving ham, turkey, and chicken, preparing all the trimmings, setting tables, readying ourselves to serve the people of the streets. When it was time to eat, Carolyn and I and our three teenage daughters mingled with homeless men and women, listened to their stories, laughed at their jokes, and watched them enjoy their meal, the food piled high on their plates. The next day, a teenage friend of my daughter Kendall asked how our Christmas was. We told her about serving the poor at St. John's. She thought about this for a while and then asked, "So you served homeless people their dinner? Was there, like, protective glass between you and them?" I guess this epitomizes the problem. Too many people, Christians included, have erected protective glass between themselves and the poor. The willingness to welcome a stranger to our table is the work of the exile. The writer of the book of Hebrews suggests that entertaining strangers can result in mystical encounters such as those experienced by Abraham, the widow of Zarephath, and the two disciples on the road to Emmaus: "Do not forget to show hospitality to strangers, for by doing so some people have shown hospitality to angels without knowing it" (Heb 13:2). Divine visitors come to us in the form of the stranger. Was Christ there in that crowd of homeless people at St. John's last Christmas?

If you've seen the harrowing film *Hotel Rwanda*, you've seen the awesome power of hospitality in a world of depravity and evil. In 1994, as Rwandan Hutus descended into a hell of bloodshed and racial violence against their Tutsi counterparts, Paul Rusesabagina, the temporary manager of the Mille Collines, a luxury hotel in central Kigali, sheltered over one thousand Tutsis from marauding death squads. Deserted by international peacekeepers, Rusesabagina, himself a Hutu, began cashing in every favor he had ever earned, bribing the Rwandan Hutu soldiers and keeping the bloodthirsty militia (mostly) outside the gates during the hundred days of slaughter during which nearly one million Rwandans were hacked to death by machete. The international community turned its back on Rwandan Tutsis, claiming to be powerless to help, but the story of Paul Rusesabagina suggests otherwise.

On April 15, 1994, a week after the genocide had began, Rusesabagina, in an interview with a Belgian newspaper, called for protection for those inside the Mille Collines, as did an official of Sabena, the Belgian owners of the hotel, who spoke on Belgian television. Rwandan authorities responded by posting some national police at the hotel.

Then on April 23, the Department of Military Intelligence arrived at the hotel and ordered Rusesabagina to turn out everyone who had sought shelter there. Rusesabagina and several of the occupants began telephoning influential persons abroad, appealing urgently for help. One of those who received a call was the Director General of the French Foreign Ministry. Before half an hour had elapsed, a colonel from the national police arrived to end the siege and to oblige the army to leave.

And then again on May 13, a captain came to the hotel to warn that there would be an attack on the hotel that afternoon. On that day, the French Foreign Ministry received a fax from the hotel saying that Rwandan government forces plan to massacre all the occupants of the hotel in the next few hours. It directed its representative at the United Nations to inform the secretariat of the threat and presumably also brought pressure to bear directly on authorities in Kigali, as others may have done also. The attack never took place.

In other words, the West had enough influence to save lives in Rwanda, but used that influence sparingly. Paul Rusesabagina provided one of the very few places of refuge, a haven of hospitality in a sea of depravity. No one who took shelter at the hotel was killed during the genocide. Rusesabagina's remarkable hospitality shames the ineffectual Western community, which stood by while hundreds of thousands were killed. He fed and housed terrified Tutsis and against all odds saved every one of them. In recent years, leaders of national governments and international institutions have acknowledged their shortcomings in Rwanda. During a visit to Rwanda in 1998, President Clinton apologized for not acting. Kofi Annan, the U.N. Secretary General, said he personally could have done more to stop it.

But the genocide in Rwanda is not an isolated incident. After the Nazi Holocaust, the international community pledged to never again allow genocide to take place. But it has happened—in places such as Cambodia (under

Pol Pot), the former Yugoslavia (under Slobodan Milosovic), Rwanda, and most recently in Sudan's troubled Darfur region, where more than seven hundred thousand people have been killed or have died from hunger and disease. According to the United Nations, another 1.5 million people have been displaced. Even though U.S. Secretary of State Colin Powell has openly named the massacres as genocide, an African Union force of only eight hundred troops and one hundred observers has been dispatched to the mainly desert region. They are there as peacekeepers and are not allowed to fire their weapons unless in self-defense.

Was Christ among those seeking refuge in the Mille Collines hotel in 1994? Is Christ among those hunted by the Sudanese Janjaweedi death squads? Who is showing hospitality?

Who are opening their tables to the hungry and the poor? Hospitality is not just about a cup of tea and some sympathy. Hospitality is a powerful force. As Paul Rusesabagina proved, it can stand against unspeakable evil. As followers of Christ, exiles should be at the forefront of offering hospitality to the hungry, to the refugee, to the dispossessed.

Another, much less dramatic, example of hospitality can be seen in a bookshop in Paris. Shakespeare & Company is a unique bookstore and private library located on the Rue de la Bûcherie across the Seine from Notre Dame. It is three chaotic floors of wall-to-wall, floor-to-ceiling books, magazines, journals, and assorted papers. Originally opened by Sylvia Beach in the 1920s in another part of Paris, Shakespeare & Company was a favorite haunt of the Lost Generation writers such as Ernest Hemingway, F. Scott Fitzgerald, and James Joyce. In 1951 American George Whitman inherited the library and relocated the store to its present site in an old grocery store. Now ninety-one years old, the curmudgeonly old bookworm has spent his adult life creating the most astonishing maze of books you could imagine.

Everywhere you look, chaos reigns. Books are stacked in the aisles up to the ceiling. There are nooks and crannies, spaces under stairwells, hidden recesses and false floors, all packed with books and papers. Winding your way up the narrow, rickety steps, you don't feel so much like a customer as an intruder, invading the private space of a strange bibliophile.

But what makes George Whitman's shop so peculiar is not just the remarkable range of stock—both new releases and first-edition classics—but the fact that the place is crawling with writers, students, and poets. Once while visiting the store, I wandered upstairs to the Sylvia Beach Library. There I discovered several people sitting at a desk by the window overlooking the courtyard below. They were hunched over a laptop computer speaking in American accents. In the corner a young woman, wearing slippers, was lying on a sofa. In a cavity in the wall, surrounded by shelves stacked with books, was a stretcher bed on which a sleeping bag had been neatly laid. In other, darker rooms (the library is bright and sunny) I found more sleeping bags, benches, and backpacks in various corners. They all belong to people whom George allows to sleep in the shop free of charge for as long as they need or like to.

The Americans whom I stumbled upon were young writers living in Paris on literary scholarships. The young woman with the slippers was a Dutch poet. At any given point in time Shakespeare & Company can be home to young romantic lovers, struggling novelists and poets trying to land a publishing contract, dancers, artists, sculptors, drifters and dreamers. George Whitman welcomes them all, without question, accommodates them and feeds them.

On a blackboard at the front of the shop George has handwritten,

How many know that in the sixteenth century this house was a monastery called La Maison du Moustier? How many know that in medieval times each monastery had a frère lampier, whose function it was to light the lamps? How many know that I am your frère lampier because when I opened this bookstore I inherited the role of the monk who lights the lamps at nightfall?

George had taken it upon himself to light the lamps in his monastery/ bookstore, to alert the weary traveler that a warm bed, a welcoming table, and a hospitable host are available inside. Over time he has opened his store (which doubles as his own home) to any "nobody" who has needed a bed and a meal. Those "nobodies" have included people such as Sartre, Beckett, Burroughs, Ginsberg, and Corso. In return they have left manuscripts and notebooks of original ideas—almost worthless at the time, but now priceless. Over the years he has collected original copies of many modern literary classics.

At his meal bench George serves hearty broths and crusty bread to his strange menagerie of international guests. Try to imagine the conviviality of such a table as artists eat and drink together, encouraging each other's work, sharing ideas, trying out poems on the small audience. Surely George's table bears a striking resemblance to Matthew's: "While Jesus was having dinner at Matthew's house, many tax collectors and sinners came and ate with him and his disciples" (Matt 9:10).

It was probably because of parties like this that Jesus was open to the charges of gluttony or avarice leveled at him by the Pharisees. Carousing and feasting with "sinners" was considered profane and ungodly, not something for a rabbi like Jesus to be involved in. But it's exactly where we would find the exile Jesus, eating with terrified Tutsis in Rwanda, with writers and artists in Paris, with the homeless at St. John's. Just as we would find him with those who've been harassed, dislocated, imprisoned, tortured, raped, or killed by totalitarian regimes. Or with the South African blacks under apartheid. Or with the victims of the nuclear ravages inflicted upon Nagasaki and Hiroshima. Or with the dead of Cambodia and Laos during the secret war of the 1970s. Or with the decades of dead in Colombia or El Salvador or Nicaragua or Guatemala or Chile or Somalia. Or with the thousands of Iraqi children who died from malnutrition during the twelve-year U.N. embargo of that country. And it's where Christian exiles should be today, lighting the lamps in our windows to alert the stranger to the fact that we are prepared to share our tables and resources with them, just like Paul, Daniel, Joseph, Paul Rusesabagina, George Whitman, Mother Theresa, Nelson Mandela, Bono, and others. There's a church in a Melbourne, Australia, inner-city area created especially for street kids, for homeless children, for drug-addicted teenage prostitutes, and the mentally ill. It's called Matthew's Party—a perfect name for a church, really. In fact, every church should be a Matthew's Party, a table for tax collectors and "sinners" to feast with the exile Jesus and his friends.

8

Working for the Host Empire

The Promise: We Will Work Righteously

> I won't take my religion from any man who never
> works except with his mouth.
>
> —Carl Sandburg

So far in this part of the book, I have suggested that exiles make dangerous promises such as "We will be authentic," "We will create communities of action," and "We will be generous and hospitable." Now we turn our attention to another such promise. Exiles will be devoted to their work, knowing that they can be called by God to work in a factory or a law firm or a school or the home every bit as much as someone can be called by God to minister as a priest or pastor. Like Daniel and Joseph, exiles will work hard for the host empire, and while doing so, they will be promising, "We will work righteously."

In 1991 a prosperous, middle-aged architect named Samuel Mockbee took a drive through America's deep South. It was to change the direction of his life. He had become disillusioned with the elitism of his profession, with its cloistered, expensive architects chasing fame and wealth with little regard for the needs of others in this world, let alone the socially disadvantaged. Mockbee somehow had held to the altruistic ideal that architecture was more than an art form. It was a social symbol. Buildings were representations of status, wealth, and security. Only the wealthy could afford the most beautiful buildings. The poor could access most other art forms—literature, film, photography, painting—but they had no access to architectural beauty.

Mockbee dreamed of the poor living in architecturally stunning new houses, and yet only the wealthy could claim to own an architect-designed home. To Mockbee, this made his profession the most elitist of all the arts. As he trundled through the most poverty-stricken rural areas of the South, he noticed hundreds of dilapidated, virtually unlivable houses and shacks, occupied mainly by African Americans. He observed a region where nearly two-thirds of the population lived below the poverty line, a state where many lived in trailer parks and hovels without running water or electricity. The social need was devastating and highly visible to any visitor—if he or she had eyes to see.

That trip from Mississippi through Alabama along the dirt roads between the wheat, corn, and cotton fields confirmed in his mind that something had to be done to throw open the doors of the architectural academy. He wanted to provide beautiful homes for the socially and economically disadvantaged. But more than creating cheap housing, he wanted to confront architectural students with the racial and cultural chasm that divided the South. He wanted to shake their values and help them to develop a concern for fellow human beings before they entered a thriving practice and lost their youthful passion for social justice. And along the way, just maybe, they'd create some darn good buildings.

That year he gave up his successful practice and formed a socially engaged architecture school called the Rural Studio in a farmhouse in Greenboro, Alabama. He was to change lives in more ways than one. Mockbee once said of his students,

> Most of these kids come from affluent or middle-class families. They think they've seen poverty, but they've only driven by it, smelled its perfume. When they shake their [poor] client's hand, and work with him month after month, then they realize this is a real person.[1]

Samuel Mockbee, known as "Sambo," was a big, barrel-chested man with a grey beard who drove an old pickup and ate breakfast in his favorite diner every day. He looked like an Old Testament prophet. And maybe he was something of a modern-day prophet after all. By his passion, eccentricity, and intelligence he inspired an emerging generation of young architects. His students at the Rural Studio were expected to walk up dusty driveways to decrepit old shacks, knock on the door, and offer the resident a brand new house. Just like that! Often the recipients of this too-good-to-be-true offer resisted the invitation because they suspected that there must have been some catch. Rich white kids just don't offer free houses to poor black folks. And yet over the years, Mockbee and his students built some astonishing homes for their "clients."[2]

---

[1]Richard Guilliatt, "This Old Shack," *Good Weekend Magazine, Sydney Morning Herald* (June 22, 2002): 45.

[2]For more photographs of the homes done by the Rural Studio see "Rural Studio," n.p. [cited 17 January 2006]. Online: http://www.ruralstudio.com.

Goat House. Photo credit: Timothy Hursley. Used with permission.

The Goat House was once a yellow stucco house, so run down that goats had taken up residence there. The Rural Studio literally cut the house in two and pulled each half apart so that a soaring, cathedral-like hall could be inserted. The inserted section—all recycled beams and cladding—rises through the middle of the original building to create a dramatic effect. Inside the addition, floor-to-ceiling windows flood the chamber with natural light, revealing an airy and comfortable space framed by natural timbers and polished wooden floors. Mockbee's students designed the unique construction and built it at a cost of just $12,000 (it was given to the client free of charge).

The Hay Bale House has a colonnaded porch on one side and three barrel-shaped bedrooms that look like hay bales lined up along the other side of the house. Its 24–inch thick walls of stacked hay bales make it easy to heat and cool inexpensively. Shep and Alberta Bryant, who had lived with their two grandchildren in a tarpaper shack with a dirt floor and leaky roof, received their new home for free.

The Butterfly House, an energy-efficient home given to Anderson and Ora Lee Harris, features a winged timber roof and screened porch made of recycled wood and tin. It was made wheelchair accessible for Mrs. Harris and was built at a cost of only $25,000. Alabama is now dotted with homes, churches, playgrounds, and community centers created by graduates of Mockbee's school of socially conscious architecture.

Butterfly House. Photo credit: Timothy Hursley. Used with permission.

Samuel Mockbee died in 2001 at the age of 57; too young for a folk hero to go. Because of his paradigm-busting approach to architecture, he'd eventually become a visiting professor at Harvard, a guest on *Oprah*, and the recipient of a $500,000 "genius grant" from the McArthur Foundation. He'd gotten famous and wealthy, not by pandering to the self-serving values of many of his peers, but by stepping out of the framework that confined most architects.

God's Apprentice-Children

Samuel Mockbee modeled exilic thinking in his approach to being an architect. Exilic thinking is the kind of compassionate creativity that looks to integrate one's work with one's sense of mission. For too long the church has fallen into the dualistic pattern of seeing someone's job as a secular endeavor while valuing his or her role within the church as holy or righteous. In this equation, only the full-time work of missionaries or clergy is sacred. There-fore the church often sees jobs such as architect, or schoolteacher or nurse, or lawyer or stay-at-home parent as completely secular. Such work is profane, religiously neutral at best. Many churchgoing people get the impression that what they spend the bulk of their time doing every week is unimportant to God in comparison to what they do for a few hours each week in the church. It's as though God couldn't be bothered with our careers, but when we turn up for a worship service, or join a church committee, or attend a Bible study, God suddenly snaps to attention. But I would argue that this is a biblically faulty view. God is as present and interested in our work life as in any area of our lives. Exiles need to wriggle free from a church that devalues the righ-teousness of their everyday work lives as well as from a world that sees work simply as the means to earn money.

God is intimately interested in the day-to-day lives of all people no mat-ter where they work. Naturally, every Christian needs to take seriously the call to work responsibly and not contribute to the suffering of others. One of the simplest ways of doing this is to see that our personal sense of mission in-volves what we do for a living just as much as what we do for our church ac-tivities. Seeing our job as our mission isn't just about using our place of business as an arena for personal witnessing; it involves recognizing that we can, in part, fulfill our calling to serve God through the very work that we do. We earn money at our jobs, of course, but our primary motivation as exiles is to do our work as an expression of our relationship with God.

Even if we work as a tiny cog in a huge corporate machine that makes as-tonishing amounts of money for a small number of people, we can see our work of valuing our colleague at the next desk as the work of God. Life is full of ambiguities, and so, for example, even the centurion in Luke 7, working for the host empire, wasn't disqualified from having faith in Jesus and being seen as an example for us all. The centurion embodies the radical nature of grace: Jesus places enormous value on the faith of a man who is quite literally in league with the most evil of all empires. Of course, some exiles will choose to leave their employment with the empire and strike out to find a job in which they can express their godly callings, but even those who feel trapped in such a system can still find nooks and crannies in which to do work that expresses their relationship with God on this planet.

My rationale for this is located in Jesus' reference to God as "Father." This occurs multiple times in the Gospels, perhaps nowhere more conspicu-ously than in his model prayer for his disciples in Matt 6:9–13: "This, then, is how you should pray: 'Our Father in heaven. . . .'" In today's world, where we are increasingly aware of gender-neutral language, the idea of being taught by Jesus to pray to God as Father might seem somewhat "politically

incorrect." We know that God is neither male nor female. Jesus himself declares that God is spirit, not physical, and is to be worshipped in spirit and in
truth (John 4:24). Although we can recognize masculine or feminine aspects
of God's character, we can't seriously think of God as male or female. God is
not a physical being, and therefore is nongendered, even though we know that
the Bible in various places refers to God's feminine or motherly characteristics as well as to God's fatherly nature. And yet references to the divine feminine in pagan and "new age" religions often cloud the issue and scare off
Christians who feel that to refer to God as Mother is to court theological heresy. The fact is that the biblical writers acknowledge the feminine as well as
the masculine aspects of God's character (see, for example, Isa 66:13). Probably, though, because those feminine aspects have been ignored by the
church for so long and are just now being rediscovered, we are anxious these
days not to overemphasize God's fatherliness. So, in a time of great contro-
versy about this subject, it may seem out of step to celebrate Jesus' references
to God as Father, but I think there is an important lesson to be learned here.

When Jesus tells us to pray "Our Father in heaven," he is doing more
than providing us an epithet by which to refer to God. He is inviting us to acknowledge an important part of our relationship with God. In Jesus' time,
sons grew up observing their fathers every day at work. Carpenters and black-
smiths often had their workplace attached to or very near the family home. A
son whose father was a farmer would grow up living on the very land that his
father was working. In this way young men learned their father's trade from a
very early age. Traditional cultures still in existence today have this same
characteristic. Fathers and sons in most tribal cultures live in what Robert Bly
calls "an amused tolerance of each other," spending hours together trying and
failing to make arrowheads or to repair a fishing net or track a clever animal. [3]
And it extends beyond father-son relationships. Young boys have plenty of
"fathers" as they grow up. Uncles loosen the son up, or tell him about
women. Grandfathers give him stories. Warriors from the village teach him
weaponry and discipline. Old men teach him ritual and soul. Each of them
is, in a sense, an honorary father.

Throughout the ancient hunter societies and throughout the hunter-
gatherer societies that followed them, and the subsequent agricultural and
craft societies, fathers and sons lived and worked together. As late as 1900 in
the United States about 90 percent of fathers were engaged in agriculture. In
all these societies the son characteristically saw his father working at all times
of the day and all seasons of the year.

---

[3]For more on this see Robert Bly, *Iron John* (Reading, Mass.: Addison-Wesley,
1990).

Only 150 years have passed since factory work began in earnest in the West, and each successive generation has seen a poorer bonding between fathers and sons. The Enclosure Act of England eventually led to the situation where the landless father had no access to free pasture and common land. This resulted in the forcing of men, with or without families, to travel to the factory for work. By the middle of the twentieth century in Europe and America a massive social change had taken place: fathers were still working, but their sons could not see them doing so. This shift has meant that today, not only do children never see their fathers at work, but also they don't feel inclined to follow in their footsteps, because their work is a mystery. When I grew up, my father left for his office before I even awoke each morning. He returned in time for the evening meal. I never once in all my childhood or adolescence went to his office or saw him at work. I once came across a photograph of him seated at his desk. I examined that picture in minute detail, exploring the papers on his desk, the pictures on the wall. When I asked him what he did all day (and I did this on multiple occasions), he would tell me the title of his role and the company he worked for. But in my childish way I wasn't asking for these cursory details; I wanted to know what he *did* with each minute of his day. As a small boy, I lacked the vocabulary to express this, and he never seemed to have the inclination to explain it.

But in Jesus' time it was much simpler. Joseph the Galilean carpenter raised his son Jesus to watch him planing a beam, measuring a table leg, slotting a tongue-and-groove into place. He arrived at the family meal table covered in wood shavings, his hands dried out by sawdust and calloused from daily woodworking. Young Jesus would have learned the trade of his father every day in incremental lessons, first by playing with wood, then by learning simple techniques, then by being apprenticed in his father's workshop. Jesus' possible career choices wouldn't have been a matter of much discussion or consideration. It was reasonably assumed that he would take up chisel, hammer, awl, and plane. Sons follow their fathers. It was as simple as that.

Recall the story about Jesus' parents, after their annual pilgrimage to Jerusalem, losing track of their twelve-year-old son. After having traveled a day's journey homeward, assuming all along that he was among their group of friends and relatives, they realize that they have left him back in the city. When they double back and finally find him in the temple three days later, they rebuke him for causing them such worry (as any parent would). But Jesus' response is one of incredulity. He is astonished that they couldn't find him. "Didn't you know I had to be in my Father's house?" he says, wide-eyed (Luke 2:49). Just as he followed his earthly father into carpentry, so he would naturally follow his heavenly Father into his temple. Sons (and today, daughters) *follow* fathers.

So, when we pray to our Father in heaven, we are confessing something powerful about our relationship to God. Whether we are men or women, we are praying that we have something of an apprentice-child relationship with God. We today confess our desire to follow God into the "family business." I want to emphasize that this is a metaphor that includes women as much as men. When women refer to God as Father, they too are saying something about their desire to follow him in their work.

We are to follow our heavenly Father into the family business. As we grow in our faith, we are to increasingly take on God's work as our own. We begin as small children, watching our heavenly Father come home covered in wood shavings each day, and slowly but surely we take on his vocation as ours, learning bit by bit until we become apprentice-children, and then fellow workers.

The Shadow of God's Work

So what is the "family business"? As followers of the living God, we are called not simply to worship and adore God, but to do the Father's work. We are called to mimic our heavenly Father, to watch him at work and to carry out that work in our sphere. Have you ever seen young children mimicking or imitating their parents? Wanting to wear the same clothes, showing an interest in the same things? Well, it should be the same with us. We should want to mimic God. And one of the primary ways we can do that is through the vocation that we choose. The term "vocation" comes from the Latin *vocare*, meaning "to call." It is the calling in our spirits that gives rise to the employment that we choose. Often we use the term "vocation" only to refer to people entering the clergy. We assume that the "calling" to do so must have come from God. God calls people into ordained ministry. We routinely refer to people "receiving the call" to Christian service, whether to church leadership or to the mission field. But when we use language this way, we are falling into the age-old trap of believing that God is primarily in the church-leadership business, and that when people become church leaders, they are following their Father into the family business. Priests, pastors, nuns, monks, missionaries—these are people following the Father's calling to work for him.

But, as I mentioned earlier, this is faulty thinking. It comes from an era when it was believed that reality was divided into two separate spheres: the sacred and the secular. This is called "dualism," and Christians have struggled with it from the early days of the church. Dualism separates the sacred from the secular, the holy from the unholy, the in from the out. The sacred realm obviously includes God and is supposed to be clearly present in church

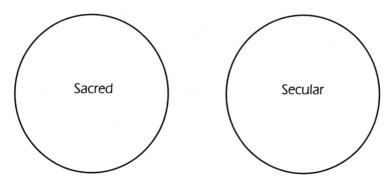

Separation of the Sacred and the Secular

services, the Mass, Bible studies, theological seminaries, and so on. The secular realm is the rest of life: having sex, gardening, going to the art gallery, eating, renovating the house, sports, working, and the like. It's not so much that God is absent from these activities, but rather, we just don't presume that God is particularly, keenly present in them. Much of our language in church reinforces this assumption. We routinely say that God was "present" in the church worship service, but do we think that God is absent when we are making love to our spouse? Many people sense God's presence in nature, when gardening or looking at a beautiful sunset, but they expect little if any such presence when they're eating at McDonald's or watching football on television. This is dualism. We routinely talk about the "world out there." What else can that mean other than that we, the church people, are "in here"? This dualism has, over 1,700 years, created Christians who cannot relate their interior faith to their exterior practice, and this affects their ethics, lifestyles, and capacity to share their faith meaningfully with others.

It also affects how we see our work. If we presume that God is most keenly present in church, then we begin to assume that God is like the greatest priest, the most perfect rector, preacher, pastor, vicar, cleric. You see, if the focus of God the Vicar is on church meetings, then it follows that for us to imitate God, like a child does his or her father, the greatest vocation that we can adopt is one of church leadership. We can easily think of a friend entering church-ordained ministry as following God, but rarely do we speak of a decision to become a computer programmer or a nurse or a filmmaker or an accountant as similarly following God's calling in our lives.

When such thinking takes root, an enormous gap develops between the special world of the full-time clergy and the mundane world of the rest of us. Earlier, we looked at Walter Brueggemann's assumptions about the feelings of alienation and rage that congregants sense toward the public discourse offered in church services. In *Redeeming the Routines,* Robert Banks identifies

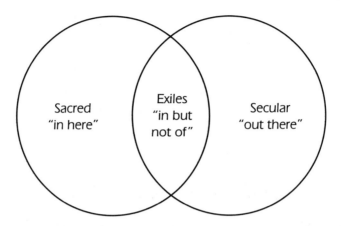

Integrating the Sacred and the Secular

the observable symptoms of this gap. When all our biblical teaching comes from (primarily male) clergy who believe that they are doing God's work and that the people in their congregations are doing some lesser kind of profane business, we end up learning a curriculum that doesn't relate to our real life. And not only is our employment seen as irrelevant, but also our pastimes and hobbies are berated as obstacles to our serving God rather than celebrated as means of doing so. Banks notes the results:

- Few of us apply or know how to apply our belief to our work or lack of work.

- We make only minimal connections between our faith and our spare-time activities.

- We have little sense of a Christian approach to regular activities such as domestic chores.

- Our everyday attitudes are partly shaped by the dominant values of our society.

- Many of our spiritual difficulties stem from the daily pressure that we experience (lack of time, exhaustion, family pressures, etc.).

- Our everyday concerns receive little attention in the church.

- Only occasionally do professional theologians address routine activities.

- When addressed, everyday issues tend to be approached too theoretically.

- Only a minority of Christians read religious books or attend theological courses.

- Most churchgoers reject the idea of a gap between their beliefs and their ways of life.[4]

Why is this the case? Because we have adopted the faulty assumption of dualism as a starting point. But in fact, the world is not divided into two realms. God is not restricted to some so-called sacred realm. God is no less present in the office or the garden or the stadium than in church services. We have to stop assuming that the only people who follow their heavenly Father into the family business are the full-time clergy. I can recall some years ago hearing a minister speak at the graduation service of a well-known seminary. Acknowledging the graduates for their decision to give up "secular" careers to "follow God into the church," he related the story of a high-up executive in the Coca-Cola Company who left his well-paid position to become a minister. When asked about his decision by the press, the Coca-Cola executive answered, "When compared with preaching the gospel, everything else is just selling lolly water." The idea that our so-called secular careers are simply a matter of selling lolly water (soft drinks) compared to the eminent worthiness of a clergy vocation is altogether unbiblical. When the preacher made that reference in that graduation service, he was effectively writing off the godly merit of what 90 percent of those present did with their lives every day of the week.

In *Redeeming the Routines,* Robert Banks quotes occasionally from the book *Christianity and Real Life,* written by William Diehl, the sales manager of a major steel corporation. Diehl writes about the gap between the secular and the sacred in church circles:

> In the almost thirty years of my professional career, my church has never once suggested that there be any type of accounting of my on-the-job ministry to others. My church has never once offered to improve those skills which could make me a better minister, nor has it ever asked if I needed any kind of support in what I was doing. There has never been an inquiry into the types of ethical decisions I must face, or whether I seek to communicate the faith to my coworkers. I have never been in a congregation where there was any type of public affirmation of a ministry in my career. In short, I must conclude that my church really doesn't have the least interest whether or how I minister in my daily work.[5]

Diehl here is assuming that the only "ministry" that he can perform at work is to share his faith with others, and even this isn't acknowledged or encouraged by his church. I suggest that there are even more fundamental

---

[4]Robert Banks, *Redeeming the Routines: Bringing Theology to Life* (Wheaton, Ill.: BridgePoint Books, 1993), 50–65.

[5]William Diehl, *Christianity and Real Life* (Philadelphia: Fortress, 1976), v–vi (quoted in Banks, *Redeeming the Routines,* 59).

ways we can be God's apprentice-children in our workplaces. But if the gap is as great as Diehl suggests, then these ways are not the ones that the church seems at all ready for. This gap is, as Helmut Thielecke calls it, a modern form of Docetism. Docetism is a dualistic heresy. It is, in essence, a Platonic way of thinking about life. The Greek philosopher Plato taught the idea of gradations of reality. Spirit or mind or thought is the highest. Matter or the material is less real. With this distinction there came to be ethical gradations as well. Matter came to be thought of as morally bad, while spirit was morally good. Meanwhile, Aristotle emphasized the idea of divine impassability, according to which God cannot change, suffer, or even be affected by anything that happens in the world. These two streams of unbiblical thought have significant differences, but both maintain that the visible, physical, material world is somehow inherently evil. And both emphasize God's transcendence and absolute difference from and independence of the material world. In other words, spiritual matters, including so-called spiritual vocations, are inherently more godly than material matters. God is far above this profane/evil world, untouched by our everyday lives. This heresy has seeped into Christian thought and has come to dominate how we view life, the church, vocation, and the very nature of God.

The Docetists were deeply influenced by this Platonic dualism and therefore taught that Jesus only *seemed* to be human. Since they believed that all matter is evil, and Jesus is perfect, pure and holy, they simply couldn't believe that the Divine Jesus could become material and dwell in a physical body. The name Docetism comes from the Greek *dokeo,* which means "to seem or appear," and the earliest proponents of this heresy adopted the position that Jesus was 100% divine and 0% human. It was as if he was God masquerading as a man, like the prince in those fairy tales who simply wears the rags of a pauper and "seems" to be a common man before finally revealing his true, regal identity.

But what we have in the New Testament is a shattering of the Platonic or Aristotelian view of reality. God takes on matter. God becomes fully human. God enters into the fray of everyday life—learns a trade, eats real food, suffers, and ultimately dies to redeem us from sin. Biblical teaching is utterly different from Docetism. And biblical teaching affirms that matter, the everydayness of life, is a place where God is more than prepared to reside. Sadly, Docetism is so pervasive in the contemporary church that it has worked its way into the very fabric of all aspects of church life. Remove this Docetism, or dualism, from church, and a great deal of what the church has built and developed over 1,700 years will fall away.

Exiles have escaped from this ancient form of dualism. They can't continue in a system that values the preacher's work but ignores their work in the local school, hospital, or office building. Armed with a more biblical world-view, exiles are prepared to recognize our role—both men and women—to be God's "sons," following God into the family business. And that business is not limited to a role within the clergy; it is any work that continues or carries on God's work in this world. We are God's apprentices, watching our Father work at the carpentry bench, taking in the methods of divine handiwork and preparing ourselves to imitate what we see. Any work that imitates God's work in this world is a noble enough vocation for the exile. Of course, we cannot do that work as nobly, as selflessly, as God would do it, but that's no reason to abandon such a vocation. We are prepared to complete just a shadow of God's work in this world. What kind of work might this entail? Let me offer a few suggestions.

Creating/Building

I have a friend, Wayne, who is a computer animator. He and three col-leagues created a series of computer-generated animated films called *Pop Pups* about those sculpted balloon animals that people twist into shape at street fairs and school parties. In the films, balloons dogs come to life, their joints squeaking like two balloons being rubbed together as they walk. The cute little balloon puppies get into all sorts of silly adventures. Wayne recently cre-ated a four-minute animated film about a sun bear walking into a bar and entering a karaoke competition. (It was commissioned by a wealthy business-man who happens to love sun bears. Go figure!) At one level, it might be seen that what Wayne does is entirely frivolous and unimportant. They're just silly kids shows. It's nothing compared with the much more godly work of overseas mission or preaching. It's like selling lolly water. But when we think about it, we realize that this is work very much like our heavenly Father's work. The Bible unquestionably tells us that God is a creator. God dreams up new worlds, creates solar systems, fashions life itself—everything from the tiny and intricately designed hummingbird to the mammoth monoliths of the Himalayas. God obviously is a creative being who builds systems, who thinks in terms of the most complicated, interrelated structures and organi-zations. If we have eyes to see it, we can quite readily understand that some-one such as Wayne is like a son following his father into the family business. He has heard all about his father's matchless work in creating worlds, and he wants to mimic his handiwork. Wayne wants to create new worlds, amazing worlds where bears sing karaoke and balloon sculptures come to life. In this way, his work as an animator reveals a shadow of God's work indeed.

I have another friend, Paul, who is a computer programmer. He builds software. He creates solutions to the computer problems experienced by technophobes like me. He builds. He creates. He fashions new ideas. As he sits at his computer screen each day, he readies himself to do the work of God, the work of creation. Another friend of mine, Mike, is an architect. He joined a firm with a strong commitment to developing environmentally sound buildings, using ecologically sustainable products, and complementing the natural world and ecosystems in which they're built. He has created and built some of the most wonderful buildings in the wilderness of Tasmania. This is the work of God, expressed through his apprentice-son, Mike. It is the same in many ways as the work of a plumber or an electrician, a gardener or a bricklayer.

History is replete with stories of people who have designed and built successful businesses and become the source of great philanthropy. In so doing, they are following the work of the Father. In 1759, a determined man named Arthur Guinness, thirty-four years of age, rode through the gate of an old, dilapidated, ill-equipped brewery situated at St. James's Gate in Dublin. He had just signed a lease on the property for nine thousand years (no, that's not a typo!) at £45 per annum (this would be about $79 US today). Mark Rainsford's Ale Brewery (as it was known then) was no different from any other, and it had been for sale for ten years, with no one having shown any interest in it. At that time, beer was almost unknown in rural Ireland, where whiskey, gin, and poteen were the alcoholic beverages most readily available. Cheap to buy, high in alcohol content, and readily available, these drinks were responsible for widespread alcoholism and indolence.

Arthur Guinness was a builder. He was an entrepreneur who could dream up business plans and marketing strategies, who could make a worthless brewery into a booming industry. He was also a devout Christian with a deep social conscience. He was concerned about the plight of young Irish drunks who wandered aimlessly around the whiskey and gin houses found on nearly every street corner. Once, while walking the streets of Dublin, he cried out to God to do something about the general drunkenness of Irish society, and he felt overwhelmingly burdened to be part of the answer to his own prayer. Like a true apprentice-child, he decided there and then to brew a drink that the Irish would enjoy and that would also be good for them.

Guinness decided to brew a beer relatively new to Ireland at that time. The beverage contained roasted barley that gave it a characteristically dark color. This brew, well known in England, was called "porter" because of its popularity with the porters and stevedores of Covent Garden and Billingsgate in London. But Guinness's recipe produced more than your average dark beer. With its rich creamy head, it's the beer we'll drink in heaven. Full-bodied, smooth, creamy, slightly bitter, it's a wonderfully delicious beverage. In fact, it's more like a meal, since it is so full of minerals and natural trace elements. It has incredible qualities to it. Guinness was so heavy and full of iron that most drinkers couldn't drink more than a couple of pints. This, coupled with the fact tht it has a considerably lower alcohol level than whiskey or gin, meant that fewer people were getting drunk.

So young Arthur Guinness made a beverage for the Irish that was good for them. Soon, his porter was overtaking the sales of Irish ales and English porters, and then it became even more popular than Irish whiskey. Today it is the national drink of Ireland. I don't doubt that many preachers today would have difficulty seeing the building of a successful brewing business as the work of God. But by following his impulse as an entrepreneur with a social conscience, Guinness showed himself to be a faithful apprentice-child, a creator and a builder.

Of course, some of us will express our God-inspired desire to create or build by taking up paints and an easel, or by writing poetry or constructing model ships. Some of us will pull the engine of our car apart and rebuild it. Others will restore old airplanes or classic motorcycles or sailboats. Where does this innate yearning to create come from? Why, it comes from us feeling apprenticed as "sons" to the master creator, God our Father. We have seen him return from the workbench, and we have hankered to try our hand at his occupation. Our hobbies, anything from sculpting statues to maintaining automobiles, are not impediments to really serving God (by going to church or Bible Study), but rather are the very means by which we follow our Father.

Nowhere is this more wonderfully seen than in the godly work of two people "designing" and "building" a child together. From the marvelously enjoyable work of falling in love, marrying, making love, and becoming pregnant, two people are undertaking an apprenticeship of sorts. They are doing what God first did. They are creating human life. Of course, we believe that all human existence issues from God, the ultimate designer and sustainer of life itself. In the act of procreation, a man and a woman intimately join God in the work of building life. And through all the pain of childbirth, through the sweat and the blood, when new life is delivered to our arms, we sense the enormous gravity of partnering our Father in his work. There is no more basic an expression of our God-inspired apprenticeship than this.

Naming/Renaming

While God is a creative God, and we "sons"—male and female—will follow God's work by creative, constructive endeavors on this planet, there is one very specific job given to humans by God at the inception:

Now the LORD God had formed out of the ground all the wild animals and all the birds in the sky. He brought them to the man to see what he would

name them; and whatever the man called each living creature, that was its
name. So the man gave names to all the livestock, the birds, and all the
wild animals. (Gen 2:19–20)

Occasionally even today a new species of some rare bird or some previously undiscovered invertebrate is identified and named. Often the creature is named after its discoverer. I recently heard a news report about the beautiful but endangered Gouldian finch. Mr. Gould was doing the work entrusted to humans by God when he named that rare little finch. Oftentimes, naming a creature after ourselves is somewhat self-aggrandizing (apparently, there's a company doing a roaring trade in selling clients the right to name a previously unnamed star after themselves). Naming that which has not been named ought to be a more selfless practice because when we do it, we are completing the work that we have been asked to do by our Father. Of course, finding a rare African finch or a minute invertebrate that lives in underground rivers in southern New Zealand is a difficult task, not readily open to anyone. But the godly work of naming is more accessible than you might at first think.

My friend Melanie is doing her Ph.D. on the effects of drought on large Australian eucalyptus. She regularly travels in a four-wheel-drive vehicle to wild terrain where she examines the telltale bark circles on old, felled trees. Annually she measures the circumferences of living trees and compares their growth in drought years with their growth at other times. She is naming information not previously named. She is searching out the thoughts of God. She is tracking down God's creative imagination, the imagination that gave rise to Australian eucalyptus. Melanie is thinking God's thoughts, and this is righteous work. Any form of research does this. Patrick, another friend of mine, did his Ph.D. on the effect of housing development on natural coastal ecosystems. Donna, an audiologist, who now works in the Dominican Republic in an ear clinic, did her master's degree on the brainwashing techniques of cults and sects in California. Patrick and Donna were naming abuses and identifying them for what they are. Once named, such practices might be less of a danger to people.

But you don't need to complete a Ph.D. to be part of this naming process. When I stood at the edge of the Great Rift Valley in Kenya and proclaimed that it was beautiful, I was naming it. I was speaking over that marvelous vista, and although I was stating the obvious, I was proclaiming that it was good. I felt an involuntary urge to speak. The beauty of that scene couldn't go unnoticed. I was impelled to name it for what it was. I've felt the same thing on a pristine beach on a deserted island in the Great Barrier Reef in northern Australia. And from the foot of the statue Cristo Redentor, overlooking Rio de Janeiro and the surrounding mountains that rise up out of the

sea. And from a turn in the road looking down the ragged, dramatic Californian coastline at Big Sur. And sitting in a roadside café surrounded by rolling
hills of tea plantations in Indonesia. Any tourist will know that when traveling alone, the thing you miss most of all is someone to turn to at those times
and say, "Isn't that beautiful!"

Earlier we looked at childbirth as an expression of the work of God in
our lives. So is the incredible honor of naming our children. And though
most people stick with standards such as Emily, Mary, Matthew, or Andrew, a few people take great advantage of their God-given work of child-
naming. I've heard of little girls called Xanthe and Amethyst, and boys
called Caruso and Gunnar. But the one that really takes the cake is Nevaeh,
given to a little girl, which has to be read backwards to get its intended
meaning. No matter what we parents come up with (and no matter what
others think of our choices), most everybody takes the privilege of naming
children very seriously. It is no light matter. We know that our children will
carry these names with them for the rest of their lives (or until they're old
enough to legally change them). We disagree with the dictum, adapted
from Shakespeare, "A rose by any other name would smell as sweet." We
know that names are important. They say something about our parents' expectations for their children. Naming our children continues the work of
God in this world.

As well as initial naming, there are various incidents in the Bible where
God renames people. It's as if the name given by the parents doesn't quite live
up to the child's God-inspired future. In chapter 17 of Genesis, God makes a
unique covenant with Abram, inaugurating the rite of circumcision and
claiming Abram's offspring as chosen people. At this point, Abram, whose
name means "exalted father," is childless, a terrible irony not lost on him, no
doubt. But then God chooses to rename him: "As for me, this is my covenant
with you: You will be the father of many nations. No longer will you be
called Abram" (Gen 17:4–5a). From that point on he was to be known as
Abraham, meaning "father of many." This is his God-given destiny, and he is
named accordingly.

Later, in chapter 32 of Genesis, Jacob has his famous all-night wrestling
match with God, who appears in the form of an angelic man. Jacob refuses to
let go until he receives a blessing. Even when his hip is wrenched from its
socket, Jacob hangs on. Unable to shake the persistent Jacob, God says,
"What is your name?" "Jacob," he replies. Then God says, "Your name will
no longer be Jacob, but Israel, because you have struggled with God and with
human beings and have overcome" (Gen 32:27–28). His new name more accurately describes his tempestuous relationships with his heavenly and
earthly fathers.

And then, much later, we see Jesus rename one of his closest disciples:

> The first thing Andrew did was to find his brother Simon and tell him, "We have found the Messiah" (that is, the Christ). And he brought him to Jesus. Jesus looked at him and said, "You are Simon son of John. You will be called Cephas" (which, when translated, is Peter). (John 1:41–42)

The name "Simon" means "to hear" and it is a reasonable name for the man who so quickly heard and responded to Christ's call, but Jesus sees a different future for Simon. Jesus sees him becoming a loyal, immovable force—a brick. So he renames him "Peter," meaning "rock." This new name is like a new set of spectacles by which Peter can look at the world. As we know, it took quite some time for Peter to live up to his new name, but live up to it he eventually did.

So when we rename people and things, we do God's work, and God is proud of us. Sometimes we live under the burden of being unfairly "named" by our families or communities. Sometimes we're named as a good-for-nothing, or a bad apple, or a daydreamer. Sometimes we live with the burden of a name that we might have once earned but no longer want to carry. It would be the work of an apprentice-child of God to rename people, to declare, "You have been known as Simon, but I see you as a rock." Teachers can do this so powerfully. They can "name" their students for good or for ill. Every school report card is a naming ceremony. Sometimes the names that our teachers give us are "could-try-harder," or "easily-distracted," or "disruptive-in-class." Such names can be very hard to shake. Teachers talk in the staff room. They pass on these names from one year to the next. You can just hear them saying, "Oh, do you have Simon in your class this year? His name isn't really 'Simon.' It's 'talks-too-much-in-class.'" And then the name sticks, year in and year out.

Godly teachers will name and rename their students. As apprentice-children to the Father, they will take this work very seriously. How many of us know the power of being renamed by our teachers, set free by a new vision of how we can be? After a particularly bad period of my own childhood when I was constantly in trouble with teachers—beaten with straps, made to stand in the corner, given regular detentions—I encountered a teacher who knew what it was to do the work of an apprentice-child. Looking at me on his first day as my teacher (and his first day at that school), he smiled and said, "I've heard all about you, son, but I don't believe a word of it." I vividly recall the sensation of a burden being lifted from my shoulders. There and then he was offering me the opportunity to start over. He was prepared to disbelieve all the names that I'd been given. I jumped at the chance to impress him so that he would rename me.

Teachers aren't the only ones who get to rename others. Therapists and counselors get to name issues in their clients' lives, and by so naming them they help those clients gain self-control. In any workplace we can name and rename colleagues and subordinates. We can value their personhood and offer the integrity of being appreciated and respected. We get to name new protocols and policies that ensure greater access and equity in the workplace. Likewise, godly parents will not just choose their child's legal name. They will rename that child every day: beautiful, darling, tiger, precious, sweetie, champ. They will call their kids "aren't-you-clever" and "how-kind-you-are." We can do the same with those with whom we work every day.

Truth-Telling

We've looked at the godly work of naming that teachers can carry out. But teaching has an even broader dimension than that. To teach is not simply to work in a university or school. To teach is to unearth the truth, to guide others in the right path. Just as God makes paths straight and confounds the foolish, so apprentice-children work to ensure that the truth comes out and that the lies of the deceitful or the powerful are seen for what they are.

I have a friend, Kip, who works for a government patent bureau. He scientifically tests whether certain products do what their designers claim they do. His job is to unearth the true nature of these products accurately, rather than simply accepting what their producers say about them in the interests of good sales. His job is that of truth-telling. Kip's girlfriend, Sarah, works as a forensic scientist with the police force. She identifies DNA and other evidence found on weapons and at crime scenes and, even more grisly, on the corpses of victims of crime. She helps to tell the truth about a situation so that justice might be done. Naturally, this should be the work of all people in law enforcement—lawyers, police officers, sheriffs, judges, and so on. We tire of the many instances of so-called truth-tellers who become corrupt and serve their own ends. We're fed up with journalists who lean toward whichever perspective their corporate bosses desire. We want truthful journalism, a truthful legal system, and truthful priests and pastors who will tell us honestly about a world in the grip of injustice and oppression. Many apprentice-children will find their way into employment that requires truthfulness, integrity, and perseverance.

One woman who has found a way to conduct a successful company and also be in the truth-telling business is British entrepreneur Anita Roddick. In 1976 she founded The Body Shop, selling a small array of around twenty-five homemade, naturally inspired products such as soaps, lotions, and creams. Roddick, always motivated by concern for the environment, assured

her customers that her products were sold with minimal packaging, and that
her ingredients were not tested on animals. She built a customer base that appreciated her values as much as her products. Today, The Body Shop is a
global network of stores franchised by the hundreds of entrepreneurs who
have bought into Roddick's vision for a just world. This has resulted not only
in great international expansion, but also in a worldwide movement of
environmentalism and anti-globalization activism.

The Body Shop's international campaigns against human-rights abuses
and in favor of animal and environmental protection, and its commitment to
challenge the stereotypes of beauty perpetuated by the cosmetics industry,
have won the support of millions of consumers, and today it continues to
lead the way for businesses to use their voice for social and environmental
change. The Body Shop's values include the following:

- We consider testing products or ingredients on animals to be morally
  and scientifically indefensible.

- We support small producer communities around the world who supply
  us with accessories and natural ingredients.

- We believe that it is the responsibility of every individual to actively support those who have human rights denied to them.

- We believe that a business has the responsibility to protect the environment in which it operates, locally and globally.[6]

Roddick's chain of shops is a fabulous example of a socially responsible
business that manages highly successful campaigns for the protection of the
environment, for human and civil rights, and against animal testing within
the cosmetics and toiletries industry. At one level, it simply sells soap, but at
another level, it is challenging the face of business itself by being prepared to
tell the truth about the environment, body image, and civil rights. Its various
campaigns are too numerous to list here, but a few examples will show the
impact that a socially responsible business can have.

In 1993, The Body Shop launched an international campaign to raise
awareness of the plight of the Ogoni people in Nigeria, and in particular of
their leader Ken Saro-Wiwa, persecuted for protesting against Shell Oil and
the Nigerian dictatorship over the exploitation in their homeland. Then in
1996, Roddick launched the "Against Animal Testing" campaign, which led
to the largest ever petition (four million signatures) being delivered to the

---

[6]See "Our Values," The Body Shop under "What's happening in the UK" [cited
17 January 2006]. Online: http://www.uk.thebodyshop.com/web/tbsuk/values.jsp.

European Commission. The campaign led to a U.K.-wide ban on animal testing on cosmetic products and ingredients in November 1998.

To celebrate the fiftieth anniversary of the Universal Declaration of Human Rights in 1998, The Body Shop launched a joint worldwide campaign with Amnesty International to highlight the plight of human-rights defenders around the world, encouraging customers to "Make Their Mark" for human rights. Three million people signed up for the campaign.

In 1999, a loyalty scheme for customers was introduced to the United Kingdom that provided incentives to customers, including the option to donate reward money to selected campaign organizations, including the World Society for the Protection of Animals and the Missing Persons Helpline. Then in 2001, "Choose Positive Energy" was a joint campaign run in partnership with Greenpeace International, which helped highlight the importance of renewable energy in the fight against global warming.

Particularly powerful has been The Body Shop's policy of encouraging volunteerism among its staff by allowing paid days off for employees to work for charities. This allows the staff to learn more about the plight of suffering people or the environment, as well as enabling the company to positively contribute to the local, national, and global communities in which they operate.

Many exiles will find themselves running organic, fair-trade coffee shops, or environmentally sound offices, or other socially aware businesses in the interests of truth-telling. Likewise, Christian novelists, playwrights, and journalists will seek to write the "truth," as Christian writers such as Flannery O'Connor, John Steinbeck, and Walker Percy have done in the past.

Healing

We readily recognize that God is in the healing business. This was amply demonstrated by God's son, Jesus, who spent a significant portion of his public ministry healing the sick. He did so not only to show compassion to those who suffered, but also as a means of demonstrating the coming of God's kingdom. So we're used to thinking of the health sector as godly work. Many Christians, trying to honor God in their career, choose to become doctors or nurses, counselors or social workers, chiropractors or physiotherapists. It makes sense to us that healing is a form of mission. We have heard those marvelous stories of medical missionaries such as David Livingstone and Albert Schweitzer bringing healing in Christ's name. My friend Iona works with clients who suffer from cerebral palsy. Often mentally alert, her clients experience a grotesque twisting of their arms and legs, their neck and face. Often they cannot speak normally or walk unassisted. Some are confined to wheelchairs. Iona finds that her job is a daily expression of God's work of healing in this broken world. Similarly, another friend, Fiona, works as a physical therapist in Cambodia, helping families to create a greater quality of life for their physically disabled children.

In 1849, Methodists John and Mary Boot, motivated by a strong social conscience, opened their first drug store in Nottingham, England. Moved by an awareness that good healthcare was unaffordable to the poor at that time, they sold herbal remedies at low prices. So necessary was this work that Boots Pharmacy has grown into a prominent chain of some fifteen hundred stores in the United Kingdom and Ireland, with a presence in twelve other countries, all the while maintaining its concern for the health and well-being of the poor.

Today, Boots invests around £50 million annually in affordable healthcare in the United Kingdom. In keeping with the deep Christian vision of their founders, Boots supports and develops health-promotion initiatives for the needy in the community. Like The Body Shop, Boots allows its staff to take paid days off to volunteer with charities that work to improve health facilities for local communities—for example, decorating drab hospital rooms or landscaping outside children's clinics. Through its "Give As You Earn" scheme, the company helps staff members to donate to community causes. In fact, the staff of Boots gives 40 percent more to charity than does the average Briton. In 2004, the company matched the £168,000 raised by staff for the charities of their choice. One Boots initiative, workshops called "Time for a Treat," provides a health boost for more than one hundred hospital patients and over three hundred hospital staff members.

Boots is also deeply committed to a rigorous environmental policy that sets greater-than-industry-standard goals for waste reduction and seeks to increase the fuel efficiency of its transportation fleet. The company has also developed a policy for the ethical sourcing of products, ensuring that it will purchase products only from customers whose corporations don't abuse human rights and don't have unsafe work conditions, unfair wage rates, or child labor or enforced labor. All this arose from the godly vision of two apprentice-children, John and Mary Boot.

But, without discounting these avenues at all, maybe we can broaden our thinking about healing. Perhaps we bring healing to a neighborhood when we rally our friends to clean up the local playground. I know of café owners and restaurateurs who bring healing to their communities by fashioning their businesses into welcoming spaces of hospitality and generosity. Aid workers bring healing when they feed the starving or help subsistence farmers develop new drought-resistant crops. A former student of mine, Nathan, works in a gym as a personal trainer. He brings healing to his clients not just by training them physically, but also by listening to them and counseling them spiritually. My wife, Carolyn, is a counselor who has been bringing healing to her clients for years, but recently she has set up a community store in a deprived neighborhood. It provides cheap clothing, free coffee and tea, and a comfortable space where people will be listened to and treated with respect.

Tony Campolo tells the story of a reformed drunk, Joe, who was marvelously converted at a Bowery mission. Joe had been an incorrigible wino, and no one who met him ever expected him to be anything other than a homeless drunk. So the transformation that occurred after his conversion stunned everyone who knew him. Filled with the Holy Spirit, Joe became the most caring person that anyone associated with the mission had ever known. He spent his days and nights at the mission serving both the homeless and the drunk, as well as the Christian workers. He considered no job beneath his dignity, whether it was cleaning up vomit or scrubbing the toilets after careless men left the bathroom filthy. Joe did what was asked with a soft smile on his face and with gratitude for the chance to help. He could be counted on to feed feeble men who wandered in off the street, and to undress and tuck into bed men who were too inebriated to take care of themselves.

One Sunday in the mission, an evangelist was delivering his evening message to the usual crowd of still and sullen men. When he made his regular appeal for people to come forward to accept Christ, one repentant drunk shuffled down the aisle to the altar and knelt to pray, crying out for God for help. The penitent sinner kept shouting, "Oh God, make me like Joe! Make me like Joe! Make me like Joe!" The director of the mission leaned over and said to the man, "Son, I think it would be better if you prayed, 'Make me like Jesus!'" The man looked up at the director with a quizzical expression on his face and asked, "Is he like Joe?"

Whether we sell shoes, sweep streets, program computers, or drive trucks, we bring healing to our world when we direct people to Jesus by the goodness, integrity, and compassion that we display in our daily lives. In this way we become "little Jesuses," apprentice-children to our Master-Father, God.

DOING WHAT WE CAN DO

At one level, Sambo Mockbee was simply an architect, but at another level, he fulfilled many of the aspects of doing his Father's work that we've looked at. Obviously, he was a creator and a builder. He fashioned marvelous buildings and taught others to do the same. As a teacher, he "named" different aspects of the architecture trade for others and, no doubt, "named" his students to inspire them to greater work. But also he was committed to truth-telling, putting his students in close proximity with poverty and injustice, forcing them to come to terms with the world as it really is. His truth-telling work has opened the eyes of hundreds of architects, giving them a proper appreciation of the hardship and the deprivation that beset many decent Americans. And, of course, he brought healing to families, neighborhoods, and whole communities. By designing and building homes, churches, community centers, and playgrounds for those who couldn't otherwise afford them, he has brought a therapeutic touch to many neighborhoods, as well as healing the prejudice or ignorance in the hearts of his architecture students.

We can't all do what Sambo Mockbee did. He obviously was a highly gifted, talented, and motivated person. Occasionally, people like him—or Arthur Guinness or Anita Roddick—come along, and the world is better off because of them. But we can do what my wife, Carolyn, does. That is, we can discover what contribution we can make as faithful apprentice-children and do it! Just as my friends Iona, Paul, Nathan, Kip, Sarah, Fiona, Wayne, Melanie, Carolyn, Patrick, Donna, and Mike do. If our chosen professions are well paid, so be it. And if so, we must make sure that we give a lot of money away in the service of others. But if our contribution is little appreciated by our society (well, not according to the pay scale, at least), we remember that the primary reason for our vocation is to complete the work of our Master-Father. It is a sacred task, not to be denigrated or ignored by our society or by our churches. As the great Danish philosopher Søren Kierkegaard said,

> What is your occupation in life? [I] do not ask inquisitively about whether it is great or mean, whether you are a king or a labourer. [I] do not ask, after the fashion of business, whether you earn a great deal of money or are building up great prestige for yourself. The crowd enquires and talks of these things. But whether your occupation is great or mean, is it of such a kind that you dare think of it together with the responsibility of eternity?[7]

---

[7]Søren Kierkegaard, *Purity of Heart Is to Will One Thing: Spiritual Preparation for the Office of Confession* (trans. Douglas V. Steere; New York: Harper & Row, 1956), 198.

PART III
DANGEROUS CRITICISM

9

Restless with Injustice

The Critique: You Have Been an Unjust Empire

CORPORATION, n. An ingenious device for obtaining individual profit without individual responsibility.
—Ambrose Bierce, The Devil's Dictionary (1911)

In the second part of this book we explored some of the promises that exiles can live out now within a post-Christendom empire: promises to be authentic, to build missional community, to be generous and hospitable, and to work as God's apprentices. Now we turn our attention to the practice of a dangerous critique, knowing that the criticism of any empire from within will land us in hot water. The following three chapters detail our obligation to censure the empire for its complicity in injustice, oppression, and environmental destruction. I will not only look at the basis for such a critique, but also explore ways the Christian community can respond practically. So what makes one topic a criticism and another a promise? On the one hand, we criticize our empire for things that we, as the Christian community, cannot do by ourselves; on the other hand, we promise to do those things that we, as the Christian community, have the power to fulfill. For example, it is reasonable to expect that Christians should commit to authenticity, generosity, and hospitality, but it's quite unreasonable to expect them to be able to end all injustice or save the environment from destruction. Promises are things that exiles can act upon immediately. These criticisms are outcries to our world that Christians must voice, knowing that things such as oppression and greed grieve God's heart. They are projects for which the empire itself must be galvanized into action, and we begin with the global tragedy of injustice.

Convincing the Western world that we live in an unjust empire became more difficult after the outpouring of generosity that followed the Indian

Ocean tsunami of December 26, 2004. Over a quarter of a million people were killed, and thousands of bloated corpses floated into ports and onto beaches in a dozen different countries. Tourists from dozens more were among the victims. Mosques and temples were set up as temporary morgues, particularly for the identification of Westerners. In Sri Lanka, Banda Aceh, and southern Thailand many locals had to be buried, unidentified, in mass graves to limit the spread of infectious disease. The world had rarely seen devastation on such a scale, and consequently, rich Western countries swung into action.

The generous response to the December 2004 tsunami is already legendary. In four days the American Red Cross collected more than $29 million for its International Response Fund. That amount didn't include the $6.2 million contributed to the agency by the ninety-six thousand visitors to Amazon's related appeal over the same period. Catholic Relief Services was usually receiving $60,000 a month in online gifts, but in the week following the disaster it was receiving $100,000 per hour. In the United Kingdom, the Disasters Emergency Committee reported collecting the equivalent of $39 million from individuals in less than one day, while the Labour government debated whether to freeze foreign debts owed by tsunami-affected nations. Finland, a country of five million people, raised $4 million in the first week. Italians raised $17 million by sending special text messages on their cell phones. Australians raised $20 million in a three-hour telethon. The Chinese Red Cross collected $3 million in four days—this from a country where the average person lives on less than $1,000 a year. Such an expression of social justice was unprecedented.

The Changing Nature of Mass Movements

It's true that in times of dreadful suffering human beings do find within themselves the capacity to be generous. When New Orleans is devastated by Hurricane Katrina or West Virginia by a brush fire, there are always Americans ready to lend a hand by donating money or volunteering time. But what incidents like the 2004 tsunami also highlight is that we have the capacity to give our time and money in enormous amounts. While making their various appeals for donations, aid agencies regularly referred to a "wave of hope" for Southeast Asia. Just as the ocean had sent a wave of destruction, we were sending a wave of support to the victims. It was easy to feel as though your small financial contribution was part of a global wave of generosity and goodwill.

However, although the language was entirely appropriate for the appeal, it obscured something else. Although the West obviously can rise to the occasion—a cataclysmic tragedy such as a tsunami—it generally does little about the enormous suffering that occurs across our planet every day. We might be good at a one-off appeal, but there is no real evidence of a general movement (or wave) of compassion or generosity sweeping through the West. There were appeals for financial support after the Bangladesh floods in 1991 (138,000 dead), the northwestern Iraq earthquake the year before (50,000 dead), the Rwandan genocide, the Ethiopian drought, the 1976 Tang-shan earthquake in China (up to 750,000 dead), and in each case money was donated, but Westerners continued to live as they always did, without allowing the scale of these tragedies to affect their ongoing spending patterns or priorities.

It was not dissimilar to the popular reaction when the Bush administration pulled together the so-called Coalition of the Willing to conduct the second war on Iraq in the light of the attacks on New York and Washington of September 11, 2001. Millions of anti-war protesters took to the streets to express their opposition to the invasion of Iraq. In New York, London, Paris, Sydney, and beyond, the streets were awash with millions of people marching against the war. And these were not just your stereotypical anarchists, hippies, and socialist peaceniks—long beards, sandals, and tie-dyed T-shirts. Suburban moms and dads pushed their babies in strollers; older people marched proudly with their teenage grandchildren; Baptists found themselves marching alongside local Islamic councils, as did Republicans alongside Democrats. For those of us who marched, it was easy to feel that we were part of a great global wave of peace that would crash at the front door of the White House or 10 Downing Street and pressure our national leaders to reverse their decision to wage war. But it wasn't to be. The Coalition of the Willing prosecuted their war with all its disastrous consequences. Mammoth though it was, the protest achieved nothing in that first month. So what did the millions of protesters do next? They evaporated.

The same could be said of the tsunami appeal. The wave of generosity was a short, dramatic burst of excitement that had no ongoing energy to sustain it. Worse still, U.S. papers such as the *New York Times* and the *Los Angeles Times* have reported that almost nothing has been done to begin repairs and rebuilding in the disaster-stricken areas. To add insult to injury, U.S. Secretary of State Condoleezza Rice, in a moment of terrible candor, was noted as saying that the tsunami was a "wonderful opportunity" that "has paid great dividends for us." Her shocking statement was seized upon by a group calling itself Thailand Tsunami Survivors and Supporters, who said that for "businessmen-politicians, the tsunami was the answer to their prayers, since it wiped these coastal areas clean of the communities which had previously stood in the way of their plans for resorts, hotels, casinos and shrimp farms. To them, all these coastal areas are now open land."[1]

There seems to be no limit to the depths to which the self-interest of wealthy nations will sink. Of course, there is a minority of deeply committed peace activists who were very much involved in the anti–Iraq War movement, as they had been involved in anti-war movements in the past. Some of them have been activists since the anti–Vietnam War protests of the 1970s. Imagine their surprise to see millions of protesters joining them on the streets of San Francisco and Seattle and New York in 2003, possibly believing that a new era for the movement had arrived, only to see it dissolve within months. The reelection of the Bush administration in 2004 confirmed their worst fears: the marches of the previous year had represented an expression of people's unhappiness with the situation but didn't translate into a cogent, ongoing movement for peace. We could conclude something similar about the explosion of munificence generated by the disaster of the 2004 tsunami in Southeast Asia.

It seems that the very nature of mass movements has changed. Whereas people once acted because they believed strongly in a cause and were prepared to invest their time, energy, and money in a collective of like-minded people, now they are more inclined to protest or donate money in short bursts to express how they "feel" about a particular situation. Protest marches and donations to aid organizations are now forms of self-expression, ways of conveying our feelings about a particular issue. By saying this, I am not dismissing the genuineness of those feelings or devaluing the contributions that people make. What I am saying is that people seem to need a valve for regular, brief responses to global issues, rather than being motivated to join long-term movements for change. Idealists must weep with anticipation at what could be done about global poverty if the wave of generosity that we saw in early 2005 could continue to sweep around the Western world.

In a post-Christendom culture that values the expression of feelings over the enlisting of oneself to a lifelong cause, we will continue to see bursts of activity like the anti-war marches and the tsunami appeal, just as we see sales for Michael Moore's books and films going through the roof. But, as impressive as these events might be, we shouldn't be fooled into thinking that a new movement of peace, compassion, and generosity is building. In fact, if such a movement is to be built, I think it's fair to say that exiles will be at its forefront, not just expressing their "feelings" about injustice, poverty, and suffer-

---

[1]Naomi Klein, "Profits of Doom," *Good Weekend Magazine, Sydney Morning Herald* (May 14, 2005): 33.

ing, but working tirelessly for the extension of God's kingdom of grace, peace, kindness, and generosity on this planet.

As we noted earlier, part of the dangerous promises that we are to make to our host empire is to fashion communities of companionship—literally, "bread sharers." There are many names for this sharing: utopia, community, nirvana, kingdom of God. It is this sharing to which Jesus calls us. Of course, Christians have always been on the frontline of overseas aid and development. After the 2004 tsunami Christian aid agencies were key contributors to the cleanup and rebuilding phases of the recovery operation. Churches were conspicuous in their generous response to the disaster. But it is important to acknowledge that global suffering occurs each and every year in two-thirds of the nations across the world, and that a proper Christian response also includes a commitment to work against the conditions that contribute to such misery and need. Granted, we cannot stop tsunamis any more than King Canut could stop the rising tide, but we can work to stop the wave of injustice being generated by Western corporations and governments. In this respect, exiles are expected to voice a very dangerous critique of their host empire.

At the World Economic Forum in Davos, Switzerland, in early 2005, rock star and activist Bono said that we are the generation that can actually see an end to extreme poverty. "That's not misty-eyed Irish sentiment," he said on air. "It's achievable. And I'm willing to spend the rest of my life toward that end." Shortly after that forum, the Group of Seven (G7), the finance ministers of the world's seven wealthiest nations, met at a summit in London. Coinciding with those meetings, Nelson Mandela launched the Make Poverty History campaign at a rally of some twenty thousand people in Trafalgar Square with these words:

> Sometimes it falls upon a generation to be great. Through your will and passion, you assisted in consigning that evil system [South African apartheid] to history. But in this new century, millions of people in the world's poorest countries remain imprisoned, enslaved, and in chains. Like slavery and apartheid, poverty is not natural. It is man-made and it can be overcome and eradicated by the actions of human beings.[2]

Sensing that British finance minister Gordon Brown's proposal to write off the foreign debt owed by the twenty-seven poorest countries might be passed, the Make Poverty History campaign erected an electronic display outside the G7 meetings that recorded second-by-second the

[2]Annabel Crabb, "Mandela Urges a Generation to Fight Poverty," *Sydney Morning Herald* (February 5, 2005): 15.

number of children around the world dying from malnutrition and disease. When Brown's proposal was indeed passed by the G7, it was a significant milestone for the debt-relief movement, which has campaigned for over fifteen years for such a decision.[3] Surely such victories ought to motivate us to share the same attitude as Bono's and Mandela's. Donations to one-off causes are excellent, but even better is a lifetime commitment to global justice and compassionate living.

The saddest thing about world poverty is that it is, as Mandela says, solvable. If the world's wealthiest nations spent just 1 percent of their income on the effects of global poverty, it could be greatly diminished.[4] Basic nutrition, health, and education would be more readily available to all for this small outlay. It also would affect the rate of infant mortality and pandemic diseases. It's not too costly to end extreme poverty. It just takes the will of these wealthy nations. And yet, since 2000 the United Nations has argued over the wording of a set of global goals for eliminating extreme poverty, defined as living on an income of below $1 a day, adjusted for relative purchasing power. While they argue, one in five of the world's population do just that— eke out a meager existence on less than $1 a day.

---

[3]The G7 is made up of the finance ministers and central bankers of the United Kingdom, the United States, France, Canada, Italy, Japan, and Germany. In some meetings, when Russia is included, it meets as the G8. Clause 7 of their resolution from London 2005 reads, "7. The Enhanced HIPC Initiative has to date significantly reduced the debt of 27 countries, and we reaffirm our commitment to the full implementation and financing of the Initiative. Moreover, individual G7 countries have gone further, providing up to 100 percent relief on bilateral debt. However, we recognize that more still needs to be done. We are agreed on a case-by-case analysis of HIPC countries, based on our willingness to provide as much as 100 percent multilateral debt relief. We also ask the IMF and the World Bank to look at the issue of debt sustainability in other low-income countries. To finance the relief of debts owed to the IMF and to enable the Fund to continue to play a role in the poorest countries, the Managing Director has stated that he will bring forward proposals at the Spring Meetings, covering the Fund's gold and other resources and in an orderly way. We look forward to his proposals. For the relief of debts owed to the World Bank and African Development Bank we will work with their management and shareholders to bring forward proposals for agreement at the Spring Meetings to achieve this without reducing the resources available to the poorest countries through these institutions. We also call on non-Paris Club creditors to provide at least their share of HIPC debt relief, and we ask the IMF to report on progress at the Spring Meetings." For a full list of clauses see http://www.finfacts.com/irelandbusinessnews/publish/article_1000374.shtml.

[4]Jeffrey D. Sachs and Sakiko Fukuda-Parr, "If We Cared to, We Could Defeat World Poverty," *Los Angeles Times* (July 9, 2003). See http://hdr.undp.org/docs/news/hdr2003/LAtimes_SFP&JS_Jul08.pdf.

AN ANTI-INJUSTICE MOVEMENT

Many conservative American Christians, seeing news broadcasts show-ing thousands of protestors demonstrating outside world-trade meetings, be-lieve the media's casting of these protesters as anti-capitalist or anti-business or, worse, anti-American. They hear the newscasters referring to them as anti-globalization protesters, and they see the images of them behaving ag-gressively, even violently. For this reason, it's been easy for the mainstream church to adopt the television networks' portrayal of them as a lunatic fringe of radical leftists. But when you take a closer, more rational look at the agenda of the so-called anti-globalization movement (notwithstanding the admittedly high-handed tactics in some quarters of it), it's hard to see why Christians have not been a more significant part of this group.

Unfortunately, the popular moniker of the movement isn't helpful. Commentators scoff at the quixotic nature of the anti-globalization move-ment, as it naïvely tilts at windmills, trying to stop the deeply entrenched juggernaut that is globalization. But such criticism is simply patronizing. Most members of the anti-globalization movement are far from naïve, being fully aware that globalization is a very present reality. They are not protesting against social progress, technology development, or global cooperation; rather, the focus of their protest is the unethical and dangerously unsustain-able way that economic globalization is being accomplished.

In addition, the reputation of the movement is not enhanced by the frag-mented nature of the various submovements that comprise its membership. Again, news reports often depict protesters as a disorganized mob that can't decide whether they're promoting AIDS awareness, advocating debt relief for poor nations, boycotting companies that use child labor, cleaning up the en-vironment, or saving dolphins from tuna trawlers. This apparent disorgani-zation emerges from the fact that the anti-globalization movement is indeed fractured by the competing agendas of different organizations. There is no hierarchy, no central leadership, no core doctrine. For this reason, some protesters feel at liberty to demonstrate violently, while others cringe at their behavior. What they share, if not agreement on tactics, is common dis-satisfaction with the current world order.

Surely this is an agenda that the followers of Jesus also share. We should be dissatisfied with our host empire as we find it. Wracked by greed, selfish-ness, injustice, and violence, this world needs a complete spiritual makeover, and exiles are prepared to abandon the prejudices about anti-globalization protesters and listen carefully to their agenda, even if that means making a very dangerous critique of our host culture. We might well find that a great deal of the critique is in keeping with the concerns of God. If we're not comfortable with the reputation of the anti-globalization movement, why not at least consider the merits of being part of an anti-injustice movement, acknowledging that the unscrupulous and dangerous forces currently supporting the globalization agenda are causing unspeakable suffering across this planet? Can we ever be comfortable in a world where there is such starvation? Can we be "at home" in a world where 12,000 women are killed each year in Russia alone as a result of domestic violence? Or in a world where there are 300,000 child-soldiers fighting in armed conflicts? Or where some 120,000 women and girls are trafficked across international borders each year? Or where Africa is home to 30,000,000 people who are HIV-positive? [5]

It's not enough that we simply share bread with the poor. Part of our companionship with the poor requires us to be peacemakers, to address the forces that foster and promote poverty and injustice around the world. We can no longer remain ignorant of the fact that Western governments are giving away power to large corporations for their own gain, leaving human rights, the environment, public health, the economy, and even democracy at risk.

Beware the Corporation

If you've seen the Canadian documentary series *The Corporation,* you understand something of the concern that many people have with the burgeoning power of big business. In this complex and highly entertaining documentary, Mark Achbar and Jennifer Abbott team up with writer Joel Bakan to examine the far-reaching repercussions of the corporation's increasing preeminence. Based on Bakan's book *The Corporation: The Pathological Pursuit of Profit and Power,* the film series is a chilling wake-up call for those of us imagining that all is well with the world. While we slept, big business survived years of mergers, acquisitions, and hostile takeovers, leading to today's major corporations being larger and wealthier than anything ever seen before. Achbar, Abbott, and Bakan observe,

> One hundred and fifty years ago, the corporation was a relatively insignificant entity. Today, it is a vivid, dramatic and pervasive presence in all our lives. Like the Church, the Monarchy and the Communist Party in other times and places, the corporation is today's dominant institution.[6]

---

[5]For the source of these facts and others about poverty, deprivation, human rights abuses, and corruption see Jessica Williams, *50 Facts That Should Change the World* (Cambridge: Icon Books, 2005).

[6]Robert Lewis, "Study Guide" for "The Corporation: a film by Mark Achbar, Jennifer Abbott & Joel Bakan," p. 2 [cited April 4, 2006]. Online: http://www.thecorporation.com/assets/TC.pdf#search= 'Today%2C%20it%20is%20a%20vivid%2C%20dramatic%20and%20pervasive%20presence.

The financial influence of the larger companies has translated into political clout, thanks to campaign contributions, personal connections, and high-priced lobbying. This has led to policies and legislation in the West that literally allow corporations to pursue profit at the expense of everything else. It is disturbing and ironic that the very companies that regularly cry out that we should "keep government out of business" have prospered so extravagantly because of their well-financed political ties.

The Corporation explains that it was only in the mid-1800s that a Supreme Court decision interpreted the 14th Amendment to the Constitution (originally intended to guarantee full citizenship to African-Americans) as allowing an entity like a company to be understood legally as an individual, even as a person. Remember that, as any CEO will tell you, the chief purpose for the existence of a corporation is to earn profit for its stockholders. Once the corporation was seen as a person in the legal sense, it began to develop something of a "personality," one of pure self-interest and greed. Over the next hundred years, corporations rose to dominance and created unprecedented wealth, unconcerned with the unintended consequences of a transaction between two parties on a third, even if those consequences included countless cases of illness, death, poverty, pollution, exploitation, and lies.

Today, fifty-one of the top one hundred economies in the world are corporations (the other forty-nine are entire countries). The largest corporation in the world is Wal-Mart, a multibillion-dollar-a-year company that has precipitated the closure across the United States of literally thousands of small businesses. Thirty years ago, any money spent in small-town America tended to circulate around that same community. Today, most of it leaves town via the huge chain stores. No doubt the stockholders of Wal-Mart are delighted, even though it has meant the devastation of numerous small communities across the United States.

Achbar, Abbott, and Bakan, conscious of the destructive personality of big business, developed a checklist using diagnostic criteria from the World Health Organization and the DSM-IV, the standard diagnostic tool of psychiatrists and psychologists, to determine the personality profile of a typical corporation. They found the following:

The operational principles of the corporation give it a highly anti-social "personality": It is self-interested, inherently amoral, callous and deceitful; it breaches social and legal standards to get its way; it does not suffer from guilt, yet it can mimic the human qualities of empathy, caring and altruism. Four case studies, drawn from a universe of corporate activity, clearly demonstrate harm to workers, human health, animals and the biosphere. Concluding this point-by-point analysis, a disturbing diagnosis is delivered: the institutional embodiment of laissez-faire capitalism fully meets the diagnostic criteria of a "psychopath."[7]

Many Christians have asked me something like, "What's so terrible about big business, anyway?" Bearing in mind that many churchgoing people often are leaders in the corporate sector, I will attempt to outline a few basic concerns that all of us should share.

They Are the Recipients of Unfair Tax Breaks

It's an acknowledged fact that the biggest corporations pay the least tax. In most Western countries legislation has ensured that with special corporate tax credits for things such as drilling for oil, issuing stock options, and depreciation of equipment, big companies can drastically minimize their tax bills. Some of America's wealthiest people pay very little personal tax at all. Despite the booming size of the corporate sector in the United States, the percentage of federal revenue from corporate tax has been going down. In 1961, only 21 percent of federal revenue was raised through corporate taxes. In 1971, it was 14.3 percent; in 1981, 10.3 percent; and in 2001, a paltry 7.3 percent. Although corporations are growing and earning increasing profits, they are contributing less and less to the federal coffers.

Corporations also receive other forms of support from federal and state governments. Some corporations have received donations of once publicly owned lands, including those with natural resources. Others have received the financial bonus of being able to patent the results of government-funded research. And many others receive quite extensive agricultural subsidies and expensive bailouts in order to keep them afloat. Naturally, the hundreds of billions of dollars in tax benefits given to the world's wealthiest businesses represent monies not spent on schools, social programs, and the poor. Of course, governments will argue that by supporting these businesses they are keeping Americans in work, contributing to the general wealth of the United States. In some cases, government bailouts are necessary to avoid mass unemployment occurring in some communities, but this accounts only for a small percentage of the corporate welfare currently enjoyed by big business.

The fact remains that some of these companies would never be able to get as large as they have without the generous support from government that

[7]"The Corporation: a film by Mark Achbar, Jennifer Abbot and Joel Bakan," n.p. [cited 17 January 2006]. Online: http://www.thecorporation.com/index.php?page_id=2.

they enjoy. Their political influence is now legendary, as corporations spend massive amounts of money to lobby elected officials to ensure the best political environment for their continued growth. In the midst of all the tabloid-TV reports about poorer families ripping off the welfare system, it's worth remembering that big corporations are now the biggest welfare recipients in the United States.

They Are Unconcerned about the Effects of Privatization

Once publicly listed, companies are under enormous pressure to make a profit for their stockholders. Slow and steady growth has been considered unacceptable. Investors want impressive and immediate returns for their money. This means that the company has to grow dramatically to increase profits dramatically. There are two general ways to do this: produce more and sell more of your product (easier said than done in today's highly competitive market), or look for new markets to expand into. One relatively simple way to create new markets is through privatization. Privatization, in its broadest sense, is the transfer of assets or services from the tax-supported and politicized public sector to the entrepreneurial initiative and competitive markets of the private sector. All over the world, formerly publicly held banks, telecoms, airlines, power companies, water utilities, prisons, and even schools are being privatized by governments. The government gets the cash infusion and loses the headache of having to administer the company. Other forms of privatization include the following:

- The outright gift or sale by government of a physical asset (a piece of equipment or a building, perhaps) to a private entity

- The sale of stock in a newly privatized company that was formerly state-owned

- The ending of subsidies and all the red tape and regulations that came with them, liberating an industry to produce for the market instead of for the government

In the meantime, corporations take over blue-chip services, such as banking and electricity production, believing them to be sure-fire businesses (everyone needs electricity, after all), and discovers that in many cases the newly privatized company should be run more "efficiently." In the interest of financial growth, the less profitable aspects of these services/companies are compromised. Also, when essential services such as these are run by profit-driven companies, the public interest is not always going to be served. For example, when prisons and law enforcement are privatized, police and prison-guard unions and other related groups lobby the government to get tough on crime, resulting in more people being jailed for petty offenses (consider, for example, California's "three strikes" legislation). Of course, when running prisons is a business, it's good for business to have more custodial sentences for offenders.

Or consider what occurs when medical care is privatized. Costs soar, and today many Americans face bankruptcy because of chronic illness. Equally worrisome is the effect of privatizing medical research: medicines are developed almost entirely on the basis of their profit potential, not their greater good. While millions of Africans die each year from the effects of HIV/AIDS, European pharmaceutical companies will not supply at-cost medications while they can produce smaller amounts for greater profit in the lucrative European/American markets. One company ceased production of Eflornithine, which was desperately needed to save lives in Africa, because its market in wealthy Western nations had shrunk so much as to make it unprofitable. Despite years of pleas from African governments and aid and medical agencies, production was resumed only when it was discovered that the drug has a profitable side effect: it can be used in creams for the removal of facial hair!

Of course, it makes sense for companies to "trim the fat," "get more bang for the buck," and "concentrate on core competencies"—all jargon for increasing profit margins. And although some level of privatization might be useful, the doctrine as a whole is now under suspicion because it is often poorly managed, done for the wrong reason, and carried out with no thought for the human cost. Why is there such an unrelenting push for privatization and downsizing at the moment? Since salaries and benefits are two of the major operating expenses for companies, a business that lays people off and/or contracts their jobs out to a supplier of cheap labor will have more ready cash available. In the highly competitive business world, it's assumed that if everyone else is doing it, so should I. This often leads to "downsizing stampedes" in an industry, and downsizing looks good on stockholders' reports. Often, share prices will rise after a major downsizing because the company is perceived as "doing something."

However, the human cost is enormous. Downsizing usually does not involve employees getting new jobs at their old salaries. In fact, the older an employee, the longer he or she may have to wait to get any job at all. Companies that have downsized usually end up replacing people in those positions, but at lower salaries. In other words, they have replaced older, more experienced employees with younger employees who are willing to work for less. The companies and the CEOs profit, while the gap between rich and poor widens.

THEY CAUSE THE GREATEST ENVIRONMENTAL DAMAGE

In *The Corporation,* the delightfully English Sir Mark Moody-Stuart recounts an exchange between himself (at the time, chairman of Royal Dutch Shell), his wife, and a motley crew of Earth First activists who arrived on the doorstep of their country home. The protesters chanted and stretched a banner over their roof that read: MURDERERS. The response of the surprised couple was not to call the police, but rather to engage their uninvited guests in a civil dialogue, share concerns about human rights and the environment, and, eventually serve them tea on their front lawn. Yet, as the Moody-Stuarts apologize for not being able to provide soymilk for their vegan critics' tea, Shell Nigeria was flaring unrivaled amounts of gas, making it one of the world's single worst sources of pollution. And all the professed concerns about the environment do not spare Ken Saro-Wiwa and eight other activists from being hanged for opposing Shell's environmental practices in the Niger Delta.

The impact of corporations on the destruction of our planet's fragile environment is astonishing. Suburban families are conscientiously recycling bottles, cans, cardboard, and newspapers, yet all our efforts in separating the recyclables from our garbage, buying recycled paper, and avoiding the use of Styrofoam cups amount to very little in comparison to the massive toll that big business takes on the environment. Consider Paul Hawken's sobering perspective:

> One of the outgrowths of Earth Day was the emphasis in the media on stories about what the consumer could do to "save the earth." . . . The popularity of the notion that it's within the power of citizens to save the earth is not surprising, because it's in the very nature of modern corporate capitalism, however inadvertently or purposefully, to put itself in the best light. While everything individuals do helps, these efforts are relatively insignificant when compared to the demands placed on the environment by corporations themselves. Consider this fact: if the items used in the households in America were all recycled, this would reduce our solid waste by only 1 to 2 percent.[8]

So the vast majority of garbage and air and water pollution comes from corporate industry and agriculture. Naturally, for this to be addressed, we need stricter and more regularly enforced environmental legislation, but as we have already noted, big business and local government are inextricably connected. Most corporations seem to be able to flout the inadequate legislation that is already in place. And local politicians have to be careful when

[8]Paul Hawken, *The Ecology of Commerce: A Declaration of Sustainability* (New York: HarperCollins, 1993), 13.

proposing new legislation because a company unhappy with tighter environment controls can just up and leave a town, resulting in lost jobs and tax revenue. Even at the federal level, politicians resist environment legislation because of the financial considerations of their sponsors.

We will look at our environmental responsibilities more fully in a later chapter, but here let's just note that the environmental record of multinational corporations has been woeful. In a hell-bent quest for greater profit, oil companies have destroyed the environment of the once pristine Fly River in New Guinea, asbestos companies have ruined the Outback of Western Australia, the Amazon is dying, global warming is threatening our ecosystem, and still the United States resolutely refuses to sign the Kyoto Protocol. We now witness the cynical practice whereby corporations employ PR firms to "greenwash" them—that is, to clean up their environmental image without affecting their environmental practices.

They Profit from Unfair Trade Agreements

The World Trade Organization (WTO) has used its power to police international trade since 1995. During that time it has developed a series of treaties called General Agreements on Trade in Services (GATS). When a nation signs a GATS treaty, there is a built-in assumption that it will work toward the privatization of essential services. GATS threatens to commercialize public resources and services and subordinate human needs for them to the interests of transnational corporations and wealthy countries. It has begun to erect new fences around the global commons, promoting the privatization of public services and deregulation of private services while eroding consumer, worker, and environmental protections. The wide-ranging provisions of GATS encompass all service sectors, from banking, energy, and telecommunications to predominantly public services such as prisons, water delivery, healthcare, and education. The treaty is also, in effect, a multilateral investment agreement because it covers direct provision of services by foreign corporations.

Admittedly, GATS does not cover any sectors that the signatory government hasn't listed in the "schedule of specific commitments," but the United States and Europe are putting heavy pressure on developing countries to continually expand their coverage, leaving services essential to human life and social stability increasingly exposed to the vagaries of international markets. And because commitments under GATS are practically irreversible, it endangers local democratic control over these services.

The ongoing development of GATS continues to be shaped behind closed doors by powerful industry associations such as the U.S. Coalition of Service Industries and the European Services Forum, working closely with the trade representatives of the wealthy governments and the WTO bureaucracy. Public debate has been minimal both in national legislative bodies and in civil society. You probably won't be surprised to learn that representatives of developing countries and citizen groups have been marginalized and excluded.

In a moment of extraordinary candor, Industry Canada, a government ministry, released a report that in one place stated, "The GATS is not just a treaty that exists between governments; it is first and foremost an instrument for the benefit of business." In fact, it is routinely admitted even by the leadership of the WTO that without the enormous pressure generated by the American financial services sector, there would have been no such thing as GATS.

Some of the individual rulings of the WTO are laughable. It declared that an American law designed to protect endangered sea turtles was an illegal barrier to "free trade" for the shrimp-fishing industry, even though their methods of fishing didn't actually threaten sea turtles at all. It disallowed a European law banning hormone-laced meat because it cut into U.S. agricultural interests. When the Commonwealth of Massachusetts sought to protest against the brutal military dictatorship of Burma (now Myanmar) by passing a law that banned public contracts to corporations that invested in that country, the WTO challenged the law. One has to question whether the trade sanctions placed on South Africa by the rest of the world ever would have happened had the WTO been active during that country's apartheid era.

The North American Free Trade Agreement (NAFTA) has a provision that allows corporations to sue governments for creating legislation that affects their profits. The Mexican government, heeding a public outcry, denied California-based Metalclad a construction permit for a toxic-waste facility, and had to pay that company $16.7 million. The Ethyl Corporation successfully sued the Canadian government for banning a gasoline additive manufactured by that company. The Methanex Corporation is suing the U.S. government because California banned a different additive. Currently, UPS is suing the Canadian government for over $200 million because it thinks that the publicly owned postal service is a barrier to the expansion of its business interests in Canada. Says Linda McQuaig in her book on the new face of capitalism,

> The growing power of corporations and diminishing power of governments these days is usually attributed to mysterious forces operating out there in the global economy, well beyond our control. Here's another possibility: governments are less powerful than they used to be simply

because they keep signing trade deals that reduce their power and enhance the power of corporations. It's likely no more mysterious than that.[9]

Euphemistically called "free trade" agreements, this global deal-making
is taking power away from democratic governments and giving it to huge
multinational corporations.

They Are Structuring an Inequitable Global Economy

The global economy is currently based on the principles of neo-liberal
economics. At the core of this economic doctrine is the push for the removal
of government controls on business. The neo-liberal economists believe that
governments should increase the freedoms enjoyed by big business in order
to allow it to create jobs and innovations that emerge only through a truly
free market, fueled by competition and entrepreneurship. It is believed that a
truly free business sector will benefit everyone, and that as the wealth built by
corporations trickles down to local neighborhoods, the net gains for everyone
will outweigh the costs in all, or almost all, cases.

These economic policies are being implemented all over the world with
the help of powerful international agencies such as the International Mone-
tary Fund (IMF) and the World Bank. Both agencies provide loans to developing countries that come with plenty of neo-liberal economic strings
attached. Currently there are strong anti-privatization movements in countries such as Nigeria, Pakistan, and Argentina, riling against the imposition
of so-called free-market principles on their economies. For example, the
structural adjustments required of Argentina by the IMF since the 1990s
have been blamed for pushing that country into its current state of crisis and
causing major problems in dozens of other countries. More recent examples
reinforce the belief that the World Bank often directs its aid for the benefit of
a privileged few, not the real victims of poverty. Naomi Klein describes the
following cases:

- "In East Timor . . . the World Bank doles out money to the government
  as long as it shows it is spending responsibly. Apparently, this means
  slashing public sector jobs (Timor's government is half the size it was
  under Indonesian occupation) but lavishing aid money on foreign con-
  sultants the bank insists the government hire. In one government department, a single international consultant earns in one month the
  same as his 20 Timorese colleagues earn together in an entire year."[10]

---

[9]Linda McQuaig, *All You Can Eat: Greed, Lust, and the New Capitalism* (Toronto: Penguin Canada, 2001).
[10]Klein, "Profits of Doom," 31.

- "In Afghanistan, where the World Bank also administers the country's aid through a trust fund, it has already managed to privatize healthcare by refusing to give funds to the Ministry of Health to build hospitals. Instead it funnels money directly to NGOs, which are running their own private health clinics on three-year contracts."[11] Klein cites the fact that the water system, telecommunications, oil, gas, mining, and the electricity sector in Afghanistan have all been directed to "foreign private investors."

- "[In Haiti] . . . in exchange for a $61 million loan, the bank is requiring 'public-private partnership and governance in the education and health sectors,' . . . that is, private companies running schools and hospitals."[12]

We are living in a world where an entrenched system of appropriation has created a situation in which poor countries that have been plundered by colonizing regimes for centuries are steeped in debt to the very same countries that plundered them, and have to repay that debt at the rate of $382 billion a year. How fair is the global economy where the combined wealth of the world's 587 billionaires exceeds the combined gross domestic product of the world's 135 poorest countries? Or when rich countries that pay farm subsidies of a billion dollars a day try to force poor countries to drop their subsidies? In 1992, the Human Development Report of the United Nations Development Program depicted the global distribution of income in the now famous "champagne glass" figure. The richest 20 percent of the world's population receives 82.7 percent of the total world income, while the poorest 20 percent receives only 1.4 percent. It is even worse today. Despite their so-called expert handling of the global economy, the WTO and the World Bank have seen the gap between the rich and the poor continue to grow.

Standing Up to All-Conquering Kings

This short glimpse of the phenomenon of globalization should reveal that globalization is not a neutral matter. It is pregnant with ambiguity, with unfair competition and unjust relationships in all areas of life, with political, economic, and cultural domination all interconnected. Often religion, instead of defending the poor, has been co-opted as part of the corporate power's hegemony.

The exile cannot return to the safety of Christendom, where the church ruled in the same way that corporations do today. We have tasted the bitter

---

[11]Ibid.
[12]Ibid.

fruit of unjustly imposed world domination. The church has lost its central place in Western society, and even though some Christian leaders yearn for those days, the wiser among us recognize that we don't want to be seduced again by that kind of ungodly power. Besides, a new force has taken that place of central control. Today the corporate sector maintains its hegemony with the same level of social engineering and control that the church once had. We don't want to return to that table. Neither do we wish to bow the knee before the economic forces that demand total authority.

The church's preferential option for (and with) the poor and the marginalized needs to be manifested concretely in all areas of life—economics, politics, culture, and ecology. We should be aware, however, that the poor are not just objects of charity; they are also agents of social change. Like all human beings, their dignity comes from being made in the image of God, being co-responsible for creation. Therefore, the best service we can offer them is to be with them in such a way as to enable them to empower themselves and to control their own lives. We are not called to live for ourselves, but rather to be open to follow Jesus by witnessing to God's sovereign authority. That will require a new way of being and living that works for global justice and commits to compassionate living. The imperialistic nature of globalization should be met with a counterstrategy: a culture of networking among communities toward a form of globalization that doesn't include the marginalization of the poor, toward building a worldwide community of justice, peace, and integrity of creation. God is calling us to be faithful disciples of Jesus in practical ways; we are called to live out risk-taking solidarity with the victims of the current forces. The credibility of our witness needs to be gained through our honest and sincere attitudes, words, and acts. And this will demand more than the occasional donation to disaster relief or the rare march in an anti-war protest.

So, short of dropping everything and moving to Indonesia to work with the victims of the globalized economy, what can we do? Without wanting to rule out moving to Indonesia, exiles will be prepared to consider the following simple, practical suggestions.

LET YOUR VOICE BE HEARD

When I discovered that all 191 member states of the United Nations had signed off on a series of eight goals to be reached by 2015, I was delighted to discover that they included the eradication of poverty, the reduction of child mortality, the combating of HIV/AIDS, and the promotion of gender equality. Called the Millennium Development Goals (MDGs), they are excellent commitments for the nations of the world to make as they enter the twenty-first century.¹³ These goals are so ambitious that their achievement will require an increase in the aid budgets of most Western nations. Still, the goals are so essential that they will be worth the minor extra expenditure. At this stage, very few developed countries have adjusted their aid expenditure to meet their responsibility to achieving the MDGs. And very few elected officials even seem to know, much less care, about these goals. When my church sent a delegation to a local politician, they were met by stunned silence. He had never heard of the MDGs, and he questioned whether pursuing them was likely to win him any extra votes (he actually said that!).

Exiles will let their elected officials know what they think about global issues. They will not allow a cycle of self-interest or apathy to overwhelm a nation's good intentions. They will agitate on behalf of the poor. Exiles might publicize or start letter-writing campaigns on issues that they care about (I remember, as a teenager, writing to the Soviet premier, protesting against the imprisonment of activist/writer Andrei Sakharov and then fearing that I'd ended up on some KGB list). For every letter they receive, politicians can reasonably assume that hundreds share your views without having written. This can have a significant impact, especially at a local level.

Take Your Vote Seriously

As mentioned earlier, given the level of sentiment against the Iraq War in the United States, it was surprising that the Bush administration was easily reelected in 2004. It is believed by many commentators that even though voters had significant concerns about the prosecution of a war in Iraq based on phantom WMDs, they voted for the Bush administration because they thought it was more likely to deliver ongoing economic stability within the United States. But it's important that our vote not be based solely on who

---

¹³The work of the Micah Challenge is to keep these goals on the agenda of wealthy Western governments in the hope of ensuring their successful achievement. The full list of goals includes eighteen subtargets and forty-right indicators of success. For a full list see "Millennium Development Goals," Micah Challenge n.p. [cited 21 February 2006]. Online: http://www.micahchallenge.org/millennium_development_goals. In brief, the U.N. Millennium Development Goals are as follows:
  Goal 1: Eradicate extreme poverty and hunger
  Goal 2: Achieve universal primary education
  Goal 3: Promote gender equality and empower women
  Goal 4: Reduce child mortality
  Goal 5: Improve maternal health
  Goal 6: Combat HIV/AIDS, malaria, and other diseases
  Goal 7: Ensure environmental sustainability
  Goal 8: Develop a global partnership for development

will lower our income tax or maintain our economic comfort. There are many other political issues that affect our long-term financial future, including those of the environment, global justice, and peacemaking. Nor should we be overtly influenced by what television broadcasters tell us. Their influence needs to be balanced with information from other sources. Responsible Christians will look into a candidate's background and past political decisions, and they will find out the sources of a candidate's campaign money. This applies especially to local candidates, as their decisions have an even greater bearing on our daily lives.

Access a Broader Perspective

News broadcasters always give an air of being responsible, unbiased journalists, but it's important that we remember who their employers are. The major U.S. television networks are owned by large corporations: ABC is owned by Disney, NBC is owned by General Electric. Even many of our local stations and newspapers are being bought out by big conglomerates. Federal media ownership laws, originally intended to protect the public's interests against monopolized news provision, are gradually being eroded. For example, the Federal Communications Commission (FCC) helped Australian Rupert Murdoch break the rules to establish a fourth network in the United States. And although there are many dedicated journalists working in the mainstream press, their editors have the power to cut and change stories as they see fit, particularly if they have to answer to their own corporate bosses. When veteran television journalist and former CBS news analyst Bill Moyers resigned as host of the PBS program *Now* in 2004, he observed,

> I think my peers in commercial television are talented and devoted journalists, but they've chosen to work in a corporate mainstream that trims their talent to fit the corporate nature of American life. And you do not get rewarded for telling the hard truths about America in a profit-seeking environment.[14]

Charles Lewis, a former producer of the CBS program *60 Minutes,* who now runs an investigative unit called the Center for Public Integrity, echoes this concern, but he goes further:

> [The current] compliance and silence among journalists is worse than in the 1950s. Rupert Murdoch is the most influential media mogul in America;

---

[14]Quoted in Robert F. Kennedy Jr., "The Disinformation Society," *Vanity Fair* (May 2005): 268. This article is excerpted from Kennedy's book *Crimes Against Nature: How George W. Bush and His Corporate Pals Are Plundering the Country and Hijacking Our Democracy* (New York: HarperCollins, 2004).

he sets the standard, and there is no public discussion about it. Why do the majority of the American public still believe Saddam Hussein was behind the attacks of 9/11? Because the media's constant echoing of the government guarantees it.[15]

In his incendiary documentary film *Outfoxed: Rupert Murdoch's War on Journalism,* Robert Greenwald examined how media empires, led by Murdoch's Fox News, have been running a "race to the bottom" in television news. Greenwald's team created a system to monitor Fox News around the clock for months to discover exactly how its shows worked. A team of volunteers around the country scrutinized every hour of Fox News programming, noting examples of bias in its coverage. The result of the intense examination of Fox News showed its clear and unrelenting bias toward right-wing views on most issues and put the lie to its signature motto: "Fair and Balanced." If nothing else, *Outfoxed* highlights the terrible dangers of ever-enlarging corporations taking control of the public's right to know. And although Fox is a chief offender, the sad fact is that almost all of U.S. television news suffers from the bias of the broadcaster and/or production team. Recall, for example, the scandal involving CBS and the false "documents" about George W. Bush's military record. Both the initial flaws by the CBS team and the marked reluctance of other networks to cover the breaking news that the documents were fabrications were journalistically outrageous. But that's what happens under the limited scope of news reporting in the United States and elsewhere. False media reports are—if I may borrow from George Orwell's 1946 essay "Politics and the English Language"—like "words falling on the facts like soft snow, blurring their outlines and covering up all the details."

Of course, freedom of the press should be a key right in every society. It ensures that citizens will be protected from disinformation campaigns. It is also a key factor in maintaining democracy. Bill Moyers puts it simply: "We don't have a vigilant, independent press whose interest is the American people. The quality of journalism and the quality of democracy are inextricably linked."[16] When we get most of our information about world events from television or newspapers, we can reasonably assume that our views will be biased by the corporations that own those news sources. In this age of corporate-filtered news broadcasts it's essential that we explore news from a variety of sources, and the best place to do that is online.

The Internet has democratized information and made fast international communication easy and inexpensive. Also, it is very difficult to censor. This

---

[15]Quoted by John Pilger in an editorial in *The Australian PhotoJournalist* 11, no. 1 (May 2005): 13.

[16]Kennedy, "The Disinformation Society," 268.

means that news agencies dedicated to independent journalism have increasingly found themselves going online.[17] Reading newspaper sites from a variety of countries is another great way to broaden the information base in your life. We all know that the major networks are inclined to broadcast only stories that are sensational and titillating. This means that they are disinclined to report on human-rights abuses or military coups unless there are dramatic images of street violence or face-to-face interviews. So much of the terrible injustice in our world goes unreported because no one had a film crew present to capture the incidents on tape. An old cliché in television news is "If it bleeds, it leads," meaning that graphic imagery will guarantee a featured spot on our television sets. Pity the sufferers of persecution without video cameras.[18]

Recently, news emerged that the Pentagon had created an Office of Strategic Influence that was considering, among other things, planting deliberately false news stories in the foreign press to help manipulate public opinion and further its military objectives. Following a public outcry, the Pentagon said that it would close the office, but this news would have been more convincing if it hadn't come from an agency that was planning to spread disinformation. The only way to ensure that we are getting closer to the truth on global events and issues is to be diligent about reading widely and responsibly.[19]

---

[17]These include *The Guardian,* one of Great Britain's last remaining independent newspapers (Guardian Unlimited, n.p. [cited 17 January 2006]. Online: http://www.guardian.co.uk/); CorpWatch, with news and stories on corporate and government activity that probably won't make your local newspaper or TV channel (CorpWatch: Holding Corporations Accountable, n.p. [cited 17 January 2006]. Online: http://www.corpwatch.org/); Disinformation, with interesting news stories and an active discussion board (Disinformation, n.p. [cited 17 January 2006]. Online: http://www.disinfo.com/site/). Other good sites include Alternet: The Mix is the Message, n.p. [cited 17 January 2006]. Online: http://alternet.org/; Common Dreams News Center, n.p. [cited 17 January 2006]. Online: http://www.commondreams.org/; Tom Paine: Common sense, n.p. [cited 17 January 2006]. Online: http://tompaine.com/; Center for Media and Democracy, n.p. [cited 17 January 2006]. Online: http://prwatch.org/; and many more.

[18]This is the rationale behind the great work of the Witness program, which is an effort to arm oppressed citizens with video cameras. For further information, see Witness, n.p. [cited 17 January 2006]. Online: http://www.witness.org/.

[19]Consider this in the light of something that Joseph Pulitzer said in his breathtaking retirement speech to journalists in 1907: "Always fight for progress and reform, never tolerate injustice or corruption, always fight demagogues of all parties, never belong to any party, always oppose privileged classes and public plunderers, never lack sympathy with the poor, always remain devoted to the public welfare, never be satisfied with merely printing the news, always be drastically independent, never be afraid to attack wrong, by predatory plutocracy or predatory poverty."

Donate Your Money Wisely

Exiles ought to carefully consider how much of their income they can give away in an attempt to be true to the biblical calls to generosity and love. But we also need to research where our money is going and in what ways it's contributing to the alleviation of suffering and to the extension of God's kingdom. Contributing a tithe to a local church that has plenty of money and is going to spend it on new carpet or a new youth hall might not be the most effective use of a gift. As Tom Sine says, "Let's quit kidding ourselves; we even tithe to ourselves. Everything we put into our churches we take back. We are not, as Bonhoeffer said, 'The church for others'; we are the church for ourselves."[20]

Be Aware of How You Benefit from an Inequitable Global Economy

How on earth can we consume ethically, since it is almost impossible to buy anything that hasn't been produced under poor labor conditions, for slave wages, or by companies with poor environmental records? Some people, overwhelmed by the complexity of the task simply choose to boycott the biggest or most famous labor and environmental offenders, such as Nike, Gap, Shell, or McDonalds. Of course, we need to acknowledge that our economic system makes it almost impossible to consume ethically, since everything that is produced within it involves the exploitation of human labor and the environment.

As we noted earlier, it is easier for wealthy people in the West to choose the "clean," "environmentally friendly," or "ethical" alternatives that the market does offer than it is for poor people, who can't afford to pay. Sadly, much consumer activism accepts without protest a strategy for change in which poor people have less power to shape a just economic system than do wealthy people. In other words, consumer activism marginalizes those who are already most marginalized by the current economic system, even as it attempts to reform that system. Any such strategy is bound to fail and result in continued injustice. Nevertheless, consumer boycotts aren't always a bad tactic. In fact, consumer boycotts that target particular corporate offenders give activists a chance to really illuminate the oppressions that capitalism allows and encourages. Says Naomi Klein,

> But capitalism, and the colonialism and imperialism that founded it, can only be challenged if we understand ourselves as people and as political

---

[20]Quoted in Mike Yaconelli, ed., *The Door Interviews* (Grand Rapids: Zondervan, 1989), 219.

agents struggling against a web of interconnected systems of domination—not merely as consumers trying to make the least evil choice. Real political change can't be bought by the dollars wealthy people can spend on niche markets. Our political power does not reside in our capacity as consumers, but in our capacity as human agents fighting on many fronts for the justice and dignity of all people.[21]

When we looked at New Realism in chapter 4, we saw how open the new realists are to the charge of hypocrisy when they seek to live ethical, authentic, and just lives in a highly complex and sophisticated world where it is extremely difficult never to make a choice that contributes to someone's oppression or suffering. But the charge of hypocrisy shouldn't stop us from at least trying to make life choices that contribute to global justice. Compassionate living is hard, and we know that, short of living on a completely self-sustaining farm in an isolated wilderness, we will buy products or services that somewhere along the line contribute to an unjust global economy. But we've got to at least try, in the name of Jesus, to be generous, peace-seeking, justice-loving followers of our Savior. As Albert Einstein once reportedly said, "We have to do the best we can. This is our sacred human responsibility." We will all do different things, but here are some possibilities:

- Support small businesses and family farms.

- Pay attention to "made in" labels to avoid products made in countries that lack fair labor laws.

- Research the backgrounds of companies and brand names (at, e.g., http://www.responsibleshopper.org).

- Choose ecologically safe products.

- Learn to see the homeless as victims of rising rents and welfare cuts.

- Talk to the people directly affected by these injustices, and to the local activist groups that support them.

You can look for groups and organizations working on specific issues in your region by checking the posts on the local indymedia site or by doing a Web search. Get in touch with groups that seem to be doing tangible work, and then attend a couple of their meetings and find out how you can contribute. Most activists groups are resource poor and need help with everything

---

[21]See Naomi Klein's website, Andréa Schmidt, "Frequently Asked Questions About Globalization and Justice," No Logo n.p. [cited 21 February 2006]. Online: http://www.nologo.org FAQs/Globalization FAQ/3. The site is based on her book *No Logo: No Space, No Choice, No Jobs* (New York: Picador, 2002).

from fundraising to the artwork for their publications, from proofreading their newspaper to helping with logistics at demonstrations.

Counterbalancing Acts

As I've mentioned before, exiles cannot pitch their tents in this host empire and settle down as if they belong here. Exiles know that this is not where they belong, and the levels of corruption, abuse, persecution, violence, oppression, and greed are a constant reminder of their own foreignness. But neither can exiles return to a sleepy, middle-class Christianity that seems unconcerned about such manifestations of evil in our world. Being *in* this world but not *of* this world means an ongoing commitment to walking a less traveled road—the road of justice, compassion, generosity. As dreadfully difficult as this sounds, the exile has to realize that for every ongoing war and religious outrage, for every environmental disaster and bogus claim about WMDs, there are a thousand counterbalancing acts of staggering generosity and humanity and art and beauty happening all over the world, right now, on a breathtaking scale, from community gardens to homeless centers, from justice discussion groups to fundraising projects. We mustn't be discouraged by the enormity of the task. God ultimately will glorify himself and vindicate the persecuted. In the meantime, we need to throw ourselves behind a movement for social justice and the environment, not because it will be profitable, but because it's right. Says award-winning Indian writer and human-rights advocate Arundhati Roy,

> The question is: How do we climb out of this crevasse? For those who are materially well-off, but morally uncomfortable, the first question you must ask yourself is do you really want to climb out of it? How far are you prepared to go? Has the crevasse become too comfortable? If you really want to climb out, there's good news and bad news. The good news is that the advance party began the climb some time ago. They're already half way up. Thousands of activists across the world have been hard at work preparing footholds and securing the ropes to make it easier for the rest of us. There isn't only one path up. There are hundreds of ways of doing it. There are hundreds of battles being fought around the world that need your skills, your minds, your resources. No battle is irrelevant. No victory is too small. The bad news is that colorful demonstrations, weekend marches and annual trips to the World Social Forum are not enough. There have to be targeted acts of real civil disobedience with real consequences. Maybe we can't flip a switch and conjure up a revolution. But there are several things we could do. For example, you could make a list of those corporations who have profited from the invasion of Iraq. . . . You could name

them, boycott them, occupy their offices and force them out of business. If it can happen in Bolivia, it can happen in India. It can happen [anywhere]. Why not?[22]

Roy's proposal to boycott corporations that profit from war is just one small suggestion. The struggle of exiles against injustice will require vision, beauty, and imagination. The point is that the battle must be joined. As the saying goes, "You can't be neutral on a moving train."

---

[22]Arundhati Roy, "Peace and the New Corporate Liberation Theology," 2004 City of Sydney Peace Prize Lecture, n.p. [cited 17 January 2006]. Online: http://www.abc.net.an/rn/bigidea/stories/s1232956.htm.

Exiles and the Earth

The Critique: You Have Not Cared for God's Creation

> Only when the last tree has died, and the last
> river been poisoned, and the last fish has been
> caught, will we realize we cannot eat money.
>
> —Cree saying

I vividly recall, as a kid, seeing the movie *Planet of the Apes* and being stunned by the dramatic final scene in which Taylor (played by Charlton Heston), the stranded astronaut, realizes that he is not on another planet as he thought, but in fact has flown through time and returned to the earth in a future where apes have taken ascendancy over humans. It's only when he happens upon the derelict Statue of Liberty half submerged on a barren beach that he finally understands this terrible fact. After recently viewing the original film, I was surprised at how corny it all was (especially James Whitmore and Roddy McDowall in those terrible latex monkey masks), but when I a young boy, that broken-down statue scared the daylights out of me. Like Taylor, I realized that the future being portrayed was one in which humankind had destroyed the very ground beneath its feet.

The End of Civilizations

Many years later, on a visit to Cambodia, I had the opportunity to have my own Charlton Heston moment. Visiting the remarkable ruins of Angkor, I found myself wandering through an abandoned civilization as it was slowly being overtaken by the lush jungles of northern Cambodia. Even in its state of decay, the central building, Angkor Wat, is unrivaled in its beauty and grace, more impressive than the Pyramids and with an artistic distinctiveness as fine as that of the Taj Mahal. But it lies empty, abandoned, like a half-buried Statue of Liberty, a testament to the former glory of the Khmer Empire. For many years, Angkor, formerly the great Khmer capital city, built between about 880 and 1225 C.E., was totally isolated from the Western world, buried under impenetrable foliage. In the 1800s the French colonialists had heard rumors from the local population about temples built by gods or by giants, though they generally dismissed them as folktales. Nonetheless, some believed that there really was a lost city of a Cambodian empire, which once had been powerful and wealthy. Finally the jungles were pierced, and French missionaries discovered the temples in 1860. As I traversed the massive buildings, I tried to imagine those missionaries and their feelings as they uncovered a lost civilization.

Angkor Wat, Cambodia. Photo credit: iStockphoto. Used with permission.

The height of Angkor Wat from the ground to the top of the central tower is an enormous 213 meters (699 feet), achieved with three rectangular or square levels, each one progressively smaller and higher than the one below, starting from the outer limits of the temple. Covered galleries with columns define the boundaries of the first and second levels. The third level supports the most prominent architectural feature of Angkor Wat, its five towers—four in the corners and one in the middle. Graduated tiers, one rising above the other, give the towers a conical shape, and near the top, rows of lotuses taper to a point. The overall profile is designed to imitate a lotus bud.

Several architectural lines stand out in the profile of the monument. Your eyes are drawn left and right to the horizontal aspect of the levels and upward to the soaring height of the towers. The ingenious plan of Angkor Wat allows a view of all five towers only from certain angles. They are not visible, for example, from the entrance.

The entire structure is surrounded first by an ornate brick wall, and beyond that by a massive square moat. As recommended by my hosts, I arrived in the dark just before sunrise and waited at the outer wall as the first rays of sun cast an eerie light across the staggering edifice. Several wild horses pranced across the grassy plain between the wall and the temple itself. They paused to drink from one of two large decorative ponds, covered by exotic floating lily pads. As I watched another day dawn on Angkor Wat, as it had every day since the thirteenth century, I felt deeply moved to have encountered this the last remnants of a once all-powerful civilization. In a flight of fancy I imagined an ancient Khmer courtier being swept magically into the future, like Charlton Heston's Taylor, to face the horror of his ruined empire.

Why did the great Khmer Empire falter? We know that Angkor was finally seized by the Thai army in 1431, and that the Khmer eventually relocated their capital to the south somewhere around Phnom Penh. There is evidence that the Khmer tried to restore the Angkor Wat (temple) around 1550 and then again in the mid 1600s, but after that it's clear that the city lay in ruins; the definite year of its abandonment and the exact reasons were not known until recently. Archaeologist Dan Penny, from the University of Sydney, set about uncovering those reasons. He says,

> Hypotheses ranging from the lure of maritime trade in the Mekong delta, environmental crises and epidemic disease have been proposed to account for the demise of this once great urban world. The recovered inscriptions shed no light on this issue, and the archaeological evidence is sparse and equivocal. Clearly a new approach is required.[1]

Penny's research focused on bringing palaeoenvironmental techniques to bear on the question of Angkor's decline. By taking sediment cores taken from the temple moats and reservoirs and natural basins in the nearby hinterland, his team has shown that the decline of Angkor was intimately related to systemic

---

[1]Dan Penny, "Palaeoenvironmental Research and the Demise of Angkor," The Comparative Archaeology Web, n.p. [cited 17 January 2006]. Online: http://www.comp-archaeology.org/WAC5%20Pre-Industrial%20Urbanism%20in%20Tropical%20Environments.htm#_Palaeoenvironmental_Research_and.

failure of the elaborate system of canals and reservoirs that collected water running off from the nearby Kulen Hills. Angkor is situated on a plain between those hills and the vast Tonle Sap Lake, which in turn drains into the south-flowing Mekong River. As the Khmer cleared the plain of vegetation for housing and for their tremendous rice production ventures, they inadvertently altered the fragile ecosystem. Deforestation and overpopulation, coupled with aggression from Thai neighbors, eventually made the awesome city uninhabitable.

The Khmer Empire isn't the only society to fail because of its excessive exploitation of natural resources. In his book *Collapse: How Societies Choose to Fail or Succeed,* Jared Diamond charts the demise of various civilizations that were driven to extinction by their failure to learn and adjust the effects that their society was having on the surrounding natural resources.[2] For example, he tells of how on Easter Island the massive square-jawed statues that dot the volcanic island are virtually the only witnesses to the collapse of the Polynesian society that carved them. When Europeans landed in 1722, Easter Island was barren and desolate. The few dozen remaining inhabitants were starving, eking out an existence in abject poverty and bitter isolation. They had no wood for canoes or fires. There were no viable crops for food. And yet, eight hundred years earlier, when Polynesian peoples first populated the thriving tropical island, it was plush with vegetation and rich in birdlife.

In Greenland, a community of thousands of Viking warriors died out, leaving only the weathered shells of stone buildings to mark the site where they had settled. In Guatemala, tourists visit the long-abandoned, jungle-covered city of Tikal, with its magnificent temples and its carved friezes testifying to the glories of a now vanished empire. In the southwestern United States, among the ruins of Anasazi settlements are even more tragic signs of a collapsing society in which starving survivors turned to cannibalism before succumbing to extinction. Diamond's litany of collapsing societies tells us something very important about our own impending global crisis, because each of these stories is about a society that literally destroyed the ground on which its people stood.

Diamond begins with an unlikely society: the state of Montana. An ardent fly-fisherman, Diamond has visited the state many times and observed its dramatic decline. Once one of the richest states of the United States, Montana now ranks among the poorest, having squandered its nonrenewable mineral resources and excessively logged its forests. For Diamond, Montana is a perfect example of why societies collapse. His central proposition is that wherever these globally disparate societies failed, the chief cause was anthropogenic ecological devastation, especially deforestation, imposed on ecosystems of limited

---

[2]Jared Diamond, *Collapse: How Societies Choose to Fail or Succeed* (New York: Viking Penguin, 2004).

resources. According to *Collapse,* many societies decline because of population growth and the desires of affluence, coupled with deforestation, habitat destruction, and overuse of natural resources. These factors have led to soil erosion and the loss of viable food sources and resources for providing shelter and defense against enemies. It's not that the environment has been incapable of sustaining these societies, but that the societies themselves have been unable to adapt to their changing surroundings. Diamond's most powerful warning is that ecocide has now come to overshadow nuclear war and emerging diseases as the single greatest threat to global civilization.

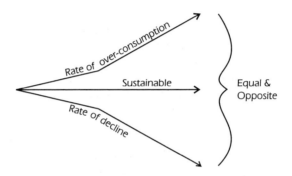

Rate of over-consumption

Sustainable

Equal & Opposite

Rate of decline

**Over-Consumption's Effect
on the Decline of a Civilization**

Diamond suggests a number of factors that can contribute to the collapse of a society and warns us today that societies still are failing because of their refusal to heed these warnings, citing Somalia, Rwanda, and Haiti, as well as Montana, as modern-day examples. First, surviving societies are concerned about whether their use of the environment is sustainable over time. This seems an obvious point, but environmental sustainability is one of the world's great blind spots. One of Diamond's single most worrisome points is the fact that failed civilizations often have been ignorant of their fate. Collapse tends to occur only a decade or two after the culture is at its peak. Such is the rate at which resources are consumed. Second, surviving societies have developed an ability to accommodate natural climate change. The Mayan, Anasazi, and Greenland cultures cited in his book were driven to the brink of disaster by food shortages caused by prolonged droughts (in the first two instances) and increasing cold (in the third). Third, societies that collapse were either forced to divert critical resources into fighting hostile neighbors rather than farming or relied too heavily on trade partners if these other cultures were unable to provide basic resources. And fourth, surviving societies have developed a capacity to learn and adjust to changing circumstances.

The book is full of disturbing questions about the sustainability of our current practices. For example, what kind of global ecological crisis is being shaped by China's rush toward North American–style affluence? Answer: a big one! Why isn't Montana the same timber-producing state that it used to be? Answer: there are few trees left. Why isn't the Dominican Republic in the same fix as Haiti? Answer: there are still trees there. And why does Australia insist on exporting wine instead of potatoes, even though the environmental cost of growing grapes is staggering? Answer: the financial returns are much better. Diamond concludes,

> Our world society is presently on a non-sustainable course, and any one of our problems would suffice to limit our lifestyle within the next several decades. Because we are rapidly advancing along this non-sustainable course, the world's environmental problems will get resolved, in one way or another, within the lifetimes of the children and young adults alive today. The only question is whether they will be resolved in pleasant ways of our own choice, or in unpleasant ways not of our choice, such as warfare, genocides, starvation, disease epidemics and collapses of societies.[3]

To wander through the eerily beautiful wreckage of the Khmer Empire is to imagine what would be left of Western civilization if it continues to disregard all the evidence of an impending global environmental disaster.

Christians and the Environment

Many of the exiles I know are deeply concerned about the state of the global environment and are ashamed of the fact that Christians around the world seem unable to speak with one voice about the looming ecological crisis confronting us. They wish there could be a form of Christian environmentalism that offers a witness to our world about the need to care for our planet. In the absence of such a thing, many turn to movements such as Greenpeace to express their environmental disquiet. If we are to develop a genuinely Christian expression of environmentalism, it should arise from an informed, thoughtful, and faithful consideration of environmental concerns from the perspective of the Christian faith. As is the case with any moral question, a Christian approach to those issues must include as its central source of insight the biblical witness. This is not to say that the biblical understanding of the world cannot be expanded by subsequent insights into the nature of things; rather, it is to say that a genuinely Christian ethic is, and must be, compatible with the witness of the Christian Scriptures.

---

[3]Ibid., 18.

It will come as no surprise to those even marginally familiar with the discussions of environmental issues carried on within the Christian community that Christians have not come together on a single approach. On the contrary, there is a diversity of approaches, each reflecting a particular understanding of the nature and significance of the environment. Even within the Christian community, the value of assuring adequate resources for future generations competes with the value of immediate economic gain. Accordingly, the one thing that can be said without fear of contradiction is that Christians do not speak with a single voice on these issues; there is at present no one expression of Christian environmentalism. There are several reasons for this.

Ignorance of the Issues

Sadly, like many middle-class people, many Christians simply do not believe that there is an environmental problem, much less a crisis. Enthused by the promise of technology to solve the practical problems of the world and in so doing to provide for the economic well-being of its occupants, many Christians, particularly conservative evangelicals, appear to be in a state of what has been termed "environmental denial."[4] If you believe that there is no problem, then naturally you see no need for a solution. Many people, Christians included, thoughtlessly drive to the local shopping mall, spewing greenhouse gases into the environment, when instead they could just as easily walk. Rarely do ministers preach about the subject. Almost as rarely do American households sort and recycle their trash. As they see it, there is no problem, and no solutions are required.

Or worse still, some Christians assume that all so-called Greens are longhaired, left-wing, unemployed loafers. They disdain environmentalists as some kind of anti-Christian, Gaia-worshipping radical movement. Maybe there has been some justification for this stereotype, but it is ignorant to marginalize the environmental movement with a caricature that dismisses Green issues as somehow "un-Christian."

Dominionism/Subjectionism

For most of its history, the Christian church has emphasized the dual relationships between God and humans and between humans and other

---

[4]Susan P. Bratton, "Christianity and Reflexive Modernity: Population, Environmental Risk and Societal Change," Global Stewardship Initiative Converence, n.p. [cited 17 January 2006]. Online: http://204.84.32.191/gsi/gsi-conf/discussion/bratton.html.

humans. The nonhuman parts of creation have been grossly ignored. We routinely speak about the "vertical" relationship that we have with God or the "horizontal" relationship that we share with others, but rarely do we include other creatures or the natural order in this way of thinking. This failure has arisen from erroneous interpretations of Gen 1:27–28:

> So God created human beings in his own image, in the image of God he created them; male and female he created them. God blessed them and said to them, "Be fruitful and increase in number; fill the earth and subdue it. Rule over the fish in the sea and the birds in the sky and over every living creature that moves on the ground."

Subjectionists or dominionists typically take this text as a call to bring the nonhuman environment into subjection for the purpose of facilitating human expansion. It is assumed by subjectionists that God created the world entirely for the purposes of human satisfaction. Any form of Christian environmentalism is viewed suspiciously because it is seen as elevating the environment to a level higher than intended by God in the first chapter of Genesis. They lodge three major complaints against environmentalism. First, many subjectionists dispute scientific claims of environmental degradations, claiming, for example, that there is doubt about the size of the hole in the ozone layer. Second, they caricature environmentalism to be essentially "new age" thinking and therefore anti-Christian. They often equate a responsible ecology with some form of Gaia or earth-goddess worship, claiming that God has given us dominion over the earth. Third, they emphasize the substantial economic costs of environmental protection policies. Christian economists from this tradition invariably speak of "resource" economics rather than "environmental" or "ecological" economics. To them, the nonhuman components of the earth are merely resources to be subdued and managed for the benefit of a sovereign humanity.

Traditional vs. Holistic Views of Creation

Domination/Subjectionism	Environmentalism
world created for humanity's purposes	humanity as a steward of created world
the environment as a resource	the environment as a responsibility
environmentalism hinders economic growth	economic growth without ecological responsibility is self-defeating
created world has worth insofar as it meets human need	created world has intrinsic value

It is often argued in high-income countries that economic concerns are at the opposite end of the spectrum from environmentalism. That is, we have to choose either economic growth or environmental protection, as if we can't have both. But as Jared Diamond argues, over any period measured in generations or centuries, long-term economic well-being is an essential component of environmental protection, and vice versa. This isn't to say that the precise dynamics of the relationship between the two isn't complex, but it can be demonstrated that they are not antithetical to one another. Nor is it to say that some criticisms of some aspects of mainstream environmentalism by subjectionists aren't valid. They certainly are, but the narrow subjectionist emphasis on economic welfare alone is excessive and ultimately costly.

There are other ways to interpret the text of Gen 1:27–28. Many scholars argue that because in Gen 1:31 all of the creation is declared to be "good," the references to its human dominion and subjection are to be understood as denoting not simply a license for use, but a responsibility to care for the creation. As Steven Bouma-Prediger observes, "Individual creatures and creation as a whole have an integrity as created by God and as such have intrinsic value as well as instrumental value."[5]

If the earth's creatures have such an intrinsic value, as I believe they do, then this makes sense of biblical phrases such as "the earth is the Lord's, and all that is in it" (Ps 24:1; cf. 1 Cor 10:26). Since everything in the world belongs to God, it is infused with a dignity and worth conferred by God's own integrity and glory. In other words, that which belongs to God, which is not limited to believers in Christ but includes all creation, shares the value that God places on it. This view leads to a model of responsible stewardship as opposed to an exploitation model. By sharing value with God, humankind has been given stewardship, not ownership, of the earth. Dominion, therefore, is properly exercised only when done in such a way as to fulfill the intent of the owner, and living as one created in the image of God requires a life consistent with God's purpose. Why is stewardship, not exploitation, God's purpose? As James Nash explains,

> The New Testament understanding of the image of God only enhances this sense of ecological responsibility. . . . Thus, when interpreted in the context of Christ, the realisation of the image and the proper expression of

---

[5]Steven Bouma-Prediger, "Creation Care and Character: The Nature and Necessity of Ecological Virtues," paper presented to the Global Stewardship Initiative Conference, October 1966. Published at http://cesc.montreat.edu/GSI/GSI-Conf/discussion/Bouma-Prediger.html. Ronald A. Smith, "Christian Environmentalism," Hardin Simmons University n.p. [cited 21 February 2006]. Online: http://www.hsutx.edu/academics/logsdon/smith/environ.html.

dominion are not manifestations of exploitation, but rather **representations of nurturing and serving love.**[6]

Only a clear and biblical doctrine of Christian stewardship will give rise to a Christian environmentalism. Such a doctrine will rightly call on all Christians to recognize and honor God's ownership of all that is and to care for creation in such a way as to honor that ownership. As Christians, we believe that the world and all that is in it is the deliberate, loving creation of God. God values it for its own sake as well as for its instrumental value to humans and to other creatures. And because God values nature, we, who want to honor and serve God rightly, will also value it.

Premillennial Eschatology

We noted that Jared Diamond's basic thesis is that certain societies collapsed because they used natural resources as if there were no tomorrow. And this is exactly what many Christian leaders in America believe who think that the rapture will occur at any minute. Trusting in a particular interpretation of the book of Revelation (in which the word "rapture" never actually appears), many Christians believe wholeheartedly that once Israel has occupied the rest of its so-called biblical lands, legions of the Antichrist will attack it, triggering a final showdown in the valley of Armageddon. At that point, true believers will be transported to heaven, where, seated at the right hand of God, they will watch the remaining inhabitants writhe in the misery of plagues—boils, sores, locusts, frogs—during the years of tribulation that follow. I think it's fair to say that many more people have adopted this view due to the mammoth success of Tim LaHaye and Jerry Jenkins's florid *Left Behind* series of novels than from reading the Bible.

The overall assumption is that with Christ's return, the world will be destroyed. If, as millions of sincere Christians believe, our planet will go up in flames come doomsday, then there is no reason for Christians to be concerned about environmental sustainability. If we believe that the world cannot be saved, then we are relieved of concern for the environment, violence, and everything else except our personal salvation. If the earth suffers the same fate as that of the unsaved and all are destroyed, what motivation is there for resisting war, working for peace, or caring for the environment? It's all going to hell in a handbasket, after all.

This was the well-publicized view of James Watt, U.S. Secretary of the Interior in the Reagan administration. He was often portrayed as believing

---

[6]James A. Nash, *Loving Nature: Ecological Integrity and Christian Responsibility* (Nashville: Abingdon, 1991), 105 (emphasis added).

something like, "God gave us these things to use. After the last tree is felled, Christ will come back." Apparently, Watt never said any such thing, and his motivation for his deplorable policies had more to do with his economic views favoring control of resources by private enterprise instead of by public governance. Nevertheless, for a generation of environmentalists, Watt has been the paradigm of the anti-environmental conservative evangelical Christian. His view on the second coming of Christ often was expressed publicly, and his record of mismanagement of the environmental resources of the United States was naturally (if erroneously) linked to his assumption that the return of Christ could be hurried along by the depletion of the earth's natural resources.

Of course, it's understandable why people in the grip of such a theology cannot be expected to worry about the environment. Why care about the earth when the droughts, floods, famine, and pestilence brought by ecological collapse are signs of the apocalypse foretold in the Bible? Why care about global climate change when you and yours will be rescued in the rapture? Why bother to convert to alternative sources of energy and reduce dependence on oil from the volatile Middle East? According to Glenn Scherer, of the online environmental magazine *Grist,* a 2002 *Time*/CNN poll found that nearly 25 percent of Americans think that the Bible actually predicted the 9/11 attacks.[7]

One can see why fundamentalist Christianity in the United States has left no space for its followers to develop a godly concern for the environment. As a result, any movement of Christian ecology is very small and largely fractured. As Anatol Lieven observes, "Fundamentalist religiosity has become an integral part of the radicalization of the right in the US and of the tendency to demonize political opponents as traitors and enemies of God and America."[8]

These enemies include environmentalists, who are routinely castigated as villains and worse by conservative Christian leaders. And yet surely this is a complete abandonment of our mandate as believers to be good stewards of the environment, caring for the earth as God's handiwork, a creation that God loves and calls us to nurture. Irrespective of one's view on the second coming, all Christians have a biblical responsibility to care for the earth. If we continue in the footsteps of the Khmer Empire or the Vikings in Greenland,

---

[7]Glenn Scherer, "The Godly Must Be Crazy: Christian-Right Views Are Swaying Politicians and Threatening the Environment," Grist Magazine, n.p. [cited 17 January 2006]. Online: http://www.grist.org/news/maindish/2004/10/27/Scherer-Christian.

[8]Quoted in Bill Moyers, "Welcome to Doomsday," *New York Review of Books* 52, no. 5 (March 4, 2005): 5.

blinded by arrogance and self-interested to the point of folly, we could see the end of our own civilization due to massive pollution, lack of natural resources, and overpopulation. What makes us think that although collapse has happened to other societies, it won't happen to us?

The Global Record of Abuse

In the 1980s, English scientist Gerry Stanhill began measuring levels of sunlight over Israel as a follow-up to data that he had collected while designing a national irrigation scheme there twenty years earlier. Even though his original research was collected for an industrial purpose, it occurred to him that the research could be repeated to see whether there had been any significant shift in levels of sunlight over Israel. What he found, to his absolute amazement, was that there had in fact been a substantial reduction in sunlight over Israel. In those intervening twenty years it had dropped by a massive 22 percent. No one had ever heard of such a thing. Every environmental scientist was convinced that the atmosphere was warming due to the increasing hole in the ozone layer. All international efforts had gone into research global warming, not global cooling. Stanhill was astonished. What could account for this marked reduction in sunlight? He began to collect similar data from across the world to see if it was a global phenomenon. First, he found that similar experiments had been done over a similar period in the Bavarian Alps of Germany and returned results comparable to his own Israel data. The more he searched, the more he discovered a widespread reduction in levels of sunlight. From the 1950s to the early 1990s sunlight had dropped by 9 percent in Antarctica, 8 percent in the United States, a staggering 30 percent in Russia, and around 16 percent in the United Kingdom. Stanhill's research was flying in the face of global-warming figures. He gave this phenomenon the name "global dimming."

Meanwhile, and completely independent from Stanhill's research, two Australian scientists discovered a worldwide decline in what is called the pan evaporation rate (i.e., the evaporation rate of water in a pan, measured meticulously by hundreds of scientists around the world). The rate at which water evaporated from an open pan was actually falling in every country where the experiments are conducted. Since sunlight is the key factor in water evaporation, the Australians concluded that sunlight levels also must be falling. Remarkably, the Australian research perfectly matched Stanhill's data about declining sunlight levels. Two independent sets of research were showing the very same thing: the sun's effect on the earth is dimming.

Since the scientific community knew that there nothing was amiss with the sun itself, it was reasonably assumed that the explanation lies in the earth's atmosphere. Recently, an international scientific team descended on the sleepy Maldive Islands in the Indian Ocean. This place had been identified as a perfect location for tests on the levels of sunlight in the atmosphere, chiefly because the northern half of the island group sits under a dark, soupy stream of dirty air sweeping down from India to the north, while the southern half sits under a pristine stream of clean air that drifts up from Antarctica. By measuring and comparing rates of sunlight in each half of the island group, scientists could determine whether atmospheric pollution contributes to global dimming. The results were frightening.

The $25 million research showed that the polluted layer—a band of soot, carbon dioxide, sulfates, and nitrates three kilometers thick—cut the sunlight by 10 percent in comparison with the clean, southern part of the Maldives. Worse than simply blocking sunlight, pollution particles, when trapped in cloud bands, turn clouds into giant mirrors that reflect the sun's rays back into space. It is assumed that this is happening all over the world. Pollution created by the burning of fossil fuels forms a thick band of soup across the atmosphere, blocking out sunlight. Furthermore, such a polluted atmosphere affects rainfall levels across the world. Global dimming means that the oceans are cooled and tropical rains are not drawn northward to parts of Africa and Asia. A cooling atmosphere leads to a reduction in monsoonal activity, and if the monsoons don't come, millions of lives can be affected by drought and famine, as we saw in the horrific 1984 Ethiopian famine. Terrible as it is to say, there seems to be a direct link between the burning of fossil fuels by our vehicles and factories here in the West and the millions of lives lost in places such as Ethiopia.

Then, in 2001, a once-in-a-lifetime opportunity occurred for a conclusive experiment to prove or disprove pollution as the cause of global dimming. David Travis is a scientist from Madison, Wisconsin, who has spent fifteen years researching the environmental effects of vapor trails emitted by jet aircraft across the United States. Each day he has measured the temperature ranges caused by the thousands of white trails that blanket the skies across America, hoping to show conclusive evidence of their damaging effect on the environment. Then on September 11, 2001, hijacked aircraft were flown into the World Trade Center in New York City and the Pentagon in Washington. As a consequence, all aircraft were grounded across America for the next three days. This had rarely happened before. With the whole U.S. air fleet stuck on the tarmac, Travis had a unique opportunity to measure the silent, pristine skies and compare them with the usually busy air traffic over the United States. As tragic as the 9/11 events were, a very small redeeming feature of the grounding of aircraft was that Travis was able to gather invaluable, and disturbing, data.

While temperature changes shift around the United States from city to city, the temperature range—the difference between the highest temperature in the day and the lowest in the evening—rarely changes much at all. What Travis found is that from September 11 to 13, 2001, during those three cloudless, vaporless days, the temperature range spiked by a full 1 degree C, a staggering jump that had not be seen in over thirty years. It has been deemed as conclusive evidence that pollution is actually cooling our planet by blocking sunlight.

So, if the levels of sunlight are dimming, why isn't the atmosphere cooling? Because of the opposite effect of global warming. We seem to be finding ourselves in a devastating situation where, by reducing greenhouse gas emissions in order to reduce global warming, we might in fact produce the opposite effect. Without the band of polluted air ringing the earth's atmosphere, sunlight levels will increase dramatically. In other words, global warming is probably much further advanced than we thought, but its effects are masked by polluted air cutting sunlight to the earth's surface. At the Earth Summit in Rio de Janeiro in 1992, global warming was predicted to increase the earth's temperature by five degrees by end of this century. With the added information about global dimming, some now suggest that it could be double that amount. An increase of ten degrees in many parts of the planet will make them uninhabitable for all living creatures. Rainforests such as those in Southeast Asia and the Amazon Basin would literally shrivel and die. Without these planetary "lungs," the earth's ecosystem would collapse. An increase of only three to five degrees will see the atoll countries of Kiribati, Maldives, Marshall Islands, Tokelau, and Tuvalu destroyed by rising sea levels. We have already seen 20 percent of the Arctic ice cap melt since 1979. Anything up to an increase of 1.7 degrees in temperature could see an exponential rise in animal extinctions. It would be devastating.

Our Local Environmental Record

Despite all this alarming information, many people remain oblivious to the emergency at hand. Even with the recently enforced Kyoto Protocol, many industrialized countries continue to flout the goals set by the international community. Kyoto was designed to reduce the six greenhouse gases. Carbon dioxide from the burning of fossil fuels is the biggest factor in climate change, but methane from agriculture and landfill, nitrous oxide from vehicles, and hydrofluorocarbons, perfluorocarbons, and sulfur hexafluoride from other industrial processes are included. The aim of Kyoto is to reduce overall greenhouse gas pollution by at least 5 percent below 1990 levels by 2012. And yet even if the Kyoto targets are achieved, the amount of emissions reduction will be tiny compared with what scientists say is needed to prevent the kind of devastating change mentioned above.

Under the rules, Kyoto could be ratified only if industrialized nations responsible for 55 percent of the total world emissions agreed to sign on. Since the United States is responsible for 36.1 percent of the greenhouse gases from the industrialized world, and since its government has refused to ratify Kyoto, it looked as though the protocol wouldn't get off the ground. Only when Russia signed on after two years of delay did Kyoto manage to get ratified in early 2005. One of the reasons for the United States' refusal to ratify is that its government felt that China and other developing countries would gain a competitive advantage because these nations wouldn't have the costs that the United States would incur to reduce emissions. By refusing to sign on, the United States is not bound by the reduction goals, but it's doubtful that the country could have managed to do so anyway, as the goal would have been a 7 percent reduction. In the period from 1990 to 2002, the United States increased gas emissions by 13.1 percent. As dreadful as this sounds, over the same period, the United States is only the ninth worst offender when it comes to increases in greenhouse gas emissions, after Spain (40.5%), Portugal (40.5%), Monaco (31.7%), Ireland (28.9%), Greece (26%), Australia (22.2%), New Zealand (21.6%), and Canada (20.1%).[9]

It is reasonable to be alarmed about the extent of environmental destruction caused by human society. Over half the electricity used in the United States is generated by the burning of coal, the single biggest air polluter in the United States. It is now estimated that there are over six hundred dirty coal plants in the country. In a typical year, just one average-sized coal plant emits as much carbon dioxide as would result from the cutting down of 161 million trees. They emit ten thousand tons of sulfur dioxide, which causes acid rain, five hundred tons of airborne particles that contribute to asthma, bronchitis, and premature death, and ten thousand tons of nitrogen oxide, which leads to the formation of smog and affects respiratory illness. Air pollution

---

[9]For a full text of the Kyoto Protocol, as well as a list of signatories, see "The Convention and Kyoto Protocol," United Nations Framework Convention on Climate Change, n.p. [cited 17 January 2006]. Online: http://unfccc.int/cop6_2/index-4.html. The United States and Australia refused to sign the protocol, instead preferring to design an Asia-Pacific Accord on the environment that also includes China, India, Japan, and South Korea. Critics of this accord claim that it merely encourages signatories to share technology in the fight against global warming and has no clear targets, unlike the 152–member Kyoto Protocol.

from dirty power plants cause nearly thirty thousand early deaths in the United States each year.[10]

Alternatives are available, but we have a society that has become entrenched in a lifestyle that our planet cannot pay for. Just 2 percent of U.S. electricity production comes from clean, sustainable, renewable sources such as wind and solar power. Yet the United States is blessed with enough renewable resources to meet more than 4.5 times the *current* electricity needs. In fact, if the United States increased its use of renewable energy to 20 percent of its electricity generation by 2020, it would be the same as taking seventy-seven million cars off the road or planting nearly 130 million acres of trees, an area the size of Colorado and Wyoming.

Besides the problem electricity production, there is our self-indulgent love affair with the automobile. And the earth is picking up the tab for our reliance on motor vehicles. They produce one-third of the carbon dioxide emitted by the United States and form the main greenhouse, or heat-trapping, gas in the atmosphere. Over the lifetime of an average car, it releases around 124 pounds of smog-forming pollutants and fifty-seven pounds of toxic emissions. As the oil crisis in the 1970s and the Gulf War and the Iraq War more recently remind us, Persian Gulf nations own two-thirds of the world's remaining oil reserves, while the United States has less than 3 percent. This makes the American car habit very expensive. Every minute, the United States sends $200,000 offshore to buy oil. This is an issue that directly affects the average driver because personal vehicles account for 40 percent of all the oil consumed in the United States.

British oil companies BP and Shell are major contributors to global pollution. For instance, BP features in the Greenpeace Filthy Fifty List and in the Friends of the Earth Secret Polluters list. In 1991, a BP-chartered tanker spewed three hundred thousand gallons of oil across a twenty-square-mile area near Huntington Beach in California. In response, the state of California drafted new legislation to improve tanker safety and tried to elicit $500 million in compensation from oil companies. BP spent $171,000 to help oppose the bill. As we noted earlier, Shell has been under immense scrutiny recently for its deplorable environmental record, in particular its use of gas

---

[10]For further details on carbon dioxide emissions see "International Carbon Dioxide Emissions from the Consumption and Planing of Fossil Fuels Information," U. S. Energy Information Administration, n.p. [cited 17 January 2006]. Online: http://www.eia.doe.gov/emeu/international environm.html#IntlCarbon. In fact, the EIA allows visitors to their site to search for specific environmental data for nearly every country in the world. See "Data," U. S. Energy Infromation Administration, under "International" [cited 17 January 2006]. Online: http://www.eia.doe.gov/emeu/international/contents.html.

flaring. In the Niger Delta, where it sources 10 percent of its oil, Shell's refusal to invest in technology results in seven hundred million standard cubic feet per day of gas being burnt off into the environment, despite a commitment to end flaring by 2008. Shell is currently fighting protests against its abuse of the environment in Texas, Louisiana, the Philippines, and the Caribbean island of Curaçao, where it is alleged that both the air and the drinking water are contaminated. Oronto Douglas, from Friends of the Earth Nigeria, is quoted as saying,

> Shell's business practices in the Niger Delta have destroyed our environment, our farmland and our fisheries. Oil spills are not cleaned up and gas flares dominate the skyline. The people in Nigeria are not benefiting from Shell's presence in our country—we are paying the price. Shell must work with local communities to clean up the Niger Delta and make sure communities receive the benefits of their operations there.[11]

Other forms of pollution are equally concerning. A recent study shows that of the 192.5 billion aluminum, glass, and plastic beverage containers generated in the United States in 1999, 114 billion were wasted. It's not that taxpayer-funded recycling programs are slacking on the job. Over the last few years there has been a dramatic increase in the number and types of beverage containers in the market. So although recycling volumes remain relatively steady, overall recycling rates are declining. And yet it has been clearly and dramatically proven, time after time, that recycling conserves natural resources, reduces pollution and energy use, creates jobs, saves taxpayer money by reducing demand on landfills and incinerators, and reduces billions of tons of hazardous waste. The fact remains that producers of beverages selling their product in states where they are responsible for collecting and processing beverage containers do an immensely better job of recycling than do producers selling in states that have no such requirements.

A recent report done by a multi-stakeholder group including recycling businesses, environmental groups, plastics manufacturers, and Coca-Cola, found that deposit systems, which transfer responsibility for recycling bottles and cans from taxpayers to producers, result in the highest level of recovery. In 1999 in the United States, the ten states with deposit laws recycled more containers than all other forty states combined, and they achieved an overall recovery rate of 71.6 percent compared to 27.9 percent in nondeposit states.

The Environmental Protection Agency in the United States continues to bemoan the fact that there is no federal system for ensuring that recycling is

---

[11]From "Behind the Shine—The Other Shell Report 2003," Shell Facts n.p. [cited 21 February 2006]. Online: http://www.shellfacts.com The 'other' Shell annual reports/Behind the Shine—The Other Shell Report 2003.

compulsory for big business. And yet recycling, which includes composting, diverted nearly seventy million tons of material away from landfills and incinerators in 2000. Few people doubt the importance of recycling, but just as few seem prepared to insist that businesses not be allowed to continue to "play" without cleaning up after themselves.

Christian Environmentalism?

As exiles, we must be prepared to practice a dangerous form of criticism against the foolhardy policies of the Western world. I recognize that many people are turned off by the environmental movement because of the abuses that they see perpetrated by so-called ecoterrorists. By destroying thousands or millions of dollars' worth of property, these extreme environmentalists believe that they can convince ordinary citizens of their message. In fact, their efforts have done the reverse. They have alienated the Green movement and caricatured themselves as irresponsible, radical, left-wing crazies. But exiles know that caring for their environment is not based on any particular brand of politics; rather, it springs from a theology that sees the intrinsic value of nature, not just its instrumental value. As we have noted, acknowledging God's ownership of the universe motivates exiles to respect, nurture, and care for that which is God's. This leads to a model of responsible and godly stewardship rather than to exploitation or subjugation. Exiles are willing to fulfill the intent of the earth's owner and live in keeping with the divine purpose for the earth.

It was Jesus who taught us to pray, "Your will be done on earth, as it is in heaven" (Matt 6:10). The idea that we have little or no responsibility for the earth or its creatures because one day we'll be raptured into heaven is a misreading of Scripture. Regardless of one's view on the nature of Christ's second coming, it is imperative that we value what God values. God valued this planet and all its creatures by creating them and calling them good in the first place.

It is interesting to note that this aspect of caring for creation is articulated in all major world religions in one form or another. This is, I believe, because God has put it in the heart of all human beings to nurture creation, as God has put in every heart a yearning for the divine. These are universal yearnings. Exiles have recognized that as an intrinsic part of their mission to critique both the mainstream church and their host empire, they must model what responsible care for the environment looks like. They are aware that Christianity has become the most anthropocentric of religions and recognize that it is entirely reasonable to view creation care as a corrective aimed at reminding the church of its duties to all of creation, instead of to humanity exclusively. This isn't to suggest that we can disregard the very human issues of suffering and injustice. As we've already noted, the nexus between poverty and environment goes largely unacknowledged within the church, and for that matter, within the secular environmental movement.

Moreover, it is important to acknowledge that the biblically based claim that the entire creation is good can imply an assertion that there is no evil in this world. Some Christian environmentalists stray into the romantic notion that all creation is pristine and perfect, just as God intended when pronouncing it good in Gen 1:31. If this is so, then should we strive to protect the AIDS and Ebola viruses from extinction? Are all species truly equal and good? Extreme biocentrists sometimes declare this to be the case, but such thinking clearly is making little headway today. Likewise, should we thank God for sending wildly devastating tsunamis and earthquakes that destroy humans and other creatures, and declare them good because they are a part of creation? Common sense tells us that creation in its present state is not unequivocally good. Also, many of the insights that ecology has provided into how nature functions reveal a creation that is far from some of the romanticized notions that seem to be widespread among environmentalists. Very few environmentalists, Christian or otherwise, have satisfactorily confronted the bad or harsh side of nature.

Creation has also suffered the effects of the fall of humankind as recorded in Gen 3:17–19 ("Cursed is the ground along with you . . ."). Jesus came to redeem all of creation. Jesus, the Word made flesh, the one through whom salvation is attained, was involved in the creation of the earth (John 1:3), along with God and the Holy Spirit. And Jesus will be involved in the full restoration of the earth. Just how this will be done, I'm not exactly sure. But it is clear that humans have an important responsibility to maintain the creation for all people and other living things until he comes again. Paul, speaking of the future glory, makes this very point:

> For the creation was subjected to frustration, not by its own choice, but by the will of the one who subjected it, in hope that the creation itself will be liberated from its bondage to decay and brought into the glorious freedom of the children of God. We know that the whole creation has been groaning as in the pains of childbirth right up to the present time. (Rom 8:20–22)

Thus Christian environmentalism will include valuing the intrinsic worth of creation by virtue of the worth conferred by its owner. But Christian environmentalism will also acknowledge the fallen condition of the earth and look forward to its final redemption in Christ, when it is "brought into the glorious freedom of the children of God." It is possible for those of us who have tasted this freedom in Christ to share it with the earth by caring responsibly for our planet. As I've mentioned, this is to be held in balance with our other concerns about human suffering and injustice.

In what ways might we make small, collective steps to care for that which God created and called good? If we want to make any difference and impact the post-Christendom West in any way, we need first to acknowledge that our use of energy in the West has reached outrageous proportions. How we use energy in the home and, above all, with our cars must be reappraised. Here are some suggestions:

In the House

- Recycle plastics, glass, and paper products.

- Replace ordinary light bulbs with compact fluorescent light bulbs. This will lower energy use and save money. Traditional incandescent bulbs waste 90 percent of the energy they use.

- When it comes time to replace a large appliance such as a refrigerator, freezer, air conditioner, washer-dryer, or water heater, look for products with the Energy Star label. They may cost a bit more initially, but the energy savings will pay back the extra investment in just a couple of years.

- Replace the old dial thermostat with one that has a programmable clock. Check to see if the water heater has an insulating blanket. Installing one will pay for itself in one year.

- Schedule a home energy audit. Many utilities offer them for free, and the expert advice can result in big energy savings.

- Choose renewable energy such as wind and solar for home or business. In many states, customers can choose an electricity provider, just like selecting a long-distance telephone provider. Other states offer options to select Green energy for all or a portion of the customer's energy. For more information on Green energy options, visit http://www .green-e.org/your_e_choices/pyp.html.

In the Car

- Keep the car's engine tuned and the tires fully inflated.

- Do not let a car idle unnecessarily for more than a minute.

- If you own two cars, take the gas-guzzler only when you can fill it up with passengers.

- When you buy your next car, buy the one that gets the best mileage in its class. Even better, buy one of the new hybrid models designed to be ecologically friendly. They generally cost the same as regular cars, have the same power and safety, save money at the pump, and cut global warming pollution by one-third to one-half. Show car manufacturers that drivers do indeed want Green cars that reduce dependence on oil.

In the Office

- Avoid plastic. Use ceramic crockery, metal cutlery, and real plants.

- Reuse paper. The blank side can be used for internal memos and reports or made into notepads.

- Recycle everything you can, including toner cartridges, magazines, and newspapers. If your office doesn't have access to a recycling collection service, take recyclables home and do the job yourself.

- If you are in charge of a business, install energy-saving devices such as motion-sensor lighting, flow-control water faucets, and double-glazed windows, and buy as much energy as possible from renewable sources.

- If you are in charge of a business, provide bonuses to employees who carpool or ride public transportation to the office.

People become environmentalists for many reasons. Their motivation may be humanitarian: they are genuinely concerned about the detrimental effects of environmental deterioration on the human race. Others may be motivated by economics: they see the need for a healthy environment so that the earth may be sustained and continue to produce wealth. Still others may be motivated by aesthetics: the beauty of the natural world inspires them to promote the protection of forests, wilderness areas, wetlands, and animals for the sake of an unspoiled environment. Some people may find all three motivations compelling. There's nothing wrong with any of these motivations, but I think that exiles, followers of the exile Jesus, will be motivated by their Christian faith. They will take seriously the biblical teaching to care for the earth. They will use the earth and its wondrous resources for living responsibly—to preserve it for the generations to come. They seek to enhance the earth for the glory of its Creator.

I like what renowned biologist Barry Commoner says in his book *The Closing Circle.* He describes the basic laws of ecology in four simple statements:

1. Everything is connected to everything else. This is the basic under-standing of ecology. All living creatures play a role in the natural scheme

of things. When humans interfere with any part of the environment, they may upset some other part.

2. Everything must go somewhere. Science states this law as "matter can neither be created nor destroyed." Matter may be changed in form, but, with the exception of nuclear energy, its quantity stays the same. One evidence that people don't understand or accept this principle is our inability to find enough landfill space as population and consumerism grow.

3. Nature knows best. If humans want to live sustainably upon the earth, they must look to nature itself and emulate the ecological principles found therein. There is harmony in the created order that can guide people to live harmoniously also. Those of us with faith can acknowledge that these ecological principles were built into creation by God.

4. There is no such thing as a free lunch. To live takes energy, which must be derived from outside living creatures. That energy comes from the sun to green plants that make the food used by all creatures. Some energy is lost in each step of the process of making and using food. One can never get out of a natural system as much energy as goes in. Scientists know this principle as "the second law of thermodynamics."[12]

These laws were built into the fabric of our world by God the Creator. Exiles will acknowledge that God has created such a world and placed humankind on earth to act as representatives, or stewards, of this creation. We have failed to protect the earth from the ravages inflicted upon it by our own human abuse. And as a result, we are flirting with global catastrophe. I readily acknowledge that those who do not share our faith in Christ are more often than not at the forefront of the movement to save our planet. They need our support. Without a basis in religious faith, however, their understanding of the environmental crisis is incomplete, and they are likely to become disillusioned and discouraged after a time.

A genuine Christian environmentalist will recognize that tending and revering the creation is part of God's divine plan for God's people. Too many Christians have spiritualized their faith to the point of marginalizing or ignoring ecology. Some people are environmentalists primarily for humanitarian or aesthetic concerns, others for economic prosperity, public attention, or political gain. Exiles, however, are environmentalists precisely because they are Christians.

---

[12]Barry Commoner, *The Closing Circle: Confronting the Environmental Crisis* (New York: Bantam Books, 1980).

11

Comforting the Oppressed

The Critique: You Have Not Protected God's Children

> The tyrant dies and his rule ends, the martyr dies and his rule begins.
>
> —Søren Kierkegaard

E xiles will be prepared to stand up and practice a dangerous form of criticism that tells their host empire that it has not been a generous enough society, and that it has not practiced justice or been careful enough as steward of the environment. They will also need to be prepared to critique their empire about the degree to which that empire has not duly acknowledged that Jesus Christ is Lord of all or protected the rights of those who serve him. In many parts of the world our brothers and sisters in Christ suffer unspeakable deprivation precisely because of their faith in Jesus. Such an abuse of human rights must attract our severe criticism, as should the governments of the developed nations that refuse to defend the rights of the most defenseless people who cannot escape the waves of persecution and violence that keep crashing upon them.

During the Babylonian exile the people of Yahweh were subjected to the most pointless and humiliating suppression by their captors. Perhaps the most famous case in point is Nebuchadnezzar's royal decree that at the appointed signal, all the people—Babylonians, Jews, and all other nationalities subjugated by Babylon—were to prostrate themselves before an enormous idol, ninety feet tall and made of gold, on the plain of Dura. Whenever the citizens and the slaves of the city heard the sound of an imperial orchestra, they were to throw themselves to the ground and worship the strange effigy. Those who refused did so on pain of death (Dan 3:1–7). This is the kind of thing that totalitarian regimes seem to enjoy: the demand that the people show themselves to be humbled by the every wish and whim of their rulers. Perhaps we are so used to hearing this idol story in Sunday school class that it has lost some of its power to shock or frighten us, but Nebuchadnezzar's decree is no different from the Nazis' requirement that Jews wear a yellow star on their clothing or the Stalinists' decree that dissident intellectuals and artists affirm the ideology of the state. And just as the Nazis and Stalinists enforced their contemptible demands with the threat of the concentration camp or the gulag, likewise the Babylonian authorities used the threat of death by fire in the imperial furnaces. You can be assured that whenever a regime installs an imperial furnace, it's not a society you want to be part of.

Nebuchadnezzar's furnace is no different from Hitler's Auschwitz or Stalin's Siberian gulags or Pol Pot's Tuol Sleng death camp or the Maoist "re-education camps" or Pinochet's interrogation rooms or the torture and internment policies of Myanmar's military junta, the Sudanese militia, the Rwandan Hutu death squads, or the apartheid-era white South Africans. The furnace is a symbol of control, of earthly power that demands absolute allegiance without question and without exception. This is why the story in chapter 3 of Daniel of Shadrach, Meshach, and Abednego and their refusal to bow down to the idol has such power today. It is the story of political and religious dissidents standing up in the face of seemingly insurmountable evil. When these insurgents declare, "Nebuchadnezzar, we do not need to defend ourselves before you in this matter" (Dan 3:16), they are looking the devil in the eye and refusing to be intimidated by his tactics. Of course, they are rescued from the furnace, and their courage and faith are vindicated. But today, in the face of torture and humiliation, incarceration and abuse, many followers of Jesus dare to stand up to such evil and they are not rescued—their suffering never ends. And yet, thousands of dissident Christians around the world can say, as those three in Babylon did, "But even if God does not [rescue us from the flames], we want you to know, Your Majesty, that we will not serve your gods or worship the image of gold you have set up" (Dan 3:18).

Even If God Does Not Rescue Us

Today, Christians around the world face this same dreadful choice: to refuse to deny Christ, even if God does not rescue them. One such Christian was Heidi Hakim Mankerious Salib, a senior in her final year at Road El Farag Secondary School for Girls in Cairo, Egypt. At seventeen, she was a committed Christian, anticipating overseas study and a new chapter in her young life. But none of this was to be. In 2004, she and her parents noticed a man watching Heidi from his balcony across the road from their home. This scrutiny aroused their suspicions, but life went on as normal until the day that man, Mustafa Ahmed Mohamed, suddenly approached Heidi and threatened violence if she didn't meet him later with her bankbook and valuables. Frightened out of her wits, Heidi complied. What happened next seems unthinkable. Mustafa, together with other members of a local Muslim extremist group, drugged, raped, and tortured Heidi for over twenty-four hours. She was forced to wear an Islamic veil, and scissors were used to deface the Christian cross she had tattooed on her wrist.

Because of their faith, the Salib family was drawn into a surreal cycle of horror. They reported their suspicions about Mustafa to the police, but when approached by the authorities, the kidnapper protested that Heidi had willingly left her Christian family to be with him, even presenting her valuables to the police as "proof" of her intentions. He continued to keep Heidi's whereabouts secret, telling police that she was free to go, but that she wanted to be with him and that she willingly wanted to convert to Islam. No charges were brought against him.

Impotent to stop this injustice, the Salibs were summoned the next day to the police station, where Heidi, obviously drugged, had been taken by her captors to officially sign a declaration that she had converted to Islam. Heidi's father and her priest protested so strongly that the local police referred the matter to a magistrate. Even though Egyptian law forbids a man to marry a girl under the age of eighteen without parental consent, the magistrate believed Heidi's dazed confession that Mustafa was now her husband. Later, it was discovered that the extremists had co-opted a local politician to their cause to keep Heidi from her parents. The Salibs were caught in a spiral of oppression and discrimination that, incredibly, was to become even worse.

Taking matters into their own hands, Mr. Salib "kidnapped" his own daughter and fled to a monastery, and eventually went to Alexandria so that Heidi could receive treatment for the effects of the drugs and the trauma that she had endured. Then, two months later, Heidi went missing while in Alexandria. The family believes that she was kidnapped by the same men. To date, the family has repeatedly contacted authorities in Egypt, including the president and the Egyptian National Council for Human Rights, with little response. Police continue to describe her as a "runaway."

Such is the cost that the Salibs have paid for their faith in Jesus. When we first heard the story of Shadrach, Meshach, and Abednego in our Sunday school classes, we casually agreed that, of course, God rescues people when they stand up to those ungodly authorities that demand their allegiance. In our carefree Christian neighborhood church it was easy to believe such things. But in a world that refuses to acknowledge that Jesus is the Son of God, exiles, wherever they might be—Egypt, Eritrea, China, Vietnam—

know that it is highly dangerous indeed to criticize the state by refusing to bow to their idols. According to the Geneva Report 2004, from the World Evangelical Alliance, there are more than two hundred million Christians who do not have full human rights as defined by the Universal Declaration of Human Rights.[1] These rights are denied to them for the simple reason that they choose to live as Christians. What these two hundred million exiles tell us by their silent, suffering witness is that the host empire can be extremely hostile when confronted with a staunch refusal to play along with the majority. The Salib family is but one example of the dreadful suffering inflicted on those whose faith is an affront to the state.

The exiles in Babylon say, "Even if God does not rescue us, we will not serve your gods," and by so doing, they speak for millions of persecuted Christians today who are not rescued from their suffering in the dramatic way that Shadrach, Meshach, and Abednego were from Nebuchadnezzar's furnace. Today, there is clear, documented evidence that Christians are suffering torments such as these:

- Imprisonment without trial

- Torture

- Home raids

- Confiscation of Bibles and Christian literature

- Physical abuse at the hands of police

- Physical abuse at the hands of non-Christian members of their communities

- Death threats

- Discrimination in employment

- Discrimination in a court of law

- Intimidation, so that they will close down churches

- Forced conversions to other religions

- Burning and destruction of churches

- Execution without trial, or "disappearances"

- Abductions and forced marriages to members of other religions

---

[1]Source: "Tears of the Oppressed," n.p. [cited 17 January 2006]. Online: http://www.human-rights-and-christian-persecution.org.

- Systematic rape of Christian populations

- Enslavement[2]

Of course, discrimination against and persecution of people from any religious background is totally unacceptable. As we noted earlier, exiles must be prepared to work toward a more just and equitable global community for all peoples. But in a world where Christians in many non-Western nations are experiencing unspeakable anguish, it is clearly part of the agenda of a biblical people to make a stand in their defense, to alleviate their suffering, and to demonstrate the power of the love of Jesus. Part of the dangerous criticism that we must make is to declare the illegitimacy of such cruel regimes. Every concentration of power requires "gods" to give credibility and legitimacy, to evoke loyalty and confidence. But someone must be prepared to say of the golden idols and imperial orchestras that they are in fact a joke because they have no spiritual power and cannot save their adherents. But remember, such criticism is dangerous because these empires have unchecked political power and have proven that they are ready to wield it against anyone who questions their supreme authority. For this reason, I believe that exiles in the West must be prepared to stand side by side with their fellow exiles in the developing world, exiles such as Damare Garang from Sudan.

Damare is a Sudanese Christian boy who was captured at the age of seven by Islamic soldiers when his village was attacked. He was sold as a slave to a Muslim family, where he became a camel boy even though he knew nothing about caring for such animals. His master taught him quickly by reinforcing his learning with severe beatings. When one of the camels absconded from Damare's care, the master threatened to kill Damare for this mistake, but he managed to restrain himself. But the very next day, while still fuming about his lost camel, he discovered that Damare had sneaked away to attend a Christian church in the village. His rage could no longer be contained, and he decided to teach the small boy a lesson that he would never forget.

What happened next is almost too dreadful to imagine. The camel owner took several rusty spikes and a hammer and held the boy down on a wooden board, where he drove the spikes through Damare's knees and feet, literally nailing him to the board. There he abandoned Damare, who was left screaming in agony.

Damare was rescued by a passerby and taken to a local hospital, where the nails and the board were removed. Later, miraculously, Damare was adopted by an army commander who took pity on the poor boy. Today,

---

[2]Ibid.

Damare is fifteen and still suffers the effects of his mock crucifixion. He limps and cannot run fast or play soccer like other boys his age, but he says that he has forgiven the man who nailed his legs to the board. He knows that Jesus was nailed to a cross for our sins, and through the Christian human rights watchdog The Voice of the Martyrs, he has asked the Christian children in America to remember to pray for the children of Sudan.[3]

The Christian community in the West enjoys such remarkable freedom. We should remain continually thankful for such a blessing, but we should also be prepared to pray for and practically support our brothers and sisters in other parts of the world whose regimes do not offer such freedom. Story after story from all corners of the globe remind us that in many places today it is indeed a terrifying thing to be a Christian. Three short examples will bring this home.

In Liberia in the late 1990s, the killing squads would look for pregnant women. When they found one, they would gamble on the gender of the unborn baby. Then to settle the bet, they would cut open the woman's womb and pull the baby out. The squads then discarded the corpses of the mother and baby by the side of the road before going off in search of another victim. During that horrific and largely unreported conflict, over one hundred thousand women were raped, often in front of their children. Many women had their breasts cut off and were left to bleed to death. Men were beheaded and their internal organs eaten by their murderers. Cannibalism was used as one of the most despicable forms of humiliation, as if the murdered victim could be further degraded after death.[4]

In Vietnam in 2003, paramilitaries arrested two village Christians, Nih (age forty-one) and So (age forty-four). Nih was known to have helped feed refugees who were hiding in the area. The two men were taken to the prison in the district of Dak Doa and tortured by beating, kicking, and electric shock. When Nih refused to answer questions or renounce Christ, the authorities stabbed him in the chest and then cut his throat. Then they took Nih's corpse to his family at Plei O Dot but refused to allow the family to perform a proper funeral, and they stated that they wanted the villagers to see what happens to those whom the government does not like.[5]

Today in the Kingdom of Saudi Arabia, where Christians make up less than 5 percent of the population, Saudi law provides that all citizens must

---

[3]See The Voice of the Martyrs, n.p. [cited 17 January 2006]. Online: http://www.persecution.com.

[4]Kenneth Cain, Heidi Postlewait, and Andrew Thomson, *Emergency Sex and Other Desperate Measures: A True Story from Hell on Earth* (New York: Hyperion, 2004), 256.

[5]See "Christian Persecution in Vietnam," n.p. [cited 17 January 2006]. Online: http://www.human-rights-and-christian-persecution.org/vietnam.html.

be Muslims. The practice of any non-Muslim religion in Saudi Arabia is prohibited, as is the owning, printing, or distributing of any non-Muslim religious material. Saudi Arabia currently has one of the worst records of all countries on human rights. Christians in particular are targeted for abuse, discrimination, and persecution. Apostasy (forsaking Islam for another religion) is a capital offense, and proselytizing can result in arrest and corporal punishment. Christian worshippers risk arrest, lashing, and deportation for engaging in overt religious activity. Christians are prohibited from entering the holy city of Mecca, and there are no official churches in Saudi Arabia. The *muttawa*—officially (and ominously) known as the Committee for the Propagation of Virtue and Prevention of Vice—are religious police who enforce adherence to Islamic norms by monitoring public behavior. They are brutal in carrying out their duties, and they intimidate and abuse citizens and foreigners. Most trials are closed, with defendants having little or no access to legal counsel. In fact, judges may legally discount the testimony of non-Muslims.[6]

The Abuse of Human Rights

I reiterate that we must be concerned about the abuse of human rights wherever it happens and to whomever it occurs, irrespective of religion. It's undeniable that Christian communities too have been responsible for human rights abuses and acts of atrocity. The terrorist activities perpetrated by so-called Christians in Northern Ireland, South Africa, and Bosnia are no less abhorrent than anything conducted by Islamic extremists or secular totalitarian regimes. By the early 1990s, Rwanda was considered to be one of the most Christianized countries in Africa, and yet it tumbled easily into nationwide bloodshed as Hutus systematically murdered hundreds of thousands of Tutsis. Less bloody was the ethnic turmoil in the Solomon Islands in 2004, but it was disturbing that the killing was carried out by churchgoers in one of the world's most Christian countries. From the Crusaders to the Conquistadors, from British colonial forces in Africa, India, and Australia to the Nazis, Christians have plenty of blood on their hands. I say again that we must be concerned with injustice wherever we see it, but it is an undeniable fact that much of the violence suffered in the world today is endured by the followers of Christ precisely because of their religious affiliation. And whenever a Christian's right to religious freedom is denied, it is common that other

---

[6]Source: "Tears of the Oppressed," n.p. [cited 17 January 2006]. Online: http://www.human-rights-and-christian-persecution.org.

human rights are violated as a consequence. These rights, as guaranteed by the U.N. Universal Declaration of Human Rights, include the following:

- Life, liberty, and security

- Freedom from torture and degrading treatment

- Equality before the law, and a fair trial

- Freedom from arbitrary arrest and detention

- Freedom of movement

- Marriage entered by free and full consent

- Ownership of property

- Freedom of expression and thought

- Peaceful assembly[7]

Even from the cases that we have looked at briefly so far, it is easy to see how these basic rights have been denied in multiple ways to the Salib family in Egypt, Damare Garang in Sudan, and Nih and So in Vietnam. But to understand the depths of the systematic abuse of Christians around the world, it will be instructive to look at two current case studies of persecution so great that some analysts have called them acts of genocide.

Case Study 1: The Horrors of Darfur

For twenty years the north African nation of Sudan, religiously and ethnically divided into the Muslim north and the Christian and animist south, has been fighting a bitter civil war. It is estimated that some 1.5 million people have lost their lives during the conflict, and the Islamic Khartoum-based government forces generally have targeted civilian villages and churches to wage its particular brand of terror. In the Longochok area of the eastern Upper Nile there has long been religious and ethnic tensions, with reports of Islamic extremists persecuting Christians, and occasional reports of the rape of Christian women by Muslim gangs and the severing of Christian women's breasts.

---

[7]For a full copy of the Universal Declaration of Human Rights (UDHR) see "Universal Declaration of Human Rights," Office of the High Commissioner for Human Rights, n.p. [cited 17 January 2006]. Online: http://www.unhchr.ch/udhr/lang/eng.htm.

But in 2000, when the government allied forces lost ground to the southern troops of the Sudan People's Liberation Movement/Army (SPLM/A), all hell literally broke loose. The government of Sudan began using local militias in a dreadful campaign to wipe out Christians and to secure their oil-rich lands in southern Sudan. The rape, torture, and murder of Christians, particularly women and children, became an entrenched tactic in the government's effort to secure the whole country. But to no avail. The southern troops held their ground, and in October of 2002 they fought the north to a historic ceasefire agreement. It looked like a breakthrough for peace, especially with the signing that month of the Sudan Peace Act, which required the Bush administration to help monitor ceasefires and sanction violations of them. But the government flouted the agreement with major military offensives in the oil-rich Upper Nile just two months later, in December of 2002 and then again in February of 2003.

In October of 2003, *Christianity Today* reported on the abuses carried out by militia sanctioned by the Sudanese government:

Chatyout Nydang is the leader of a Muslim militia that helps the Sudanese government wipe out Christians in southern Sudan. In July relief-and-development agency director Dennis E. Bennett spoke with an elderly southern Sudanese man in the eastern Upper Nile about life in territory that Nydang patrols. "Routinely, anyone Chatyout's men catch walking to church is beaten and told to convert to Islam, or next time they'll be beaten harder or killed," the approximately 65–year-old Nuer tribesman, Jon Giang-giang, told Bennett. After finding a Nuer Bible in his backpack, Nydang's men recently beat Giang-giang until he was unconscious. Bennett, executive director of Servant's Heart, says they left Giang-giang in a pit for more than two days.[8]

That same year, Janjaweed Arabs, a Sudan-backed militia, began driving some two million villagers from their homes in the western Darfur region in an attempt at ethnic cleansing designed to suppress local rebels. Satellite imaging has documented hundreds of burned-out villages. In remote border camps, displaced families live under plastic sheeting with grossly inadequate food and water. They have just enough food to starve—slowly. Already, twenty children a day may die in these camps, where seventy people sometimes share one pit latrine. By 2005, the attacks on Christians in the south were reaching staggering proportions. The so-called peace accord could do nothing to stop more than ten thousand deaths per month, with somewhere

---

[8]Jeff M. Sellers, "Submitting to Islam—or Dying: Ceasefires and Peace Talks Bow to Greater Powers in Sudan," Christianity Today, no. 10 (August 2003):100 [cited 17 January 2006]. Online: http://www.christianitytoday.com/ct/2003/010/26.100.html.

between 210,000 and 350,000 lives being lost in Darfur, according to a recent U.N. estimate.

Eyewitness accounts detailing the militia attacks are horrifying. Children have been murdered in front of their parents. Hundreds of Christian women have been raped in a crude attempt to impregnate them with "Arab babies." This is ethnic cleansing in its most heinous form.

In 2004, U.S. Secretary of State Colin Powell appropriately labeled the Darfur crisis as genocide. Also, the U.N. Security Council passed resolutions demanding an end to violence. Then in January of 2005, Sudan's leaders and southern rebels signed a new peace accord, only to see it evaporate as violence continued in the southern border region. Once again, women are the targets, with reports of militia cutting off the ears, lips, and breasts of southern women. The attackers also often abduct children to serve in their army. Captured children, mostly Christian, are trained to kill. They are put through a perverted baptism-like ritual by their captors and told that it will magically make them immune to the penetration of bullets. Paul Aciek Ater, a Sudanese pastor in Kansas, says of the people in Darfur, "They are God's children, and they are suffering terrible injustice."[9] Says the advocacy group Save Darfur,

> Not since the Rwanda genocide of 1994 has the world seen such a calculated campaign of slaughter, rape, starvation and displacement. Government-backed militias, known collectively as the Janjaweed, are systematically eliminating entire communities of African tribal farmers. Villages are being razed, women and girls raped and branded, men and boys murdered, and food and water supplies targeted and destroyed. Victims report that government air strikes frequently precede militia raids. According to the findings of the United Nations Commission of Inquiry, January 25, 2005, "government forces and militias conducted indiscriminate attacks, including killing of civilians, torture, enforced disappearances, destruction of villages, rape and other forms of sexual violence, pillaging and forced displacement, throughout Darfur. These acts were conducted on a widespread and systematic basis."[10]

---

[9]"Hotel Sudan Isn't a Film—Yet: Genocide in Darfur Must Be Stopped," *Christianity Today*, no. 5 (May 2005):26 [cited 17 January 2006]. Online: http://www.christianitytoday.com/ct/2005/005/21.26.html.

[10]"Current Situation," Save Darfur n.p. [cited 21 February 2006]. Online: http://savedarfur.org/go.php?q=currentSituation.html.The Save Darfur Coalition is an alliance of over one hundred diverse faith-based, humanitarian, and human-rights organizations that was formed in response to the massive crisis in the Darfur region of Sudan. Its mission is to raise public awareness and mobilize efforts to end the atrocities and reduce the suffering in Darfur and nearby refugee camps.

Case Study 2: Persecution in Paradise

The beautiful Maluku Islands lie in the eastern part of the Indonesian archipelago, about 1,700 kilometers from the capital, Jakarta, and once were known in the romantic adventure stories of Jack London and others as the Spice Islands of the former Dutch East Indies. Their history and their relationship to the nation of Indonesia, of which they now are part, are a story of mistrust, violence, and religious persecution.

The Malukans have been a thorn in Jakarta's side since they declared independence in the 1950s. In fact, they have always had a sense of being different from other Indonesians because of their close association with the previous colonial power, the Netherlands. After the Dutch drove out other European rivals to monopolize the spice trade in the Malukus, they set about building ties with the local populace. Local sultanates were allowed to remain intact, and the Dutch proselytized energetically, converting much of the population to Christianity. They set about creating the best education system in their Indies empire. Christian Malukans became the backbone of the colonial army, and they earned notoriety for their involvement in the Dutch struggle to put down the Indonesian independence movement.

When that independence was won in 1949, Jakarta was quick to exact revenge by sending in an invasion force that took more than a decade to completely crush the Malukan independence forces. About forty thousand Malukan ex-servicemen and their families took refuge in the Netherlands after the Indonesian troops finally put the rebellion down. There, they continued to lobby ineffectually for independence. However, this led neither to recognition of their cause abroad nor to a revolt in the Malukus, and the islands remained generally quiet throughout the next thirty years.

Whereas some 87 percent of Indonesians are said to be Muslim, in the Malukus the split between Muslims and Christians is more or less even. The islands had long been held up as a model of religious harmony. For centuries, local Muslims and Protestants lived in peace, observing traditional laws, but a purposeful policy of religious migration soon upset the fragile social structure. New immigrants, mainly Muslims from Sulawesi, Indonesia, began to tip the demographic and religious balance. Violence, when it came, was unexpected. In January 1999, a petty dispute between a Christian and a Muslim on a minibus in the port city of Ambon exploded into violence. Muslim lynch mobs went on a killing spree, burning churches, houses, and businesses. More than 350 people died in three months, and tens of thousands were made homeless. But this was nothing compared to what was to come.

By the end of 1999, youths as young as twelve armed with semiautomatic weapons were fighting pitched battles in the streets of Ambon. The port and the town went up in flames. Around twenty thousand of the islands' 110,000 people were uprooted as entire villages were razed. Since the attacks began, around eight thousand lives have been lost. And it could have been much worse. In May of 2000, the Indonesian government blocked Ahlus-Sunnah Wal Jama'ah, a loose grouping of hard-line Muslims, from sending a vigilante army to the islands. The group, which organized military training camps, claimed to have mustered ten thousand fighters to attack the Christian families that had remained on the island group. For the last few years, Jakarta has had limited success in quelling the attacks, using a policy that mixes negotiation, arrests, and port blockades. Muslim militia have continued to move from one island to the next, attempting to purge them of all Christians. Women have been kidnapped and raped. Property has been destroyed. Families have lived in continual fear for their lives. In one case, two thousand Muslim warriors systematically purged all the Christians on the remote island of Doi, northwest of Halmahera. One of the villages attacked had a population of just four hundred, who were forced to endure days of murder, looting, and burning. Those who had escaped into the jungle were hunted down like wild animals. Only those who converted to Islam were permitted to live.

What Can Be Done?

Sometimes it seems that these situations are so intractable and their historical roots go so deep that there's nothing we can do to help suffering Christians around the world. But that is not the case. In the Malukus especially, advocacy and relief efforts have been launched in the United Kingdom and Australia that have gone a long way toward motivating the Indonesian government to act to stop the bloodshed and restore peace.[11] Christians in the West have considerably more political muscle than we often realize, and while conservative Christians might be exercising it locally in the areas of the debates on abortion and gay marriage, exiles should not forget what they can do for the suffering church around the world. Here are some suggestions:

First, Look!

Qoheleth ("Teacher"), the writer of Ecclesiastes, bemoans the presence of such violence and persecution:

---

[11] "Understanding the Crisis," Cry Indonesia Website and Resource n.p. [cited 21 February 2006]. Online: http://cryindonesia.rnc.org.au Understanding the Crisis.

I saw the tears of the oppressed—and they have no comforter; power was on the side of their oppressors—and they have no comforter. And I declared that the dead, who had already died, are happier than the living, who are still alive. (Eccl 4:1b–2)

What a tragic realization: for the oppressed, death is more desirable than clinging to the misery of life. It reminded me of the stories that emanated from Rwanda, after the genocide there, that Tutsis were paying for bullets to give to their murderers so they could be shot rather than hacked to death by machetes (the Hutus' preferred method). As bleak as Qoheleth's vision of oppression might be, at least he looked! And herein lies an important lesson of the Christian exiles of the West. We must be prepared to look at the tears of the oppressed. No longer can we turn a blind eye to the misfortune of our brothers and sisters in the Malukus, Darfur, Egypt, Saudi Arabia, Vietnam, Eritrea, China, North Korea, and beyond. Western Christians can play a vital role in helping to stop violence and start peace in these places, but it begins with our preparedness to become internationally aware. Places such as Liberia or Rwanda or the Ivory Coast, for example, are not attractive holiday destinations. They have no oil or other important resources needed by us in the West. Many Westerners cannot even locate these nations on a map. So it's easy for us to remain ignorant of their plight. Exiles in the West must become global Christians, citizens of the whole planet, aware of the oppression suffered by the defenseless in various corners of the globe.

Develop a Theology of Persecution

Whenever we encounter terrible suffering, as did the writer of Ecclesiastes, it can bring on a serious existential crisis. Some years ago I visited an evil, evil place: Tuol Sleng, the Khmer Rouge's detention and torture camp in Phnom Penh. Formerly a school, it was converted by Pol Pot's henchmen into a depraved place of unspeakable suffering. Today it is a memorial to the thousands of Cambodians who were tortured there before being executed in the infamous Killing Fields outside the city. Bizarrely, the Khmer Rouge photographed every one of their torture victims as they entered Tuol Sleng, so that when the Vietnamese army liberated the city, it found thousands of these passport-sized pictures strewn around the camp. Today these pictures cover the walls of the torture chambers—pictures of men, women, grandparents, and children. The experience of looking into the horror-filled faces of hundreds of victims, like ghosts staring blankly at me, was too much to bear. The walls and floors are still bloodstained, the crude torture devices still intact. I stumbled from buildings into the silent yard and wept, wondering how God could allow such suffering.

All the more, we wonder why God's children, the followers of Jesus, should have to endure such torment. At these times it's important to develop a theological understanding of persecution. Of course, the Bible has much to say about persecution, including the fact that it is a likely prospect for those who follow Jesus. Indeed, the apostle Paul writes, "In fact, everyone who wants to live a godly life in Christ Jesus will be persecuted" (2 Tim 3:12). Elizabeth and James Scott, good friends of mine, head up the ministry of Tears of the Oppressed in Australia. They have listed a series of biblical principles that we need to keep in mind in developing a theology of persecution:

- The prophets were persecuted (Matt 5:12).

- Jesus predicted his own persecution (Mark 10:33–34).

- Jesus was persecuted (Mark 15:16–20).

- Those who follow Jesus will also be persecuted (Mark 10:30; John 15:20; 1 Thess 2:2; 2 Tim 3:12).

- Persecution occurs where the gospel is preached (Acts 8:1–3).

- Jesus warns his followers in preparation for persecution (John 16:1–4).

- In the midst of suffering, there is blessing (Matt 5:10, 12).

- Those who suffer in the name of Christ may be insulted, falsely accused (Matt 5:11).

- Persecution may be severe physical punishment (2 Cor 11:16–29; 4:7–18).

- Those who are persecuted must forgive their oppressors, because the oppressors do not know God and do not know what they are doing (Luke 23:34: John 16:3).

- Persecutors, by God's grace, can repent and turn to God (1 Tim 1:13).

- Christians should pray for their persecutors and bless them (Matt 5:44; Rom 12:14).

- Jesus does not abandon his people to persecution, but sends his Holy Spirit (John 15:26–16:4).

- A time will come when God will be glorified, and all suffering and persecution will cease (Rev 22).[12]

---

[12]"A Theology of Persecution," Human Rights and Christian Persecution n.p. [cited 21 February 2006]. Online: http://www.human-rights-and-christian-persecution.org/theology.html.

Pray for Those Who Suffer and for Those Who Cause Suffering

If you ask those who have been persecuted for their faith what you can do for them, more often than not they will ask you to pray. They have seen the miraculous power of prayer. They have seen prayer make a real difference to the circumstances of those who suffer, including the release of incarcerated Christians. Says Tears of the Oppressed,

> Through prayer, torture comes to an end. Through prayer, families find safety. Through prayer, false charges are dropped. Through prayer, people can be sustained and preserved through all manner of evil. Through prayer, world leaders can have a change of heart. . . . Prisoners have often said they have been conscious that people are praying for them, when they were suffering torture, or threats, or were alone in their cells.[13]

Remember also Paul's words: "Bless those who persecute you; bless and do not curse" (Rom 12:14). We should pray that those who oppress others will find the love of Jesus. This echoes Jesus' words when he tells us to pray for those who persecute us, so in our prayers we need to remember the oppressor as well as the oppressed.

Advocate Politically

Powerful Western nations such as the United States and the United Kingdom, as well as the United Nations, and other peace advocates must talk less and act more. In a small step forward for Darfur, the U.N. Security Council passed a resolution recently to refer those suspected of war crimes in Sudan to the International Criminal Court in The Hague. The perpetrators of genocide must be stopped and brought to justice. They must know that the international community will hold them accountable for their horrific crimes. In other words, we must communicate to the oppressors that we too have seen the tears of the oppressed, that their actions are being observed, and that they cannot get away with such bloodshed.

For this reason, advocacy is essential. American evangelicals are currently in a rare position to be heard both in Washington and at the United Nations. In fact, international relief groups are well aware that when American evangelicals speak with one voice, policymakers in Washington pay attention. And high-level pressure gets results overseas. This is not to place all the international responsibility on the shoulders of Americans. Christian exiles in Great Britain, Australia, New Zealand, Canada, and Europe must also force

---

[13]Ibid.

their governments to look at the oppression in places like Darfur. Explore the advocacy work done by organizations such as Tears of the Oppressed, Micah Challenge, Save Darfur, and The Voice of the Martyrs and use the resources that they offer, including template advocacy letters and the addresses of various embassies and influential bodies.

A few minutes spent writing a thoughtful letter to a government official—a secretary, a governor, a member of a parliament or a congress, an ambassador, an embassy official—can make a difference to the plight of persecuted Christians. People in power can give the order to make a change, or they can influence those who have the power to make a change. Five minutes spent writing a letter to a person in power may mean five years' less torment for a suffering Christian.

Remember, a handwritten letter can have great impact because it conveys a heartfelt and personal commitment to the cause. But even a typed letter will have immense value in the hands of authorities if you have drafted it yourself.

Provide Practical and Spiritual Comfort for Victims

Qoheleth twice declares " . . . and they have no comforter" in chapter 4 of Ecclesiastes. We ought not let it be said of our brothers and sisters around the world that no one comforted them. We can write letters to Christians in prison. It's true that sometimes letters are intercepted by prison authorities and never make it to the prisoners' hands. But we shouldn't let that stop us. A letter from a Christian in the West not only demonstrates personal concern for a particular person, but also it makes the authorities aware that the world is watching their actions. It also offers the hope to the prisoner that someone is doing something about his or her plight. Sometimes these letters can result in better treatment or more food for prisoners. On the other hand, of course, they may sometimes have the opposite effect. We can't be sure. So it's essential that we follow the advice of analysts working for human-rights watchdogs. Nonetheless, when the letters are passed on to suffering Christians, they can come at just the right time to lift their spirits. And we can also write letters to the relatives of prisoners. This will reduce their sense of isolation, and they can share our letters when they visit prisoners.

In addition, we can do much to alleviate suffering by supporting efforts to rebuild war-torn communities. For example, Washington-based Faith McDonnell, director of the Church Alliance for a New Sudan, says, "Islamists in Sudan have not given up their jihad-in-Africa campaign. Are we willing to get in there and help southern Sudan? To build schools, churches, hospitals, roads? Are we willing to help train pastors? Will we force the cessa-

tion of genocide in Sudan?"[14] By rebuilding war-ravaged Sudan, we give the persecuted communities a greater chance, and we provide a possibility that the millions of refugees will be able to return to their homeland. The Sudan Council of Churches USA, based in Kansas, has thirty-eight member congregations that are stepping up to the task of rebuilding. They have helped to lead mission teams to a refugee camp in Chad. The organization Cry Indonesia has advertised the plight of the Malukan Christians, and Sydney-based Bridge to Hope has established a ministry of providing interest-free loans for Christian refugees to establish microenterprises in their new communities. These initiatives provide comfort to those whose lives have been devastated by persecution.

The Other Side of Persecution

Up to this point, I have barely mentioned the persecution of Christians in China. As we know, even with the more recent relaxing of the restrictions placed on Chinese Christians and the lifting of the Bamboo Curtain, the church in China continues to suffer for its faith. But unlike the devastating effects of the genocide in Darfur, the flames of Chinese persecution have forged a very muscular and confident underground church that has grown remarkably, even miraculously, over recent decades. This is the other side of persecution: the purifying effect on the suffering church.

Paul Hattaway is the director of Asia Harvest,[15] a Christian ministry committed to serving the Chinese church. His book *Back to Jerusalem* has provided the world with a surprising glimpse of the emerging missionary church of China, where preparations are currently underway to send out thousands of missionaries to the West.[16] Hattaway reports on the testimony and vision of three Chinese house-church leaders who believe that the Chinese will complete the task of world evangelism by taking the gospel via the various "silk roads" west, through the Muslim lands, and back to Jerusalem, thus completing the circuit of Christian expansion from west to east over the past two thousand years. According to Hattaway, this vision is the driving force of their lives and ministries. In fact, they see it as the destiny to which God has called the Chinese church, the very reason they exist: to preach the gospel and establish fellowships of believers in all the countries, cities, towns,

---

[14]Quoted in "Hotel Sudan Isn't a Film—Yet."

[15]Asia Harvest, n.p. [cited 17 January 2006]. Online: http://www.asiaharvest.org.

[16]Paul Hattaway, *Back to Jerusalem: Three Chinese House Church Leaders Share Their Vision to Complete the Great Commission* (Carlisle: Piquant, 2003).

and ethnic groups between China and Jerusalem, which includes the largely Muslim former member states of the Soviet Union, as well as Pakistan, India, Afghanistan, and, of course, the Middle East. How remarkable that the church that Mao and the Chinese Communist Party spent fifty years oppressing is now planning to send missionaries to reach the people of other nations.

Collectively, the three Chinese leaders discussed by Hattaway have spent a total of almost forty years in prison for their faith, and through their sufferings they have learned much about God's character and work. They are indefatigable, resilient, and deeply spiritual. Their faith has been hardened by years of oppression, and Hattaway is confident that the vision of these leaders will come to fruition. He believes that he is chronicling the formation of a new, major missions movement across the globe:

> Today there are hundreds of Chinese missionaries working outside China in the Middle East, North Africa, Central Asia, the Indian subcontinent, and Southeast Asia. Thousands more are in training. The total membership of major house church networks [currently supporting the Back to Jerusalem movement] came to 58 million people in 2000, while the net growth rate of each church group was reported to be between 12.5 per cent and 17.5 percent per year. Some experts estimate that thirty thousand Chinese are coming to Christ each day, which works out to more than ten million new believers annually.[17]

The history of the Chinese church is a fascinating one. The arrival of Christianity in China can be traced to the Nestorians in 635 C.E., though in the modern era, Catholic missionaries arrived in the 1300s, five hundred years before the arrival of Protestants such as Robert Morrison and Hudson Taylor. By the 1920s, more than ten thousand foreign missionaries were scattered around China. Persecution broke out against Christians throughout China in the 1950s. There was no limit to the savagery inflicted on Chinese Christians, and by 1953, almost all foreign missionaries had been expelled or martyred.

Church historians and missiologists now believe that the communist authorities unwittingly paved the way for the spread of the gospel by removing much of China's idolatry, attempting to deny the supernatural (when people experienced miracles), constructing transportation systems, unifying the language by adopting Mandarin, developing large-scale literacy projects, and creating a hunger for the printed word through controlling the media. So much so, that today it is estimated that there are eighty to one hundred mil-

---

[17]Ibid., 2.

lion Protestants and at least twelve million Catholics, compared to 1949, when there were about seven hundred thousand Protestants and three to four million Catholics.

Those persecuted Chinese church leaders who share the Back to Jerusalem vision have, rather ingeniously, claimed that the spread of the gospel globally has happened, generally speaking, in a westward direction. From Jerusalem in the first century, it spread west through Asia Minor and northern Africa, eventually to Rome and Western Europe. From there it spread to the Americas and the Pacific, and eventually to the Far East. They say that practically all of the remaining areas of the world that have never been penetrated by the gospel are situated west and south of China. Furthermore, they believe that God has told them that when the gospel takes root in those nations between China and Jerusalem, the work of global mission will be complete, having circled literally the entire globe. Even if their reading of church history and their claims that God has spoken to them are questioned, reading Hattaway does make us wonder whether God has raised up the Chinese church under communism for this very moment in history.

Today there are hundreds of Christians inside China learning foreign languages such as Arabic and English in preparation for missionary service outside China. But they also believe that the past fifty years of suffering, persecution, and torture of the house churches in China is all part of God's training for this moment in history. Says one Chinese church leader,

> We never pray against our government or call down curses on it. Instead, we have learned that God is in control of both our own lives and the government we live under. There is little that any of the Muslim, Buddhist, or Hindu countries can do to us that we haven't already experienced in China. God is calling thousands of house church warriors to write their testimonies with their own blood. We're totally committed to planting groups of local believers who meet in homes. We have no desire to build a single church building anywhere! This allows the gospel to spread rapidly, is harder for the authorities to detect, and enables us to channel all our resources directly into gospel ministry.[18]

It seems that we are seeing a Christian fundamentalist zeal forged in the fires of communist China that can match the fundamentalist zeal of Middle Eastern Islam. Either this will result in significant global conflict or Chinese Christianity will be the very thing that India, Bangladesh, Afghanistan, and the Middle East need in order to hear the gospel of Jesus Christ. The persecuted Chinese Christians cannot be accused of being wealthy

---

[18]Ibid., 57.

imperialistic missionaries, spreading a dogma of Western greed and immorality. In fact, they will be an affront to everything that such nations assume Christianity to be.

According to the movement, Jerusalem has been connected to China by road for more than two millennia, ever since the long-reigning Emperor Wudi (138–87 B.C.E.) opened up the Silk Road. The Chinese leaders of Back to Jerusalem believe that this was part of God's providence for the present-day strategy. They also believe that they are called not only to go westward through the Muslim world, but also to take the gospel to the ethnic minorities in Southwest China and the nations of Southeast Asia. Their vision also includes the Northern Asian countries of Japan, North Korea, and Mongolia, with certain church networks focusing prayer and preparation on these specific areas. To achieve this, they have picked their most experienced workers, those who had suffered much hardship for the kingdom, and sent out the first thirty-nine workers. Thirty-six were arrested in their first few days as missionaries. Their training included standard missionary training, such as how to reach across cultural barriers, how to witness, and how to reach specific people groups. But it also includes surprising learning, such as how to suffer and die for Jesus, and how to escape from custody (can you imagine Western seminaries including such subjects?).

This zeal not only grips the leaders and missionaries from Back to Jerusalem, but also affects whole congregations. In spite of their poverty, the house churches involved have collected tens of thousands of dollars to support these missionaries. It is currently estimated that together, these churches had approximately one million "full-time" Christian workers in their churches. They believe that the very least they can do is give a tithe of these leaders to foreign missions. As a result, they have arrived at the figure of one hundred thousand, and they plan to send that many missionaries out of China.

As extreme as all of this may sound to some, it is an example of the positive difference that decades of persecution can make. Let's face it, when American missionaries go to Iran or Syria or Kazakhstan, their message about Jesus is easily misunderstood. In many Muslim nations in the Middle East, Northern Asia, and the subcontinent, Christianity is inextricably linked to current Western values. Muslims in, say, Uzbekistan routinely assume that the greedy and sexually promiscuous cultures that they observe in America and Europe are the epitome of Christianity. They see white European or American missionaries to be as much an expression of cultural imperialism as Coca-Cola or MTV. They can discount the message of Jesus on the basis of the culture that they believe it has created. But if these crazy, fundamentalist Chinese Christians have their way, they will soon be flooding through countries dominated by Islam, Buddhism, and Hinduism. These new missionaries will share a set of very conservative, almost puritanical, lifestyle values similar to those of the fundamentalist Muslims among whom they will live. And they will have been hardened by oppression and able to withstand persecution far better than Western missionaries who have never known adversity. Frankly, I have no idea what will come of it all, but it is a reminder to us that God can use even something as dreadful as the Maoist persecution of the church for his own glory.

Thou Shalt Not Stand Idly By

Elie Wiesel was born in Romania in 1928. He grew up in a small village, his world revolving around his loving family, his religious studies, and the tightly knit community. But his family, his village, and his innocent faith were destroyed by the deportation of Romanian Jews by the Nazis in 1944. Wiesel went on to survive the horrors of Auschwitz, Buna, Buchenwald, and Gleiwitz.

After the liberation of the camps in April of 1945, Wiesel spent a few years in a French orphanage, and in 1948 he began studies in Paris at the Sorbonne. He eventually became a journalist, writing for the French newspaper *L'arche*. During this time, Wiesel met Nobel laureate François Mauriac, who eventually influenced Wiesel to break his vowed silence and write of his experience in the concentration camps. He has since become the author of thirty-six books dealing with Judaism, the Holocaust, and the moral responsibility of all people to fight hatred, racism, and genocide. His statement "To remain silent and indifferent is the greatest sin of all" stands as a succinct summary of his views on life and serves as the driving force of all his work. He is also often quoted for having written, "Let us remember, let us remember the heroes of Warsaw, the martyrs of Treblinka, the children of Auschwitz. They fought alone, they suffered alone, they lived alone, but they did not die alone, for something in all of us died with them."

In 2004, the Darfur Emergency Summit was convened at the City University of New York by the American Jewish World Service and the United States Holocaust Memorial Museum. Elie Wiesel, the survivor of one holocaust, was invited to speak about another holocaust, this time the one happening in Sudan. The Darfurians are a predominantly Christian ethnic minority, being persecuted by the Muslim north. Wiesel's defense of these Christians is breathtaking, and I include just his conclusion to end our look of this topic. I trust that it will inspire you as it did me:

> How can a citizen of a free country not pay attention? How can anyone, anywhere not feel outraged? How can a person, whether religious or secular, not be moved by compassion? And above all, how can anyone who remembers remain silent?

As a Jew who does not compare any event to the Holocaust, I feel concerned and challenged by the Sudanese tragedy. We must be involved. How can we reproach the indifference of non-Jews to Jewish suffering if we remain indifferent to another people's plight?

It happened in Cambodia, then in former Yugoslavia, and in Rwanda, now in Sudan. Asia, Europe, Africa: Three continents have become prisons, killing fields and cemeteries for countless innocent, defenseless populations. Will the plague be allowed to spread?

Lo taamod al dam réakha is a Biblical commandment—"Thou shall not stand idly by the shedding of the blood of thy fellow man." The word is not akhikha, thy Jewish brother, but réakha, thy fellow human being, be he or she Jewish or not. All are entitled to live with dignity and hope. All are entitled to live without fear and pain.

Not to assist Sudan's victims today would for me be unworthy of what I have learned from my teachers, my ancestors and my friends, namely that God alone is alone: His creatures must not be.

What pains and hurts me most now is the simultaneity of events. While we sit here and discuss how to behave morally, both individually and collectively, over there, in Darfur and elsewhere in Sudan, human beings kill and die.

Should the Sudanese victims feel abandoned and neglected, it would be our fault—and perhaps our guilt.

That's why we must intervene.

If we do, they and their children will be grateful for us. As will be, through them, our own.[19]

---

[19]Elie Wiesel, "On the Atrocities in Sudan," Save Darfur n.p. [cited 21 February 2006]. Online: http://savedarfur.org/misc/ElieWiesel'sStatement.doc.

PART IV

DANGEROUS SONGS

Exiles at the Altar

The Song: To God Be the Glory

To love another person is to help them love God.
—Søren Kierkegaard

n the work that I do around the world with missional churches I am regularly asked about how exiles should worship. Even after I've told about the exciting experience of creating communitas, fashioning missional communities, eating together, living compassionately, serving the poor, and honoring our work as sacred activity, someone still wants to know what a missional church worship service would look like. In fact, barely a week goes by when someone doesn't contact me and ask to come and "check out" our community, smallboatbigsea. This request is always followed by the next question: "What day and time do you meet?" What assumption lies behind such a request? Answer: that we are primarily defined by a weekly meeting, and that if you attend that meeting, you can see all you need to see to get an understanding of our community.

I confess that I have been guilty of this myself. A few years ago, when doing research for *The Shaping of Things to Come,* I contacted a Christian faith community in California and asked if I could meet their leadership team and attend their weekly gathering. Their reply initially confused me, but today it makes perfect sense. They said that they would allow me access to their community and its leaders only if I agreed to live for four days with them. I wasn't sure I had a spare four days and was annoyed that they would be so uncooperative. I just wanted to look at their worship service and interview their leaders, but reluctantly I agreed. It was a profoundly important time because it taught me that a genuinely missional community operates at multiple levels and different times, as any organic, dynamic web of relationships would. Their corporate worship times, when viewed in isolation, weren't that big a deal (neither are the worship times for smallboatbigsea), but having spent several days with them, I found their corporate gathering to be a rich and fulfilling time of connection with God because it was representative of the interconnections between the members and their ministries. In a very real sense, if a missional church has a public worship service, it is literally the tip of an iceberg—a very small, visible part of a much larger body. Today, when people say that they want to check us out, I suggest the four-day option, but few are willing to take it. Why can't we think of churching together as a web of relationships? Why are we obsessed with the singular event rather than seeking the rhythm of a community churching together?

The Impact of Christendom

Partly this issue emerges because after seventeen hundred years of Christendom we cannot clearly imagine church as anything other than a weekly worship gathering. Remember that in the period of Christendom, after the Edict of Milan in 313, whereby the Roman emperor Constantine began introducing measures designed to replace paganism with his favored Christianity as the imperial religion, the role of mission recedes into the background. By the Middle Ages, all people in Europe were considered to be Christian by virtue of their infant baptism. There was no longer any need for the church to be missional. So, if it could no longer provide a missional contribution to European Christendom, it would retreat to the one primary function it could still offer: rituals for worship. This became the Christendom-era church's specialty.

For pretty much the whole period of this era, average Christians expressed their faith almost entirely by their attendance at Mass, although the meaning of "express their faith" needs some explanation. There were laws during this era that required regular church attendance, so any expression of faith was more likely an expression of one's Christian heritage or culture. Many people attended services because they had to, because it was culturally expected, and not necessarily out of a deep personal faith in Jesus. Stuart Murray quotes Augustine complaining about "depraved persons who in mobs fill the churches in a bodily sense only," and Martin of Braga, who referred to people who played dice games or talked throughout church services.[1] It's easier to understand this kind of unruly behavior when you enter an Italian or a French church today. Even the most modest chapels are huge buildings, with the area in which the liturgical performances take place set far back from the space provided for con-

---

[1]Murray, *Post-Christendom*, 68.

gregational seating. Attendees were treated as nothing more than disinterested spectators, which many of them were.

Furthermore, by the end of the twelfth century, everyone in Christendom had been divided into parishes large enough to support a church and a priest but small enough to allow easy access to the parish chapel for services. Tithing became mandatory, so everyone was "taxed" to support the parish church and its priests. It was a brilliant system for ensuring both ecclesiastical administration and pastoral care. The laity was expected to pay its tithe and attend Mass. The clergy were expected to perform sacramental rites such as baptism, marriage, funerals, and weekly Mass, as well as provide spiritual and pastoral care for the laity. There was no need for evangelism or for ministries of social justice, aside from some basic services provided for the poor. The result of nearly two centuries of Christendom is that Christians have become used to the idea that their faith is primarily about attending meetings—worship meetings, weddings, funerals, prayer meetings, and so on. Even today, in our thoroughly post-Christendom world, when the essential work of the church in providing religious, liturgical services has become irrelevant, Christians (including many exiles) can't separate the idea of Christianity from the weekly Mass or worship service. Even those who have ceased attending church services have great difficulty imagining what it means for a group of believers to church together without picturing a liturgical meeting of some kind.

In *The Shaping of Things to Come*, Alan Hirsch and I had much to say about the sinister nature of buildings. We quoted Winston Churchill's maxim "First we build our buildings, then our buildings build us." We were keenly aware of how church buildings shape the communities that meet in them, but more disturbing than such buildings themselves is the Christendom-based assumption that went into their design and creation. It is an assumption that locates the central purpose of the Christian community in the act of corporate worship. I submit that this is unbiblical and emerges more from the cultural forces just described than from the teaching of Jesus or his first followers. Without buildings or priests or ancient liturgies, these early Christians found their reason for being not in a weekly worship service, but in their corporate commitment to glorify God in Christ. As French theologian Jacques Ellul points out,

> For the Romans, nascent Christianity was not at all a new religion. It was "antireligion." This view was well founded. What the first Christian generations were putting on trial was not just the imperial religion, as is often said, but every religion in the known world.[2]

---

[2]Jacques Ellul, *The Subversion of Christianity* (trans. G. W. Bromiley; Grand Rapids: Eerdmans, 1986), 55.

It can be justifiably said that their example also puts contemporary Christianity on trial. Although our roots as a movement emerge from anti-religion, the current expression of church life is centered very much on religious meetings, liturgies, "priests" (whether preachers or worship leaders), buildings, and events. The employment of staff and the construction of buildings then create a vicious cycle. The congregation has to keep attracting people to the services in order to fund the building and the staff. Even when congregations want to break from this model, their financial commitments prevent them.

The Chief End of Humankind

But there's another powerful reason for our obsession with corporate worship meetings, and it lies in a misunderstanding of Reformed teaching on worship. The Westminster Confession famously states, "Man's chief end is to glorify God, and to enjoy him forever." This statement is particularly well known by Christians today, even those who've never read the Westminster Catechism or don't even belong to the Presbyterian tradition. Most Christians seem quite certain that the primary purpose of all humankind is to glorify God. And they seem equally certain that the primary mechanism for glorifying God is through corporate Christian worship. But is this really the case? The Reformers certainly overturned much of the works-based theology of the pre-Reformation church, but they did so without challenging the broadest assumptions of Christendom. They still required attendance at religious meetings, even if their meetings were different in theology, tone, and liturgy from those that preceded them.

Since the Westminster Confession codified our chief end as being to glorify God and enjoy him forever, many people from the Reformed tradition have assumed that our highest purpose is to worship God, and to worship God is to do so in a properly conducted Christian worship service. Such a properly convened and conducted service might include various elements, but central to its purpose is the proper preaching of the Word of God by a properly trained and accredited teacher/priest. For many Christians today, attendance at such a gathering is the chief end of humankind. It follows, then, that for these Christians, the idea of evangelism is almost entirely bound up in an assumption that our primary goal is to invite unbelievers into such a meeting, at which they can hear the correct preaching of the Bible in the context of a worshipping community.

The Pentecostal movement of the twentieth century did nothing to correct this assumption. In fact, Pentecostals are equally in the thrall of the gathered worship meeting as the highest calling of the Christian. They sing,

"Better one day in thy house than a thousand days without." What else can this mean other than that one day in church, worshipping with other believers, is better than anything else in the world? This, supposedly, is our chief end. I've had more than one young student tell me in all sincerity that they believe that heaven will be an eternal worship meeting in which we gather with angels and the saints of history to sing and adore God for all time. I'm sure they're shocked when they see me blanch at the idea.

But I'm not certain that this is what the Westminster Confession says anyway. The statement in question implies that our primary purpose as Christians is twofold: glorifying and enjoying God. So what does it mean, first, to glorify God? Is it limited to singing worship songs and attending services? God's glory is generally understood to have two components: essential glory and declarative glory. The essential glory is that of God's own self, intrinsic glory. Westminster says that glory is essential to the Godhead, as light is to the sun. In other words, it's impossible for God *not* to be glorious. The Scriptures are full of references to God being a "God of glory" (e.g., Acts 7:2) and having a glory that is complete in itself. God's glory cannot be added to or shared with another. In Isa 48:11, Yahweh says, "I will not yield my glory to another."

Second, there's God's declarative glory. This is the glory that is ascribed to God, or that creation labors to bring to God. This is the bit that we can contribute. Since we can't add a thing to God's essential glory, our contribution is to add to God's declarative glory. Thus, to glorify God means to exalt God's name in the world and magnify God in the eyes of others. But still we might ask, "Can this be done via corporate worship meetings alone?" The Westminster Catechism states that we glorify God in four primary ways: appreciation, adoration, affection, and subjection.

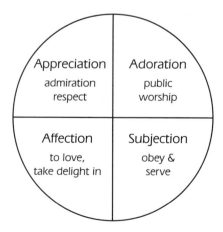

Declaring the Glory of God

- **Appreciation.** This is to **esteem** God, to value God above all in our thoughts and admiration, to venerate God in our imagination, thinking, and belief. When we admire and respect God in this way, we glorify God.

- **Adoration.** This is to **worship** God in a formal, liturgical sense in a public, corporate setting. The Westminster Catechism, based on the Confession, makes copious references to Old Testament injunctions to worship correctly in the temple and in the exact method prescribed by the Lord. The Confession assumes that adoration must be done in a properly constituted worship service.

- **Affection.** This is to **love** God, to offer a love of delight, as we take delight in a friend. This is to love God indeed, with our hearts set upon God. It is an exuberant love. It is superlative; we give glory to God when we offer the best of our love.

- **Subjection.** This is to dedicate ourselves to **serve** God through our actions. This can take various forms: Bible study, prayer life, witness, compassionate living, generosity and hospitality offered in God's name. To obey the divine will through service brings glory to God.

I think that the Westminster Confession has got it pretty much right. We glorify God in a number of ways: esteem, love, worship, service. In other words, when I feed the poor or share my food with a neighbor, I am glorifying God. When I study the Bible, I am glorifying God. When I take a prayer walk along a beach and give thanks to heaven for all its blessings, I am glorifying God. When I sit in the Impressionist Room at the Getty Center in Los Angeles and feel deep affection and admiration for the divine beauty in Van Gogh's irises, Monet's haystacks, and Cezanne's apples, I am glorifying God. When I visit an orphanage in Vietnam, filled to overflowing with unwanted children dumped on the streets of Saigon, I am glorifying God. When I write to my government representatives demanding that they procure greater overseas aid, I am glorifying God. When I attend a gathering of fellow believers to sing or pray or undertake some other corporate worship activity, I am glorifying God. So, although attending worship meetings is *one* of the ways we glorify God, it is not the only way.

To Enjoy God Forever

The second part of our purpose, according to the Westminster Confession, is to enjoy God forever. What a delightful suggestion! When we make the glorifying of God our chief end, our eyes are opened to the myriad ways we can enjoy God here on earth. A trip to an art gallery becomes a worship time. A time of feeding the homeless becomes an act of communion with God. A day in the house of the Lord is great, but so is the thousand days outside. Enjoying such sweet, everyday communion with God is a riddle and mystery to most people, but those of us who have experienced God's marvelous grace in Christ can't imagine how anyone could enjoy life without the enjoyment of God. Personally, I can't imagine enjoying physical health, great friends, good fortune, or earthly pleasures without enjoying God. It's said that the higher the lark flies, the sweeter it sings. Surely this is a picture of the believer who enjoys life because he or she enjoys God, and vice versa. The higher we fly by the wings of faith, the more we enjoy God. This kind of enjoyment can be sensed in the pleasure of a deep and satisfying time of corporate worship. There's nothing quite like the joy experienced when we raise our hands and our voices and together with others sing in praise of God as if with one voice. But we can't limit our enjoyment of God to these experiences. When we trim the edges of our lawn, cut back the hedges, and fertilize the flowerbeds, sensing a powerful communion with the God of creation, we are enjoying God. When we pray with dear friends for the needs of another and feel deeply connected with fellow believers in this single cause, we are enjoying God.

To enjoy God also means to embrace the slow and ongoing work of sanctification, of orienting every part of your world to the glory of God. Our abandonment to lust, greed, or other ungodly sensual pleasures doesn't glorify God. Aristotle called sensual lusts brutish, because when any lust is violent, reason or conscience cannot be heard. These lusts besot and brutalize us. In the King James Bible, Hosea puts the matter bluntly: "Whoredom and wine take away the heart" (Hos 4:11). It follows that a heart captured by such pleasures is incapable of being fully directed toward God's glory. To enjoy God also means to embrace the "pain" of a life of discipline and devotion. Denying unhelpful, destructive impulses is an expression of the enjoyment of God, as it gives glory to him. So does feeding the poor, taking in the homeless, visiting the sick, dressing wounds, cleaning the soiled. I heartily endorse that our chief end is to glorify and enjoy God, as long as we understand it to mean more than just corporate worship.

If heaven really is an eternal worship service, I'm having trouble getting excited about that. This is not to say I don't want to worship God. I do, but I want to see worship as something that includes appreciation, affection, and subjection, as well as adoration. Isaiah's vision of the new heavens and the new earth paints a different picture from that of angels and humans dressed in white robes, hands in the air, singing praises to God forever. Speaking of the age to come, Isaiah says,

The sound of weeping and of crying will be heard in it no more. Never again will there be in it infants who live but a few days, or older people who do not live out their years; those who die at a hundred will be thought mere youths; those who fail to reach a hundred will be considered accursed. They will build houses and dwell in them; they will plant vineyards and eat their fruit. No longer will they build houses and others live in them, or plant and others eat. For as the days of a tree, so will be the days of my people; my chosen ones will long enjoy the work of their hands. They will not labor in vain, nor will they bear children doomed to misfortune; for they will be a people blessed by the LORD, they and their descendants with them. (Isa 65:19b–23)

Here is a vision of a new city, a redeemed world of justice, plenty, love, mercy, fruitful labor, and an equitable distribution of resources. It will be a magical city in which "the wolf and the lamb will feed together, and the lion will eat straw like the ox" (Isa 65:25), and everyone will have plenty and live together in harmony. The image of the redeemed city appears also in Revelation:

Then I saw "a new heaven and a new earth," for the first heaven and the first earth had passed away, and there was no longer any sea. I saw the Holy City, the new Jerusalem, coming down out of heaven from God, prepared as a bride beautifully dressed for her husband. And I heard a loud voice from the throne saying, "Look! God's dwelling place is now among the people, and he will dwell with them. They will be his people, and God himself will be with them and be their God. 'He will wipe every tear from their eyes. There will be no more death' or mourning or crying or pain, for the old order of things has passed away." (Rev 21:1–4)

The rest of the chapter is an enchanted, dreamlike description of a pristine, perfected metropolis, a city that needs no temple to worship God because God himself will be in the midst of the people. To enjoy God means to seek to fashion such a world as this here and now. A world of health and peace for sick infants. A world in which workers can enjoy their own homes and their own lands and not be at the mercy of greedy landlords. A world in which we don't need temples or churches or synagogues or mosques, because God is present with us always. A world in which mourning and crying are absent. That's the kind of world in which we could enjoy God forever.

God's Chief End

But there's even more to enjoying God than this. If our ultimate goal is to glorify and enjoy God, what is God's role? It has often been suggested that God's chief end is the creation, preservation, redemption, and regeneration of humankind. Therefore it is often taught that our primary efforts ought to go into the same thing. If God exists to redeem humankind, then surely we the redeemed must likewise make this our chief concern. This kind of thinking leads many Christian teachers and writers to conclude that evangelism is our primary task. But pastor and writer John Piper, in his highly influential book *Desiring God*, takes a slightly different stance. He suggests that the salvation of humankind is not God's primary goal:

> God's saving designs are penultimate, not ultimate. Redemption, salvation, and restoration are not God's ultimate goal. These he performs for the sake of something greater: namely, the enjoyment he has in glorifying himself.[3]

Piper goes on to suggest that God's enjoyment of God's own glory is the basis for what Piper calls Christian hedonism, the foundation of which is God's allegiance not to us, but to the divine Trinity. God revels and delights in God's own glory. Of course, this gels with biblical texts such as Prov 16:4: "The Lord works out everything for his own ends." God has the right and power and wisdom to do whatever makes God happy. As the psalmist says, "Our God is in heavens; he does whatever pleases him" (Ps 115:3). And God cannot be frustrated in this task. Therefore, God is never deficient or needy, never gloomy or discouraged. The Bible makes this point repeatedly:

> I am God, and there is no other; I am God, and there is none like me. I make known the end from the beginning, from ancient times, what is still to come. I say, My purpose will stand, and I will do all that I please. (Isa 46:9b–10)

> I know that you can do all things; no purpose of yours can be thwarted. (Job 42:2)

As Piper points out, since God is completely self-sufficient and absolutely sovereign, God is always full and overflowing with energy for the sake of people who seek happiness in God. This seeking of happiness in God is Christian hedonism, the pursuit of joy based in the task of glorifying God. Piper continues,

> If none of God's purposes can be frustrated, then he must be the happiest of all beings. This infinite, divine happiness is the fountain from which the Christian Hedonist drinks and longs to drink more deeply . . . the foundation of Christian Hedonism is the happiness of God.[4]

Piper's inventive reworking of the Westminster Confession is that the chief end of humankind is to glorify God *in order* to enjoy God forever. When

---

[3]John Piper, *Desiring God: Meditations of a Christian Hedonist* (Portland, Ore.: Multnomah, 1986), 33.
[4]Ibid., 34.

we throw ourselves into a lifestyle consecrated to God and aimed at bringing God glory, the secondary, natural consequence is that we will be filled with joy and pleasure because we drink from the happiness of a glorified God. And the converse is also true. The great business of life is to glorify God by enjoying God. There's no distinction to be made between duty and delight, as though they were polar opposites. For the follower of God, duty is delight.

This is the model revealed to us in the example of Jesus. He embraces the duty of the cross because of the delight that it brings his Father. This seems to be a disturbing idea, that a father could derive delight from his son's suffering. But in a broad or global sense, this is what happens. No doubt, God hated the pain and the suffering. God hated the sin that Christ carried. But if we use a wider lens, we see that the Father delighted in the sin-covering, death-conquering obedience of his son, Jesus. So it is with all pain and sin even today. Through the narrow lens, we see that God grieves for our suffering, but, as Piper points out, "it does not thwart his plans, or diminish his deepest delight."[5] God's joy at the fulfillment of the ultimate purpose—the glorification of God—overtakes the narrow view of suffering.

The point is that God's pursuit of praise from us and our pursuit of pleasure in God are one and the same pursuit. God's quest to be glorified and our quest to be satisfied reach their goal in this one experience: our delight in God that overflows in an obedient, godly life. For God, a life of devotion to divine glory is the sweet echo of God's own excellence in the heart of the people. For us, praise and godliness are the summit of satisfaction that comes from living in fellowship with God. God is for us!

To Please God

Instead of saying that our chief end is "to glorify God and to enjoy him forever," I suggest an even simpler maxim: "The chief end of humankind is to please God." That is, we contribute to the happiness that God derives from God's own glory. Surely this was the chief end of Jesus' own ministry. He models for us what a human life lived entirely for the pleasure of God looks like. In fact, at various times God can't help but explicitly declare pleasure at the Son's life of obedience. These incidents are particularly noted in Matthew's Gospel. At Jesus' baptism in the Jordan River, the very public inauguration of his public ministry, the heavens open and the Spirit of God, resembling a dove, descends on him. As if this display of affirmation isn't enough, a voice from heaven is heard to announce, "This is my Son, whom I love; with him I am well pleased" (Matt 3:17). Later, on the mountain of the

---

[5]Ibid., 41.

transfiguration, Jesus' face and clothes shine like the sun before Peter, James, and John, and again a voice from the enveloping cloud repeats the same validation, but adding, "Listen to him!" (Matt 17:5). Then, at his resurrection, Jesus emerges from the tomb, his appearance like lightning and his clothes as white as snow (Matt 28:3). Though no audible voice is reported, we know that the resurrection is God's ultimate seal of approval on the work of his Son. So, at the beginning, middle, and end of Jesus' ministry, God announces great pleasure in Jesus. And Jesus literally glows because of it.

We might consider it audacious to expect that we could bring God pleasure in the same way that Jesus did. Most of us are used to sensing that we bring God disappointment or sorrow through our failings and disobedience. Maybe once or twice in our lives we felt that the Lord was deriving enjoyment from us—once or twice, no more. We strive ever harder in worship services to praise God with greater intensity, hoping to please God. But maybe God is more readily pleased than we think. Maybe the God-pleasing work of Jesus' sacrifice for our sins washes away all the condemnation due us. God's purposes are accomplished regardless of our failures. God's pleasure is something that we cannot diminish. When we are reconciled to God through faith in Christ, the disappointment and sorrow that we thought God felt toward us is overwhelmed by the tsunami of pleasure that God receives from being glorified by Christ. Freed from condemnation, we ought to be renewed in our vision that this is the one end for which humankind is made, and that everything else that we may be or do or strive for is a means to this end. All our service to others, all our corporate worship, all our sorrow for sin, every sacrifice, every aspiration—all must be offered to the higher service of pleasing God. And even when we let God down, God is still enjoying God's self because God sees through the wide lens. We have an eternally exultant, cheerful God.

With a big, robust faith in our happy God, we should be able to see all manner of things as opportunities to bring God more enjoyment. G. K. Chesterton was noted as having quipped, "I think God is the only child left in the universe, and all the rest of us have grown old and cynical because of sin." Like a child giggling with the attention paid by its parents, God derives enormous pleasure from receiving attention. The Scottish athlete and missionary Eric Liddell, portrayed by Ian Charleson in the film *Chariots of Fire,* is quoted as having said, "I believe God made me for a purpose, but he also made me fast. And when I run, I feel his pleasure." With this kind of faith, exiles should be able to acknowledge that the whole of our lives can be God-directed and therefore God-glorifying. When our chief end is to please God, running fast isn't about personal glory or being the best in the world; it is about giving pleasure to God. Likewise, a life lived in order to give God pleasure will mean that our choices, our preferences, our desires become subservient to our greater end.

Thus, loving the Lord or enjoying the Lord or obeying the Lord or even accepting the Lord's salvation in the first place—all these are means of serving the chief end, which is to please the Lord. Nurses please God when they perform the God-glorifying work of healing the sick. Teachers do it when telling the truth to their students. Runners do it when running fast. And as we cooperate more and more with God's unstoppable goal of self-glorifying, we bring increased pleasure to God and to ourselves. Like Jesus, we will literally glow.

Why is it that many worship pastors seem to suggest that the primary way we give God pleasure is through sung worship? Was Liddell worshipping God on the track at the Paris Olympics? Do I worship God when I meet with my local politician to raise his or her awareness of global poverty? Do we worship God when we choose to protect the environment over which we've been granted stewardship? I think so. Our whole lives are to be lived in praise of God, as expressions of God's glory, adding to the enjoyment that God has in God's self and in the outworking of the divine purposes on this planet.

See You Next Sunday

Of course, none of this rules out corporate or public worship times. In fact, it predicates them. We give glory to God by appreciation, affection, subjection, *and* adoration. This aspect of adoration is essential, but it has been my hope to reset it as one of the essential ways we glorify God, not the only way. My view is that worship services ought to be corporate expressions of the overflow of the regular life of a community that churches together at some level every day. If we are a community—a web or network of relationships—that is chiefly concerned with pleasing God, then our gathered times will reflect that. Unfortunately, the church-growth gurus have been pressuring congregations to market their worship services as "seeker services" in the hope that they can attract people back to church on Sundays. But this is a serious theological misunderstanding, for it contorts the meaning of the words "worship," "evangelism," and "church." As we've noted, the term "church" does not indicate a place that one goes to; instead, it signifies something about the nature of a group of people, that they are called out by God for his purposes. I also think that such marketing belittles, not inflates, the idea of corporate worship. Surely, when we participate in corporate services, we worship God precisely because he is worthy of our praise, not as a marketing device for attracting Christians disgruntled with other churches (let's face it, this is mainly who is attracted to such services).

In her book *A Royal "Waste" of Time: The Splendor of Worshiping God and Being Church for the World,* Marva Dawn builds a biblical case against those who advocate turning worship into the congregation's evangelistic tool, because this notion lets all the believers cop out of their responsibility for reaching out to their neighbors by actually being church.[6] It is Dawn's assumption that when a community of believers, churching together, meets to worship, they are formed more deeply into the people of God. And when this happens, they are more likely to impact their neighborhood by the quality of their lifestyles and relationships. She believes that good worship forms a people whose way of life is a warrant for belief. I'd like to think so, but I'm not convinced. I cannot buy the assumption that the corporate encounter with God that the worship service provides forms people to be more like God and therefore to be more genuinely a missional community. I think that it is debunked by the thousands of church services from which Christians emerge to carry on with their lives as thoughtlessly and as selfishly as any nonbeliever. As I mentioned in part 2, I think that a corporate commitment to mission galvanizes community/communitas. I also think that worship issues more powerfully from a missioning communitas than mission issues from a worshipping community.

In Craig Van Gelder's book *Confident Witness—Changing World,* contributor Mary Jo Leddy reports that the poet-president of the Czech Republic, Vaclav Havel, was asked to account for the remarkable success of the so-called Velvet Revolution against the communists in the former Czechoslovakia. Havel answered like this: "We had our parallel society. And in that parallel society we wrote our plays and sang our songs and read our poems until we knew the truth so well that we could go out to the streets of Prague and say, 'We don't believe your lies anymore'—and communism *had* to fall."[7] So, for Leddy, in a post-Christendom culture the church must worship as a similarly parallel society. Our gathering together, then, is an opportunity to speak our language, to read our narratives of God at work, to sing authentic hymns of the faith in all kinds of styles, to chant and pour out our prayers until we know the truth so well that we can go out to the world around us and invade that world with the message of our friend Jesus. The people of the Velvet Revolution became a parallel society precisely because of their commitment to the mission of overthrowing the communist regime. The mission gave rise to the parallel community, which in turn gave rise to plays, songs, and poems

---

[6]Marva J. Dawn, *A Royal "Waste" of Time: The Splendor of Worshiping God and Being Church for the World* (Grand Rapids: Eerdmans, 1999).

[7]Mary Jo Leddy, "The People of God as a Hermeneutic of the Gospel," in *Confident Witness—Changing World: Rediscovering the Gospel in North America* (ed. Craig Van Gelder; Grand Rapids: Eerdmans, 1999), 309.

of the revolution. Exiles, like the underground Czech revolutionaries, are formed by biblical narratives, which tell a different story from that of the surrounding culture. By embracing the mission of subverting that culture for the glory of God, exiles are formed into a community that will develop its liturgies and rhythms of worship accordingly.

It is my view that the correct order of things goes like this:

Knowing Christ

propels us into mission

which invites us to church with each other.

Knowing the dangerous stories of Jesus cannot but force us up out of the rabbit hole and into the world in which we find ourselves. The example of Jesus, when authentically understood and appropriated, makes us ill at ease with comfort and security. It propels us into the lives of others. It sends us out to serve someone or something other than ourselves. In short, it lands us with the mission of practicing generosity, hospitality, justice, and peace. The next link in the chain comes when we find ourselves in the liminal experience of mission, of being in over our heads, and we reach out to fellow believers to support us on that journey. That's when we fashion rhythms and frameworks of churching together. These rhythms emerge out of the social context in which we find ourselves. Worshipping together is essential because when we trust God in that liminal, missional space, we see God at work, self-glorifying, and we want to adore God for being a wonderful, happy, gracious God. True worship (as distinct from simply singing songs) emerges from the texture of a missioning community. The idea of worshipping with fellow believers and then bidding them farewell for the week in the parking lot—"See you next Sunday"—is the very antithesis of the experience of the earliest Christians.

The satirical Christian website Ship of Fools pokes merciless fun at the whole church-as-event mindset with its "mystery worshipper" stunt.[8] Seven years ago, it started sending out "spies" to attend church services around the United Kingdom and began publishing reviews and ratings on the website.

---

[8]"The Mystery Worshipper," Ship of Fools, n.p. [cited 17 January 2006]. Online: http://www.ship-of-fools.com/mystery/index.html.

The exercise was inspired by the market-research techniques of supermarket chains that send "mystery shoppers" into their own stores to gather consumer feedback. Like newspaper food critics, Ship of Fools mystery worshippers report on the "quality" of the services that they attend. Churches are judged on the warmth of the welcome, the length and content of the sermon, the music, and even the after-service coffee and the softness of the pews. Mystery worshippers also describe the moment in the service that brought them closest to heaven and the moment closest to "the other place." Each year, Ship of Fools awards ecclesiastical "Oscars," with categories such as best sermon, best use of music, and best overall church. For the church being rated, the only clue that a Ship of Fools volunteer has visited is a calling card, dropped discreetly into the collection plate, bearing the picture of a masked man in Lone Ranger pose. As ridiculous as it sounds, it's the perfect stunt for lampooning the consumer-driven, event-based approach to worship that we have now in the mainstream church.

Just in case you think that "mystery worshippers" is a bit irreverent or even sacrilegious, here's an exercise that I often use with people in my seminars. I ask them to take a sheet of paper and rule a line down the middle. At the top of the left column, they are to write the heading "Audience," and on the top of the right column "Church." I then ask them to write in the left column the attributes of an audience—as, for example, at a cinema, theater, or concert. In the right column they are to list those attributes that the New Testament says should feature in a Christian church. Most often, the lists look like this:

Audience	Church
Critical (you've paid money and you want a decent show)	A family of deep, trusting relationships
Unconnected to anyone else (highly individualized)	A body of interconnected, interrelated parts
Expectant (hoping the show will be good)	Everyone is gifted and expected to contribute
No relationship with performers	Compassionate, caring
Facing the same direction	Generous, hospitable
Focused on receiving not giving	Focused on giving
Generally passive	A high priority on unity
Easily bored	A royal priesthood, everyone enjoying access to God
Expected norms (you'll be silent; you'll stay seated until the end)	

Having completed the list, people then choose which column best describes their experience of church. Eight times out of ten, they choose the left column. And they're not happy about it. Exiles are tired of belonging to an audience, of paying their money and expecting a decent show, decent preaching, decent music, comfortable seating. They're tired of turning up each week but knowing hardly anyone, of facing the front and watching the "performers" do their thing. In short, they're beyond Christendom-style, platform-driven worship.

Alternative Worship?

As I said earlier, none of this, of course, precludes corporate worship. In fact, it is essential that collectives of exiles gather together to worship God, inspired as they are by their liminal experience of mission. Worship times will be an expression of the collective overflow of our lives together, and they can take whatever form the community sees fit. They will not be the sum total of that community's life, but rather its overflow. It should take days to "check out" a missional community, not the ninety minutes of a worship service. Will missional communities worship differently from mainstream churches? I strongly suspect so for the reasons already mentioned, and there are clues that a revolution is occurring in worship and is being led by exiles.

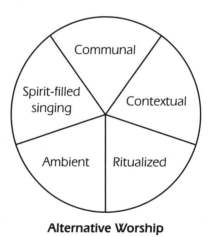

Alternative Worship

Exiles have reacted against worship that is platform-led, culturally dissonant, safe and repetitive, highly cognitive, and musically bland. They are also disturbed by what they see as a capitulation by the church to the spirit of modernism, based in foundationalism, and expressed in forms of worship that tended to rely heavily on words and reasoned argument. Singing and sermons, the two centerpieces of the Protestant church, are used mostly to convey doctrine. Gone is the sense of mystery, wonder, and awe. Exiles are beginning to fashion worship experiences that emphasize congregational involvement with multiple opportunities for group interaction. In fact, in some quarters this style of worship is called "fishbowl worship" because the worshipper enters fully into a curated zone; that is, a space that has been pre-designed by the worship team to include a variety of worship experiences that can be engaged in by the worshippers at their own pace. As an art curator designs an exhibition space, worship curators design zones in which the worshipper is literally surrounded by worship experiences. Many exiles have tried to rediscover the disciplines of contemplation and meditation, to emphasize relationships and community, transcendence and mystery, the experiential and the symbolic. Such worship is highly creative, deeply God-focused, and wonderfully playful and meaningful at the same time. This is a style of worship through which I find a deep connection with God. But as I have said earlier, my primary goal is not the revitalization of corporate worship. I see this as part of a broader need for a complete renovation of the church. With that in mind, I suggest that the worship of exiles often contains the following aspects.

Communal

Worship that is platform-led is, by nature, elitist. It reinforces the dualism between clergy and laity that exiles have rejected. It is designed by a small team of "experts" and conducted by those with the particular talent necessary to pull it off—chiefly, musical talent. In fact, in much of church parlance today, worship *is* music. Ask people what worship is like in their church, and they'll probably describe its musical style. Exiles yearn for a worship experience that acknowledges the contributions of all, not just the talented. This isn't to say that some people aren't peculiarly gifted to bring teaching or song-leading, but rather to recognize that we can learn through multiple experiences, not just monologues, and we can adore God in multiple ways, not just singing.

There should be opportunities for anybody to contribute at any level, including the design stage. And the gathering itself should acknowledge the important contributions of many by allowing people access to make them. Steve Collins is one of the most respected voices in the United Kingdom on the changing shape of worship. He says,

> Each part of the worship is seen as a gift from the person or persons creating it to God and to the rest of the worshippers, so there is a high level of

openness to new contributions. This also requires a trust that people will
play their part with care and appropriateness, a trust which seldom proves
misplaced.[9]

This communal aspect of worship will ensure that any leadership is not
separated from the congregation in any way, nor the congregation reduced to
an audience with the experts appearing from backstage like performers. Ideally, the space should be arranged so that there is no specific "front," and the
focus of activity may move from one part of the space to another, or may be
in many places at once. Again, Steve Collins:

> Direction proceeds by invitation, with no obligation to take part or to all do
> the same thing at the same time. The elements of the service are usually all
> built carefully around a theme, so teaching occurs through everything that
> happens, rather than being concentrated in a sermon given by a single au-
> thoritative voice. There is room for discussion and sharing, in small groups
> or with the whole congregation.[10]

Paul's directions to the Corinthians regarding worship typically are taken
completely out of the context in which they were written. Everything that
Paul says to them on this subject, particularly in chapters 11–14 of 1 Corinthians, implies that the worship gathering occurred around food and in a
communal, egalitarian spirit. It's true that the Corinthians were abusing this
arrangement, and Paul rebukes them for these abuses, but his counsel makes
much more sense when read against its original context rather than that of
today's platform-led services.

Paul begins by sketching a situation in which some members of this
factionalized congregation arrive early and eat all the food and drink all the
wine, while others are left with nothing (1 Cor 11:21). His directions for how
to conduct the remembrance feast (1 Cor 11:23–26) are couched in his understanding that the "service" will occur around tables, on lounges and cushions,
with enough food to satisfy everyone. We regularly hear these words quoted by
ministers in communion services with everyone sitting in pews, facing the
front. Then we distribute tiny cubes of bread and thimbles of juice. And yet,
Paul was outraged that some Corinthians were leaving their gatherings hungry!
His injunction that people examine themselves before eating (1 Cor 11:28)
seems to indicate that they should consider how they might be guilty of contributing to the factionalism and greed. It probably has less to do with personal
piety and more to do with communal responsibility. If judgment was to come

---

[9]Alernative Worship.org, n.p. [cited 17 January 2006]. Online: http://www
.alternativeworship.org/.
[10]Ibid.

upon them, it was because of their selfish and discriminatory practices that allowed some members full access and others none at all.

> So then, my brothers and sisters, when you gather to eat, you should all eat together. Those who are hungry should eat something at home, so that when you meet together it may not result in judgment. (1 Cor 11:33–34a)

Reinforcing further that worship is to be communal, not elitist, Paul then launches into his well-known teaching about spiritual gifts and his favorite image of the church as a body made up of many different parts, each one contributing to the whole (1 Cor 12). No doubt this teaching is applicable beyond the community feast, but bear in mind that it's included in a discussion about the Corinthians' worship life. Messages of wisdom and knowledge (1 Cor 12:8), gifts of healing (1 Cor 12:9), prophecy, discernment, tongues and their interpretation (1 Cor 12:10) are all mentioned in the context of the remembrance meal and form the bridge to Paul's teaching about the church as a body. In other words, the remembrance feast and the communal worship time were to allow for the expression of multiple gifts from many people. It is no small matter that in the midst of this discussion Paul includes his beautiful ode to love in chapter 13. Today we habitually quote it at weddings in regard to the love shared between a man and a woman, but marriage is foreign to Paul's context here, and he intended it to describe the tone and tenor of a communal worship gathering. With some people prophesying, others speaking in tongues, and still others expressing great faith or great works of service, Paul declares that patient, kind, selfless, truthful, perseverant, protective love should characterize their gatherings.

As we've already noted, community is a place of honesty, commitment, and support where people grow in intimacy and trust through their shared commitment to serve others. Many exiles have banded together because of their shared dissatisfaction with the culture of mainstream worship. But as they begin to work together, serving each other and those beyond themselves, creating worship and exploring theology, they draw together as intimate communities. This is much less possible in the mainstream church, where a few experts design and conduct worship services, and the rest of us basically play the role of audience.

Contextual

There is much talk about "relevant" worship these days. It often refers to the need to play music that matches the playlists on popular radio stations or to prepare sermons based on contemporary social or personal issues. But contextual worship is more than this. It is worship that emerges from the rhythms of the culture or subculture that the community has felt sent to serve.

And those who form incarnational communities to witness into sub-cultures soon find that their worship needs to be rethought, not only to be accessible to those they wish to reach, but also to the people they have now become.

In the United Kingdom in the 1990s there developed a new movement called "alternative worship." Most, if not all, of the chief proponents of this movement were exiles from the mainstream church, which they came to believe was unable to provide an environment for the expression of an authentic postmodern spirituality. For many of them, the U.K. club scene was a much more openly spiritual environment, reflecting the importance of dance music, clubs, and raves for adults under forty, especially in the United Kingdom, where club culture has been predominant since the late 1980s. Clubs and raves created a multimedia and multisensory environment that could carry tremendous spiritual and emotional impact for young adults. Club culture also has an intense, if often superficial, sense of togetherness and an unfocussed but genuine concern for spirituality. The early proponents of alternative worship began to create Christian worship gatherings that approximated this same energy. That's not to say that they launched church services with frenetic music and dancing. The model they borrowed from club culture was the "chill-out" room—a space with a quiet, soothing ambience for resting away from the intense heat and sound of the dance floor. Chill-out rooms showed what a church in the emerging culture might be like—a reflective, relaxing place to think or talk quietly, visually and sonically rich but gentle, a relief from noise and activity.

Today, British alternative worship has been exported around the world via the work of people such as Steve Collins, Paul Roberts, Jonny Baker, and Mark Pierson.[11] But its origins are to be found in an attempt to fashion

---

[11] Steve Collins, from the Grace service in London, and Paul Roberts, from Resonance in Bristol, manage the website Alternative Worship.org, n.p. [cited 17 January 2006]. Online: http://www.alternativeworship.org/, the standard exploration of the subject on the Internet. Steve also manages an excellent site that collects photographs from a number of alternative worship gatherings around the world (Smallfire.org. n.p. [cited 17 January 2006]. Online: http://www.Smallfire.org/). It's an excellent visual introduction to alternative worship. Jonny Baker, also from the Grace service, has co-authored *Alternative Worship: Resources from and for the Emerging Church* (Grand Rapids: Baker, 2004), which is chock full of ideas, readings, liturgies, and poems for use in alternative worship services. It includes a very helpful CD-ROM. Mark Pierson, formerly of Cityside Church in Auckland, has co-authored *The Prodigal Project: Journey into the Emerging Church* (London: SPCK, 2001), which also includes a CD-ROM, and has put together *Fractals,* a CD-ROM full of ideas for alternative worship. It's available at "Fractals," Proost, n.p. [cited 17 January 2006]. Online: http://www.proost.co.uk/fractal.html.

worship in a way that substantively paralleled the culture from which it was emerging.

In the United States, a similar movement has occurred in which warm, ambient coffee houses with wireless Internet connection, free newspapers and magazines, comfortable couches and easy chairs have increasingly dominated the young-adult market, particularly in university towns. Chilled-out music, an unrushed atmosphere, and good coffee create a zone where young people relax, recharge, recreate, and meet others. As a result, "café churches" have sought to replicate that unhurried and friendly atmosphere, where discussions take place over good food and drink in comfort. People come and go as they please, and there is no formal beginning or end to proceedings apart from opening and closing times. There can be background music, art on the walls, maybe even a live act—but not one that kills all conversation. So-called emerging churches particularly on the West Coast have used this subculture to great effect, allowing art-based prayer stations, discussion groups, and freeform gatherings.

Contextualizing worship involves more than choosing to play pop music in church instead of classical hymns. It involves a serious incarnational attempt to enter, know, love, and enjoy the culture that you have been sent into. Then, whatever worship style or venue you use will naturally reflect the lifestyles, rhythms, and interests of that culture.

Ambient

Gone are the days when a worship service in the West simply needed a band, a platform, and enough seating for the congregation. People today, particularly young people, are multisensory in their engagement with their world and highly sensitive to the ambience of a particular environment. Restaurants, coffee shops, shopping malls, and even workplaces have taken seriously the impact for good and ill that a certain ambience can have. This is not a trivial matter of interior decoration. To take the ambience of a worship space seriously is to take seriously that God can be worshipped with all our senses. Some of the areas we need to consider include the following:

- **Visual arts**. The image has great power in Western culture today. Attuned as we are by television and film, we are greatly stimulated by pictures, perhaps at least as much as by words. This takes the emerging church back to its roots, where imagery such as stained-glass windows, icons, illustrated books, and sculpture was used to convey truth and rouse the believers to worship. The use of projectors, television stacks, art installations, art-based experiences (e.g., painting your prayers), as well as the inclusion of ambient-style imagery (usually called "visual wallpaper"), aren't luxuries, but are essential to creating wor-shipful environments for exiles.

- **Rediscovered Christian traditions.** Along with the newly realized power of the image comes the rediscovery of the interactive experience as a basis for worship and learning. Says Steve Collins, "In particular, the shift of our society towards an image-based culture, where the visual is the central means of communication, causes us to look again at how the Church communicated through imagery and ritual in the past. And our ecological anxiety causes us to look again at Celtic understandings of the wholeness of creation and humanity's place in it. Many more recent traditions, especially those which make encounter with God cerebral or rationalistic, have ceased to be relevant and give the impression that Christianity has nothing to offer the world anymore. In a time of great cultural change it becomes necessary to look at the whole of Christian tradition and discern what might be newly valid or ripe for reinterpreta-tion, and what needs to be laid aside for a time."[12]

- **A new approach to music.** At the moment, music is used almost exclu-sively for the purpose of corporate singing. This seems a terribly limited use of a highly stimulating medium. Listen to the way music features in films or television programs. It forms an underlying soundscape that heightens our perception of the narrative being played out. Likewise, news broadcasters such as Fox News and CNN have come to understand the impact of put-ting a soundtrack behind their stories. Worship for exiles will use music much more broadly than as a platform-based pop or rock band. Such a use of the "worship team" necessarily attracts the focus of the participants' to the stage, forcing them back into the role of audience members. Ambient music can underscore a corporate worship time brilliantly, particularly when the music comes from our own CD racks at home. Our personal music col-lections, much of which these days has a distinctly spiritual element to it, can also become the soundtrack of our worship life.

Ritualized

At smallboatbigsea we regularly install a labyrinth prayer walk in our gallery space. A labyrinth is a geometrical pattern that has one well-defined path leading into the center and back out again. Unlike a maze, there are no tricks to the pattern, no intersecting paths or dead ends. The most famous, and most often used design, measures over twenty feet in diameter and is modeled after the pattern of inlaid stone built into the floor of Chartres

---

[12]"Innovation and Tradition," *Small Ritual*, n.p. [cited 1 June 2006]. Online at http://www.btinternet.com/~smallritual/section6/theory_steve_tradition.html.

Cathedral in France in the early 1200s. As participants walk the path, they encounter a series of worship experiences wherein they pause and listen to a piece of music and a meditation. They also undertake some symbolic action or ritual. At the center of the labyrinth is a communion table, with bread and wine, allowing a time for silent reconnection with Christ before beginning the journey back out and past more worship stations.

Labyrinths are an ancient Christian spiritual practice, and following the path into and out of the labyrinth becomes a walking meditation and a metaphor for our spiritual journey as individuals and within community. Ours is not the only Christian community using a labyrinth. In fact, they have become enormously popular around the world. Recently, one was permanently installed in Grace Cathedral in San Francisco. And "alt worship" maestros such as Jonny Baker and Steve Collins installed a temporary labyrinth in St. Paul's Cathedral in London to great acclaim. Their labyrinth then went on a tour around various cathedrals throughout England. People are rediscovering ancient rituals, such as prayer beads, the *lectio divina* form of Bible reading, and Celtic worship practices, and fusing them with ambient spaces filled with projected visual wallpaper, dance music, and chill-out zones. In this way, people are giving the design and conduct of worship back to the congregation itself, allowing ordinary Christians to mix and match practices from a variety of traditions and eras.

Spirit-Filled Singing

Having shown that worship can be much more than a sing-along and a sermon, let me return to the subject of congregational singing. As I've said, I think that we emphasize it far too much, almost to the exclusion of anything else. Nevertheless, I don't see it as redundant or unhelpful. Far from it. Congregational singing has been one of the very legitimate modes of the Christian worship of God throughout our history as a movement. But the current obsession with what's called "praise and worship"—multiple, discontinuous songs strung together—is a relatively new innovation. The history of Christian singing is much richer.

Paul's best-known reference to communal singing appears in Col 3:16:

Let the word of Christ dwell in you richly as you teach and admonish one another with all wisdom, and as you sing psalms, hymns and spiritual songs with gratitude in your hearts to God.

So, what exactly did Paul mean by "psalms, hymns and spiritual songs"? He uses the same phrase in Eph 5:19. We have no early Christian documents dealing with congregational music or singing. There is considerable evidence that the New Testament contains passages that probably were hymns or chants or public confessions of faith,[13] but the earliest text we have of an extrabiblical Christian hymn is dated around 200.[14] Not until about 560 are there substantial descriptions of Christian liturgy and its music, although writers such as Ignatius of Antioch (d. 110), Tertullian (d. 220), Clement of Alexandria (d. 212), and Augustine (d. 430) discuss music practice in their time at some length. What surprises many scholars today is that a great deal of their attention was given to improvisation and charismatic utterance. For example, Tertullian describes how much of their chanted singing was improvised: "Anyone who can, either from holy Scripture or from his own heart, is called into the middle to sing to God."[15]

While biblical scholars have puzzled over the exact meaning of Paul's threefold reference to psalms, hymns, and spiritual songs, some authorities on the music of the early Christian period have sought to explain it from a historical-cultural point of view. Musicologist Egon Wellesz believes that the three forms were stylistically differentiated. Based on a study of early Jewish music and later recorded Christian chant, he offers the following definitions:

- Psalmody: the cantillation of the Jewish psalms and of the canticles and doxologies modeled on them

- Hymns: songs of praise of a syllabic type, i.e., each syllable is sung to one or two notes of the melody

- Spiritual songs: "alleluia" and other chants of a jubilant or ecstatic character, richly ornamented[16]

If we take the reference to psalms to mean the singing of Old Testament psalms and the like, and if hymns were sung or chanted versions of Christian doctrine such as Paul includes in Phil 2:6–11 ("Who being in very nature God . . ."), what are these spiritual songs? It seems to me that today we still sing psalms and hymns (whether contemporary or classical), but are we missing something that Paul's churches included in corporate worship?

The Greek expression for "spiritual songs" is *ôdai pneumatikai* or "pneumatic odes"—literally, "songs upon the breath." Some scholars, including

---

[13]See Col 1:15–20; Eph 5:14; Phil 2:6–11; 1 Tim 3:16.

[14]John S. Andrews, "Hymns," in *The New International Dictionary of the Christian Church* (ed. J. D. Douglas; Grand Rapids: Zondervan, 1974), 494–96.

[15]John Andrews, "Music in the Early Christian Church," in *The New Grove Dictionary of Music and Musicians* (ed. Stanley Sadie; 20 vols.; London: Macmillan, 1980), 4:363–64.

[16]Egon Wellesz, "Early Christian Music," in *Medieval Music up to 1300* (vol. 2 of *New Oxford History of Music;* ed. Dom Anselm Hughes; London: Oxford University Press, 1954), 2.

Egon Wellesz, consider these "songs upon the breath" to imply improvisation. Improvising on a single word such as "alleluia" was common practice in Near Eastern cultures during the time of Christ and later became formalized in the *jubilus* of the Catholic Mass. The final syllable ("ah") of the word "alleluia" was prolonged in a kind of wordless improvisation. Both Jerome and Augustine speak of the practice, with Jerome describing it as neither "words nor syllables nor letters nor speech." Augustine said of it,

> It is a certain sound of joy without words . . . it is the expression of a mind poured forth with joy. . . . A man rejoicing after certain words which cannot be understood, bursteth forth into sounds of exultation without words so that it seemeth that he . . . filled with excessive joy cannot express in words the subject of that joy.[17]

What can "words which cannot be understood" refer to? Perhaps Augustine was speaking of simple improvisation or some kind of ecstatic expression. There is evidence that the earliest Christians engaged in some kind of extended chant that was regarded as an ecstatic praise, a pure, wordless jubilation. This seems not to have been the wild, fervent frenzy that is seen in some churches today, but rather a gentle, marvelous expression of connection with God. Nonetheless, it is worth keeping in mind Paul's cautionary advice:

> For if I pray in a tongue, my spirit prays, but my mind is unfruitful. So what shall I do? I will pray with my spirit, but I will also pray with my understanding; I will sing with my spirit, but I will also sing with my understanding. (1 Cor 14:14–15)

The improvisation might continue (in the spirit), but Paul doesn't lose control of his mind. He is conscious of what he is singing, and the expression of the sounds, though spiritually moving, is still intelligible to others. And here Paul is back on familiar ground. For him, the remembrance meal and corporate worship time were to be thoroughly communal, not distancing or excluding anyone. He continues,

> Otherwise when you are praising God in the Spirit, how can the others, who are now put in the same situation as an inquirer, say "Amen" to your thanksgiving, since they do not know what you are saying? You are giving thanks well enough, but the others are not edified. (1 Cor 14:16–17)

If indeed spiritual songs were ecstatic utterances or wordless improvisations during which the worshipper felt caught up in wonder, love, and praise, Paul seems anxious that they form a smaller part of the corporate experience,

---

[17]Quoted in Gustave Reese, *Music in the Middle Ages* (New York: Norton, 1940), 64.

so as not to alienate others. But the fact remains that they are still part of the corporate gathering. They are God-directed, God-glorifying. And though the singing of spiritual songs seems to have blessed the worshipper greatly, that was a by-product of the exercise. Spirit-filled, God-glorifying corporate singing is essential for any community of faith. Today, unfortunately, many churches sing inanities such as the following in "Make a Joyful Noise":

> Make a joyful noise, unto the Lord
> Make a joyful noise, unto the Lord
> Make a noise! (3x)
> Make a joyful, joyful, joyful, joyful, joyful
> (waaaaaaaaaaaaaaa!) noise.

Sure, it's fun (apparently), upbeat, and easy for the youth service to remember. Songs like this one make the worshipper feel good, but certainly they do not teach or admonish worshippers or glorify God. In fact, they say absolutely nothing about God's character. Exiles have given up on singing dippy, meaningless songs. They can't bear songs that make us the center of the universe, such as "I choose you, God" or "You can be my Lord." They're blasphemous, self-seeking, ungodly. And just because they make people feel good doesn't mean that they're acceptable. Collectives of exiles, living with the liminality of mission, enjoying communitas, serving others, and eating with each other, desperately need to be sustained by Spirit-filled, God-honoring worship. A few songs and a long sermon won't do it. A communal, ambient space, centered around a convivial meal table, reflecting local culture, using ancient and modern rituals, and infused with spiritual singing will be a wonderful expression of the overflow of lives lived daily to please our happy, joyful, all-powerful God.

While in Kenya several years ago, I heard about the "singing wells" of the Borana people. The Borana are a nomadic tribe that ekes out an existence in the arid lowlands in southern Ethiopia, near the border of Kenya. They use deep, hand-dug wells to provide water for themselves and their livestock. A ladder, made of acacia tree trunks, is lowered into the well, and each rung is manned by one of the Borana people. The larger wells accommodate eight to ten workers, the lowest of whom fills a bucket and passes it up to the person on first rung, and so on. Buckets are quickly passed up this human chain to be emptied into a large trough near the lip of the well. To develop a rhythm, the man or woman at the bottom begins chanting a traditional song. The rest of the chain picks up the song, their voices reverberating inside the deep well. No one is ever without a bucket; they're either moving a full one up or lowering an empty one back down. Thousands of liters a day are moved by a song. Now, that's how to sing! Imagine a communitas of Christian exiles, joined together in a shared missional project, singing praises to God in a way that keeps them going, bringing water to an arid empire.

13

The Songs of Revolution

The Song: Jesus Ain't My Boyfriend

Some people say the world has had enough of
silly love songs. . . .

—Paul McCartney

At a conventional church service recently all my worst fears about the romantic nature of contemporary worship were realized. On the screen appeared the following lyrics, which most people around me sang with furrowed brows, closed eyes, and meaningful looks of intensity on their faces:

The simplest of all love songs
I want to bring to you,
So I'll let my words be few—
Jesus, I am so in love with you.[1]

I balked. I couldn't bring myself to tell Jesus that I am in love with him. In fact, I had such a sense of revulsion that I had to think long and hard about why this was disturbing me so much. Maybe the lyric isn't meant to be taken too seriously (I can be guilty of thinking too much about these things), but it occurred to me that I'm not only not in love with Jesus, I'm not actually "in love" with anyone in my life at the moment. I'm not in love with my children. As a matter of fact, I've never "fallen in love" with any of my children. I have loved them with an intensity of love that I never knew I was capable of. I have loved them more than life itself since each of them was

---

[1]Matt Redman, "Let My Words Be Few," from the album *The Father's Song* (Survivor, 2000).

born. I have never at any moment in their lives questioned my unconditional, unreserved love for them. But "fall in love" with them? No. Never.

I love my mother dearly, but I haven't "fallen in love" with her. There are
many people in my life that I love very much, but I'm not "in love" with
them either. I wouldn't even say that I'm "in love" with my wife, Carolyn,
whom I have loved deeply and faithfully for more than half my life. I was
once in love with her. Actually, I was head over heels in love with her, but I
discovered that it's a fleeting and unreliable set of emotions. I'm not suggesting that being in love with someone isn't deliciously exciting, even exhilarating. It's a marvelous feeling, but it never lasts. It might be the kind of
emotional elation that throws members of the opposite sex together, but it
doesn't carry the kind of emotional provisions that can sustain that relationship. Real loving is something much richer, deeper, more robust, more powerful than anything experienced when we're "in love" with someone. In fact,
Scott Peck says that in any relationship, real loving can begin only when the
feelings of being in love dissipate. Once those fabulously carefree romantic
feelings ebb away after a time, then a couple is forced to confront the much
more genuinely loving choice to remain faithful and true.

So, what does it mean to sing to Jesus that we are in love with him? Is it
that we have intense and exhilarating feelings of attraction toward him? That
our legs go to jelly and our stomach churns whenever he walks in the room? I
have no doubt that when we first encounter Jesus and his saving grace, there
are intense feelings of spiritual pleasure, even bliss. This certainly was my experience. I also have no doubt that in our life-long journey with Jesus there
will be times of spiritual communion of a similar intensity. Sometimes during corporate worship or personal times of reflection and prayer, I feel deep
gratitude and a wonderful attraction to the person of Jesus. But I have never
felt myself falling in love with him. Now I'm waiting for a Cole Porter-
inspired hymn to Jesus. You know, "Birds do it, bees do it, / Even educated
fleas do it, / Let's do it, let's fall in love."

The satirical website Lark News takes an even more cutting perspective
than this. It's faux advertisement for a mythical upcoming worship release reads,

> The groundbreaking—some say risqué—album includes edgy worship songs
> such as "My Lover, My God," "Touch Me All Over," "Naked Before You," "I'll Do
> Anything You Want," "Deeper" and "You Make Me Hot with Desire."[2]

The disturbing fact of this bit of humor is that it's not that far from the
truth (as is the case with the most biting satire). It is increasingly common to

---

[2]LarkNews.com, n.p. [cited 21 February 2006]. Online: http://www.larknews
.com/april_2003/secondary_exclusive.php?header=header&page=walmart_cd.

refer to our relationship with God or Jesus in the most explicitly sexual fashion. And why do so many people buy into this nonsense? Imagining God or Jesus to be a beautiful man who wants to "partake of our body" is creepy enough, but even more disturbing is how many of the new worship writers are hip young men. For instance, the members of the popular worship band Delirious?—all young men—are notorious for romanticizing their expression of Christian faith with lyrics such as "All I want is you / All I want is you now," and "And the wonder of it all is that I'm living just to fall / More in love with you," and even more explicitly,

> There's a song that everyone can sing
> There's a prayer that everyone can bring
> Feel the music 'cos it's time to dance
> People all across the world
> With a heartbeat for holiness
> Feel his pleasure
> We are God's romance[3]

Falling in Love with God?

Is it appropriate to express our devotion to Jesus or to God in such romanticized, sexualized, and, dare I say it, feminized ways? I mean, are we really God's romance? Do the writers of the Bible ever employ this kind of language? And has there been a tradition of writing love songs to Jesus in the history of hymnody? Let's turn to the Bible, for there are a number of places in biblical literature where it could be argued that something of this highly sexualized language appears.

The writings of Old Testament prophets such as Jeremiah, Ezekiel, and especially Hosea do present God's relationship with Israel as being like a marriage between a man and a woman, although in every case it is presented as an unhappy or faithless marriage. Hosea's personal domestic situation mirrors God's unsatisfactory "marriage" to Israel. Jeremiah reiterates this powerful sexual/romantic imagery of Israel as the whoring wife of faithful Yahweh:

> "If a man divorces his wife and she leaves him and marries another man, should he return to her again? Would not the land be completely defiled? But you have lived as a prostitute with many lovers—would you now return to me?" declares the LORD. (Jer 3:1)

---

[3]"God's Romance," Delirious, n.p. [cited 17 January 2006]. Online: http://www.delirious.org.uk/lyrics/songs/godsromance.html.

Nowhere is the image of Israel as an unfaithful wife more sexually explicit than in chapter 16 of Ezekiel. In this deeply disturbing allegory of infidelity, Ezekiel imagines the story of a king who finds an abandoned newborn girl wallowing unwashed and bloodied in an open field. He rescues her from certain death and brings her to his court, where she grows into a beautiful woman. He takes her as his bride and lavishes the riches of his kingdom on her. The language used by Ezekiel is overtly sexual. It sounds like an erotic love story, but it takes a very nasty turn when the princess turns to prostitution and then sacrifices to pagan idols the very children whom she has borne to the king. It is a sordid and violent tale of Israel's unfaithfulness. Even though God has rescued them from obscurity and lavished wealth on them, they have betrayed God in the worst possible ways. Although the imagery may be sexual, it can hardly be called romantic. In fact, these are "hymns" to human frailty, unfaithfulness, and disobedience.

Another well-known source for romantic and sexualized language in the Bible is, of course, Song of Songs, which for most of the history of the church has been interpreted as an amorous allegory of the love of God for God's people, or that of Christ for the church, or that of Christ for the soul. In this interpretation, the lover/Solomon character is assumed to be God/Jesus, while the beloved/female voice is, well, ours. The sensuous and suggestive imagery employed by the voices in Song of Songs implies that God's love for us and ours for God can be of such a deep intensity that it mirrors that of an infatuated pair of lovers. In fact, I suggest that the only biblical basis for a hymn such as "Jesus, I Am So in Love with You" can be found here in Song of Songs, if you employ this allegorical interpretation.

However, in contemporary interpretations Song of Songs has been seen much more simply, as a linked chain of lyrics depicting human love in all its spontaneity, beauty, and power. Recent interpreters have scoured Egyptian and Babylonian love songs, traditional Semitic wedding songs, and Mesopotamian fertility songs looking for parallels and resonances with the biblical Song of Songs. Their conclusion is that Song of Songs belongs to biblical Wisdom literature, and that it is wisdom's description of a *human* amorous relationship. The lovers experience moments of separation and intimacy, anguish and ecstasy, tension and contentment—all very normal, really. And in its normality it is a marvelous biblical affirmation of human sexual and romantic love. It is hardly a model for Christian worship. Some years ago I preached from Song of Songs in the chapel service at the seminary where I teach. I asked two students, a husband and wife, to read selected sections of the text, he taking the part of the lover, and she the beloved. After reading some of the more suggestive verses about the woman's allurements and the man's burning passion, they closed the Bible and spontaneously turned to each other and kissed right there in front of the audience. It was a perfect conclusion to the reading, which is indeed about human desire and attraction.

New Testament writers make no reference to Song of Songs, nor to being in love with Jesus, but there is one image that might imply a romantic aspect to the Christian experience of worship. Jesus' reference to himself as a bridegroom, an image taken up later by Paul, could be construed as implying a sexual component to the church's relation to Christ. In Matt 9:14–15, Jesus responds to a question from the disciples of John the Baptist regarding the less-than-ascetic lifestyle of his own disciples. Specifically, they wonder whether his disciples fast. Jesus' joyous response is, "How can the guests of the bridegroom mourn while he is with them?" Although the primary intent of the response is to address the concern that his disciples do not fast, it introduces the idea that Jesus sees himself as being like a bridegroom. The question is whether he saw himself as the *church's* bridegroom. His response here refers more to the joy that his disciples felt at being in his presence (as great as that of guests at a wedding) than to the specific nature of the relationship between Jesus and his subsequent followers—that is, the church. That said, when John the Baptist himself employs similar imagery, as he does in John 3:27–30, it very much refers to Jesus' relationship to his followers. When informed that Jesus' fame is growing, John explicitly presents himself as something like the best man at a wedding. Jesus, he says, is the bridegroom, and the bride—the people—belongs to him, not to the best man. This is the very imagery that Paul employs in his various references to the church as the bride of Christ. Nowhere is this more sexually implicit than in 2 Cor 11:2:

> I am jealous for you with a godly jealousy. I promised you to one husband, to Christ, so that I might present you as a pure virgin to him.

Paul clearly sees himself as something like the father of a bride. He has prepared his virgin daughter—the church in Corinth—for her wedding day to Christ. He "promised" her to him, as a father in the Middle East would to a successful suitor. The language certainly is romantic, but like the references in Hosea or Jeremiah, it is being written to an unfaithful people. It is not a sentimental reference to being "in love" with Jesus; rather, it is a call to increasing faithfulness to Christ. It seems that every time romantic husband/wife imagery is used in Scripture, it refers to the unfaithfulness of humans (versus the steadfast faithfulness of God). It is in virtually every case a call to deeper obedience to God or Christ. Hardly romantic or emotional, it is a hardheaded call to action, holiness, and obedience. Likewise, the triumphant reference in chapter 19 of Revelation to the wedding of the Lamb of God:

> Let us rejoice and be glad and give him glory! For the wedding of the Lamb has come, and his bride has made herself ready. Fine linen, bright and clean, was given her to wear. (Rev 19:7–8)

Any such references to the marriage between Christ and the church are nearly always made in the context of a discussion of the need for the church to remain pure, faithful, and obedient. In this respect, they are earthy, gutsy calls for practical lifestyle changes, not amorous, ethereal expressions of romantic love. This mirrors the language of the prophets in the Old Testament, the obvious exception being Isa 54:5–7, in which it is God who is seen as the deserter who promises to return to Israel his bride. Otherwise, whenever God or Jesus is called our "bridegroom," you can be sure that what follows is a call for renewed holiness on our part.

But when it comes to the expression of a particularly intimate relationship between God and the church, we have another term in the New Testament, also favored by Jesus and Paul: "*Abba,* Father." We overhear Jesus employ it in the garden of Gethsemane, as he asks his Father to take the cup of suffering way from him (Mark 14:36). We read Paul's encouragement to use it in Rom 8:15: "For you did not receive a spirit that makes you a slave again to fear, but you received the Spirit of sonship. And by him we cry, '*Abba,* Father.'"

The term is expressive of a particularly close relationship to God as Father. Jesus knew such intimacy with God, and we, Paul tells us, by the Spirit can know the same intimacy. He goes on to commend us not as slaves, but as children of God, co-heirs with Christ. In fact, Father/child language for the divine/human relationship runs throughout the New Testament. It is far more common than the references to the bride of Christ, and it describes an equally intimate relationship. In fact, it could be argued that in the first century, the relationship between a father and his son was even more intimate and more foundational to society than that of husband and wife. It's hard for us to imagine this in contemporary Western culture. Even with the breakdown of the family unit and disturbing divorce rates in Western nations, there is still a cultural allegiance to the husband/wife and father/mother as the primary relational building block of society. This was not necessarily so in the time of the first Christians. They would have seen the father/son institution as crucial, an intimate relationship of genuine affection and obedience. Paul explains it beautifully in Galatians:

> What I am saying is that as long as heirs are underage they are no different from slaves, although they own the whole estate. They are subject to guardians and trustees until the time set by their fathers. So also, when we were underage, we were in slavery under the elemental spiritual forces of the world. But when the set time had fully come, God sent his Son, born of

a woman, born under the law, to redeem those under the law, that we might receive adoption to sonship. Because you are his sons, God sent the Spirit of his Son into our hearts, the Spirit who calls out, "**Abba**, Father." So you are no longer slaves, but God's children; and since you are his children, he has made you also heirs. (Gal 4:1–7)

This is a wonderfully expressed summary of the gospel itself. It describes our state as former slaves, but now daughters and sons of God. It describes the role of Christ in buying us back into the household of his Father. But more than simply becoming the legal children of God, we are ushered into a deep, intimate relationship with our Father. We are his much-loved children, brothers and sisters to his son, Jesus. It is naturally assumed that a son will obey his father, so not only is intimacy implied, but also faithfulness and obedience. So, it seems bizarre to me that when the New Testament writers so clearly prefer Father/child imagery to describe the church's relationship to God, the contemporary church is singing love songs to God our Father.

What Love Is and What Love Isn't

Part of my aversion to the current predilection for romanticized language in worship is that it represents a complete capitulation to the values of the songs of our host empire. The anthems and hymns of post-Christendom are more often than not vacuous love songs sung by attractive performers barely out of puberty. Heard on every FM radio station around the world, these songs deify sex and romantic love as the highest expressions of human intimacy. And now we have the writers of contemporary Christian worship songs expressing faith in the same terms. Consider, for example, "And I'm madly in love with you. / Let what we do in here fill the streets out there. / Let us dance for you."[4]

Such language implies that we can speak to God in the same manner in which we would speak to a romantic partner, or more specifically in the same way a lovelorn teenager would speak to a romantic partner. And here's my main objection: being *madly* in love with someone is such an impermanent, unstable, unreliable sensation that to express such "love" to God is disrespectful at best. When I hear an exuberant sixteen-year-old declare her undying love for her boyfriend, I don't really imagine that this is a love that will conquer all obstacles, last for decades, or survive well into her old age. I think of it as a fabulously exciting, but quite temporary, sense of deep attraction to a cool guy. Besides, it is surely the most gullible of all emotions. As I said

---

[4]Steve Fee, "Madly," from the album *Sacred Space* (independent release, 2005).

earlier, compare this to the permanent, unconditional love that we feel for our children. We simply don't speak about falling in love with our sons or daughters. So how can those of us who know better sing these teenage-style love songs to God?

Surely, exiles need to recover a more biblical understanding of the nature of Christian love for God. If loving God is not just about singing love songs, what more is involved? This requires us to develop a clearer idea of what love is and what it isn't, something that is sadly lacking in a world more influenced on this topic by the songs of Britney Spears and Christina Aguilera than by the teaching of the New Testament. Jesus' teaching on loving God is really very surprising when compared with the soft, emotional expressions that we see presented in church. In fact, it is a much tougher, more practical, more actional understanding of love than we are used to. In Matthew's Gospel, Jesus is confronted by the religious leaders of his time:

> Hearing that Jesus had silenced the Sadducees, the Pharisees got together. One of them, an expert in the law, tested him with this question: "Teacher, which is the greatest commandment in the Law?" Jesus replied, "'Love the Lord your God with all your heart and with all your soul and with all your mind.' This is the first and greatest commandment. And the second is like it: 'Love your neighbor as yourself.' All the Law and the Prophets hang on these two commandments." (Matt 22:34–40)

Jesus proves his orthodoxy (for now) to the Pharisees by responding with a quotation from the law. Loving God is the greatest commandment, he says, agreeing (with one slight word change) with Deut 6:5; but note that he elevates the commandment to love your neighbor as yourself to the same level as that of loving God. This is in no way contrary to conventional Jewish teaching, but it underscores the fact that for Jesus, it is impossible to love God apart from expressing that love physically and practically into the lives of our neighbors. This is an unmistakable aspect of the spirituality of Jesus: devotion to God is expressed primarily by obeying Jesus' teaching and loving others.

> If you love me, you will keep my commands. (John 14:15)

> Whoever has my commands and keeps them is the one who loves me. (John 14:21)

> Jesus replied, "Anyone who loves me will obey my teaching. My Father will love them, and we will come to them and make our home with them. Anyone who does not love me will not obey my teaching. These words you hear are not my own; they belong to the Father who sent me." (John 14:23–24)

The link between loving God or Jesus and obedience to their commands is unbreakable. It is not primarily about some emotional depth of feeling for God. Loving God is to be expressed in action, in choice, in a volitional commitment to do the will of God. Therefore, to serve the poor, to show generosity and hospitality, and to share Christ with others are expressions of loving God. We love God when we are faithful to our spouses. We love God when we reject greed and covetousness. We love God when we rescue the suffering. This was so obvious to Jesus' first followers that it appears throughout the New Testament. John continues the theme in his first epistle:

> Whoever does not love does not know God, because God is love. This is how God showed his love among us: He sent his one and only Son into the world that we might live through him. This is love: not that we loved God, but that he loved us and sent his Son as an atoning sacrifice for our sins. Dear friends, since God so loved us, we also ought to love one another. No one has ever seen God; but if we love one another, God lives in us and his love is made complete in us. (1 John 4:8–12)

Paul is equally as aware of this central Christian teaching when he defines love this way:

> But God demonstrates his own love for us in this: While we were still sinners, Christ died for us. (Rom 5:8)

At the core of Christian belief is an understanding that God has shown us the supreme expression of love in Jesus' self-sacrifice on the cross. If you want to know what God's love is like, look to the Easter event. Nowhere is God's love better demonstrated. We should have known this all along, of course, because Jesus himself spelled it out to his disciples in the hours before his arrest:

> As the Father has loved me, so have I loved you. Now remain in my love. If you keep my commands, you will remain in my love, just as I have kept my Father's commands and remain in his love. I have told you this so that my joy may be in you and that your joy may be complete. My command is this: Love each other as I have loved you. Greater love has no one than this: to lay down one's life for one's friends. (John 15:9–13)

Note again the explicit connection between love and obedience. The language is much more obviously rooted in the father/son imagery that we looked at earlier. A good son would never abandon or betray his father. This is why Jesus' parable of the Prodigal Son is so shocking to its original audience; sons just don't do that, they don't abandon their father. They fulfill their father's wishes. This same language is employed by Jesus to describe "Christian" love. It is expressed by obedience and sacrifice. And just in case we are wondering how to fulfill such a high calling, Paul explains that the means by which we discharge our duty to love is through the Holy Spirit: "God has poured out his love into our hearts by the Holy Spirit, whom he has given us" (Rom 5:5b). And here we have it. The very same Holy Spirit of love who sustained Jesus through Gethsemane and beyond is the same Spirit of love given to us today. We, like Jesus' disciples, are called to love as Christ did: sacrificially, extravagantly, humbly, to the point of personal pain, even to death.

God's love, then, is not an abstract idea, nor is it a feeling, no matter how intense. It is a passionate commitment of God's will to what is good. In fact, the history of God's dealings with Israel in the Old Testament is a clear demonstration of how often God's love/action overrides his feelings of disappointment, anger, and frustration. God loves so that others might be reconciled to him, and, to quote Jesus again in John 15, so that their "joy might be complete." So, how are we to love God? By following his example, by "dying" for others so that they might know the joy of eternal life. Love and action are inseparable to God, as they should be to us. Therefore, the supreme expression of our love for God is the embracing of the mission of Jesus: to serve others, to feed the hungry, to empower the lowly, to heal the sick, and to direct people to a relationship with God as "*Abba,* Father."

Love, then, in the Christian framework, is an action. It is a verb, not a noun. To love is to *do* something for others, not necessarily to *feel* something for them. It is to desire their spiritual growth, so that they might blossom and grow and become everything that God intended them to be in the first place. And, interestingly, this is also how we love God, by serving God's creation.

This is not to suggest that there won't be feelings attached to our service of God and others. Nor is it to suggest that the expression of such feelings in communal singing isn't appropriate. But surely these feelings, like the "undying love" of a teenager, are transitory and unreliable. Corporate worship, though it might express human emotions and intense feelings, ought to call us onward to a greater, ever deeper commitment to love God by serving others. If that is its objective, it will be worthwhile to consider the concrete ways we express our love for God. In his devotional book *Sunrise Sunset,* Rowland Croucher devises a list of "tests" for measuring our love for God.[5] I will adapt and utilize them here, though their explanation will be my own. We love God in the following ways.

---

[5]Rowland Croucher, *Sunrise Sunset: Prayers and Meditations for Every Day of the Year* (San Francisco: HarperSanFrancisco, 1996), 35. See also Croucher's *Rivers in the Desert: Prayers and Meditations for the Dry Times* (Sydney: Albatross/Lion, 1992), in which this material first appeared.

We Love God by Loving Others

Rowland Croucher rather provocatively suggests the following maxim: You love God just as much, and no more, than the person you love least. Ouch! But clearly, given the Scriptures that we have looked at, this is not an unreasonable equation. Our love for God will clearly and directly be expressed in our love for others, including the poor, the oppressed, and the marginalized and those whom no one else cares to love. This surely is one of the most conspicuous features of Christ's own life and ministry, and we cannot fail to recognize our calling as his followers to do likewise.

We Love God by Obeying Jesus

"Anyone who loves me will obey my teaching," said Jesus. Remember that Jesus taught us not to be angry with others, not to look at anyone with lust, to turn the other cheek, to love our enemies. He taught us that when engaging in spiritual disciplines such as prayer, fasting, and giving to the needy, we must do so discreetly, not making a big display of our so-called righteousness. He taught us not to worry, but to trust in God. He taught us not to judge others, but to root out hypocrisy in our own lives. He taught us to deny ourselves and to embrace the sacrifice of the cross. He also taught us that it is impossible to earn our way into God's good graces, and that in all these things we will let ourselves and God down. That was the reason for his own sacrifice on the cross: to redeem us from our failure to live up to God's standards. But having done that, and having poured out his Spirit upon us, he now invites us to express our love and gratitude for him in our increased obedience to his commands. We don't obey Jesus to earn salvation—that is a free gift. We obey his commands out of love and thankfulness for his grace and forgiveness.

We Love God by Lingering in God's Company

When my wife, Carolyn, read Gary Chapman's book *The Five Love Languages,* she realized that "time spent" was her primary love language.[6] I can best show love to her by lavishing time on her, by being present with her and enjoying her company. Forget buying flowers and writing love poems to her. She

---

[6]Gary Chapman, *The Five Love Languages: How to Express Heartfelt Commitment to Your Mate* (Chicago: Moody, 1996). According to Chapman, the five primary ways we express love to our partners are (1) words of affirmation, (2) gifts, (3) quality time, (4) acts of service, and (5) physical touch. He suggests that all of us favor one or two over the others and that our partners need to learn our "love language" to communicate love most effectively to us.

wants my time. Well, in many respects, time spent with God is also an expression of our love. We spend time with God in prayer, fasting, and contemplation. By employing the skills of practicing the presence of God (as we observed in chapter 3), we indicate that we love God 'through daily companionship.

We Love God by Speaking about the Things of God

It's simple: from our mouths issues the overflow of our hearts. We can't help but talk about those things that excite our imaginations or fill our hearts. Whether it's a hobby we enjoy or a sports team we support or a project we're working on, we openly talk about the things that captivate our attention. Try to stop new parents from talking about their baby. It's natural to speak about that which we love. So, likewise, the degree to which we speak about the things of God is an indication of our love for God.

We Love God by Longing for the Return of Christ

This was a central tenet of the thinking of the first Christians. They longed for the return of Jesus, and it became part of the lens through which they viewed life and faith. Paul writes to the Colossians,

> Set your minds on things above, not on earthly things. For you died, and your life is now hidden with Christ in God. When Christ, who is your life, appears, then you will also appear with him in glory. (Col 3:2–4)

He also expresses something of this deep desire for the return of Christ in 2 Timothy:

> Now there is in store for me the crown of righteousness, which the Lord, the righteous Judge, will award to me on that day—and not only to me, but also to all who have longed for his appearing. (2 Tim 4:8)

We Love God by Forsaking Other Gods and Idols

The earliest Christians competed with the claims of the host empire on key fronts. First, they opposed polytheism and, against great odds, defended their belief that there was only one, true God, revealed to us in Christ. Second, they vehemently opposed idol worship. Today, we must carry on that fight. Our host empire today is equally polytheistic and inclined to idol worship. Whether it's the idols of greed, lust, violence, or hatred, we are regularly tempted by the "gods" of our culture that demand our higher allegiance. Our god might be our stomach. It might be our wallet. It might be our racism or our fear. We love God when we seek to eliminate such idolatry from our lives.

We Love God by Laying Down Our Life

Christians must ask themselves, "Who or what am I prepared to die for?" This is not an overstatement of the case. Jesus, in commissioning his disciples in chapter 15 of John, makes this clear when he says, "My command is this: Love each other as I have loved you. Greater love has no one than this: to lay down one's life for one's friends" (John 15:12–13). To love each other as "I have loved you" implies that our decision to love God might invite us to sacrifice our life to that cause, just as Christ freely did at Golgotha. No one imagines this ever to be the case in the West, but our brothers and sisters in China, Saudi Arabia, Vietnam, Indonesia, Pakistan, and elsewhere live under such a threat as an everyday part of their life in Christ. We must not forget this.

We Love God by Loving What God Has Created

As we noted earlier, it is not possible to be a faithful follower of the living God and not be concerned about the earth, about God's creation, the care of which has been entrusted to us. God spoke the universe into being, and if we love God, we will love that which has been created. We must also recognize that every human being is a creation of God, loved by God, and worthy of respect and dignity. One way we can show our love for God is to be concerned for the rights of human beings, God's creation. We shouldn't limit our area of concern to other Christians, but it continues to amaze me that Christians in the West have such little concern for the plight of their brothers and sisters in other parts of the world, in particular the persecuted church. As we observed earlier, news reports about the terrible atrocities inflicted upon Christians because of their faith in Jesus are numerous. In Vietnam, there is the case of the so-called Mennonite Six—six members of a Mennonite house church in Ho Chi Minh City who have been arrested for holding public church meetings in their homes. They have been the victims of severe human rights abuses for their faith. In the West Papuan region of Indonesia, there are genocide fears for Protestant Christians. A massive repatriation program has seen thousands of fundamentalist Muslims move to West Papua to alter the religious and social makeup of the region. There are reports of elderly Christians being murdered and churches burned to the ground. Combine this with news of the rape, torture, and illegal confinement of Christians in Pakistan, the abduction and forced conversion to Islam of young Egyptian women, and the imprisonment of Eritrean Christians in metal shipping containers to force renunciations of their faith in Jesus.

Wherever the church takes root in a host culture, we can be sure that this is a creation of God. It is God's work to birth the church around the world.

And we know that God loves the church. Surely, then, one of the ways we can express our love for God is to love that which God loves: the persecuted and suffering church around the world.

We Love God by Forgiving Others

Having introduced the template for Christian prayer to his disciples in Matt 6:5–13, Jesus concludes with an ominous warning: "For if you forgive others when they sin against you, your heavenly Father will also forgive you. But if you do not forgive others their sins, your Father will not forgive your sins" (Matt 6:14–15). Central to any request for forgiveness from God must be a willingness to forgive those who have "sinned against" us. It is hard not to harbor bitterness or a desire for vengeance (even one that is never acted upon) toward another who has hurt us. But Jesus both teaches and models that a godly lifestyle involves continual forgiveness toward our enemies. We see this in his declaration on the cross: "Father, forgive them, for they do not know what they are doing" (Luke 23:34). We see it also in Paul's persistent forgiveness for the Corinthians who continually misunderstand him, doubt him, and even outright reject him:

> So I made up my mind that I would not make another painful visit to you. For if I grieve you, who is left to make me glad but you whom I have grieved? I wrote as I did so that when I came I would not be distressed by those who should have made me rejoice. I had confidence in all of you, that you would all share my joy. For I wrote you out of great distress and anguish of heart and with many tears, not to grieve you but to let you know the depth of my love for you. (2 Cor 2:1–4)

There's no question that the Corinthian Christians had been a source of much emotional pain for Paul. At various points he is forced to defend himself, both the nature and the quality of his ministry in Corinth. He bears the brunt of mockery and scorn from certain parts of the community there. And yet, he resolutely expresses his love and concern for them. This is one of the obvious prices of Christian loving.

Oh, the Deep, Deep Love of Jesus

This quick survey of the biblical teaching on loving God should make it obvious that Jesus had in mind a much more actional, outwardly expressed model of love than the more emotional one expressed by many worship songs today. But is there a problem with expressing our feelings of love for God? Certainly not, as long as we recognize that these feelings, as wonderful as they are, are not the essence of the Christian faith. That faith is best expressed through action. If we are singing emotional songs without living out our desire to love God in the active ways we've just explored, then our faith is, as Paul declared, merely a resounding gong or a clanging cymbal. But Christians throughout the ages have sung corporately about the very emotional sensation of experiencing Jesus' love. Consider Samuel Trevor Francis's classic hymn "O the Deep, Deep Love of Jesus":

> O the deep, deep love of Jesus, vast, unmeasured, boundless, free!
> Rolling as a mighty ocean in its fullness over me!
> Underneath me, all around me, is the current of Thy love,
> Leading onward, leading homeward to Thy glorious rest above!
>
> O the deep, deep love of Jesus, spread His praise from shore to shore!
> How He loveth, ever loveth, changeth never, nevermore!
> How He watches o'er His loved ones, died to call them all His own;
> How for them He intercedeth, watcheth o'er them from the throne!
>
> O the deep, deep love of Jesus, love of every love the best!
> 'Tis an ocean full of blessing, 'tis a haven giving rest!
> O the deep, deep love of Jesus, 'tis a heaven of heavens to me;
> And it lifts me up to glory, for it lifts me up to Thee!

Although it doesn't express the same sexually charged element of contemporary worship songs, it certainly is full of emotional imagery and an intensity of feeling that matches anything written more recently. But what about Charles Miles's beloved hymn "In the Garden"? It sounds like a standard love song of its era, with the charming and innocent image of a pair of lovers walking hand in hand through the park:

> And He walks with me, and he talks with me,
> And He tells me I am His own,
> And the joy we share as we tarry there
> None other has ever known.

But just because it has happened in past eras of the Christian movement, does this necessarily make it right? To stay with Miles's imagery for a while: surely the deep, deep love of Jesus was indeed most obviously expressed in a garden, but not in the form of a furtive lover's embrace, but rather in Jesus' tough decision in the garden of Gethsemane to pursue his love for his Father all the way to the cross. The deep, deep love of Jesus is stained with sweat and blood, anguish, humiliation, and the betrayal of his friends. Let's sing about that love. Let's sing in a way that inspires us to similar measures of selfless sacrifice and devotional living.

This book began by looking at the ways in which the exiled Jews in Babylon sustained their faith and remained true to their one God, Yahweh. We looked briefly at the songs sung by their prophets in exile, in particular those of Isaiah. These songs are not mawkish or cloying love songs; rather, they are dangerous songs, revolutionary songs—songs of uprising sung into the very faces of Israel's oppressor, Babylon. It certainly would have been illegal to sing these songs in public or to teach them to children. That's why they were dangerous: they could incite a people to fight for freedom. They begin with a promise from Yahweh, and they build to a crescendo of revolution.

In Isa 41:13–14, the prophet sings,

> "For I am the LORD, your God,
>   who takes hold of your right hand
> and says to you, Do not fear;
>   I will help you.
> Do not be afraid, you worm Jacob,
>   little Israel, do not fear,
> for I myself will help you," declares the LORD,
>   your Redeemer, the Holy One of Israel.

Israel is a worm in Babylon, a despised and lowly community of slaves and prisoners. The song accurately portrays their feeble condition as exiles, but it also dares to dream of Yahweh as their redeemer. The Hebrew background to the term "redeemer" refers to the idea of an obligated family protector, a powerful relative with the means to rescue family members who get themselves into trouble. In the book of Ruth, we see a human expression of this idea in the obligation that Boaz feels for Ruth, his relative by marriage. As Boaz was to the Moabite widow Ruth, so Yahweh will be Israel's family protector. Isaiah portrays God at times as a father to Israel (Isa 63:16; 64:8) and at other times as a husband (Isa 54:5), though not in the sexual terms of, say, Hosea. Instead, Isaiah sees God as a husband-protector to the unfaithful Israel, one who cannot turn his back on his people even in their darkest hour of need. In the dangerous songs of Isaiah, Yahweh, as the family protector or redeemer, promises to commit treason against Babylon. Throughout the book we hear God singing about the seditious acts that he will perform in the interests of Israel's freedom:

> God promises to redeem their property to them and restore their land ("Your descendants will dispossess nations and settle in their desolate cities") (Isa 54:1–3).

> God will set them free from the slavery of Babylon ("I will bring your children from the east and gather you from the west. I will say to the north,

'Give them up!' and to the south, 'Do not hold them back'") (Isa 43:1–6;
52:11–12).

God will avenge them against those who have persecuted them ("I will
contend with those who contend with you") (Isa 49:25–26; 64:4).

God will restore the posterity of Israel well into the future ("I will reward
them and make an everlasting covenant with them") (Isa 61:8–9).

The singing of such promises in Babylon was tantamount to treachery,
but as Isaiah himself says, "For Zion's sake I will not keep silent, for Jerusalem's sake I will not remain quiet" (Isa 62:1). The true revolutionary cannot
keep silent even in the face of persecution by unjust regimes. We have seen
this in the example of Dr. Martin Luther King Jr., who in spite of monumental opposition refused to be silent about the injustices of his host empire. In
Memphis he concluded his famous "Mountaintop" speech by recounting the
threats that had been made against his life, including the unsuccessful assassination attempt on him at a book signing where he was stabbed within milli-
meters of his heart. He reported that his plane to Tennessee had to be
guarded all night to ensure that a bomb could not be hidden with the lug-
gage. He openly acknowledged that death threats had been made against him
in Memphis. Then, refusing to be silenced, he concluded,

> Like anybody, I would like to live a long life. Longevity has its place. But I'm
> not concerned about that now. I just want to do God's will. And He's al-
> lowed me to go up to the mountain. And I've looked over. And I've seen
> the promised land. I may not get there with you. But I want you to know
> tonight, that we, as a people, will get to the promised land. And I'm
> happy, tonight. I'm not worried about anything. I'm not fearing any man.
> Mine eyes have seen the glory of the coming of the Lord.[7]

The songs of the revolutionary Isaiah are no less dangerous. And we
know that King eventually did pay the ultimate price shortly after he spoke
these words. But exiles know that in the face of open rejection, even persecution, the word of the Lord must be sung. The Civil Rights movement in the
United States was a sung revolution, going as far back as the Spirituals, religious songs that spoke of freedom and vindication for God's people. And before Dr. King began singing his revolutionary hymns, another, much more
unlikely exile was already singing a devastatingly dangerous song. Her name
was Billie Holliday, and in the late 1930s she recorded a scornful, haunting

---

[7]For a full transcript of the speech see Martin Luther King, Jr., "I've Been to the
Mountaintop," American Rhetoric, n.p. [cited 17 January 2006]. Online: http://
www.americanrhetoric.com/speeches/mlkivebeentothemountaintop.htm.

anti-lynching anthem called "Strange Fruit," a song that Holliday would continue to sing until her death in 1959. Today it is considered to be one of those songs that literally changed America. At first, it sounds like any wistful torch song, but a close listen to the lyrics packs an emotional punch. Consider its caustic open lines: "Southern trees bear strange fruit / Blood on the leaves and blood at the root / Black bodies swingin' in the Southern breeze / Strange fruit hangin' from the poplar trees." The imagery of murder and racism in the American South is graphically portrayed by a blues singer whose own life epitomized the social struggles of African Americans in the twentieth century. The devastating second verse is hard to listen to: "Pastoral scene of the gallant South / The bulging eyes and the twisted mouth / Scent of magnolia, sweet and fresh / The sudden smell of burning flesh."

No one song will do or say it all, but it's worth noting that no significant movement has been without its music, whether it be the French revolutionaries singing "La Marseillaise" ("Grab your weapons, citizens / Train your battalions / Let us march / May impure blood / Water our fields!") or the Bolsheviks and the Maoists singing their revolutions into being ("The east wind is blowing / The war drums are sounding / Who fears who in today's world? / It's not the people who fear American imperialism / But American imperialism who fears the people").

In the 1980s, in Leipzig, Germany, six opponents of the Berlin Wall gathered in the Church of St. Nicholas to sing and pray for freedom. By 1989 their numbers had swelled to twelve thousand people, spilling out of the church into the streets of Leipzig. An East German communist leader was noted to have said, "We had planned everything, we were prepared for everything, but not for singing and prayers."

After the assassination of Philippine opposition leader Benigno Aquino in 1983, the opponents of dictator Ferdinand Marcos overwhelmingly elected Aquino's widow, Corazón, to the presidency, only to see Marcos refuse to hand over power. They began a singing people's movement that ousted Marcos from office four days later. The streets of Manila were packed with protestors singing and chanting for change. South Africans sang in the face of entrenched apartheid. Ukrainians sang outside their parliament when their ousted government refused to cede power to the properly elected opposition party. Even the early American revolutionaries sang against the tyrannies of English occupation in every bit as caustic a fashion as Billie Holliday sang against the horrors of black lynching. Consider the revolutionary hymn "God Save the Thirteen States":

> Oft did America
> Foresee with sad dismay
> Her slav'ry near.

Oft did her grievance state,
But Britain, falsely great,
Urging her desp'rate fate,
Turned a deaf ear.
We'll fear no tyrant's nod
Nor stern oppression's rod,
Till time's no more.
Thus Liberty, when driv'n
From Europe's states, is giv'n
A safe retreat and hav'n
On our free shore.

That's telling 'em!

Isn't the radical teaching of Jesus as revolutionary as any of these examples of political upheaval? Hasn't he called us to a revolution of grace, peace, and justice? And hasn't he told us that if we love him, we will *follow* him, we will obey his commands? His message is a call to insurgency, to mutiny against the values of this, our host empire. This is a world to which we don't belong. This is Babylon. We have been called by the Revolutionary One to demonstrate our love for him with action, with insubordinate acts of generosity and kindness, with a struggle against injustice, with an activist's vision for a renewed world in which God is acknowledged as the one, true God, and every knee is bent in service to him. Isn't this the ultimate goal of the deep, deep love of Jesus?

A Mature and Committed Love

In 1977, the novelist Madeleine L'Engle wrote her memoir, *The Irrational Season*.[8] It's a beautiful description of her journey of faith through the seasons of the year and the seasons of the heart. In a chapter entitled "To a Long-Loved Love" she reflects on her marriage to actor Hugh Franklin after nearly thirty years together. It is no starry-eyed hymn to an untroubled love affair. Instead, it is a beautiful description of a mature and committed relationship that has survived disappointment and failure. It comes closer to describing true love than any pop song or Valentine's Day greeting card. She begins,

It's an extraordinary thing to me that Hugh and I have been married for 29 years. It is also, I believe, a good marriage, although much of it would not seem to be so in terms of the kind of success commercials would hold out to us. However, our own expectations of marriage were false to start out with.

---

[8]Madeleine L'Engle, *The Irrational Season* (New York: Seabury, 1977).

> Neither of us knew the person we had promised to live with for the rest of our lives. The first bitter lessons of marriage consisted in learning to love the person we had actually married, instead of the image we wanted to have married.[9]

This mirrors not only my own experience in marriage, but also my experience in serving Christ. He and I have been "married" now for about the same period that L'Engle and Franklin were together when she wrote this memoir. And I must confess that Jesus hasn't turned out to be the man I thought I had wed either. My romantic images of gentle Jesus, meek and mild, have evaporated. He has turned out to be a much more strange and unpredictable God than I had imagined in my teenage years. I thought that he would love me in an eternally warm and comforting fashion, safe in his arms of love. But it has turned out that he has kicked my butt many times and forced me to grow in ways I'd never imagined. His love has been demanding, tough, uncompromising. I don't mean to imply that he hasn't been wonderfully generous and patient with me. But his is a love that wouldn't leave me as I was, insisting that I grow up and make changes that touched the core of who I thought I was. In every case, this has been for my greater good, but it has hardly been all chocolates and roses. And have I been disappointed in him? Oh yes, many times, though certainly not as often as I suspect he has been disappointed in me. But our love has survived disappointment and failure and grown stronger through it. L'Engle continues with her reflection on her marriage:

> I've learned something else about family and failure and promises: when a promise is broken, the promise still remains. In one way or another, we are all unfaithful to each other. . . . We do break our most solemn promises, and sometimes we break them when we don't even realize it. . . . I can look at the long years of my marriage with gratitude, and hope for many more, only when I accept our failures.[10]

I don't mean to suggest that Jesus has completely failed me as such, but it has felt like a failure at times. When I have begged him for things that I know are biblically part of his will, and he hasn't come through, I have felt floundering and betrayed. I have felt anger at him and hurt by his silence. I remain true, though, knowing that I too have broken many, many of my feeble promises to him. The fact remains that, as L'Engle wisely says, a promise broken is a promise nonetheless. After nearly thirty years together with Jesus, my identity and purpose in life are so bound up in my relationship with him that

---

[9] Ibid., 56.
[10] Ibid.

I cannot unravel all that history and find myself again apart from him. We're a partnership now, for life—for better, for worse. Only a writer of the consummate skill of Madeleine L'Engle could describe this so beautifully:

> My love for my husband and his for me is in that unknown, underwater area of ourselves where our separations become something new and strange, merge and penetrate like the drops of water in the sea. But we do not lose our solitudes, or our particularity, and we become more than we could alone.

> This is mystery. I cannot explain it. But I have learned that it makes up for our clashes, our differences in temperament, our angers, our withdrawals, our failures to understand.

> No long-term marriage is made easily, and there have been times when I've been so angry or so hurt that I thought my love would never recover. And then, in the midst of near despair, something has happened beneath the surface. A bright little flashing fish of hope has flicked silver fins and the water is bright and suddenly I am returned to a state of love again—till next time.

> I've learned that there will always be a next time, and that I will submerge in darkness, but that I won't stay submerged. And each time something has been learned under the waters; something has been gained; and a new kind of love has grown. The best I can ask for is that this love, which has been built on countless failures, will continue to grow. I can say no more than that this is mystery, and gift, and that somehow or other, through grace, our failures can be redeemed and blessed.[11]

There is something richer, deeper, and wiser in these words than the froth and bubble of newly found love. The first blush of falling in love leaves the lovers with the staunchly held view that they will love each other this deeply, faultlessly and forever. Worship songs based on this kind of gullible, naïve, simplistic view of love never move me. My relationship with God through Jesus has at times left me disillusioned, disappointed, and confused. But the sum total of all these years together has left me with the same kind of love for God that L'Engle describes for her husband. Our love has been built on countless failures, but it's a love that continues to grow deeper, like an ocean, a dark fathomless sea with regular flashes of hope and joy and even triumph. Can I sing about that, please? Can I sing about the mystery of God's grace in the face of anger and pain? Can I worship God for being faithful through the hardship of exile and separation? As with the battle songs of

---

[11]Ibid.

revolution, can I be inspired to continue with this life-long journey of service, devotion, and friendship in spite of the struggles and difficulties of remaining faithful to God on foreign soil? Where are the worship songwriters who can fashion a new voice for the exiles who cannot sing the romantic nonsense we hear sung in too many churches today?

Many contemporary songwriters love passages such as the song of praise recorded in chapter 42 of Isaiah:

> Sing to the LORD a new song,
>> his praise from the ends of the earth,
> you who go down to the sea, and all that is in it,
>> you islands, and all who live in them.
> Let the wilderness and its towns raise their voices;
>> let the settlements where Kedar lives rejoice.
> Let the people of Sela sing for joy;
>> let them shout from the mountaintops.
> Let them give glory to the LORD
>> and proclaim his praise in the islands. (Isa 42:10–12)

Yes, they usually love this kind of stuff, but for some reason they fail to recognize that it was written to people under oppression, to exiles who were tired of the yoke of slavery, who were disappointed with God and who yearned for freedom and vindication. They often fail to read on and see that the song reaches a crescendo when God appears like a mighty warrior who sings his own song in response to the song of praise just recorded. God's song, however, is not a hollow, emotional ditty, but a wild, tempestuous hymn of sedition and revolution:

> For a long time I have kept silent,
>> I have been quiet and held myself back.
> But now, like a woman in childbirth,
>> I cry out, I gasp and pant.
> I will lay waste the mountains and hills
>> and dry up all their vegetation;
> I will turn rivers into islands and dry up the pools.
> I will lead the blind by ways they have not known,
>> along unfamiliar paths I will guide them;
> I will turn the darkness into light before them
>> and make the rough places smooth.
> These are the things I will do;
>> I will not forsake them.
> But those who trust in idols,
>> who say to images, "You are our gods"
>> will be turned back in utter shame. (Isa 42:14–17)

Here is the very word that exiles need to hear. It is a call to believe that the lowly exile will ultimately be vindicated for his or her faith in God, that present experience is not the final word. It is a call to believe that the utter pointlessness of reality TV cannot satisfy our yearning for real life. It is a call to believe that the fake relationships that people have online, using false names and pretending to be something other than they are, are not the way we were meant to relate to one another. It is a call to believe that it's simply not right that the richest 20 percent of the world's population receives over 80 percent of total world income. It affirms that it is evil that tens of thousands of people die of starvation every day, while we live in a nation where 60 percent of us are overweight or obese. God's song, sung like a woman in labor, gives birth to a new hope, a hope that we, as exiles, are never to be "at home" in a world of obscenely powerful corporations and technocrats, of ever-increasing militarization, of unspeakable greed and avarice.

And finally, it warns us that we, as exiles, must at all costs refuse to trust in the idols of our host empire. We cannot trust in the promises of our post-Christendom empire. We must not say to those corporations in whom we have invested our money, "You are our gods." We must not say to the shopping malls that have become our primary source of entertainment, "You are our gods." We must not say to the fast-food outlets that line the highways into our communities, "You are our gods." We must not say to Hollywood, the Democrats, the Republicans, the televangelists, *People* magazine, the *National Enquirer,* Wal-Mart, McDonalds, or our television sets, "You are our gods." Those who do so will be turned back in utter shame.

Epilogue

CROSSING THE JORDAN TO GO HOME

And so John the Baptist appeared in the
wilderness, preaching a baptism of repentance
for the forgiveness of sins. The whole Judean
countryside and all the people of Jerusalem went
out to him. Confessing their sins, they
were baptized by him in the Jordan River.

—MARK 1:4–5

John's role as forerunner to Christ's ministry is well known, a role through which he fulfills the prophecy that a messenger would be sent by Yahweh to prepare the way for the Lord's appearance. In this passage at the beginning of Mark's Gospel we catch a glimpse of hundreds of Judeans, including many from Jerusalem itself, gathering by the Jordan, making their confession, and being plunged by John beneath the water's surface. The response was overwhelming as Judeans collectively repented of their sin and prepared themselves for the Lord. But what exactly did John's baptism mean to these Judeans? Surely not what we think of baptism today!

It would be many years before Paul would imbue the act of baptism with distinctly Christian meaning in chapter 6 of Romans, where he describes the immersion in water as mirroring being "buried" with Christ and then raised to new life (Rom 6:2–4). But this was not what John was calling people to. At that time, the death and resurrection of Christ were yet to occur, and they seemed inconceivable in those early days of Jesus' public ministry. John was preaching repentance baptism, not an altogether unknown concept to his audience, although they would have known primarily of baptism for Gentile converts. Some Jewish sects, such as the Essenes, were known to use baptism as a rite of purification for preserving their moral and religious purity, but it was not a mainstream rite.

What, then, was John up to? And why was he using the Jordan River? The baptizing of Gentile converts or the ceremonial washings used by the Essenes were conducted privately, using normal drinking water. Why was John calling his adherents into the wilderness to be washed in the muddy river waters? Well, it takes an exile to see the importance of this moment in history.

As we know, the Babylonian ruler Cyrus released the first of the Jewish exiles to return to the ravaged land of their ancestors in 537 B.C.E. They immediately set about establishing an altar in the ruins of Jerusalem and laying the foundations for a new temple. More than ten years later, during the reign of Artaxerxes, the Jewish leaders Ezra and Nehemiah were sent to Jerusalem to administer the formation of the new state. The exile was over. Israel was to be rebuilt. For all exiles, who had longed so deeply for the reestablishment of the temple and the freedom of God's people, this was the moment they had waited for. But it was a moment that became truly real only when they finally crossed the Jordan River and returned home.

This is what makes John's ministry at the Jordan so powerful. In his time, over four hundred years after Ezra, Israel again was held captive. This time it was not on foreign soil, but captivity to an invader that now occupied all lands west of the Jordan. The Roman occupation was every bit as much an exile as their bitter experience in Persia had been, and the yearning for freedom was no less great than it had been in the time of Cyrus. Jews dreamed of a day when they could again cross the Jordan—metaphorically this time— and be home again. Now, a voice cries out in the wilderness, just as the exilic prophet Isaiah had predicted, demanding that Israel ready itself for the appearance of its liberator. John's baptism was a call for the Jews to prepare themselves spiritually for their exile to end. As they confessed their sins and repented of their wrongdoing, John led them across the Jordan, preparing them to go home to freedom, grace, and intimacy with Yahweh. John's preparatory work is to turn people's hearts toward home. So that when Jesus announces that the kingdom has come and declares the forgiveness of sins, those who yearn for home will see that their exile from God ends right now in Christ.

Our sins are forgiven. The gulf that separates us from home with God has been closed. This is the good news of which Jesus spoke so liberally and demonstrated so powerfully in word, deed, and symbol. Our exile from God is over. We have crossed the Jordan River and returned to where we belong.

In all our talk about exiles in a post-Christendom empire, we must not lose sight of the fact that we indeed have found our way home, led there by our trusted guide and Savior, Jesus. Even though our culture has drifted as far from the things of God as had Babylon or Rome, our citizenship belongs across the Jordan. We carry our home in our hearts. For our home is that place of reconciliation with God made possible by Jesus' work on the cross and in his resurrection.

So hold on, exile. Hold on to those dangerous memories of God. Keep making those dangerous promises. Keep practicing that dangerous critique of the host empire. Keep singing those dangerous songs. Our day will come. When the dogs are barking, it's time for cats to be circumspect, to walk on fences and trust that this is not the final word on the matter. In the meantime, keep your balance. And hold within you the sure hope that home is found in the presence of our gracious, loving, forgiving God. Let me leave you with a contemporary blessing, one that makes sense to the exile, to the sojourner, and to the pilgrim heading resolutely home again:

> May you grow up to be righteous,
> May you grow up to be true,
> May you always know the truth
> And see the light surrounding you.
> May you always be courageous,
> Stand upright and be strong,
> May you stay forever young.[1]

---

[1]Partial lyrics from Bob Dylan, "Forever Young," *Planet Waves* (Sony, 1974).

RESOURCES

Books, Websites, and Movies for the Road

On Understanding the Post-Christian Empire

- David Boyle, *Authenticity: Brands, Fakes, Spin and the Lust for Real Life,* London: Flamingo, 2004
- Douglas John Hall, *The End of Christendom and the Future of Christianity,* Harrisburg, Pa.: Trinity Press International, 1995
- Stuart Murray, *Post-Christendom: Church and Mission in a Strange New World,* Carlisle: Paternoster, 2004
- Lesslie Newbigin, *Foolishness to the Greeks: the Gospel and Western Culture,* Grand Rapids: Eerdmans, 1986
- Lesslie Newbigin, *The Gospel in a Pluralist Society,* Grand Rapids: Eerdmans, 1989
- Ray Oldenburg, *The Great Good Place: Cafés, Coffee Shops, Community Centers, Beauty Parlors, General Stores, Bars, Hangouts and How They Get You Through the Day,* New York: Paragon House, 1989
- Neil Postman, *Amusing Ourselves to Death: Public Discourse in the Age of Show Business,* New York: Viking Penguin, 1986

On Being Faithful in Exile

- Walter Brueggemann, *Cadences of Home: Preaching among Exiles,* Louisville: Westminster John Knox, 1997
- Rodney Clapp, *A Peculiar People: The Church as Culture in a Post-Christian Society,* Downers Grove, Ill.: InterVarsity, 1996
- Jacques Ellul, *The Subversion of Christianity,* trans. G. W. Bromiley, Grand Rapids: Eerdmans, 1986

330   **EXILES**

- Michael Frost and Alan Hirsch, *The Shaping of Things to Come: Innovation and Mission for the 21st-Century Church,* Peabody, Mass.: Hendrickson, 2003
- Craig Van Gelder, ed., *Confident Witness—Changing World: Rediscovering the Gospel in North America,* Grand Rapids: Eerdmans, 1999
- Stanley Hauerwas, *A Community of Character: Toward a Constructive Christian Social Ethic,* Notre Dame, Ind.: University of Notre Dame Press, 1981
- Martin Hengel, *Acts and the History of Earliest Christianity,* trans. J. Bowden, London: SCM, 1979
- Philip Jenkins, *The Next Christendom: The Coming of Global Christianity,* Oxford: Oxford University Press, 2002
- Jürgen Moltmann, *The Open Church: Invitation to a Messianic Lifestyle,* trans. M. Douglas Meeks, London: SCM, 1978
- Michael Riddell, *Threshold of the Future: Reforming the Church in the Post-Christian West,* London: SPCK, 1998
- Rodney Stark, *The Rise of Christianity: A Sociologist Reconsiders History,* Princeton, N.J.: Princeton University Press, 1996
- Pete Ward, *Liquid Church,* Peabody, Mass.: Hendrickson, 2002

On Missional Community

- Archbishops' Committee on Mission, *Mission-Shaped Church: Church Planting and Fresh Expressions of Church in a Changing Context,* London: Church House, 2004
- David Bosch, *Transforming Mission: Paradigm Shifts in Theology of Mission,* Maryknoll, N.Y.: Orbis, 1991
- Darrell L. Guder, ed., *The Missional Church: A Vision for the Sending of the Church in America,* Grand Rapids: Eerdmans, 1998
- Lesslie Newbigin, *The Open Secret: An Introduction to the Theology of Mission,* rev. ed., Grand Rapids: Eerdmans, 1995
- Alan J. Roxburgh, *The Missionary Congregation, Leadership, and Liminality,* Harrisburg, Pa.: Trinity Press International, 1997

On Food

- Linda McQuaig, *All You Can Eat: Greed, Lust, and the New Capitalism,* Toronto: Penguin Canada, 2001

- John Piper, *A Hunger for God: Desiring God through Fasting and Prayer,* Wheaton, Ill.: Crossway, 1997
- Eric Schlosser, *Fast Food Nation: The Dark Side of the All-American Meal,* New York: HarperCollins, 2002
- Slow Food Movement website: www.slowfood.com
- World Hunger website: www.worldhunger.org

On Ecology

- Barry Commoner, *The Closing Circle: Confronting the Environmental Crisis,* New York: Bantam, 1980
- Jared Diamond, *Collapse: How Societies Choose to Fail or Succeed,* New York: Viking Penguin, 2004
- Paul Hawken, *The Ecology of Commerce: A Declaration of Sustainability,* New York: HarperCollins, 1993
- James A. Nash, *Loving Nature: Ecological Integrity and Christian Responsibility,* Nashville: Abingdon, 1991
- Clean Air Council website: www.cleanair.org
- Shell Facts website: http://www.shellfacts.com

On Global Justice

- Naomi Klein, *No Logo: No Space, No Choice, No Jobs,* New York: Picador, 2002
- Jeffrey Sachs, *The End of Poverty: How We Can Make It Happen in Our Lifetime,* London: Penguin, 2005
- Joseph Stiglitz, *Globalization and Its Discontents,* New York: Norton, 2003
- Jessica Williams, *50 Facts That Should Change The World,* Cambridge: Icon, 2004
- The Corporation website: http://www.thecorporation.com
- Jubilee research website: www.jubileeresearch.org
- Liberty UK website: www.liberty-human-rights.org.uk
- Micah Challenge website: http://www.micahchallenge.org
- Naomi Klein website: http://www.nologo.org/faqs/

On Religious Persecution

- Cry Indonesia website: http://www.cryindonesia.org
- Save Darfur website: http://www.savedarfur.com
- Tears of the Oppressed website: www.human-rights-and-christian-persecution .org. See also http://www.tearsoftheoppressed.org
- The Universal Declaration of Human Rights (UDHR): http://www .unhchr.ch/udhr/lang/eng.htm
- The Voice of the Martyrs website: http://www.persecution.com

On Alternative Worship

- Jonny Baker, Doug Gay, and Jenny Brown, *Alternative Worship: Resources from and for the Emerging Church,* Grand Rapids: Baker, 2004
- Dan Kimball, *The Emerging Church: Vintage Christianity for New Genera-tions,* Grand Rapids: Zondervan, 2003
- Alternative Worship website: http://www.alternativeworship.org/index.html
- Small Fire website: http://www.smallfire.org

Emerging/Missional Church Blogs and Websites

- Andrew Jones: http://tallskinnykiwi.typepad.com/tallskinnykiwi
- Jonny Baker: http://jonnybaker.blogs.com
- Emergent Kiwi (Steve Taylor): http://www.emergentkiwi.org.nz
- Living Room (Darren Rowse): http://www.livingroom.org.au/blog
- Maggi Dawn: http://www.maggidawn.blogspot.com
- Neurotribe (Steve Said): http://www.neurotribe.net/blog
- Next Wave (Charlie Wear): http://charliewear.next-wave.org
- The Ooze (Spencer Burke): http://www.theooze.com/blog/index.cfm
- Vintage Faith (Dan Kimball): http://www.vintagefaith.com

Films Worth Watching

- *Babette's Feast* (Denmark, 1987)
  A marvelous tale of grace, generosity, and the place of food in a commu-nity controlled by strict religiosity.

- *Smoke* (United States, 1995)
  A slice of life illustrating the power of friendship, community, storytelling, and smoking.

- *Big Night* (United States, 1996)
  The story of a clash between two Italian restaurateurs: one a purist, the other prepared to compromise to give his customers what they want.

- *Fight Club* (United States, 1999)
  A very popular film about the subversive nature of community and the meaninglessness of suburban contemporary life.

- *Chocolat* (United States, 2000)
  A depiction of the clash between the traditional church and an emerging community of grace and love.

- *The Lord of the Rings* trilogy: *The Fellowship of the Ring, The Two Towers, The Return of the King* (New Zealand, 2001)
  An epic story of a community (or fellowship) built by common commitment to goals greater than the capacity of any individual to achieve alone.

- *Whale Rider* (New Zealand, 2002)
  A brilliant film about tradition, myth, and culture, and one who embodies these things while at the same time shattering them.

- *Super Size Me* (United States, 2004)
  A documentary by Morgan Spurlock, who eats nothing but McDonald's food for a month, that examines the American addiction to fast food and its health effects.

- *Ladder 49* (United States, 2004)
  Not necessarily a brilliant film, but a graphic portrayal of communitas as forged among a group of Baltimore firefighters.

Also by Michael Frost

Have You Read?

The Shaping of Things to Come*: Innovation and Mission for the 21st-Century Church*
Co-authored with Alan Hirsch

Most people in the Western world are not interested in what the Church has to offer . . . even though they are very open to the issues of God, faith, and meaning. This book explores why the Church needs to recalibrate itself, rebuild itself from the roots up. It examines real-life stories gathered from innovative missional projects in the United States, Australia, New Zealand, Canada, and England. The authors present vital modes of missional learning for the established Church as it seeks to orient itself to the unique challenges of the twenty-first century.

"This book is a bountiful multi-course meal, each serving presented with charm and class. It will satisfy even eclectic appetites, and please the most discriminating palates. Four Stars!"
—*Leonard Sweet*

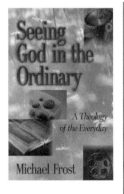

Seeing God in the Ordinary*: A Theology of the Everyday*

Seeing God in the Ordinary is an appeal to recover the place of imagination in the Christian life, to rediscover the use of metaphor in a prose-flattened world, to see God in the ordinary. By a careful examination of film, literature, and other aspects of contemporary culture—as well as the Gospels—Frost argues for a robust faith that embraces human experience in all its forms, that is open to the intuitive, and that has the capacity to fill us with wonder and astonishment.

"Frost has produced a probe of a world 'not-yet-holy,' but being made so by the presence of God's holiness in the day-to-dayness of our lives. A suggestive read!"
—*Walter Brueggemann*